RESTLESS ENERGY

RESTLESS ENERGY

A Biography of William Rowan 1891–1957

Marianne Gosztonyi Ainley

Véhicule Press
MONTRÉAL

This book has been published with the assistance of a grant from the Canadian Federation of the Humanities, using funds provided by the Social Sciences and Humanities Research Council of Canada, and a grant from The Canada Council.

Cover design: J.W. Stewart
Interior design and imaging: ECW Type & Art
Printing: Imprimerie d'Edition Marquis Ltée
Frontispiece drawing of juncos by William Rowan, 1920s, courtesy of University of Alberta Archives.

Dépôt légal Bibliothèque nationale du Québec and the National Library of Canada, second quarter 1993.

CANADIAN CATALOGUING IN PUBLICATION DATA

Ainley, Marianne Gosztonyi, 1937–
Restless energy : a biography of William Rowan, 1891–1957

Includes bibliographical reference and index.
ISBN 1-55065-027-0

1. Rowan, William, 1891–1957.
2. Ornithologists — Canada — Biography.
3. Conservationists — Canada — Biography.
4. Educators — Canada — Biography. I Title.

QL31.R69A46 1992 598'.092 C92-090428-9

Véhicule Press, P.O.B. 125, Place du Parc Station,
Montreal, Quebec Canada H2W 2M9

Printed in Canada on acid-free paper.

For David

CONTENTS

ILLUSTRATIONS

PREFACE

AS A NATURALIST and a student of the history of science I have known about William Rowan's work for many years, although I cannot remember when and where I first heard about his pioneering bird-migration experiments. By the early 1980s, when I was working on a history of Canadian ornithology, I found that Rowan's ground breaking work had been discussed in zoology textbooks, cited in scientific papers, and included in Erwin Stresemann's *Ornithology: From Aristotle to the Present*. He was always described in larger-than-life terms. Evidently, Rowan had not only been one of Canada's foremost biologists, but he had also played an important role in the history of science. There was, however, very little information about his life and career. The formal obituaries in learned journals discussed his scientific research, his eminence as a teacher, and his impact on other scientists. Anecdotal descriptions of his antics in the field, published in Robert Lister's *The Birds and Birders of Beaverhills Lake*, presented him in a different light, as a character, a lively, somewhat erratic person.

In the course of my own research I came across Rowan's correspondence with ornithologist Percy A. Taverner. This was an eye-opener. I was amused by Rowan's colourful turn of phrase and fascinated by his discussions of science, the position of Canadian scientists in a North American context, and attitudes towards wildlife and conservation.

In July 1984, I was writing my dissertation at a borrowed cottage in Piedmont, Quebec. On a warm, sunny day, surrounded by the sounds and smells of the Laurentian mountains, I suddenly realized that William Rowan, who was trained in England but had worked in Canada on a number of important problems in biology, deserved a full-scale scientific biography. At the time, I was looking for a project that would combine the histories of science, ornithology, and people's experiences. The life and work of this internationally recognized Canadian scientist seemed to be a perfect focus.

I already knew that Rowan's letters and diaries were at the

University of Alberta Archives. With the encouragement of historian of science Trevor H. Levere, I began my inquiries. I wrote to Dr. David A. Boag, one of Rowan's students, to ask if he knew whether anyone else was already working on a biography. He replied, "I know of no one who is writing a biography on Professor Rowan. He was indeed a . . . pioneer in Canadian ornithology and a biography would be a valuable contribution." I was further encouraged by W.O. Rowan, the scientist's son, who informed me that the family "would be pleased to see a biography."

In the fall of 1984, I submitted a detailed research proposal to the Social Sciences and Humanities Research Council of Canada and was delighted when, in April 1985, I received notice that I had been awarded a one-year research grant. I immediately set about arranging to spend two months in Western Canada working in various archives, interviewing people, and seeing as much as possible of Rowan's enormous outdoor laboratory (the prairies, lakes, and muskegs), which provided the subjects of his research.

Later trips took me to the various parts of England, where Rowan lived and studied and explored the natural world around him, and to the ranching country of Alberta where Rowan first discovered "his beloved wilderness," a discovery that led to his determination to become a scientist.

My work was greatly facilitated by the support and cooperation of many people. My husband David was my companion in most of my travels, read various versions of the manuscript and, for the better part of seven years, with our children Vicky and Mark, shared my involvement in the Rowan biography.

William Rowan's children gave me encouragement, friendship, and invaluable information. Without them it would have taken me much longer to work my way through the complexities of Rowan's life. I feel fortunate indeed to have met Julian and Niva Rowan, Erich and Josephine Rowan Traugott, Gerdine Rowan McPhee, W.O. Rowan, Reginald Benchley, and the late Sylvia Rowan Benchley. Other family members, including Athalie Abraham, Mary G. Brodrick, Pauline Loveridge, and Marjorie Rowan provided me with important primary material on the Bush and Rowan families.

I appreciate the prompt and cheerful assistance of Gertrude MacLaren, Maureen Aytenfishu, and the late James M. Parker, all of the University of Alberta Archives. I thank those who shared their memories of Reta and William Rowan with me, including David A. Boag, Bruce Collier, Merva and Wally Cottle, Gerdine Crawford, Nancy and Charles Eddis, Elsie Park Gowan, Mary and Cy Hampson, Joan Hochbaum and the late H. Albert Hochbaum, Barbara and Otto Hohn, Edgar T. Jones, Silver Keeping, Al Oeming, Ralph Nursall, Verna and David Stelfox, and the late Robert Lister. While I was in England, Edith and Walter Ainley and Dorothy and Ronnie Craven opened their home to me and helped me to retrace Rowan's activities. Arthur Nightall was a mine of information about Bedford School.

Other people whose assistance was important include Eleanor MacLean, Ann Habbick, and Jennifer Adams from the Blacker-Wood Library, McGill University; I. Achermann-Knoepfli, vice-mayor of Binningen, and Howard T. Emery, Q.C.; Janet Pieschel and Tom Gooden from the Glenbow-Alberta Institute; and Ron Rutschke, Susan and Doug Clark, and Karen and Roy Clark, who guided me around ranches and taught me ranching history. David Jones helped with the history of the Canadian Pacific Railway, Mark Woolforth with photographs, and C. Budden provided information on the records of University College, London. Gene Christman sent invaluable material from the Museum of Vertebrate Zoology, Berkeley, and W.E. Godfrey, Henri Ouellett, Michel Gosselin, and Stuart MacDonald turned my research at the National Museum of Natural Sciences, Ottawa, into a series of satisfying experiences.

I shall always be grateful to the late Michael G. Hogben for his encouragement and interest in my work, and to Jane Atkinson, Tina Crossfield, Barbara Meadowcroft, and Nancy Schumann who read parts, and John Cranmer-Byng, W. Earl Godfrey, and Martin McNicholl who read all, of the manuscript and offered helpful criticism. I would also like to acknowledge the friendship and support of Sheila Arthur, Mary E. Baldwin, George Gardos, Mary Gilliland, Susan Hoecker-Drysdale, Stuart Holohan, Mary and Stuart Houston, Alison Li, Richard Mackie, Patricia Morley, Bob Nero, Iola Price and Tony Keith, Trevor H. Levere, Nellie Reiss, Marion and J.B. Steeves, and John H. Thompson.

My final thanks go to Simon Dardick, Nancy Marrelli, and Mary Williams, for their encouragement and help in completing this biography.

INTRODUCTION

WILLIAM ROWAN has been considered a Renaissance man, a man of integrity, a famous biologist, a flamboyant showman, a challenging teacher, and often a nuisance. His work as a scientist has been highly regarded by biologists all over the world, and his experiments have been covered in numerous zoology textbooks. Who was this scientist? What was he like as a person, a family man, a colleague, a friend? Why was he so well known to contemporary scientists, and why do we still find written references to his scientific work while, apart from anecdotal descriptions about his escapades in the field, little is known about the details of his life?

Convinced that William Rowan was an important subject for a biography, I went to Edmonton in July 1985 to see the environment where he lived and worked; to talk to the people who knew him as friend, teacher, and colleague, and who admired him as a world-renowned scientist, highly respected wildlife artist, and outstanding conservationist. Inevitably, other facets of his character came to light: his integrity, his kindness, his egotism, his unfailing need to criticize mediocrity, his ability to inspire others, his love of beauty and of nature. I learned of his exquisitely designed conservation stamps, Christmas cards, and hand-painted menus; of his great skill as a self-taught sculptor and musician, and as a builder of model sailing boats and a unique single-gauge model railway. I found that he had been well known as a radio personality, and as the man who tried to make crows fly the wrong way. Nearly thirty years after his death, William Rowan was still very much alive in Edmonton, and even those who had never set eyes on him could tell a few choice stories about his escapades. Indeed, as I gradually discovered, Rowan was an unusual individual — a Renaissance man in Alberta.

William Rowan was born in Switzerland in 1891 of Danish-Irish parents. His life was one of extremes and contradictions. He knew luxury and comfort in European mansions, but revelled in roughing it in the wilds of Alberta. He spent his early childhood in the lap of luxury, but later lived the life of a typical overworked and underpaid Canadian university professor.

While a young man, Rowan showed extraordinary promise as an original thinker and innovative scientist. His early research, conducted under unusually difficult conditions, is still cited in numerous books as "pioneering" and "ground breaking." In later life, he felt that he had to waste much valuable time on money making projects to help support his growing family of three girls and two boys. Although this multitalented man often resented the time he had to spend on nonscientific activities, he managed to create wildlife art treasured by collectors all over North America and Britain, broadcast nature programs that educated and entertained two generations of listeners in the western provinces and the northwestern United States, and write, for commercial publications, articles that are still admired for their outstanding style and evocative language.

William Rowan knew the exhilaration of successful scientific discovery. His findings almost instantly changed the course of migration research and led to the establishment of the discipline of photobiology. He also knew the depths of extreme despair, for personal and financial problems as well as World War II and the Cold War severely disrupted his life. At the University of Alberta, he struggled for over three decades to maintain high standards in teaching and research in spite of low salaries and lack of administrative support. Rowan found, as have many "prophets" throughout history, that it is easier to be recognized abroad than at home, particularly by those with power to fund scientific research.

Restless Energy explores Rowan's experiences as a European-trained scientist in the Canadian West, details his difficulties with unimaginative administrators, including the well-known H.M. Tory, and follows in some detail his scientific experiments as well as his growing awareness of, and concern about, social issues affecting the future of humanity. This biography also addresses the effects a scientist's intense involvement in work has on his or her spouse, and underlines the ways in which the experiences of educated immigrant men and women in the West differ from one another.

It is hoped that the reader will appreciate why, in spite of recurring difficulties, Rowan remained an outstanding and challenging teacher. Why, although he was often discouraged to the point of physical illness, he never gave up his science or his art. Why did he not leave the University of Alberta, and work in the United States or in Britain, countries whose granting agencies had long supported his research? What were the advantages of living and working in Western Canada that helped to counteract pettiness and animosity in the workplace or difficult situations at home. What was Rowan's relationship with his "beloved wilderness," the muskegs, prairies, and mountains of Alberta? How and why had the wilderness provided him with artistic inspiration and a giant outdoor laboratory for scientific research? What was the character of this scientist that he could attract the friendship of so many men and women? Some of them were down-to-earth, such as the ferryman Joe Dawkins, others famous in international artistic, scientific, and business circles, such as the actor Anna Neagle, zoologist Sir Julian Huxley, and oil magnate Eric Harvie.

It has been an exacting and exciting task, trying to recreate the multifaceted personality that was William Rowan. During his lifetime his inquiring mind and restless energy took him into many different areas of work and study: conservation, science, art, and philosophy. Unlike some biographers who suffer from a dearth of primary material, I have been overwhelmed by the volume of the William Rowan Papers. It was a challenge to make my way through the often contradictory information provided by Rowan's own correspondence, and by the interviews about him.

Rowan's fame as a scientist has overshadowed his other attributes and accomplishments. In this biography I have tried to illuminate the complex web of his life, his approach to nature and science, the minutiae of his scientific research, his many victories and self-doubts, and his relationships with his family and friends. I know, perhaps more than anyone, that no single work can do justice to Rowan's manifold activities and accomplishments. This is my interpretation of the life and work of this fascinating, complex man. At a time when we badly need histories of Canadian science, I hope that this book will stimulate further research.

I

The Lap of Luxury, 1891-1908

WILLIAM ROWAN CONDUCTED his first migration experiment in 1901. He was ten years old. In the midst of the noisy upheaval generated by the move of his large family from France to England, he characteristically found time to pursue his own interests. For his first experiment he trapped about a dozen flies, placed them in a wire-mesh cage (actually a borrowed tea infusion ball) and put the "cage" in his own pocket. As he explained to his amused family on board the train, he was in the process of "migrating French flies to England." Nearly sixty years after that August day, his oldest brother recalled that when Billy "opened this 'cage' ONE utterly exhausted fly stepped out, the rest were dead."[1]

Although he never referred to the event, this is the first recorded instance of William Rowan's lifelong interest in the field of animal migration in which he achieved world renown. No matter that this very first experiment was conducted with makeshift material, or that it proved inconclusive. Rowan's ability to think about a scientific problem and to pursue research under difficult circumstances was already there, even in early life. It became William Rowan's hallmark throughout his long and chequered career.

From his early childhood, Rowan enjoyed railway travel, whether on board luxurious coaches or simple bone shakers. Railways contributed to Billy's youthful adventures, and trains were his preferred mode of transportation in adult life. When Rowan built a unique single-gauge model railroad system in the Rocky Mountains of Canada, the railway even added to his fame.

William Rowan's family had been connected with railways since the middle of the nineteenth century. His father and his grandfather were both railway men. Grandfather Frederick James Rowan (1817–1884) came from a "pedigreed Irish" family that included many illustrious members in "His Majesty's Services, the Church, Medicine and the Law."[2] But Frederick James Rowan chose a different career. He trained as a technical engineer in England, and after his marriage to Mary Wickham Betts, whose brother was a railway contractor, "he became associated with the influential firm of Railway Contractors Peto, Brassey & Betts."[3] In 1859 the firm obtained the contract to build the Danish state railway, and Frederick James Rowan went to Denmark to supervise the work. Later, he established a railway carriage factory at Randers, Jutland. He was highly regarded by the Danes for connecting their country to most of Europe, for having slowed down the advance of the 1864 German invasion of Schleswig Holstein by delaying the delivery of the rolling stock, and for popularizing yacht racing in Scandinavia.[4]

William Robert Rowan was born in Omagh, Northern Ireland in 1841 and, like his own father, became a railway engineer. He took over the family business in 1874, introduced steam tramways and light railways in many parts of the world, and served as directing engineer for the Franco-Algerian Railway Corporation and other railway companies.

Secrecy surrounds the circumstances of William Robert's first meeting with Gerdine Atalia Jacobsen (born in 1851), a small, blond, determined girl with dazzling white teeth and a wry sense of humour. Their descendants know little about Gerdine's early life and the details of the Jacobsen-Rowan romance. There is some sketchy evidence that eighteen-year-old Gerdine eloped with the tall, handsome Irish engineer, and that theirs was a happy, albeit often stormy relationship, punctuated by William Robert's frequent absences on business.[5]

Having sole responsibility for her growing family did not daunt Gerdine Rowan. She led a comfortable existence in a series of beautiful Continental mansions, surrounded by numerous servants including a governess for the girls, a tutor for the boys, and a nanny for her babies. By 1890 there were four children, Ellen (Nellie), born in 1879, Agnes (Moussie), born in 1885, Arthur, born in 1887, and Frederick (Fretsie), born in 1890. The family had settled in the outskirts of Basel, Switzerland in 1889, where William

1. William Robert Rowan, 1890s.
Courtesy of the Rowan family.

2. Agnes and Nellie Rowan, late 1890s.
Courtesy of Mary Brodrick.

Robert Rowan bought a seventeenth-century step-gabled house and about three thousand square metres of land. Although William Rowan later maintained that he was born at Schloss Binningen (a castle originally built in the Middle Ages), the sale contract of 24 July 1889 states that the house bought by William Robert Rowan was a medieval tenant's house, known as the Schlössli (meaning "small castle").[6]

With the birth of William in 1891 and of Harry (Hansie) in 1894 the family was complete. The Binningen area was ideal for bringing up children, and provided a perfect background for one of the twentieth century's great naturalists. Contemporary tourist books mentioned Binningen (meaning "wild man") as a stop in the picturesque Birsig Valley on the way to Fluhen. Now only a few minutes journey by car, from the bustling, ancient city of Basel, in 1890 it would have been a one-hour train ride. Binningen's accessibility by steam railway made it a favourite excursion and holiday place for British travellers.[7]

William Rowan, variously called Willie or Billy by his family and friends, was born at the Schlössli on 29 July 1891. His birth was attended by the family doctor and a nurse, although there is no evidence that his forty-year-old mother had trouble with the delivery. In fact, the birth of a fifth child in the days of large families was far from a noteworthy event. This particular birth created much excitement, however, because of the child's appearance. He was born with dark hair, while his siblings were fair, and had two teeth at birth, which the family doctor considered a sign of future cleverness. The infant was therefore regarded as a super baby, and received special treatment from other members of the Rowan household.[8]

William Rowan was introduced to the outdoors early. While most newborns at the time were kept indoors for several weeks, Billy, born in midsummer, was soon taken outside by his nurse. This was the only period of his life when he was well protected from the elements. On sunny days the nurse carried the precious bundle in her arms, tightly encased in a white bunting bag, face well covered with a lace shawl to keep out both gnats and the harmful rays of the August sun. A tilted sunshade, lined with green material, held by the fiercely protective nurse, shielded him from the inquisitive glances of his curious siblings. In fact, as his sister Agnes, six years old at the time of his birth, recalled, the other children had to earn the privilege of peeking at the super baby.[9]

Billy grew up to be a quiet, thoughtful little boy who spent much time out-of-doors playing with the family's dogs or watching birds. In time, observing nature would take precedence over personal grooming, fixed mealtimes, and all indoor activities. He frequently escaped into the garden to watch the large, long-legged white storks.[10] He did not yet know that storks, nesting in Europe but wintering in Africa, are called long-distance migrants. He simply observed their large platform nests on neighbouring roofs, and listened to their noisy greetings, so loud that they could be heard even inside the Schlössli. Although storks are usually silent, in the mating season they engage in a remarkable visual and auditory display.

In the 1890s the white stork was still a common sight in many Continental villages. The large nests on the chimneys of thatched cottages were part of the general landscape. On a youngster of Billy's interests and temperament, the long, red, rapierlike bills of the parent storks, which they used in their deafening, intricate fencing manoeuvres, must have left an indelible impression. The parent storks' careful feeding of the young with wriggling frogs, snakes and lizards, that they airlifted in their beaks, inculcated ideas of the interrelationships of living organisms. Young Billy Rowan, observing many aspects of the stork's nesting behaviour, easily acquired the foundation of a lifelong interest in the breeding biology of migratory birds.

Storks were just one of many species of colourful birds seen at Binningen throughout the year. Others, such as the striking black-beige-and-pink hoopoe and agile blue and great tits, made the Binningen area a paradise for a budding naturalist. There were forests and meadows in the district, and in the garden the Rowan children had their own flower beds. Not surprisingly, however, Billy's suffered from lack of care.[11]

With their father absent so much of the time, the responsibility for the children's education remained the domain of their mother, who believed that youngsters should develop their own interests. Although she could be strict, she was indulgent with those she loved, and allowed her children a freedom unusual for the times.[12] Languages were an important part of European culture, and the

3. The Schlössli, 1918.
Courtesy of I. Achermann-Knöepfli.

young Rowans learned German, French, and English, as well as reading and arithmetic, from various tutors and governesses. This left them with free time to dream and to play.

When the elder Rowan's business shifted to France, he sold the Schlössli and, in 1898, moved his family to the outskirts of Paris. The children took the move in their stride. For them it simply involved exchanging one estate for another. Instead of the Schlössli, they now lived at the Château Plessis-Trevise, about thirty kilometres southeast of Paris, where the staff spoke French instead of German.[13]

The magnificent estate in the Val-de-Marne consisted of the actual Château surrounded by a moat, a guest house for thirty people, stables and even a pheasantry. For the young Rowans, it was an idyllic existence. Their favourite spot was a deep circular pit under a small, tree-covered hill, which served as an ice cellar and which became the site of games played by the four Rowan boys during the Boer War. Arthur, the eldest, prompted by what he had read in the English newspapers, formed an imaginary company to trade with South Africa. The division of labour was along strongly hierarchical lines: Arthur was both director and general; Fred was the scout and the second in command; Billy, already the Renaissance man, had three roles — those of the enemy, the horse, and the cook; and Harry, the youngest and ultimately the most financially successful of the brothers, was the banker and journalist.[14]

Billy enjoyed playing his roles. He liked being the enemy because it meant that he could disappear to find nests. As the cook, he showed imagination; in later life he would provide unusual game dishes for special occasions. He began his adventures as a gourmet with sticklebacks, fished from the moat with an old teapot on a string, and pickled with laurel leaves in an old jar. Being a horse was more strenuous, as it involved "dragging a four wheel go-cart across the moat to the ice cellar."[15] Meanwhile, Arthur occupied the headquarters located in a tree, and used the electric bell he had rigged up to summon his underlings.

Although William Robert Rowan usually spent the hot month of August with his family at their country house in Boulogne, August 1900 was an exception. He stayed in London on business. In mid-September he became sick, and by the time he joined the family at Boulogne he was gravely ill with double pneumonia. Within a week he was dead.[16] After his burial in the Rowan vault at Kensal Green (London), the family, their happy, secure existence suddenly in ruins, returned to France. Mrs. Rowan had to settle her affairs, sell the Château, find a new place to live, and, as she was determined to fulfil her late husband's wishes, provide the children with a good English education. Although her husband lived most of his life on the Continent, he often said he planned to send the boys to an English boarding school, possibly Eton or Harrow, where in addition to getting a good education they would receive proper discipline.

Gerdine Rowan liked the idea of English schools. England was neutral territory for her, as she and her husband had severed ties with both the Irish Rowans and the Danish Jacobsens. But after the loss of her husband she could not face sending her boys to a boarding school. On the advice of family friends she found the perfect solution in Bedford, where the boys could attend Bedford School, a public school with a more modest reputation, as day students, while Agnes could study at Dame Alice Harpur, the excellent local girls' school.[17]

The family first lived at Armstrong Cottage, 41 St. John Street, while waiting for the completion of a more suitable new house. By 1902 the Rowans had moved to 12 Merton Road, one of three new houses built on that street in 1901. While the Rowan's new home, a red-brick detached house, could not compete with either the Schlössli or the Château it was spacious enough and ideally situated on the edge of town. There were fields and small woodlots, the Great Ouse River was within easy walking distance, and the boys' school could be reached on foot in less than three minutes.[18]

Bedford was indeed a fortuitous choice. The attractive old town in the fertile Ouse Valley is only eighty kilometres north of London, and not far from Cambridge and East Anglia. The town has a long and varied history beginning in Roman times, and is famous for its connection with John Bunyan. It is still possible to identify many of the natural features of the area mentioned in Pilgrim's Progress.[19]

Bedford School, a sixteenth-century public school, was modernized in the mid-nineteenth century when it became a combined boarding and day school, catering mostly to the sons of army officers. In the 1890s the reorganized school moved to the edge of town in order to accommodate more students. Although the open green spaces around the handsome, well-appointed red-brick buildings have long since disappeared, the large playing fields are still in use.[20]

It was a strange new existence for the young Rowans. On the Continent, private tutors had allowed them to proceed at their own speed. Now the five school-age children found themselves in strictly regulated school environments where their fluency in languages did not compensate for their lack of knowledge in other subjects.[21]

The school records show that the four boys entered Bedford School on 20 September 1901. Arthur attended the Big School while the three younger ones were placed in the Preparatory School, dubbed "the Incubator," or "Inky." Billy and Fred stayed together in the Inky until July 1902; but at the beginning of the next term, in the Big School, their paths diverged. Fred, who planned to become an engineer, studied science, while Billy, with his mother's encouragement, took classics, French, and English in preparation for the civil service.[22]

The boys came in for much ribbing during the first few weeks. They still wore their French clothes and spoke French and German more fluently than they did English; not surprisingly, they were called Froggies.[23] They were not allowed to play rough games. Bedford School had an excellent sports program, but as all the Rowan boys had had hernias as infants, Gerdine Rowan would not allow them to play rugby or other violent games. Instead, they played tennis and cricket, and enjoyed swimming and boating. Once they had acquired the obligatory school uniform — flannel trousers, sports coat, school cap, and dark blue tie — they were physically indistinguishable from the other students.[24]

Natural history continued to fascinate Billy. He explored the countryside with his brothers and friends, discovering the similarities and differences between France and England. The boys collected birds' nests and eggs, water bugs from ponds, and harmless snakes, which they kept at home. The house at 12 Merton Road was home for the Rowans, Miss Stone, the children's former nanny, and a changing collection of animals and other treasures. Their pets included cats, rabbits, pigeons, and even a chameleon, which lived for a long time in a floral centrepiece on the dining-room table.[25]

It was about this time that Billy took up sketching both natural-history specimens and the surrounding countryside. He may have received some private instruction, because a 1904 certificate in the William Rowan Papers testifies to his having passed into division 2 of the Royal Drawing Society. His sister Agnes recalled that when Billy was eleven years old, his talent in drawing was discovered by one of the schoolmasters.[26]

Billy, who had a good ear for music, took piano lessons for awhile, but refused to practise.[27] He was very upset when his mother stopped his lessons, although, characteristically, he never questioned her decision. Instead, determined to show her that he could teach himself music, he continued to strum by ear. Nearly forty years later, the journalist Barbara Moon reports, he claimed that "his parents had forbidden him concerts because of the moodiness that always ensued."[28] However, since Billy had no father by this time, one must question the accuracy of his recollection.

Moodiness is a state not uncommon in teenagers, whether induced by music or not. In fact, Billy Rowan's moodiness could well have been due to other factors, such as the increasingly religious tone of the Rowan household.

The Rowan children were members of the Church of England. While they were living abroad, either Gerdine Rowan or her husband read the Sunday service, but there is no indication that either of them was particularly religious. After the family moved to England, Gerdine Rowan increasingly found solace in religion.[29] The major turning point came during the summer of 1902, at the fashionable seaside resort of Cliftonville, a select part of Margate on the southeast coast of England. Fred Rowan recalled, in 1959, that they made many friends through the Children's Special Service Mission, which held daily services on the beach. He added that their mother was a "good Victorian and threw herself heart and soul into Church, and us with her."[30] The children were not all equally influenced by their mother's religious enthusiasm. While Fred became devout, Billy, always of a critical mind, could not accept the church's tenets. For his mother's sake, however, he tried to share his family's new-found joy in Christianity. So Billy played the harmonium during the beach services, while remaining critical, as he would for the rest of his life, of the church's dogmas and rituals.

By his early teens, Billy was finding his home atmosphere increasingly religious and restrictive. He found school equally restrictive. Indeed, for a very bright boy, his school results were mediocre. His best mark was in mathematics, which he found a challenging subject. He could admire its logic, the neatness of its laws and derivations. Twenty years later he would apply such logic to the formulation of the original hypothesis for the research that would make the name William Rowan well known in zoological circles.

As an adolescent in Bedford, Billy was mostly concerned with the outdoors, yearning for the opportunity to sketch and photograph birds and other animals. His dreams of outdoor adventures were fuelled by numerous nature books, such as the nature encyclopaedia Fred won in school, and works by the brothers Richard and Cherry Kearton, and the British-born Canadian naturalist Ernest Thompson Seton. He resolved to spend his adult life studying nature. As he later recalled, a career in the civil service, "stewing behind Government bars," did not appeal to him, and he "took an unexpected escape to the Wild West."[31]

The idea of escape may have been prompted by Richard Kearton's visits to Bedford School in 1903 and 1905. It was around this time that Billy began to have a recurrent dream in which he was let loose on an estate with a bird's nest in every bush.[32] Whether this dream was precipitated by Kearton's illustrated lectures or was an outcome of Billy's increasing frustration at school and at home we shall never know, but it is clear that he still grieved for the freedom he enjoyed at Plessis-Trevise and Binningen.

Kearton's lectures, illustrated with slides taken by his brother Cherry, were extremely popular in Britain. In a country where amateur naturalists have long contributed to the study of botany, geology, and zoology, the Kearton brothers' success as nature photographers and interpreters held the promise of a career for aspiring young naturalists such as Billy, unable to envisage a life behind closed doors. Judging by the review of "Haunts and Habits of British Birds" (Kearton's second lecture, delivered at Bedford School on 4 November 1905) in the school's magazine, the *Ousel*, the lecturer "encountered a large audience all agog for an entertainment equal in interest to the last lecture he gave us (Nov. 14, 1903)."[33] The slides of merlins and owls, an osprey at its nest, and a tree pipit feeding its cuckoo fosterchild, entranced the young audience. Many of the boys had already read of the Keartons' adventures while photographing wildlife in their popular books, inexpensive enough to be easily accessible to schoolchildren. The books and school presentations gave practical advice to aspiring young nature photographers. The Keartons were among those in Britain who pioneered the use of hides, tentlike contraptions designed to conceal both photographer and camera.[34]

Not surprisingly, Billy was fascinated by the possibility of seeing animals at such close quarters, and never forgot the Keartons' advice to choose cameras of "strength and stability rather than elegance, for natural history photography demands the withstanding of far greater strain and wear and tear than ordinary studio work." He also learned about photographic techniques, and the public relations work needed to become a successful nature photographer, such as obtaining permission from landowners for photographing on their estates, and maintaining a good relationship with gamekeepers.[35]

Ernest Thompson Seton's visit to Bedford School on 10 February 1906 introduced Billy to the sights and sounds of North American animals. Seton's lecture was entitled "Wild Animals I Have Known" (as was his successful 1898 book). According to a report in the *Ousel*, the author showed slides of Canadian mammals such as the pronghorn antelope, cottontail rabbit, skunk, and racoon. The lecture finished with an exciting and "realistic Moose Hunt in which trumpeting, beating of horns and revolver firing played a considerable part."[36]

Billy was captivated. He had already read Seton's animal stories. He had encountered other books and stories of the Wild West of Canada, which were popular in Britain at this time. Magazines such as *Boy's Own Paper*, published by the Religious Tract Society (which had a circulation of more than one million), carried regular features on Canada's wildlife, Canadian Indians, and the Canadian Pacific Railway (CPR).

Beginning in the late nineteenth century, CPR agents and Canadian government clerks in search of potential settlers published numerous colourful advertisements extolling the virtues of the Canadian Prairies. The young men to whom this literature was addressed were motivated to emigrate by a variety of factors. These included the inhibiting effects of the British class structure, unemployment, and the attraction of the wild, open spaces.[37] For Billy, the open spaces promised, as they had for many others before him, the idea of freedom and adventure, escape from the restrictive realities of everyday life in Britain. They also offered a chance to evade the life of a civil servant, which he contemplated with increasing distaste.

According to Patrick A. Dunae, young British immigrants were deliberately solicited, partly to "strengthen Canada's imperial connection," and partly to "help to counter the growing numbers of American and European immigrants in the West."[38] Billy capitalized on this trend, although he was far from ready to settle in Canada. Captivated by Seton's lectures and pictures, fascinated by the literature of the Wild West, he sought adventure rather than a career, an escape from home (and a postponement of decisions about his future) rather than a life of toil.

Although Billy was not quite fifteen years old at the time of Seton's visit to Bedford School, he may have felt old enough to go west immediately. Accordingly, he began to mount a campaign worthy of his military forbears to obtain his mother's permission for a trip to Canada. He knew that his mother understood him, considered him to be the most unique and creative of her children, and would always encourage his interest in natural history. He was lucky that Gerdine Rowan also had an adventurous nature. Although her children did not know it, she had rebelled against her own background when she eloped with her dashing Irish engineer. She may have thought a short trip to Canada would cure Billy from contemplating other adventures, and he would then settle down to a secure job in the British civil service. She agreed that he could go, but insisted he finish school first.[39]

With his mother's permission thus won, Billy resigned himself to two more years of school, but spent all his spare time outdoors, in preparation for the Wild West. He roamed the Bedford district, sketched birds and mammals, and, after acquiring a box camera, began to take and develop his own pictures. He read voraciously on Canadian subjects in the *Boy's Own Paper*, and in books by J. Macdonald Oxley, R.M. Ballantyne, W.H.G. Kingston, and others.

Meanwhile, Gerdine Rowan did some research on her own. She wanted Billy to have his adventure and promised to finance it for awhile, but she also wanted to ensure that he would be well looked after. She needed to know that a trustworthy person would keep an eye on the inexperienced boy, and that Billy would come to no harm in the Canadian West, a region much wilder in her imagination than in reality. So she began some discreet inquiries about some friends of her friends who had settled in Western Canada and were willing to take on her adventurous son for a year or two. The records are silent on the chain of events that led to an agreement between Gerdine Rowan and rancher Bryce Hamilton Bunny, an agreement that stipulated that William Rowan was to spend two years as a ranch pupil, lodging with the Bunnys, a proper British family. There, in the Crawling Valley, Alberta, he would experience the seemingly glamorous life of a cowpuncher while having plenty of opportunities to observe and photograph wildlife.

Billy Rowan's last year at Bedford School (1907–1908) was spent in the London stream, which prepared boys for the London matriculation, although Billy did not actually sit for this exam. Then life became a whirl of visits and shopping — preparations for the life of a cowpuncher. Arrangements were made for his passage on a Canadian Pacific Railway steamer to Quebec City, and by rail to Gleichen, Alberta, where someone from Bunny's Ranch would meet him. In August 1908, seventeen-year-old William Rowan, made the journey to Liverpool, where he embarked on the next stage of his life.

2

A Life of Adventure, 1908-1911

FROM THE UPPER DECK of the ocean liner in Liverpool harbour, Rowan happily watched the busy scene: passengers milling at the railings or coming aboard in a steady stream, porters struggling with luggage, and gulls screaming above the din and clatter of the harbour. On this cloudy August day in 1908, after years of anticipation, Rowan was finally on his way to Canada and a life of adventure.

Rowan's passage on the *Empress of France*, one of the many Canadian Pacific liners transporting emigrants and visitors from Liverpool to Quebec City, was paid for by his mother. From the travel brochures he knew that his passage would take about six days, and from his readings in natural history he had learned that he was likely to see whales and seabirds while sailing up the famous St. Lawrence River to historic Quebec City. He enjoyed the prospect of seeing places visited in the early 1850s by Sir William Rowan, his famous great-great-grandfather who, in 1853, had been appointed deputy governor-general of Canada.

In contrast to the British civil servants, European visitors, and numerous immigrants who thought that Canada had practically no history, Rowan looked forward to seeing places where history was still new and therefore tangible, where in the not-too-distant past European merchants traded with Indians. He knew the main item of trade was fur, and he wanted to photograph the famed North American mammals: beaver and bison, cougar and grizzly bear. In his imagination he saw himself pursuing mammals on horseback over the hills of Alberta, protected by the famous Northwest

Mounted Police. For added protection, he would rely on his revolver, bought on expert advice in England for six pounds sterling. Thus equipped, he felt equal to the challenges of frontier life. But on the *Empress of France* he had no need for weapons. Although Rowan took with him only a flat-topped steamer trunk of the type commonly used by emigrants, his accommodation was comfortable. Like the other first-class passengers, he slept in a luxurious stateroom and dressed for dinner, which was served in the ship's ornate dining room.

It was natural for Rowan, the son and grandson of railway engineers, to travel on a railway-company-owned steamship. The Canadian Pacific Railway (CPR) was popular in England, and with good reason. It was favoured by European emigrants because its ships were comfortable, inexpensive, steady, and fast. They regularly picked up passengers at Antwerp or at a British port, and not only carried them to Canada, but also sold them land on the Prairies.[1] By the time Rowan sailed from Britain, steerage had disappeared and third-class passage — which included the use of cabins, lounges, and dining saloons — was used to transport most emigrants to the New World. Accustomed to luxury travel on European railways, Mrs. Rowan would not allow her seventeen-year-old prospective cowpuncher to sail third class. Thus, instead of sharing his cabin with unknown emigrants, most of whom were peasants, Rowan slept alone, in first class comfort. Instead of being served pea soup, salt herring, corned beef, or boiled salt fish in third class, Rowan ate roast beef, lamb, or fresh seafood, and indulged his taste for ice cream.

From the very first morning, when the vibration of the ship woke him as it left the bustling port of Liverpool, Rowan spent most of his time on deck, watching seabirds, hoping for a glimpse of whales. He soon got his sea legs, and did not suffer from the seasickness that afflicted most passengers on the rough North Atlantic crossing. Only multiple helpings of the rich ice cream made him ill, but he soon recovered, and by the time the ship reached Canadian waters off Newfoundland, he was spending practically all his waking hours propped against the railing of the ship, his slightly myopic eyes scanning water and air for signs of wildlife.[2]

In later life, Rowan often recalled his first view of the Gulf of St. Lawrence and the trip along the river to Quebec City. The wind had dropped, the air was mild, and the distant blue hills, studded with church steeples and colourful wooden buildings, provided ample material for both his camera and sketchbook. His visit to the old part of Quebec City was Rowan's first experience of a part of Canada where French was the language of everyday life. The familiar language and European-style architecture made him feel at home. In contrast, on his train journey from Quebec City to Alberta, he got his first real view of a different world, where the sights and sounds were novel and exciting. Rowan eagerly observed the thickly forested slopes of the Canadian Shield, low in comparison with the Swiss Alps, which he had seen in his early childhood. Sitting in his comfortable leather seat, which at night converted into his sleeping couch, he happily watched the hills and lakes. He observed ducks, geese, and entire loon families on the lakes, and red-tailed hawks soaring over open land or forest, or perching on trees along the railway line.

Groups of German- and Slavic-speaking immigrants got off or on the train during its many stops. There were numerous family groups — lured to the West by the advertisements of the Canadian government and the CPR, seeking free land for themselves and their children. Other immigrant groups consisted solely of women and children, the youngsters impatient to run around and explore, their shawled mothers frightened to let them out of their sight.[3] There were also young men — some, no doubt, prospective ranch pupils like Rowan, whose parents paid an annual fee of one hundred pounds sterling to enable them to live and work on a ranch among cowboys.They were to learn about the seemingly glamorous, but in truth gruelling, life of a ranch hand. Many of the ranch pupils came from well-to-do English families — seduced, like Rowan, by visions of the rolling hills, wooded coulees, and unending open sky of the West. Some were remittance men, wastrels whose respectable families gladly paid an annual remittance to keep their embarrassingly unconventional sons at a safe distance from home.[4]

Rowan, though he later jokingly referred to himself as a typical remittance man, did not belong to this category. He was a young man seeking adventure and escape from a loving but overly religious mother in a country inhabited, he thought, by the wild animals Ernest Thompson Seton had so eloquently described. However, Seton's Manitoba of the 1880s had changed considerably by the beginning of the twentieth century. When Rowan arrived in 1908, the westward thrust of homesteaders had already begun to alter the endless, fenceless horizon of early ranching days. The immigrant families he encountered en route were to alter further the character of the West young Rowan was seeking.

It is unlikely that Rowan thought about immigration policy and homesteading advances as he avidly contemplated the landscape of this new country. Dark forests, with patches of dead trees (remnants of forest fires), were lit up with the pink spires of fireweed. Goldenrod, black-eyed Susans, and purple asters dotted the small meadows. Wooded swamps, where darting swallows gathered for their fall migration, also showed evidence of muskrat and beaver. Wet meadows and ponds provided wallowing and drinking areas for the moose, and dead snags made excellent lookout posts for the bald eagle, belted kingfisher, and other species of birds. Once the train passed Lake of the Woods, the country flattened out, and clumps of willows gave way to farmland. Frequent stops enabled the travellers to stretch their legs, gather wildflowers and berries, and view the numerous tiny railway stations, many with beautifully kept gardens. Rowan used these stops to photograph the people and the landscape, but there was no time for animal photography.

The hundreds of miles of windswept prairie, with its ripening fields of wheat and blue pools of flax, its occasional farm buildings and the limitless arching sky, filled Rowan with an excitement he was to retain all his life. Soaring Swainson's hawks, their tilted wings forming a shallow *V*, vied for attention with other hawks sitting on telegraph poles. Ducks, geese, and shorebirds, unidentifiable from the distance, fed busily in prairie sloughs. Dust devils swirled over the flat land. Farther west he saw the real prairie: clumps of grass, wildflowers, grazing horses and cattle, and occasionally a small band of pronghorn antelope.[5] In vain did Rowan strain his eyes for a view of the legendary plains buffalo or grizzly bear. They had long retreated from their former habitats, squeezed out by Eastern Canadian and European settlers.

For anyone else seeking the kind of adventure promised in early twentieth-century boys' literature, the journey would have proved a disappointment.[6] No outlaws or bands of Indians attacked the train. In fact, the journey was smooth and comfortable, allowing Rowan to concentrate on the much-dreamt-about, but still new, strange, and overpowering countryside. No amount of reading and dreaming could have prepared him for the sheer size of the country. Every section of the landscape was huge: the dark forests and rock outcrops of the Canadian Shield, the muskegs of northern Ontario, the farmland of eastern Manitoba, and the increasingly rolling countryside of western Saskatchewan and southeastern Alberta. Everything was on a scale unimaginable for someone used to the Continent and Britain.

Rowan's first view of Alberta certainly did not match the romanticized notion he had of it for several years. "On the bald-headed prairie," he recalled nearly half a century later "the aftermath of the drastic winter of 1906–7 was everywhere still in evidence, particularly in the coulees full of skeleton[s] of starved cattle and horses."[7]

Indeed, the winter of 1906–1907 was remembered by ranchers as one of the worst in a quarter century. Ranching became a big business on the western plains in the 1880s, when cattle driven up from Montana were first turned loose on the mixed and short-grass prairie in what is now southwestern Saskatchewan and southeastern Alberta. This area, thanks to a climatic phenomenon unique to it — the Chinook winds — could provide year-round natural feed for the grazing cattle. Chinooks can vary from being gentle breezes to being winds of eighty kilometres per hour. They can last for days on end, melting the snow cover and exposing clumps of grass, the cattle's food supply.[8] This is a great advantage in cattle country, since neither shelter nor extra food is needed to supplement the natural grass feed. But on rare occasions the Chinook fails to appear. The severe winter of 1886–1887 was long remembered as one of great hardship for cattle and ranch owners; that of 1906–1907 surpassed all others in previous recorded history. The Two-Bar Ranch lost nearly 80 percent of its cattle in 1906–1907: the herd dwindled from 11,000 head to a mere 2,200. The BU Ranch lost 12,000 head of cattle — half of its herd.[9]

Rowan could not see all the devastation from the passing train, but he saw scattered skeletons along the railway line. Watching them through the large window of his luxurious coach, he was forced to focus his attention on the uncomfortable realities of life and death in this gently rolling short-grass country. Indeed, the skeletons seemed an integral part of the landscape through which the train had been steadily climbing ever since leaving the bustling depot at Winnipeg. Fortunately, there were plenty of other sights vying for his attention: pencil-straight Richardson ground squirrels (also known as gophers or picket pins), long, bushy-tailed, ubiquitous coyotes, and "lovely little kit fox[es] still to be seen."[10]

On a sunny afternoon in late August, Rowan jumped off Canadian Pacific train number 1 at Gleichen, Alberta, a busy trading centre for ranchers, railway men, and Blackfoot Indians. Rowan's arrival went unnoticed by the *Gleichen Call*, a weekly newspaper founded in 1907, which regularly detailed the comings and goings of notable ranchers and other local people. It listed the names of land seekers, but ranch pupils, casual ranch hands and drifters came and went unnoticed.

In Gleichen, Rowan was met by Ernie Brooks, who worked for Bryce Hamilton Bunny, the owner of a two-and-a-half-section ranch in the Crawling Valley.[11] Brooks brought along extra horses for Rowan and for supplies, and took the new ranch pupil to various outfitters where he could finally buy his western gear: a dun-coloured, flat-brimmed Stetson, dark leather chaps, and spurs.[12] Though seemingly a raw, dusty western town, Gleichen had several good hotels and restaurants, and numerous feed stores, liveries, and hitching posts. Its general stores were full of goods, and while Brooks ordered supplies for his boss, Rowan was able to mail his postcards and replenish his photo supplies at A.R. Yates's post office and drugstore.

The trip across country from Gleichen to Bunny's was more than eighty kilometres, and would take nearly ten hours on horseback, so the experienced ranch hand and the young ranch pupil spent the night in Gleichen. They set off early next morning, following the Lord Lorne Trail. Laid down by the Northwest Mounted Police, the trail crossed what is now the Trans-Canada Highway, and east and north of Gleichen forded the Crowfoot Creek. Heading towards the northeast, by the Wintering Hills, the Two-Bar Trail (as it was also called) led towards the Red Deer Badlands and the Crawling Valley. There was much to see. Tepee rings indicated that there had been Indian settlements near smallish coulees. Rutted cart tracks, made by the early settlers and still used by the ranchers to transport supplies picked up at Gleichen, crisscrossed the prairie.[13]

Though the tide of homesteaders had already encroached upon

4. Bunny's House, Crawling Valley, Red Deer, Alberta, 1908. Drawing by William Rowan. *University of Alberta Archives, William Rowan Papers.*

the eastern section of the Prairies, Rowan saw few signs of civilization on his first all-day ride in southeastern Alberta. Later he recalled that at the time of his arrival only half a dozen gates had to be opened between Gleichen and Bunny's ranch. Wildlife was abundant. He observed many birds, some of which he identified from his Chester Reed pocket guide as western meadowlarks. Swainson's and red-tailed hawks soared over the prairie looking for prey. He watched western kingbirds flycatching from the poplars and alders growing in the coulees. There were plenty of mammals, such as jackrabbits, and Rowan noted that "Badgers, later to become almost non-existent, were everywhere, and gophers, their main diet, sizzled."[14] He had his first close look at the characteristic plants of the district: wolf willow, buckbrush, and sage, the dry-looking pussyfoot, and the prickly wild rose hidden among the bunchgrass. At the approach to Bunny's trail, Rowan marvelled at the panorama of the Red Deer River Valley, the horizontal layers of its eroded sides pinkish buff in the afternoon sun.

The sight of the rolling country and its wildlife surely compensated Rowan for the discomfort of sitting for hours in the hard, western saddle. He was soon pitched into the life of a ranch hand, because Bunny's ranch, as the old-timers now recall, was run with military precision: Rowan and Brooks returned just in time for milking.[15]

B.H. Bunny bought Charlie Bray's two-thousand-head cattle ranch in 1903, replaced the cattle with Percheron horses, and, in 1907, went to England to "acquire a wife and a piano."[16] He obviously succeeded, as the 18 April 1908 issue of the *Gleichen Call* announced the arrival of "Bryce H. Bunny and Bride from England." Soon, a big house was built on a stone foundation. By contrast to the bunkhouse, which had furniture constructed of barrels and boxes, the new home seemed quite civilized. Like many other ranchers' homes, it now had real furniture, curtains — and a piano. Unlike most of them, it also had electricity and hot water.

There was much for a ranch pupil to learn. He was typically a young man, fresh from an English public school, whose family paid one hundred pounds per year for his board and ranch training.[17] Rowan soon participated in a roundup, held during the first week of September. He became used to chuckwagon meals and learned to ride in all sorts of weather, and to smoke and roll cigarettes (a habit he maintained all his life). Later, Rowan also learned how to observe, and prevent harm to livestock, to brand cattle or dip it for mange. He became tough and self-sufficient, qualities that stood him in good stead during his later period in Alberta. He learned to eat enormous meals and to go for long periods on very little food. He developed a fondness for thick cream, and for periodic socials, get-togethers with singing, where his mellow baritone was much appreciated.[18]

Rowan found life at Bunny's ranch exhilarating. He loved the clear air, open countryside, encounters with neighbouring cowboys and ranch hands, and, always the indigenous plants, birds, and mammals. Though the life of ranch hands was far from luxurious, by sharing it Rowan learned much about wildlife, Canada, and himself. He had more space, both physical and emotional, than ever before. He had companions — mostly men less educated than himself — men with a clear reverence for the rolling prairie and the freedom it offered. Although as a ranch pupil Rowan was expected to participate in all ranch activities, he had precious moments for contemplating the land and the sky and, without knowing that it was called ecology, the interrelations of climate, plants, and animals — including humans.

There were other things in his cowpunching days that he benefited from in later life. One that became particularly important was his ability to talk to people from all walks of life. During his sheltered childhood in Switzerland and France, Rowan's companions were his four brothers and two sisters, tutors and governesses, plus an assortment of servants. During his days at Bedford School, Rowan had spent much time with his brothers Fred and Harry, and also with those of his schoolmates who shared his enthusiasm for natural history. He met few people from other social classes, apart from tradesmen and servants. The ranchers and cowboys he met in Canada came from a variety of backgrounds. Some were ex-army officers, a few had served in the Northwest Mounted Police. They all shared a love of the outdoors, and many knew the names of the plants and animals Rowan was seeing for the first time.

He immersed himself in the varying sights, sounds, and smells of the land. His schoolboy training in natural history enabled him to classify many plants and animals, and he later maintained, exaggerating somewhat, that "the average English school boy who collects eggs as a hobby, could be dumped out here on the prairies amongst birds he has never seen before, and would make [few] howlers in identification."[19]

Rowan may have acquired excellent natural-history training in England, but in 1908 he showed little evidence he would later prefer studying birds rather than mammals. He observed, described, and photographed mammals at every available opportunity. He often watched a small band of pronghorn antelope while riding on the range. He was told, by the rancher Jack Clark, that in the 1880s, when Clark first came west, antelopes were still a common sight, but the buffalo was already on the verge of extinction. Rowan later noted that in 1908 timber wolves were still doing damage, and at campfire gatherings people were regaled with stories of a famous wolf, "the old one with a scarred face, said to be as big as a pony." Rowan often searched for this legendary wolf, but he never found it — he only heard its howl.[20]

The life of a ranch pupil was far from comfortable, but Rowan, despite being born into the "lap of luxury" (his own term), complained remarkably little. One suspects that having persuaded his doting mother to let him go alone to Canada, Rowan deliberately minimized the extent of his discomfort. Like the other ranch hands, Rowan slept in a log house covered with a sod roof. The dirt floor was bare. At other times Rowan would sleep in a tent or on the open range, using a cowboy's bedroll, described by an old rancher as: "a canvas sheet just over twice as long as the blankets and about six inches wider than the width of the blankets. It had a row of snaps and rings on the sides." The cowboys would spread the sheet, put the blanket on one half, fold the sheet on top of it, snap the sides together, roll it all up and tie it with a rope.[21] This practical arrangement was a far cry from the soft feather beds Rowan had as a child. He did not mind using a bedroll, however, and the whole experience served as an excellent preparation for his Spartan adult expeditions, during which he would often sleep, without even a bedroll, in leaky tents, prickly haystacks, or on the hard, bare ground.

Sleeping out-of-doors, under the crystal clear western sky, Rowan felt happy; he listened to the sounds of cattle and horses, coyotes and wolves. In spring and summer, he woke in the early morning to the flutelike song of the western meadowlark, the tinkling sound of the horned lark, and the winnowing of snipes. He often listened to the honking of migrating wild geese. These experiences reinforced his previous interest in wildlife and imbued him with a lifelong love of southern Alberta. Among the gently rolling hills and wooded coulees he felt free from the restrictions, as he perceived them, and the many demands of a loving but stifling family environment. For nearly two years he lived the life of an apprentice cowpuncher, becoming self-sufficient and increasingly at ease with outdoor living.

Rowan frequently wrote letters to his mother, partly to communicate his new experiences, partly to allay her fears concerning his well-being. In the spring of 1910, although his two years as a ranch pupil had not yet been completed, his mother persuaded him to return home for a visit. Why Rowan agreed is unclear. Possibly ranch work had lost its appeal. He did miss his family, was curious about their new house in St. Albans, Hertfordshire, and wanted to explore the surrounding countryside, a promising area, his brother Fred wrote, for nature photography.

Rowan boarded a Canadian Pacific liner at Quebec City, and enjoyed once again the luxury of first-class travel. He was impatient to see his family, who would meet him at Liverpool. He wanted, as he so often did in his life, to impress others, and impressed the Rowans were, his brother Fred recalled, particularly by his clothes: he disembarked at Liverpool in "Chaps, Stetson and all!"[22] Even in England, a country used to eccentric clothes and behaviour, Rowan's cowboy garb must have raised a few eyebrows. He wore faded work pants and cracked leather chaps. A large, colourful bandanna was casually knotted around his neck. As he descended the gangway, the family noted that he appeared taller than before. Though Rowan may have grown, his new height was probably due to his high-heeled cowboy boots and pinched-crown hat. He was quite a sight, and his family was delighted to see him.

During the summer of 1910, Rowan found there were few people around to keep him company on his country rambles. Some of his old friends had remained in Bedford, others worked in London or had entered university. His eldest brother, Arthur, was in India, and his sister Nellie, a missionary, lived in China. Agnes, though at home, was busy with her own life. Fred was preparing for his matriculation exams, and Harry was still at school. Rowan thought he had returned only for a visit, but soon realized that his mother expected him to make new plans for his future.

While he was still unsure about what to do with his life, discussions with family and friends, and, especially, his desire to please his mother, convinced him to follow Fred's example, and study for the University College, London entrance exams. His dilemma about the future came to the fore because, like many other multitalented young people, Rowan seemed unable to commit himself to a single career. His interest in the outdoors and wildlife was perhaps, at the time, more aesthetic than scientific, but he certainly considered becoming a naturalist. His other choices were music and art.

Though Rowan lacked formal training, he played the piano, composed songs, and at odd moments contemplated becoming a musician. His wildlife drawings had always been praised by his schoolmasters, and everyone else who had seen them, and he loved sketching and painting. But was he good enough at music or art to train for a professional career? At age nineteen, Rowan could not answer this question, but he did know that he could not envisage his future in the consular service. In spite of the fact that such a career offered good opportunities for travel and plenty of leisure time for outdoor activities, he was repelled by the idea of spending his life within the narrow confines of a government bureaucracy.

Matriculation examinations could be taken three times a year. Rowan aimed to take his in September, in English, French, German, and math, with a view to pursuing science. Although these were his favourite subjects at Bedford School, Rowan was always an indifferent student, and had been away from formal studies for two years. To help him prepare for the exams, Mrs. Rowan engaged a tutor. For relaxation, Rowan could explore the charming old city of St. Albans, with its tree-lined avenues, old Roman wall, magnificent cathedral, and fifteenth-century clock tower.[23] He could clear his head of his studies among the undulating hills and mature woodlots of the Hertfordshire countryside. From his third-storey window at 19 Clarence Road, which overlooked a large park, Rowan could hear the songs of the chaffinch and the wren. He could also hear the whistles of the trains. The station was less than a kilometre away, and a trip to London was cheap and easy.

By the end of the summer, Rowan was ready to tackle the exams; it would be a four-day ordeal, his brother Fred informed him. On a Monday in mid-September, nervous and pale after having suffered from stomach cramps and nausea as was usual for him in stressful situations, Rowan began the three-hour test in English. The following day he wrote the math exam, and two days later those in French and German. He returned to St. Albans exhausted but elated. He was confident he had passed.

The long ordeal over, Rowan relaxed by playing the piano, roaming the district, and visiting family and friends. The results were posted on the first of October (and later published in a supplement of the *University Gazette)*; Rowan learned that he had passed in the second division. While not a brilliant result, it ensured admittance to University College, London.

It is not known what Rowan did during the winter of 1910–1911. Perhaps he travelled on the Continent, as he often intimated in his later correspondence. He was still hesitant, not ready to begin a lifelong career, and somehow convinced his mother that he needed more wandering time. Rowan set off from Liverpool to Quebec City in early March of 1911. He had changed since his first crossing in 1908. He was older and more aware of the need to make the right decision about his future. Characteristically, he postponed the decision until after he had revisited his old haunts in Alberta. The trip was to be brief, and his mother stipulated that he was to earn his living and pay his own return fare.

Rowan noticed significant changes along the Canadian Pacific route across the country. Some were due to the climate, the sun and snow of the Canadian spring. The bright, snowy landscape practically blinded him, yet he welcomed the warmth through the train window, a pleasant change from the chill of the North Atlantic crossing. Despite the strong sunshine, the snow hid the rocks of the Canadian Shield, weighed down branches in the forests, and blanketed the new farms in Manitoba.

The snowdrifts obliterated most landmarks. Rowan, who rented a horse at Gleichen, soon lost his bearings and rode nearly fifteen kilometres in the wrong direction. Finally, guided by the sun, he cut across the country to reach Bunny's ranch. Much to his dismay, wildlife was scarce. During an entire day in the saddle Rowan only saw one coyote, one kit fox, and two hawks.

Unlike his previous trip, the 1911 visit to Alberta was not undertaken to acquire ranching experience, and after ten days Rowan decided to return to Winnipeg. The scarcity of birds and wild mammals (there was no sign of antelopes or deer, no howl of wolves) precipitated his early departure. Rowan soon found that in contrast to the lack of wildlife in Alberta, there was much for a naturalist-photographer to see in southern Manitoba. To his delight, in late March Rowan found numerous game birds, including the now-rare prairie chicken, around Otterburn. At Emerson in late April, he watched the wild geese "passing north daily in their arrow shaped flocks." He was thrilled when he saw three sandhill cranes and wondered why these long-necked, broad-winged, heron-size birds flew west, not north like the geese. He observed ground squirrels all over the landscape, and thirty or forty snipes, and a glimpse of one large mink added zest to his delighted observations.

"There is no use crying over spilt milk," wrote Rowan in his 1911 diary-cum-field notebook, regretful that he had not kept notes during the 1908–1910 period. To remedy this, he began to keep more-or-less detailed accounts of animals and their habitats. He was more erratic or careless in recording the kinds of events that would aid us in retracing his itinerary. Thus we do not know where he stayed in Emerson and Otterburn, but learn that from the end of May he worked in Winnipeg at the Hudson's Bay Company store "for a month or so, selling socks, dressing windows, and working in the advertising office." These activities occupied him six days a week. On Sundays he photographed animals in various Winnipeg parks, sometimes alone, sometimes accompanied by Manitoba government taxidermist Edward W. Darbey. One of Rowan's favourite places was Manitoba Park, where he could photograph bison. For Rowan, the sight of these huge, shaggy animals was well worth the long streetcar journey from the centre of Winnipeg, where he lived at 558 Ellice Avenue, in a room rented from Henry F. Wilson, a carpenter.[24]

Rowan loved the bustling city, advertised in 1910 as "The Gateway to the Golden West."[25] To him Winnipeg was indeed a gateway to the Canadian West and the freedom it implied. Later it was to become the gateway to his life as a professional scientist in Canada. For the moment Rowan was satisfied by watching the bison, strolling along the banks of the Red and Assiniboine rivers, cycling along specially built paths in Elm Park, or simply lolling on the grass, admiring well-dressed young girls taking the air on Sunday afternoons.

Sometime during the summer of 1911, Rowan became acquainted with the outdoor editor of the *Manitoba Free Press* and began to sell advertising for the newspaper. He continued to spend his free time in the city parks, among the elms, oaks, birches, and poplars that grew in profusion. Like many other young men, he also tried boating on the rivers. He soon realized, however, that he preferred canoeing in the wild country, and, when time permitted, he went on overnight camping trips along the Red River, north of the city.

During the long, light summer evenings Rowan often took the electric streetcar to some distant spot to photograph wildlife. It was during one of these evenings that he met Alex G. Lawrence, who introduced him to Canadian birds and became his lifelong confidant and friend. A chemist trained in Britain, Lawrence settled in Winnipeg in 1910, at age twenty-two. He worked as a clerk in the city health department, and in his spare time set out to discover the natural features of the Manitoba landscape, to learn the names and habits of its wildlife. A keen photographer from early childhood, he also spent much time in the city parks. It was inevitable that the two young men should meet. They clicked instantly, and remained friends until Rowan's death in 1957.[26]

Rowan and Lawrence discussed photography techniques, plants, animals, and life in general. Lawrence, whose scientific training was evident in his approach to natural history, was the best companion Rowan found in Canada. The two men frequently visited Darbey's taxidermy shop at 233 Main Street which, like many other taxidermy establishments across Canada (in places where there were no museums of natural history), served as a gathering place for both budding and experienced naturalists. Among the mounted specimens of bison, moose, and deer, all of impressive size, one could also find freshly killed birds from the Winnipeg area. Others were already prepared and mounted in lifelike positions. At Darbey's, Rowan took detailed notes and made pen-and-ink and watercolour sketches. He could also examine the differences in plumage and size, and note the variations among the specimens from different geographic regions. Information was also available about when and where the specimens were killed, and about the relative abundance of birds and mammals. In this way, Rowan acquired a basic Canadian natural-history education, similar to the training students in large cities received in natural-history museums.

Excursions with Lawrence and others resulted in Rowan collecting birds, making sketches, and, more importantly for his future work, achieving a new awareness of the association between animals and their breeding and feeding areas. Rowan's acute observations concerning the differences between plants and animals found in parts of Alberta and southern Manitoba, his quick grasp of the relationships between geology, climate, plant cover, and animal life, convinced Lawrence that his enthusiastic young friend had a future in science.

At a time when his mother's letters urged him to "get together as soon as you can the money for your passage and come home,"[27] Lawrence advised Rowan to concentrate on science. Prompted by his mother and convinced by his friend, Rowan arranged to return to England in time to enroll for the 1911–1912 session at University College. It did not bother him that he could only afford third-class fare, but he regretted leaving his friends in Winnipeg. He had no inkling that eight long years would pass before he would again set foot in the Canadian West. He only knew that his roaming days were over.

3

Science It Is, 1912-1915

BACK IN ENGLAND, Rowan enrolled in the honours zoology course at University College, London, a secular university founded in 1826 to provide education to the large proportion of the nonconformist urban middle class excluded from Oxford and Cambridge because of its religious beliefs.[1] University College, London was Mrs. Rowan's choice for her younger sons, albeit an unlikely one for a deeply religious mother who originally planned to send all her sons to Cambridge. Arthur, the eldest, went up to Cambridge in 1905 to read classics, but he spent more time on costly social activities than on his studies. Mrs. Rowan, though upset, paid his debts. She also changed her plans and moved from Bedford to St. Albans, a city closer to London, to enable her younger sons to live at home while going to university. Fred, the first of three Rowan boys to go to University College, enrolled in engineering in 1910, Bill started zoology in 1911, and Harry began his medical studies in 1912.[2]

Zoology had been taught at University College since the institution first opened its doors in 1828. The department had attracted many eminent scientists, such as Ray Lankester, the first zoologist to introduce laboratory work and to advocate research, and W.F.R. Weldon who, with Francis Galton and Karl Pearson, initiated the use of extensive quantitative measurements, which led to the creation of the new science of biometrics.[3] In 1911, the head of the Department of Zoology and Comparative Anatomy was the embryologist Dr. James Peter Hill. Among the other outstanding scientists at University College were chemist Sir William Ramsay, and botanist Francis Wall Oliver.

Like all students entering first year, Rowan asked the provost (or secretary), Sir Gregory Foster, for permission to take certain courses. Science students chose courses exclusively from the science curriculum, and Rowan registered for the introductory courses in chemistry, physics, botany, and zoology.[4] Classes were held from Monday to Saturday inclusively. The inorganic chemistry course given by Ramsay conflicted with a botany course given by Oliver, so Rowan soon dropped chemistry and never studied it again. He persevered with F.T. Trouton's physics course, but as the practical class consisted only of demonstrations and excluded experiments by the students themselves, Rowan lost interest in physics. He was more enthusiastic about his zoology and botany courses.

In J.P. Hill's introductory zoology course (lectures and laboratory) students learned sectioning, staining, microscopic examination, and comparative description of specimens.[5] Oliver's botany course consisted entirely of lectures, but interested students could participate in field excursions, or in the activities of the Natural Science Society, established by the professor in 1905.[6]

Though Rowan knew that to succeed at university one needed commitment, self-discipline, and a clear set of priorities, he still viewed the prospect of settling down to serious work with mixed feelings. He had chosen science as a career, but had no intention of giving up his other interests. The proximity of the Slade School of Art, a part of University College that occupied the same building as the zoology and botany departments, was one of the original attractions of this particular college for Rowan, and from Fred he knew that music was an important activity at the student union.

Despite his initial misgivings, Rowan soon succeeded in making the adjustments needed to effect the transition from the freewheeling life-style of a cowpuncher and nature photographer to the disciplined one of a conscientious university student. At twenty, he was somewhat older than most of his classmates and he had been away from the schedule-bound life of a student for over three years.

At first, Rowan was also ambivalent about living at home, in the half-timbered, three-storey house facing Clarence Park, but he soon found life at home easier than he had anticipated. His mother's warmth and humour and the presence of old Nanny Stone provided a stable, comfortable base, and the countryside was full of potential for nature study.

5. Gerdine Atalia Rowan, circa 1912.
University of Alberta Archives, William Rowan Papers.

It was annoying, however, to have to leave social events to return home for the 10 p.m. curfew. Mrs. Rowan laid great stress on punctuality, and her sons wanted to avoid upsetting her. So, they made a game of beating the clock, which she permanently kept ten minutes fast throughout their college years. Characteristically, while they resented the imposed curfew, they never voiced their objection.[7]

As class attendance was compulsory, Bill and Fred had to commute to London five or six times a week, exchanging the verdant countryside around St. Albans for overcrowded classrooms and laboratories. The one-hour train ride took them through delightful Hertfordshire villages, green fields, and the suburb of Camden Town. From London's King's Cross Station, the young Rowans could reach the college buildings on Gower Place in a few minutes. There, they parted company till evening. The Department of Mechanical Engineering was in the south wing of the college, while the Department of Zoology and Comparative Anatomy was on the first floor of the north wing, or north cloister.

Rowan was busy. Judging by his soft, black, linen-covered practical zoology and practical botany notebooks from the 1911–1914 period, preserved among the William Rowan Papers, students received thorough grounding in the subjects taught by professors Hill and Oliver. The many pen-and-ink and watercolour illustrations found in Rowan's notebooks are indicators of his own deep interest in both science and art. The fine detail and flowing lines of these zoological and botanical drawings presaged his later art work, much praised by collectors.

Rowan had a quick and logical mind, but his school and college records never did justice to his actual knowledge of the subjects he studied. At Bedford School, the annual exams were only tests, and, as sports were far more important than good marks, he never developed the skills needed to be successful.[8] Although poor at exams, at University College Rowan acquired knowledge that he was to use effectively throughout a long and productive scientific career. In Hill's course he had familiarized himself with the structure and physiology of invertebrates, the zoology of vertebrates, and the detailed anatomy of the dogfish, frog, and rabbit. In the first year he also heard lectures on vertebrate embryology and the theory of evolution. He liked Hill's teaching methods, which included the use of visual aids, and during his own teaching career Rowan was to use similar methods.[9]

Although Rowan acquired a thorough knowledge of contemporary biological theory and great precision in laboratory work, he received no training in experimental zoology. He already had considerable first-hand experience with living animals, however. As a growing boy he had kept birds, mammals, and amphibians as pets. He observed other species in their own environments on the Rowan family estates in Switzerland and France, around the cities of Bedford and St. Albans, and in the open country of Manitoba and Alberta. Through his observations of plants and animals he had developed an ecological awareness that, by 1911, had already become an integral part of his view of nature.

In Oliver's botany courses Rowan obtained scientific grounding in ecology. The Professor, as Rowan was to refer to him, was a pioneer of paleobotany and ecology. A tall, ruggedly handsome man, Oliver was slow and circumspect in his lecture delivery, but vigorous and enthusiastic out-of-doors. His interests in fieldwork and plant ecology led to his initiating, since 1904, a summer field course for senior students on salt-marsh vegetation of the Brittany coast. In 1910 Oliver changed the study area to Blakeney Point on the north Norfolk coast, where advanced students and staff could study plant life in relation to habitat conditions.[10]

It was natural for Rowan, with his enthusiasm for outdoor nature study, to become one of Oliver's favourite students. The two men had much in common. They shared a deep love for the natural world, and for outdoor activities such as swimming and boating, cycling and hiking. A colleague recalled that the outwardly shy Oliver was "something of a rebel, disliking all authority, rules and regulations, and liked to be a law unto himself, a trait that was liable to impair his judgement."[11] Rowan shared these character traits with Oliver, indeed the above description could well have been of Rowan, who also enjoyed thumbing his nose at authority. Like his beloved Professor, Rowan never took care of himself, had an inquiring mind, and a "perennial adaptability to new surroundings, the never-failing capacity to ignore discomforts and drawbacks and to see only the advantages of his immediate environment."[12] The similarity of their interests soon drew Oliver and Rowan even closer together. For Rowan, the Professor became a kindly surrogate father. Later he was to become his lifelong friend.

Rowan had his first introduction to systematic fieldwork at the Blakeney Point field station at the end of April 1912, just before the beginning of the third term. He was the only junior student and the only zoologist in a group of botanists, that consisted of professors F.W. Oliver and E.J. Salisbury and a number of female and male senior students. On subsequent expeditions, other zoology students would join the group to work on the faunistic studies Oliver had instituted. Rowan relished the intellectual stimulation and good companionship provided by these field trips. He was to retain his love for such outings all his life.

Blakeney Point, near Cley-Next-the-Sea on the Norfolk coast, has been a National Trust reserve since before the First World War. It consists of 548 hectares of land, most of it a four-and-half kilometre-long shingle spit, a narrow shale-covered piece of land, part of a beach that is nearly three times as long. The point is a tern breeding colony. It is also an excellent area for the observation of migrant land birds, and the salt marshes and clumps of several types of marsh grass have long provided outstanding staging areas for migrating waders (or shorebirds). In 1912, cars were still scarce along the narrow lanes and twisting streets of nearby Cley, but bicycles were numerous. The walker could safely travel the roads to admire the wooden windmills built at the edge of the saltmarsh, and the picturesque houses constructed of flint, their small windows shut tight against the North Sea winds, their tiny front gardens a riot of colour. Blakeney Point and the Cley marshes had not yet been discovered by bird-watchers, thousands of whom now frequent the area year-round. The carefully maintained walking paths and permanent hides that now cater to naturalists were still to come.[13]

On Blakeney Point there was a wooden laboratory building, but most of the time staff and students slept in simple tents and erected their own portable canvas observation hides. On this first, memorable visit, Rowan only noted his observations on the ringed plover and the oystercatcher. He was too busy to describe the various study areas, such as the pebble beach (called "shingle"), the continuous fields of glasswort, and the muddier sections which were carpeted with low-lying plants such as the sea-blight. On subsequent visits he noted these, as well as the open sand dunes and unprotected and narrow-mouthed salt marshes, the seabirds that bred in the "embryo" dunes, and rabbits and other rodents in the older dunes. There were crabs, shellfish, and insects, and, as he was to find out, a never-ending variety of ornithological rarities.

On the following trip, from 1–3 July 1912, Rowan took nearly one hundred bird photographs and prepared a full report on the wildlife of Blakeney Point for Oliver. His first year at university over, Rowan was ready for a real vacation, to explore the fields and forests of Hertfordshire. He climbed oaks, sycamores, and beeches to find birds' nests, watched juvenile kingfishers around the sand and gravel pits, and sketched wildlife at every possible opportunity. He even had time to laze around and play the piano.

In late September 1912, Rowan was back at college, studying botany, zoology, physics, and geology. Physics and geology, though fascinating to him, proved to be difficult for someone without any previous scientific training. Although he failed the physics exam in June 1913, Rowan had become interested in light, particularly phosphorescent and ultraviolet light. He had also learned much about the importance of temperature, a factor that, together with light, was to feature prominently in his later scientific work. But all that was still to come. For the time being physics seemed to Rowan of less immediate use than geology, particularly in view of his growing interest in ecology.

In Britain, the discipline of ecology owed much of its development to Oliver, Salisbury, and A.G. Tansley (a former student of Oliver), who established the British Ecological Society in 1913.[14] In Oliver's course Rowan found that a knowledge of the geological features of a given landscape was useful in understanding the interrelationship of rock and soil with vegetation and animal life. Although Rowan did not have the benefit of geological field excursions, by his third visit to Blakeney Point, in January 1913, he had begun to view with sharpened awareness the relationship of coastal vegetation and its bird and mammal life with the underlying geology.

Rowan's field notes became more detailed. Although he occasionally referred to other activities, or his impressions of people and places, the notebooks rarely mentioned his studies at University College. Perhaps this was because, at the time, University College tended to separate laboratory and field studies in zoology. Rowan's zoology and botany notebooks are the only reminders of the lectures and laboratory work he completed in Hill's and Oliver's classes.

The daily notes Rowan took at Blakeney Point indicate his interest in detail, his approach to research, and his ability to work hard. It is evident that Rowan endured, without grumbling, adverse weather conditions, blown-down tents, and long, tiring walks. The scientific and social opportunities the field excursions offered greatly outweighed their discomfort. He worked hard and played hard. He spent many hours observing animal behaviour and the interactions of plant and animal life, such as huge flocks of linnets feeding in the glasswort marshes, and rabbits eating the emerging asters.[15] He helped the Professor put up fences around study plots, and took his turn at kitchen duty. He played bridge the odd evening. He photographed the scenery, the birds, and the destruction of coastal vegetation by rabbits. He also took many photographs of the party of botanists.

Back at the college, Rowan studied for the intermediate science examinations with mixed results. Although he passed botany and zoology, he failed physics and geology. His failure may be attributed partly to his lack of examination skills, partly to his growing absorption in ornithology, and partly to his increasing involvement in student-society activities. In his second year, Rowan spent much time out-of-doors, sketching and photographing birds; he joined the Hertfordshire Natural History Society and became honorary secretary of the University College Natural Science Society. He participated in student musical events and mildly flirted with a number of girls, members of the Women's Student Union.

Kitty Marsland, who later married Harry Rowan, jokingly called William Rowan a philanderer,[16] but although he had certainly met many girls on his travels, there is no evidence of his having had an early love affair. During his years as a cowpuncher, Rowan had known emancipated older girls who went to Western Canada to become independent from their families, and worked as governesses or teachers in the ranching community. Some even put in land claims for themselves.[17] At University College he encountered a practically new species, the determined female scientist. Belonging to this category were zoology students Winnifred Smith, Dorothy M. Simmons, and Kathleen M. Parker, and botany lecturers Ethel

N. Thomas, B.Sc., and Sarah M. Baker, Ph.D.[18] It is not known whether or not Rowan had a romantic relationship with any of them. He soon became good friends with Parker, however, and later cooperated with her on a study of the breeding biology of the common tern.

The summer of 1913 was a time of intensive fieldwork for Rowan. He undertook this work partly to overcome his disappointment at having failed two examinations, and partly to compensate for having missed out on an exciting expedition to Brazil. Rowan had been selected, as he later recalled, from the entire Department of Zoology, including staff and students, as field naturalist and collector for a Brazilian expedition to be led by J.P. Hill. When a hoped-for Royal Society grant failed to materialize, Rowan's place was taken by another zoology student, who could pay his own way.[19]

Rowan's fieldwork at Blakeney was too absorbing to leave him much time to mope about the lost opportunity. With Parker, he conducted a biometrical study of 203 clutches of late-nesting common terns.[20] Julia Bell, a graduate assistant in Karl Pearson's biometrical laboratory, helped with the final analysis. The results of their study were published in *Biometrika* in 1914 and 1919.[21]

Although bird studies began to occupy much of Rowan's time, he developed a keen scientific interest in other animals and their habitats. This is apparent from notes he took during a vacation he spent with his family in 1913 at Tenby, on the southern coast of Wales. The study of marine organisms formed part of the zoology course at University College, but students only encountered such organisms as preserved specimens, or sections of such, under microscopes in the laboratory. A four-day trip on a trawler during his vacation gave Rowan the opportunity to observe marine life (for example, dogfish, blue shark, and ray) in its natural environment. He collected starfish for his friend G.E. Bullen, curator of the Hertfordshire County Museum. The sights and raucous calls of gannets, guillemots, puffins, and other seabirds, never ceased to delight him. Rowan had his first view of phosphorescent sea plankton in Wales, and this inspired him to write: "The sea was like pea-soup with plankton, and brilliantly phosphorescent at night. Porpoises were abundant. As they jumped they looked as though they were lit up with electricity."[22] At twenty-two Rowan was not only an acute observer, but had the skill to describe his experiences vividly.

He began to read voraciously about scientific matters. In his third year as an honours zoology student, Rowan enrolled in more advanced courses in his main subjects, zoology and botany. He borrowed and bought a number of advanced texts, some of them old and valuable.[23] As his love of science deepened, his other major interest, art, was eclipsed. His careful photographs, skilful pencil drawings, and delicate watercolours were now only used to illustrate his notebooks.

In early 1914, after having spent part of his Christmas holidays observing birds around St. Albans, Rowan plucked up enough courage to visit Mr. Lloyd, the owner of nearby Astwick Manor. This lovely old house is between St. Albans and Hatfield on a large estate that Rowan felt ought to prove fruitful as a study area. Lloyd, impressed with Rowan's knowledge and enthusiasm, gave him permission to take photographs all over the estate, and two of the gamekeepers promised their help.[24]

Photographing nesting birds at Astwick and elsewhere required much patience and involved waiting in the hides for hours for the right picture, as well as hiking, cycling, and tree climbing.[25] Rowan definitely preferred fieldwork to library work, but was quite willing to study in the evenings, provided he could spend his days observing birds. It was during this period of intense outdoor activity that he developed the habit of reading and writing late into the night.

Rowan passed his intermediate zoology, elementary botany, and junior geology exams in early June of 1914, but, for the second time, failed physics. He soon recovered from fatigue, dejection, and the stomach cramps and bouts of vomiting he habitually suffered during periods of stress. Yet another field excursion to Blakeney Point made up for the trying times.

Under Hill's tutelage in embryology, Rowan's interest in nesting birds became more scientific, and Blakeney Point provided the perfect locale for studies in breeding biology. From a movable canvas hide Rowan observed nesting dotterels, a species of plover now only found on the Norfolk coast during migration. He photographed young oyster-catchers and little terns, and recorded his first attempt at colour photography.[26]

The notes Rowan took during another cooperative study of the tern colony in July 1914 predate by a decade his groundbreaking research on the breeding biology and migration of birds. As a student, in 1914, he may not have chosen his own topic for investigation, but his observations and notes demonstrate an awareness of daylight as an ecological factor, that influenced the activities of a tern breeding colony.

There is no evidence that the fateful events that took place in Sarajevo in June 1914 had any impact on Rowan at the time. The group at Blakeney must have heard news of the murder of the Archduke Francis Ferdinand and his wife Sophie, yet they carried on with their scientific work, perhaps unaware of the larger implications of this occurrence. Indeed, how were they to know that the tradition of scientists' neutrality would be forever changed by the outbreak of the First World War?[27]

Rowan left Blakeney Point for St. Albans on 20 July, while Europe was still at peace, to do fieldwork and visit with family and friends. How he and his brothers viewed events unfolding on the Continent, and England's subsequent declaration of war, is not recorded. We know, however, that on 1 September 1914, twenty-three-year-old William Rowan, frustrated at not being able to enlist in the regular army because of his myopia, joined the London Scottish Regiment. Instead of entering his final year at University College, London, he went to training camp, which was situated in Richmond Park. Mrs. Rowan was proud that all her sons had enlisted (Arthur in the intelligence service, Fred in the Royal Engineers, and Harry in the Royal Navy), but viewed the prospect of another war with trepidation. In her youth, German forces invaded her native Denmark, and although Mrs. Rowan had no first-hand experience with other wars, for her, as for many other women, war was a game played by men — which greatly affected women.

The family viewed Bill's enlistment as a typical impulsive gesture. Rowan's own recollections concerning his reasons for enlisting offer a different perspective. Nearly thirty years after the event, he wrote to W.C. Allee, "I welcomed the war in 1914 as a godsend to effect another escape" from serious work.[28] This is an extreme statement, especially from someone deeply in love with science. But William Rowan was given to extreme statements. The truth must have been less colourful. Undoubtedly, the war offered escape from

6. "Brothers All." (left to right) Harry, Willie, Fred, and Arthur, circa 1915.
University of Alberta Archives.

the monotonous everyday routine for a large number of men. But Rowan's life at the time was varied and interesting. Although he had twice failed his physics examination and did not excel in other subjects, he gained much satisfaction from his growing knowledge of science, his scientific publications, and his much-praised nature photography. He made new friends at university, met many well-known naturalists, and even hosted Ernest Thompson Seton at a dinner, paid for with funds received for one of his early articles, which was accepted by the journal *Knowledge*.[29]

Like many other young men at the time, Rowan was probably infused with patriotic fervour. He would have considered it his duty to do his share, and despised as cowardly any attempts to shirk such a duty. Moreover, he was never one to be left out or left behind. When his brothers and friends joined up, he was determined to do so himself. Despite his unruly dark hair, already receding from his domed forehead, and his comical little moustache, Rowan looked younger than his age. His slight build belied his energy, his well-developed leg muscles could carry him over any terrain without fatigue, and, his weak eyes notwithstanding, he was a good shot.

Under the circumstances Rowan was happy to enlist, though he was likely to remain in Britain. He was proud of his uniform, similar to that of the regular Highland regiment, but with a kilt of hodden grey and, uncharacteristically, took great care not to crease it.[30] There are no entries in Rowan's field notebook between 1 September 1914 and 4 March 1915. He was occupied with regimental matters until his first major leave, in March 1915, when his mind turned once again to science. While his brief attempt at fieldwork was unsatisfactory, going to London to see his professors proved more rewarding.[31]

Did Rowan regret having joined the London Scottish instead of continuing with his studies? Did a cold winter in temporary barracks erected in a muddy, bleak place dampen his original enthusiasm? Judging by his almost immediate reimmersion in scientific activity on his first long leave, it seems evident that whatever regrets he may or may not have had, his mind craved the challenge that by this time only scientific investigation could provide. At the zoology department, no doubt following Hill's advice, he obtained some tadpoles and axolotl eggs.[32] Axolotls (or mole salamanders), widely distributed throughout North and

Central America, are a commonly studied laboratory species. The adults thrive in captivity, feeding on earthworms in terrariums, and the larvae are easily raised in aquariums. These characteristics made the axolotl the perfect species for Rowan to study at home.

At 19 Clarence Road, Rowan set up his laboratory, actually an aquarium, in his room and spent several hours every day observing the development of the amphibians.[33] His study was terminated prematurely after he accidentally poisoned the axolotl and frog tadpoles.[34] As there was no time to start another study before his return to camp, he conducted some fieldwork in the district.

In April 1915, Rowan developed what was diagnosed as German measles, and was granted three weeks of sick leave. His recuperation was rapid. Within ten days he was at Astwick Manor, photographing birds' nests. Back at camp he continued his bird observations.[35] At the end of June the army doctor found that Rowan's heart was strained, and recommended a week's leave. This soon had to be extended.[36]

The notes Rowan took during his sick leave do not present the picture of a man with a weak heart, under a doctor's care. Instead, the reader is impressed by the energy and zeal of the field naturalist, forever walking, cycling, and tree climbing. What was called a "strained heart" or "soldier's heart" was, at the time, a common cause of sick leave and discharge from the army, and British doctors prescribed physical activity as a remedy.[37] This perfectly suited Rowan who, by this point, preferred ornithological fieldwork to life in camp. On this sick leave, Rowan even went to Blakeney Point (on a borrowed Triumph motorcycle) for four days, where he photographed young birds, "wagtails in nest, Rock pipit, and also Sheldrake,"[38] before returning home. From home he proceeded to camp, where he was found unfit for service.

As a batman in the Royal Scottish Rifle Volunteers, Rowan had never been exposed to danger, and did not have to face bayonets, shells, poison gas, starvation, and disease. The feeling of that he had had of being of service to his country soon palled, and his reaction to his impending discharge from the regiment was one of relief. The official reason for Rowan's discharge from the London Scottish Regiment, as stated on his discharge certificate, was vague — he was declared "no longer fit physically for war service" — and more than seventy years later, the British Ministry of Defence would still not disclose the pertinent medical information.[39] So, it remains unclear whether Rowan had been discharged because of the heart murmur he had developed earlier in 1915 (as he later often intimated), or because of the recurrent intestinal problems from which he suffered during periods of stress.

Whatever the exact cause, on 9 November 1915, after one year and sixty-eight days, William Rowan, without having seen a single minute of action, without even having had a glance at the enemy, was discharged from the 3/14th Battalion, London Scottish Regiment. Described on the discharge certificate, as five feet six inches tall, with a fresh complexion, dark hair, and grey eyes, Private Rowan had proved himself to be honest, sober, trustworthy, and hardworking. His military character was very good, even though his health, apparently, was not.[40]

4

In Search of Employment, 1916-1919

DURING THE GLOOMY WINTER of 1915–1916, Rowan's career plans underwent a number of short-lived changes. Added to the insecurity of the war, there was a new worry about the family finances, and this affected Rowan's view of his own future. Since William Robert Rowan's death in 1900, the Rowan family had lived well on income from sizeable investments, most of them in French government bonds and stocks. By late 1915, due to the devaluation of the French franc, these funds were much diminished and Rowan had to face the unpleasant prospect of a penniless future. He became depressed.

Mrs. Rowan, already worried about her children (Nellie in China, Agnes in London, and three sons in active service), also suffered from depression. The two resolved their difficulties in characteristically different ways. As it had done so often before, Mrs. Rowan's faith sustained her through the darkest days of that winter. Although Rowan, an agnostic since childhood, could not turn to his mother's god, he soon recovered, at least superficially, from his depression. The resilience of youth was on his side, and though his future as a scientist remained uncertain, he arranged to reenter University College, London.

Mrs. Rowan was a practical woman, and once again changed her lifestyle. She gave up the large, three-storey home on Clarence Road and rented Lulworth, a charming, small, stucco-and-brick house on Carlisle Avenue, next to the McOustra family whose children Oswald and Marjorie (later Mrs. Fred Rowan) were already friendly with the young Rowans.

Lulworth was located near the Abbey Church, the museum, and shops. A brisk twenty-minute walk could take Rowan to the railway station. He could easily get to London, and resumed his studies by taking the advanced zoology and botany courses the university offered to B.Sc. pass and honours students. At University College at the time, evolution was not taught as a separate course but formed part of the various life-science courses. Rowan had hoped to take the advanced zoology course on evolution at King's College, but it was not offered in 1915–1916. He became serious about physics and, determined to pass the course once and for all, spent many evenings in his room wrestling with physics problems.

In his spare time Rowan tramped and cycled all over the district on his quest for ornithological discoveries, but underneath the seemingly carefree exterior he cultivated for his mother's sake, he continued to worry about his future and, in his correspondence, often hinted at having periods of poor health. The fact that Rowan was so physically active during the winter of 1915–1916 suggests, however, that he was not seriously ill. Possibly, the mental preoccupation and physical exercise involved in his studies and fieldwork proved therapeutic.[1]

Always a keen photographer, Rowan, in the autumn of 1915, bought a secondhand Thornton-Picard reflex camera with a telephoto attachment for ten pounds sterling. He was convinced that it was a bargain as it was in excellent condition,[2] and he was soon photographing scenery and wildlife with renewed enthusiasm, particularly at Symondshyde Great Wood, part of Lord Salisbury's estate.

This extensive woodland had been in the Salisbury family since 1853. In Rowan's time, access to it was strictly controlled by a number of gamekeepers who patrolled the oak-beech forest, looking for poachers among the moss-covered trees. In 1915, Symondshyde must have been a haven for a nature photographer, as the unpaved roads were more likely to show the hoofprints of horses and game than the tire marks of automobiles. The persistent song of the chaffinch and the calls of foraging blue tits were not yet drowned out by the voices of picnicking schoolchildren. Noisy radios and cars had not yet arrived.

Rowan's studies provided an acceptable alternative to active service. He also embarked on a series of lectures for wounded soldiers.[3] The *Union Magazine* reported that on 2 June, William Rowan

> delivered a lecture on Camera Hunting in which he vividly described the difficulties of obtaining good photos of wild animals. His illustrations, however, were so successful as to convince the audience that the difficulties are not unsurmountable to him.[4]

Rowan was encouraged by his success as a lecturer but was unclear about the future of such work. His childhood heroes Richard Kearton and Ernest Thompson Seton were renowned natural-history lecturers without university degrees, and this profession, which had appealed to him a decade earlier when he was a student at Bedford School, still seemed an interesting choice to him, if he decided not to pursue a career as a scientist. It combined field observation, photography, and popular teaching methods, and Rowan knew that he had the knowledge, artistic eye, and lively delivery that were the hallmarks of a natural-history lecturer.

Taxidermy was another possibility. It was an integral part of ornithology and mammalogy, and taxidermists were valued employees of natural history museums. Though much of the work had to be done indoors, and the arsenic used to preserve animal skins was known to be unhealthy, even dangerous, there was always the possibility of going on museum expeditions as a naturalist-collector.[5] Taxidermy was likely to be less lucrative than lecturing, but it could provide steadier work. Rowan had a third option. He could become a schoolteacher. While he knew that without a degree he could not hope to find a good teaching post, becoming a teacher appealed to him more than becoming a civil servant, a possibility he was unwilling to consider.

Rowan would have liked to discuss his career problems, but who could advise him about his future? Though he talked easily to all sorts of people, he confided in only a few. In his childhood, as indeed later in life, he had many companions with whom he exchanged ideas on nature, science, and art, but he would not or could not share with them his inner feelings, his desires, and his doubts. F.W. Oliver, his favourite professor, had always been sympathetic, but as a scientist and teacher he was likely to try to

7. William Rowan self portrait, watercolour, 1916.
University of Alberta Archives.

persuade Rowan to continue with his studies. Fred, now in the Royal Engineers, was Rowan's closest confidant, but during the winter of 1915–1916 he was not available for heart-to-heart talks. Only his mother was there.

Mrs. Rowan often guessed the root of Bill's problems, as the two were similar, except in the area of religious belief, in many ways. They loved family life but cherished their independence; they shared a sardonic sense of humour and a love of art, music, and nature. Both could be rigid, exacting, impatient, stubborn, impulsive, and kind. They often masked their kindness with brusqueness, and their concern for others with seeming self-centredness. Although during the winter of 1915–1916 both Rowan and his mother fretted about one another's health, Rowan, as usual, avoided burdening her with his problems, and was reluctant to worry her further with his fears about the future.[6]

As was so often the case in his later years, Rowan found it easier to discuss his problems through correspondence than face to face. During the spring of 1916, he wrote letters to a number of people in which he discussed the various possibilities open to him in natural-history lecturing and taxidermy work. Typically, Rowan slanted the letters to impress upon the recipient both his need for a position and his expertise in the field in question.

Rowan's letters to Canada were prompted in part by his desire to plan for his future and in part because a late-March gale of snow and sleet reminded him of the wild Canadian blizzards he had experienced during 1908–1910 on the Prairies. He informed his old friends of the family's loss of fortune, of his own precarious health, of the possibility of not being able to complete his studies, and of his desire to find employment in Canada. Rowan told E.W. Darbey that he was looking for a position in taxidermy, possibly in Winnipeg, and implied that he had already taken up taxidermy work. To A.G. Lawrence, he not only poured out his fears and hopes but greatly exaggerated his financial difficulties. Hoping to obtain bookings, Rowan also wrote to Gerald Christy, owner of a well-known British lecture agency.

The eagerly awaited letters of reply did not immediately help Rowan to resolve his problems. Christy informed him that because of the war he could not offer Rowan steady employment.[7] So, his successful lectures to wounded soldiers notwithstanding, a lucrative future in this area seemed unrealistic. Lawrence greeted Rowan's letter with an enthusiastic and prompt reply. He wrote,

> I am awfully sorry, old man, to hear that your family have been affected seriously by the war; you have my deepest sympathy, but I am more sorry to hear about your health, for after all that is our chief asset. I sincerely hope that the outdoor life will fix you up proper and that you will get out of the doctors' hands with all speed. Rotten luck not being able to go on with your degree work . . . you must make the best of life and I'm glad that you have chosen the profession of a naturalist as you are eminently suited for it.[8]

Lawrence also wrote of the bad winter, of French Canadians resisting conscription, of prohibition in Manitoba, and of the impending vote for women.[9]

Darbey replied that he was pleased that Rowan had taken up taxidermy but could not offer him employment. He told Rowan of the Manitoba government's plan to open a natural-history museum, and advised him to "keep on plugging" to become efficient.[10] By this time, however, Rowan had given up the notion of becoming a taxidermist, a career for which, in any case, he had no formal training. He also rejected the more serious idea of becoming a natural-history lecturer.

Whatever he wrote to Darbey and Lawrence, there is no evidence that Rowan's formal studies were in actual jeopardy. In fact, by the summer of 1916, Rowan even ceased to mention ill health. With care the family maintained a relatively comfortable lifestyle, and there was no suggestion whatsoever of Rowan quitting his studies. While he remained concerned about his future, his success as an unpaid lecturer and the fact that he passed the physics exam improved his morale.

After a difficult winter, Rowan could look forward to a summer of bird study. His field observations and early scientific papers brought him in touch with many eminent British ornithologists, including H.F. Witherby, editor of *British Birds*. Rowan attended the meetings of the British Ornithologists' Union, and Witherby visited Rowan in St. Albans and accompanied him on field excursions — a great honour, indeed, for the young ornithologist.[11] It may have been due to Witherby's influence that Rowan started ringing (banding) birds, particularly European kingfishers and sand martins.[12]

At the end of the summer, Rowan returned to Blakeney Point, and, despite what he called "intermittent spells in bed," he began his last session at University College.[13] There, he not only prepared for his final examinations (he fully expected to obtain his degree in 1917), but also reimmersed himself in student-union activities.

During the autumn of 1916, Rowan submitted to the provost the subject of his proposed honours examination topic. There is no record of the original title. A slightly modified one, accepted by the college authorities, was "The General Structure and Classification of Birds, and the Bionomics and Distribution of the British Species."[14] Rowan's chosen topic shows both his own orientation and the influence of the morphologist-embryologist J.P. Hill, the botanist-ecologist F.W. Oliver, and the biometrician Karl Pearson. Although the scientific study of birds at British universities was still in its infancy and ornithology was not an academic subject, by 1917, Rowan evidently considered birds not only as fit objects for descriptive natural-history studies, but also for biological investigations, for establishing hypotheses, for constructing theories.[15]

At age twenty-six, after years of interrupted study, William Rowan obtained his first professional degree. With a B.Sc. Honours in Zoology (third class) he became an accredited scientist. Now he had to find employment. It was time to become independent and self-supporting, as his plans included marriage to Miss Reta G. Bush, of the Holt, Morden, Surrey.

Sometime during 1916 William Rowan fell in love with twenty-two-year-old Reta Bush, a second-year student at the Slade School of Art. The statuesque, chestnut-haired Reta was a talented artist, singer, and cello player. An active member of the student musical and choral societies since 1915, she sang at the June 1916 Dramatic Society soirée. Rowan heard her performance, and wangled an introduction through Kitty Marsland, brother Harry's fiancée, who had known Reta since their Wimbledon High School days.

Reta, the fifth child of Maud M. Simmons and Richard Arthur Bush, a wealthy manufacturing chemist, was born on 23 October 1894 at Hall Place, near Mitcham, Surrey. Her parents soon recognized her artistic talent and provided her with private lessons. Reta graduated from Wimbledon High School for Girls in 1913, and soon passed her London matriculation exams in English, French, mathematics, chemistry, and modern history.

At the outbreak of the First World War, Reta was in Germany with a friend. Naïve, with idealistic notions concerning war among civilized people, she was surprised to hear a German pastor incite his parishioners to fight. Although in later life Reta rarely discussed her frightening experiences as an English national caught in Germany, she became a pacifist at the time, and remained one all her life. After her return to England, Reta enrolled at the Royal Drawing Society, and studied to become an art teacher. She received her certificate in 1915, and entered the Slade School of Art for further training in sculpting, drawing, and painting.[16]

Reta's first impressions of Bill Rowan, a short, exuberant man, older than most students, are not recorded. He was not conventionally handsome, but his dark hair, chaplinesque moustache, fine grey eyes, and great energy were attractive to women. He had a good sense of humour, a pleasant baritone singing voice, and drew well. By accident or design, the two met frequently and soon became friends.

There were more female students than ever before at University College, and it became easy for male students to meet them. The war provided women with more opportunities to acquire higher education, because many more were now being admitted to fill the places vacated by the men who had departed for war. Male students, however, had mixed feelings about being outnumbered by females. Rowan's "Topical Sketch," a short play written for the student union and performed in December 1917, reveals a male ambivalence about the changing proportion of students. "Women in the classes, women in the lab, women even in the dissecting room . . . . They say they're to have keys to our sacred Union Lounge because their own is crowded out," complains Smith, a character in the play.[17] Did he speak with Rowan's voice? At first reading it seems that Rowan's alter ego is the ex-student Freddie Brown, a soldier on furlough, rather than Smith. Brown wears a kilt, like Rowan did, and is keen on meeting girls. He arranges an introduction to a Slade student, Miss Jones, a "Nice girl! Great Sport!"[18] On further reading, it is evident that both Smith and Brown represent Rowan's views, and these Rowan probably shared with most male students. Rowan's play shows an early indication of what was to become a lifelong attitude towards women, and typically concentrates on the sexual rather than intellectual relationships of male and female students. He emphasizes their meetings at various student-society gatherings, at tea between lectures, in the libraries, and in the Flaxman Gallery. They flirt, they kiss, they contemplate marriage. They do not discuss intellectual issues.

Rowan's ambivalent attitude to women became more obvious later in life. Though during his university years and throughout his professional career Rowan worked and cooperated with women as equals, he considered most women to be soft, warm, loving scatterbrains.[19] Whatever his thoughts about women in general, by early 1917 Rowan was undoubtedly serious about Reta Bush. He referred to her in his fieldnotes with increasing frequency, and there are photographs of Rowan, Reta, Kitty, and Harry walking in the woods while Harry was on furlough from the Royal Navy. Within a few months, Reta had become the woman who "alone matters."[20] Their relationship provided Rowan with the impetus to once again consider science as a career, and to persist in his search for a position. Reta accompanied him on field trips and helped him to collect clutches of bird eggs for study. The spring and summer were full of plans that included Reta.

Rowan was always unconventional, and by 1917 he showed a predilection for the unusual, the anomaly in science. He had no liking for repetitious, puzzle-solving activity — for what Thomas Kuhn was to call "normal science."[21] Rowan, believed, as did many highly original scientists, that puzzle solving was merely a means to an end. This belief was later at the root of his search for anomalies in science, for discrepancies between empirical facts, current hypotheses, and speculative theories. In 1917, he was delighted to find an unusual clutch of sparrow's eggs consisting of two identical ones and two that were markedly different. That there was a developmental reason for the differences in the eggs was confirmed by Professor Hill, who found that "every one of the four had abnormal blastoderms, or abnormal cleavage" but Rowan was unable to examine the internal abnormalities because Hill threw away the eggs. Clearly aware of the importance of priority in scientific discovery, Rowan remarked, "it is probably the first time in history that an abnormal clutch of eggs has been examined internally. The coincidence [of outward and internal abnormality] is extremely remarkable, the more the pity that a careful and accurate description has been rendered impossible."[22] As Rowan had not published any scientific papers since before the war, he was annoyed by Hill's failure to save the clutch for further study.

Rowan's relationship with Reta matured during the summer. They visited each other's families at Morden and St. Albans. Later, they went to Blakeney Point in a mixed company of students. Reta participated in all camp activities. She cooked for the group, washed dishes, and collected data. She also helped Rowan with his watercolour painting.[23] The Blakeney Point trip was the happiest that Bill Rowan had ever experienced, because before it he and Reta had never spent more than two or three days together. It was also a scientifically important visit because it allowed Rowan to be at the point for the first time during the height of the autumn migration in September.

In his later writing and interviews Rowan frequently recalled that it was while recuperating at Blakeney Point during the war that he became fascinated with the periodic migration of large numbers of birds. This made a good story, but was only partly true. The autumn bird migration had actually attracted his interest nearly two years after he had been released from the Royal Scottish Regiment, and he certainly was not recuperating from injury or illness. It is true, however, that the experience of observing the large-scale movement of migrating birds at Blakeney Point would in time change the course of his life, as the impression it had made upon him was indelible. In his diary he recorded the considerable migratory movements he had seen by daylight and by moonlight. He also noted that the conclusion of the happiest of the Blakeney visits opened a new epoch in his chequered career.[24] This was ushered in by a renewed search for employment.

In the autumn of 1917, William Rowan, B.Sc., began to peruse the appropriate columns of *Nature* and the *Times* and talk to his professors who, through the old-boys' network, periodically heard of lucrative positions opening up at various public schools and colleges. There was not much hope for a university post in 1917. Student enrollment had dropped during the war, and the few available positions in zoology had already been taken by earlier graduates. There was the possibility of a teaching post in a secondary school, and Rowan applied to both Bedales School, a progressive, coeducational institution near Petersfield, Hampshire, and to a temporary school-cum-sanatorium at Eastby, near Skipton in Yorkshire.

Dr. Catherine Arnott, headmistress of the new school at Eastby, was keen to employ Rowan to teach about fifty working-class boys who, because they were susceptible to tuberculosis, needed an open-air life. The school already had a woman teacher for the junior boys, and Arnott was anxious to find a man with an interest in the outdoors because nature study and gardening were an important part of the curriculum.[25]

This was an ideal post for Rowan. Although Eastby, six kilometres from the old market town of Skipton, could be dull for most city people, he liked the idea of the short working hours, the emphasis on outdoor activities, and the possibility of taking photographs and doing fieldwork in the Yorkshire Dales. Rowan visited Eastby on a bleak December weekend, and noted that the sanatorium, built of local grey stone, was beautifully situated.[26] The stillness of the snow-covered countryside suggested freedom.[27] The strong resemblance between the endless horizon of West Yorkshire and that of the less-hilly, but equally open ranching country of Alberta he loved so much, was unmistakable.

The area has not changed much in the intervening years. Though the sanatorium extension, a wooden structure, has disappeared, the original grey-stone building still nestles under Eastby Crag. Few trees impede the view across Halton Moor. To the north, Thorpe Fell rises to a height of 506 metres above the winding Wharfe River, still full of trout. On the bracken-and-heather-covered moors, the red grouse and the meadow pipit still shelter in the low, dense vegetation. Waterfalls cascade in thin streams and, in the marshy areas above Eastby Reservoir, round-leaf sundew and butterwort still attract tiny insects with their sticky, dewy leaves. The area is ideal, as it was in Rowan's time, for outdoor pursuits, a haven for ornithologists.

Without waiting for a reply from Bedales School, Rowan jumped at the opportunity to work at Eastby. He could gain teaching experience, spend almost all his time out-of-doors, and even get paid for it. By 4 January 1918, when J.H. Badley, headmaster of Bedales School, wrote to offer Rowan the post of biology master, the latter had already agreed to teach two terms at Eastby.[28]

Arriving at Eastby in January 1918, Rowan immediately began to survey the area. He sketched and photographed its natural features, made a bird-list, and contacted local gamekeepers. The initial excitement over, within a few weeks he was depressed and feeling sorry for himself away from his loved ones. In a letter to Kitty Marsland, he mentioned that a fight with Reta was further exacerbating his loneliness.[29] He soon recovered because he enjoyed teaching and the freedom it gave him to spend so much time in what was to become, for Rowan, one of the most promising birding spots in England. His self-confidence was also helped by the correspondence he carried on with the headmaster at Bedales School, who still wanted Rowan as a teacher. For the first time in his life, Rowan was assured that, by using his scientific training, he would be able to have a decent income with which to support a wife and family.

The often-gloomy Yorkshire winter, so much greyer and damper than winters in southern England, soon ceased to bother Rowan. He tramped all over the moors, accompanied by his young charges, or Miss Taylor, the school nurse, and Miss Forbes, the other teacher.

Rowan frequently went home for visits and soon made up with Reta. The prospect of a lovely spring in Yorkshire further lifted his spirits. He happily observed the arrival of numerous spring migrants: greater golden plovers, snipe, large flocks of lapwings, and skylarks that sang over the open moors. For Rowan, prone to overreaction, Eastby Crag and its district seemed the most productive spot in England. He was proud to show his visiting mother the entire district. Mrs. Rowan shared her Bill's enthusiasm for the meandering Wharfe, the narrow, twisting lanes enclosed by drystone walls, and the glorious vistas from hilltops rising three hundred to four hundred metres above the valleys.

Most of the district was accessible by train or bicycle, and Rowan used his bike to visit Birch, gamekeeper on the estate of the Duke and Duchess of Devonshire, to obtain permission to photograph birds. The picturesque ruins of historic Bolton Priory are part of the estate, which also encompasses tenant farms, woods, and moors.[30] A Roman aqueduct has been an integral part of the scenery for nearly two thousand years. Rowan loved the triangle defined by Bolton Abbey to the east, Crookrise to the west, and Thorpe Fell to the north; it extended eight to ten kilometres in each direction over hilly terrain, in which he found more than seventy nesting species of birds.[31]

In spite of the inherent ornithological interest of the district and the easy teaching load, Rowan never considered the Eastby teaching post as anything but temporary. He visited Bedales School in early March, met Mr. Badley, the tall headmaster who reminded him of his own father, and was offered a post as of September 1918.[32] Rowan was to teach biology to students twelve to nineteen years of age, until they reached "university scholarship standard" or were prepared for "Higher Certificate Exams." The work included classroom teaching and as much fieldwork as possible, and seemed tailor-made for Rowan. Though the annual salary of 150 pounds sterling was less than he would have earned as a university lecturer, the prospects were good and his pay was to rise to 180 pounds within two years.[33]

With his future thus fixed, Rowan returned to his teaching and nature study in Yorkshire. The stomach ailments and depression (always signs of stress for Rowan), which he had initially experienced at Eastby, disappeared as he photographed wildflowers and scouted the moors for birds' eggs, accompanied by his students.[34] In August, at the close of his second term, Rowan left his post at Eastby with mixed feelings. He regretted having to end what he called the most profitable bird season of his life, but looked forward to meeting his family at Deganwy, in North Wales.[35] Once Reta joined the party a few days later, Rowan's happiness was complete.

"I got a most depressing little room with a window near the ceiling out of which we cannot see unless we climb on to the bed or chair," noted Rowan at the end of his first day at Bedales School on 19 September 1918. Although the place impressed him so favourably during his initial visit the previous March, he felt "most awfully sorry not to be back at Eastby."[36]

Rowan wrote of his impressions to his brother Arthur, and, rationalizing the reasons for his change of employment, added: "I was extremely happy, but the chances of T.B. infection were too great in my state of health." At Bedales School he suffered from a "most intense longing for the moors." While this upset him, he was also intrigued by the way the school was run along what he called the "most cranky lines." At Eastby, Rowan's pupils were "ripping little gutter jumpers" from working-class families living in overcrowded, sooty row houses.[37] At coeducational Bedales School, the students came from well-off families, and Rowan was expected to be friendly with them and call them by their first names.[38]

He soon got used to the school system. In spite of the longer working hours and his depressing little room, he found that the school's relative proximity to London and St. Albans meant that "it won't be so lonely here."[39] The spectre of his own loneliness bothered Rowan much less than the impending loneliness of his mother. Mrs. Rowan, like her son, got fed up with life from time to time, though she had always recovered quickly from what the family referred to as her "breakdowns."[40] But towards the end of the war, worries over her children and her finances eventually took their toll, and, as Bill wrote to Arthur, she felt "the stress of these trying times pretty badly." He added, "as to myself, I am much better for the moment [but] I get so completely fed up with life when my insides return all that goes into them."[41]

Rowan soon began to enjoy teaching biology, conducting field trips, and instructing his students in the elements of farming. He liked all his colleagues and many of his pupils. He felt a special affinity for Woolacott, one of the big boys, a clever, reserved lad, keen on natural history, who had already published notes in the *Entomologist*. The two spent much time together, and from their discussions Rowan found the boy was practically a misogynist. This, he noted, "seems unnatural and calls for a deeper explanation."[42] Because of his busy schedule, however, Rowan had to postpone investigating the causes of the boy's attitude.

Understandably, Rowan was distressed when, a few weeks later, Woolacott informed him he would probably be expelled. Rowan promptly arranged to see the headmaster to intercede on Woolacott's behalf, but was too late. Woolacott shot himself that afternoon. Rowan blamed himself for not getting to the root of the boy's problem, and was most deeply touched to find that Woolacott had left a pile of beautifully made entomological slides, representing many hours of careful work, on Rowan's desk.[43] While he was profoundly affected by these events, Rowan appeared to have recovered from his wretchedness. He bounced back after spending a weekend at St. Albans with Reta, during which they announced their engagement to his family. Reta showed off her ring of two rubies and three diamonds, chosen in London a few weeks earlier. Moreover, after more than four years of war, Armistice Day had arrived. Rowan wished to be in London to toast the occasion, but had to be content with the school celebrations, held a few days later.[44]

Throughout his first year as a schoolteacher, Rowan kept up his correspondence with Darbey and Lawrence. Early in 1918 he notified them of the impending arrival in Winnipeg of Dr. Charles Henry O'Donoghue, who had been an assistant zoologist at University College, London during Rowan's student years. In Canada, like in other British colonies, there had always been a shortage of university graduates, and the older schools (McGill University and the University of Toronto) traditionally employed British and American professors. The newer universities in the West soon emulated this policy. The system worked well, because British and American graduates were often anxious to acquire experience abroad.

O'Donoghue was hired as the head of the Department of Zoology at the University of Manitoba, and with his wife, Elsie Joste Smith, sailed to Canada. In April, Lawrence informed Rowan that everyone was delighted with O'Donoghue.[45] Lawrence also wrote about the remarkable spring they were having — the birds had arrived earlier than ever — and the news from his old stomping grounds, as always, turned Rowan's thoughts to Canada. He had not yet given up hope of returning, and in O'Donoghue found a new source of information about positions available at Canadian universities. In the meantime, J.P. Hill advised Rowan to continue ornithological studies and keep his "eyes on the M.Sc. in the not too distant future." Hill also told Rowan of a vacant demonstrator position at Armstrong College at Newcastle-on-Tyne, and promised to mention his name to the professor in charge of filling it.[46] Rowan was appreciative, but uninterested. If he were to give up his job at Bedales, it would be for a university position in England or Canada, or some other lucrative and/or exciting opportunity abroad.

At the time, Rowan was still unsure whether he was destined to become a schoolmaster, a museum curator, an explorer, or a scientist. Although happy enough to take the posts at Eastby and Bedales schools, he had not given up on a career in science. He even toyed with the idea of working at a zoo. There was a restlessness in Rowan that could be attributed to his being intellectually unchallenged by teaching in a secondary school, no matter how progressive, congenial, and well-paying such work may have been.

Rowan wrote to O'Donoghue, ostensibly to inform him of his engagement to Reta, in reality to inquire about the possibility of there being ornithological work for him in Canada. O'Donoghue was forced to discourage Rowan's hopes regarding a university post, but told him of a government opening.[47] New in Canada, O'Donoghue did not know that this position was created following the ratification of the Migratory Bird Convention Act between Canada and the United States. The 1917 act protected economically useful birds, such as waterfowl, game birds, and insect-eating birds. It was to be administered by a dominion ornithologist. The post was advertised in the Canadian press at an initial salary of $2,200 per annum, or about the same as that of an assistant professor.

O'Donoghue advised Rowan to write a letter applying for the position, explaining that he had heard about it from a friend in Canada, and "make[ing] the most of" his Canadian visits and his acquaintance with E.T. Seton. He told Rowan to stress his "return to England to obtain a degree" as well as his "engulfment in the army and . . . desire to return to Canada."[48] So Rowan wrote to the Canadian government offices in London to inquire about the job. He followed O'Donoghue's advice and provided details of his education, emphasized his recent election as member of the prestigious British Ornithologists' Union, and added a list of his publications.[49] These, in the *Journal of Ecology*, *Biometrika*, *British Birds*, and the transactions of various natural-history societies, were truly impressive for someone at the beginning of his career.

Rowan also obtained a number of letters of recommendation from professors and friends. These documents are doubly interesting, because they both reveal the impression Rowan had made on his referees and indicate the qualifications British scientists considered important in applying for overseas jobs. Hill stressed Rowan's qualifications in zoology, his wide knowledge of ornithology, his artistic talent, his excellence as a lecturer, and his "driving power and considerable organising ability."[50] Oliver wrote about Rowan's resourcefulness as a naturalist and his knowledge of bird protection. Dr. P. Chalmers Mitchell, secretary of the Zoological Society of London, praised Rowan's aptitude for fieldwork and his capacity for executive work.

The anxiety of waiting for news about the Canadian position threatened to overshadow Rowan's Christmas and New Year's celebrations. But Reta spent part of the holiday in St. Albans, and Rowan's spirits lifted with the good company, good food, and good music. They spent many hours in the field, but during one of their hikes, Rowan, inadequately clothed as usual, caught a chill that soon turned into pneumonia. While recuperating at home, he received news of the appointment of Hoyes Lloyd, a dynamic thirty year old, as dominion ornithologist. Lloyd was trained in science (although in chemistry, not in zoology), knew his Canadian birds, and was a good administrator and public speaker.[51] Rowan was upset and let everyone know about it. He grumbled to Reta, to his mother, and to various friends. He complained to Darbey, to Lawrence, and to O'Donoghue, among others.

After a short visit to Eastbourne to recover, and then to experience what he called a "slice of heaven" at Reta's family home in Morden, Rowan returned for his second term at Bedales School. Though he was unsettled, he had to remain there whether he liked it or not, in order to fulfill his obligations as biology master. Rowan became determined, however, to search for a more challenging job, preferably overseas. Letters from his Canadian friends were encouraging. There was the prospect of a job in Winnipeg, in the newly founded natural-history museum.

O'Donoghue had turned into an important contact by virtue of his position in Manitoba. He was a practical man, and his letters to Rowan were full of useful information about how things are done in Manitoba. The astute O'Donoghue soon perceived the extent of political manoeuvreing and subterfuge prevalent in the hiring practices of the time. He cautioned Rowan that although Darbey would be glad to help, he should not rely on getting a museum job.[52] O'Donoghue even contacted the *Manitoba Free Press* on Rowan's behalf, but was told that the newspaper already had enough outdoor reporters, and was only in need of someone to take a desk job, hardly what Rowan had in mind. As the new professor of zoology at the University of Manitoba, O'Donoghue felt that he was overworked, and requested that a lecturer be appointed to assist him. He told Rowan to look out for the job advertisement in *Nature*.

From his letters to Rowan it is clear that O'Donoghue regarded his younger friend as an impractical dreamer. He warned him that life for Reta would be difficult in Winnipeg: "with you away all day and perhaps picking up dollars in the evening as well she would have a pretty thin time in a strange place."[53] These were prophetic words, but Rowan, in his desire to get back to Canada, did not consider their implications for the future, and it is unlikely that he ever showed Reta this correspondence. Had she seen it, perhaps she would have thought more seriously about her future in Canada, alone with her beloved Bill, but away from her other loved ones. In retrospect, it is evident that they were both extremely naïve and idealistic. Marriage for them was to be heaven, with lots of time together. O'Donoghue's warning that "there is no doubt that a woman has to work harder out here than in the old country" remained unheeded.

Rowan was unlikely to pay attention to a letter that told him that "it is only fair to the lady that she should consider these things before she comes to what for some time will be a lonely land and without some of the comforts she has been used to." Rowan's suppression of O'Donoghue's advice, that he consider his future wife in making plans points to one of his shortcomings: his inability to discuss his plans with those closest to him and directly affected by his arrangements. This was a weakness he never overcame. O'Donoghue knew his young friend well, because he added, "Now in spite of the 'gloomy doom' tone of this I suppose you will be coming out . . . ," and recommended that Bill and Reta bring a lot of clothing, particularly woollen things. He told them that everything was expensive and it was even hard to get good dinnerware.[54]

Before Rowan had a chance to digest all of O'Donoghue's news, he received another letter in which O'Donoghue informed him that the position of lecturer had been approved and was to be advertised in both the *Times* and *Nature*.[55] Though the zoology lecturer's salary was sixteen hundred dollars per year, six hundred dollars less than Lloyd's starting salary as dominion ornithologist, the post carried much less responsibility.

Highly stimulated by the possibility of a Canadian job, Rowan wrote an application, listed all his accomplishments, and enclosed copies of three articles. He mailed the required letters of reference (earlier ones by Hill and Oliver, and new ones from the headmaster and the "Head of the Science Side" of Bedales School). The Bedales School recommendations described Rowan as a keen, efficient, and stimulating teacher, and cited his popularity with his pupils.[56]

By now, having decided to return to North America, Bill Rowan was not content to apply for just one position. He well remembered his painful disappointment earlier in the year, and decided to inquire elsewhere in the New World, including the New York Zoological Gardens. He considered working in the United States, because he was assured by an American correspondent, that the country "was swimming with money [and] that the opportunities here as probably in Canada, are good for the man of either muscle or brains."[57]

In later life Rowan often recalled that in 1919 he was "simultaneously appointed Curator, Zoological Museum, University College London[;] Zoologist to the New Guinea Expedition[;] and Lecturer in the Department of Zoology, University Manitoba."[58] In fact, these three appointments did not occur simultaneously. In August 1919 Rowan was offered the post of assistant in the Department of Zoology at University College at an annual salary of two hundred pounds sterling.[59] Duties included instruction, practical demonstration, and assistance in the Museum of Zoology and Comparative Anatomy: thus the post was not that of museum curator, though Rowan recalled that it had been. The appointment was, like all others advertised by University College, open to both men and women.[60] This was highly unusual at the time, because while women students were accepted as equals at some coeducational universities, they rarely found that the positions were open to both sexes.

No records remain of either Rowan's application for the job of zoologist for the McNeil New Guinea Expedition, or his letter of acceptance. In his University of Alberta staff file, however, there is mention of Rowan having been chosen for this job out of more than one thousand applicants. Apparently, he was to go as the university's representative, but as the expedition was to be outfitted only in 1920 and Rowan was anxious to marry Reta, he accepted the job as zoology assistant at University College.

The year at Bedales School was finally over, and Rowan received the congratulations of staff and students on his new appointment. Though they regretted his leaving — he was a good and very popular teacher — no one was about to stand in the way of his career advancement. He travelled to Blakeney Point to celebrate his new post in the company of Professor Oliver, Reta, and a number of old friends and colleagues. The weather was glorious and there were many birds, including a stone curlew, now rare even in East Anglia. He and Reta swam, painted, dug for shells, hunted for snails, and sailed. It was an idyllic, carefree vacation for Bill Rowan and his fiancée in the congenial company of scientists.

In early September, just a few days after Rowan began his new duties, he wrote in his notebook: "Got a cable from O'Donoghue this morning . . . to say that I had been appointed to the Zoological Staff in the Winnipeg University to sail immediately."[61] Eight years after he had left Winnipeg to study zoology in England, Rowan would return as lecturer of zoology at the University of Manitoba. No matter that he was only to be what he called "second in command" to O'Donoghue — Rowan was finally embarking on a scientific career.

5

"Second in Command": The University of Manitoba, 1919-1920

THE CANADIAN PACIFIC ocean liner *Metagama* left Liverpool on 15 October 1919. On board were Mr. and Mrs. William Rowan, heading for Canada, the Prairies, and a new life. The previous month had been a busy one for Rowan who had to relinquish his new post at University College, London to accept the one at the University of Manitoba.[1] Though he was to be second in command to Professor Charles H. O'Donoghue, who was unlikely to resign his own position, Rowan saw this opportunity as a gateway to a scientific career in Canada. For once, stress and excitement had no detrimental effects on his health; he was optimistic about his future, delighted to be returning to Canada, and extremely happy to be married to Reta.

The weeks prior to their sailing they spent shopping, packing, and making numerous arrangements. This included buying and carefully packing household goods, and obtaining suitable clothing for the Canadian winters. In preparation for his new duties at the University of Manitoba, Rowan also assembled teaching materials (textbooks, his own lecture notes, and even his old examination sheets), and took a crash course from his friend G.E. Bullen in modelling laboratory animals. Bullen used all sorts of scrap material when supplies ran short;[2] this was a valuable lesson for Rowan, who would later have to construct all his own teaching aids, and often use cast-off materials to improvise experimental equipment. The experience also benefited him later, when he became involved in modelling and sculpting.

On 24 September 1919, Reta Bush and William Rowan were married at Morden Church, with only family members and close friends in attendance. Arthur Rowan was the best man, and Agnes Rowan and Reta's sister, Deeda Bush, the bridesmaids. The newlyweds soon left to spend their honeymoon in Skipton. In glorious weather they cycled all over the Yorkshire Dales, or walked among the purple heather and yellowing bracken of the moors. They enjoyed a prolonged honeymoon, because, happily, a railway strike prevented their return to the south of England. When the strike extended to all transport workers, even the sailing date of the *Metagama* was postponed.

When Bill and Reta finally boarded the ocean liner at Liverpool, only Mrs. Rowan saw them off. In contrast to the many passengers who became seasick, the Rowans were good sailors and spent hours on deck walking, admiring the spectacular waves, or resting, well bundled, on deck chairs.[3] They savoured their meals, danced nightly to the orchestra, and made friends with other passengers. They enjoyed the intimacy married life offered them. Rowan, as became his custom, noted various details (speed, daily distances) of this crossing.[4] Reaching the St. Lawrence River, Bill was happy to show Reta the familiar Quebec scenes of forests, mountains, and fishing villages.[5]

In Quebec City, Bill and Reta had coffee at the Château Frontenac. In Montreal, they ate at the Windsor Hotel, and went sightseeing with a friend of the Bush family. They admired the view from the top of Mount Royal, and strolled along fashionable Sherbrooke Street. In the evening they boarded the train that was to take them to Winnipeg.[6]

Reta Rowan's first impressions of Canada were favourable. The landscape of the St. Lawrence Valley and the Old World architecture of Quebec City and Montreal appealed to her artistic sense. She luxuriated in the autumn sunshine.[7] Journeying along the edge of the Canadian Shield, the Rowans watched the seemingly endless stretch of dark conifers, interspersed with grey granite, for two days before Reta got her first view of the snow-covered Prairies.

They arrived in Winnipeg on 27 October 1919. The station and

8. William and Reta Rowan, September 24, 1919.
Courtesy of the Rowan family.

the freezing temperatures under a brilliant sky were familiar to Rowan, though not to his wife, who, to her credit, was delighted rather than discouraged. Rowan proudly noted that her "sole comment was one of relish at the prospect of immediate skating."[8] Such outdoor exercise had to wait until after they had settled themselves. As a first step, the Rowans moved in with Elsie and Charles O'Donoghue at 133 Monck Avenue.

In Winnipeg, after an early cold snap, everything, including the rivers, was frozen hard.[9] The cold did not bother Rowan when, the morning after his arrival, accompanied by O'Donoghue, he took his first walk in the city in more than a decade. Later Rowan observed that although Winnipeg had grown, it was

> still suffering from pre-war barbarism in certain respects. Smoking, for instance, was yet prohibited in the majority of restaurants, while Winnipeg's leading store neither sold tobacco nor permitted the sale of classical pictures in which the figure was more than a little exposed.[10]

O'Donoghue was delighted to show the University of Manitoba to Rowan, its bustling, urban campus near the court house and provincial jail teeming with students. The university had more students that year than ever before. The sudden increase in enrollment was caused, in part, by changes in the university entrance requirement and a general reevaluation of education throughout the province, and in part by the return of war veterans.[11] Inevitably, classes were overcrowded. Larger buildings were needed.

In October 1919, construction was already in progress on the new laboratories at a site the university had chosen on Broadway. Zoology was to have its home there, together with botany, chemistry, physics, and civil and electrical engineering. The promise of up-to-date equipment and space in new quarters remained, however, cold comfort for faculty and students, who were teaching and attending classes in the old, overcrowded buildings. Even the president admitted in his report that the day-to-day realities of that year included "class rooms, with place for 48, now seating 72," and laboratories overflowing into other rooms.[12] As the Department of Zoology consisted solely of O'Donoghue and Rowan, and there were 267 students, most classes had to be repeated. Rowan soon found that he had to teach about thirty hours per week; laboratory sessions were held in poorly lit, cramped quarters; and research was impossible under the circumstances.

Fortunately, Rowan got on well with O'Donoghue, a good zoologist with a delightful sense of humour. He found the work quite pleasant, despite the unsatisfactory conditions. Rowan thrived on hard work and intellectual challenge, and the laboratory work (in preparation for teaching in the practical class) excited his scientific curiosity. He noted that the North American species of the frog used for dissecting was larger than the one used at University College. It had several curious features, such as a "persistent pronephric duct in the male, which looks like an oviduct somewhat underdeveloped. The vascular supply of the skin is also phenomenally well developed, no doubt something to do with their wintering habits."[13]

Within a week of his arrival, Rowan was already caught up in the fascinating details of his work in zoology. Reta, in the meantime, went apartment hunting and found a small, unfurnished flat. Their household goods had not yet arrived, but Rowan was unconcerned, even if they had nothing to eat with but knives.[14] He was finally in Canada and that was all that mattered.

What Reta thought is not recorded. Like many other women immigrants, she had to adjust to a new life. In her tiny new home, far both in comfort and actual distance from her childhood one at Morden, she had to become a Canadian homemaker. As there was not yet much to do, she had time to visit the famous Hudson's Bay Company store, to take walks along the rivers, and to dream about her future.

The Rowans socialized with Lawrence, the Darbeys, the O'Donoghues, and other members of the university community. After Bill's piano and Reta's cello arrived with their furniture, the Rowans held musical evenings with friends, and in January sang at a church social.[15] Weekends also meant excursions. A typical example was their first. Bill and Reta took the streetcar along Portage Avenue to Assiniboine Park to photograph animals, but saw only a few white-tailed deer and bison.[16] In the clear, dry, invigorating air, the young couple in their English woollens (topped with fur coats bought in Winnipeg), fitted into the snowy landscape well. Though looking at animals in enclosures was not like seeing them in the wild, they attempted to ignore the fences. Eventually, with cold feet, frosted spectacles, and fingers numbed by the icy metal of his camera, Rowan was forced back to reality.[17]

During the Christmas vacation there were daily excursions on snowshoes or on foot. Reta soon found that sunshine, even at thirty degrees below freezing, was much preferable to the greyness and dampness of England, and she cherished these outings as they meant more time with Bill. She learned to love the countryside — the flat and snowy fields, the big arching sky, and the spectacular sunsets. The land's openness was a welcome change from the closed-in quality of the English countryside with its high hedges. And Winnipeg, its wide streets lined with (now-bare) box elders, its winding rivers, and numerous parks, had a unique charm.

All too soon their first holiday was over, and Rowan was immersed again in teaching. He carried on with added zeal when he learned he had been granted an M.Sc. by University College, London, on the basis of his published papers.[18] On weekends they snowshoed for exercise, photographed mammals, and watched winter birds. Rowan became familiar with the feeding habits of the pine grosbeak and black-capped chickadee, and observed a white-breasted nuthatch "sit still for a long time on some given spot as though trying to thaw it out and then proceed to peck on it."[19] He watched evening grosbeaks congregate on bare branches. Bohemian waxwings, in flocks of two to three hundred, flashed red, white, and yellow wing feathers, and were easy to identify without field glasses by their plump grey bodies, erect crests, and square, yellow-tipped tails.

Accompanied by Alex Lawrence, Bill and Reta took advantage of the fine weather to visit outlying areas, such as Kildonnan East and Deer Lodge. Reta had her first close look at the "prairie mixed with poplar bluffs and other trees."[20] Even a freezing gale, which followed the March thaw, could not deter the Rowans and Lawrence, cooped up indoors during the week, from getting out into the country. In the absence of automobiles, they took advantage of Winnipeg's extensive electric streetcar system. From their usual meeting place at Eaton's department store, near Portage and Main, they could travel to different places.[21]

During the long spring evenings, Rowan, always accompanied by his wife, stepped up his field excursions. One day, on a trip to what is now the Tuxedo golf course, a dead skunk aroused Rowan's curiosity. The animal appeared unharmed. Rowan thought it had "shot off its battery on death for it stank like skunk only can." Unconcerned with the penetrating stench, and perhaps unaware of just how long the stink would linger, Bill and Reta wrapped the skunk in paper and put it in their haversack to carry it. Then Rowan, deciding that a streetcar was out of the question, set off with Reta on the fifteen-kilometre walk to Darbey's shop on Main Street. The hike took three hours, because no passing truck would take them with their cargo — at any price. Finally, the weary couple with their malodorous parcel reached Portage Avenue. Walking along this busy street they were entertained by the comments they provoked, some of which were "very amusing and some quite rude." Darbey's customers cleared off with great haste when the Rowans passed through the taxidermy shop and dumped the skunk in the backyard. Bill and Reta watched the exodus with glee. It was a priceless lesson in animal physiology and in human behaviour, and Rowan vowed that it was the last time "I carry a Skunk through Winnipeg."[22]

Rowan brought with him to Canada a renewed optimism about his future as a scientist. He brought his camera, sketchbook, binoculars, a well-thumbed Chester Reed bird guide, and unbounded enthusiasm for Canadian wildlife. In his luggage he also carried a letter of introduction from English zoologist D.M.S. Watson (who had married Rowan's friend Kathleen M. Parker) addressed to Dr. C. Gordon Hewitt, consulting zoologist to the Canadian government.

Hewitt was one of a handful of Canadian civil servants with a keen interest in wildlife and conservation. Formerly a lecturer in economic zoology at the University of Manchester, Hewitt had become dominion entomologist with the Canadian Department of Agriculture in Ottawa in 1909.[23] In this capacity he was concerned with the economic value of insects and birds, and the importance of bird protection. He became a key figure in the establishment of the 1916 Migratory Bird Treaty, and its 1917 ratification as the Migratory Bird Convention Act, between the United States and Canada.

Soon after his arrival, Rowan wrote to Hewitt, and enclosed Watson's letter. Hewitt's reply was encouraging: "It is a pleasure to know that by your arrival the all too small body of working zoologists in Canada has been increased and I am particularly glad that you are interested in birds."[24] Hewitt, the first Canadian government scientist with graduate training in zoology welcomed the arrival of Rowan, Canada's *first scientifically trained ornithologist.*

Hewitt recommended that Rowan get in touch with Canadian and American ornithologists. Rowan wrote to Percy A. Taverner, naturalist and assistant zoologist at the Victoria Memorial Museum (renamed the National Museum in 1926), and a self-trained man. Though an excellent field naturalist and a competent museum systematist and taxidermist, he had no formal training in basic biological theory or even in laboratory techniques. The same can be said of most nineteenth- and early-twentieth-century Canadian, British, and American ornithologists.[25] (There were, of course, trained zoologists at various Canadian universities, but they were more interested in invertebrate zoology, or marine biology, than in birds and mammals). Rowan informed Taverner that he was "a member of the British Ornithologists' Union and [had] accepted the appointment here especially to do work for the next few years or probably for the rest of my life, on the birds of Canada, for which my previous stay here aroused an enormous enthusiasm." He mentioned his plan to do fieldwork in remote parts of the country, and asked Taverner's assistance in obtaining government publications on birds.[26] Taverner replied, "I am glad another naturalist of ornithological inclination has come to Canada and hope that you will be a permanent fixture. There is such a great amount of work to do in the Dominion and competent workers are so few that every addition to the rank is an important accession."[27]

Taverner was in a good position to know what ornithological work needed to be done in Canada. Active in bird study since the mid-1890s, he was hired in 1911 by the federal government to coordinate Canadian ornithological observations and build up the museum's collections. Hampered by the lack of money and personnel, Taverner was well aware of the many blank spaces in Canadian ornithology. He firmly believed, however, that Canadian avifauna offered a fine field for original research in life history, geographic distribution, and economic ornithology.

Taverner's letter fuelled Rowan's initial enthusiasm for fieldwork. In contrast to Taverner, however, Rowan knew very little about the state of ornithological studies in the New World. Rowan fully intended to become an outstanding member of the Canadian ornithological community, but there was no such cohesive community! As Taverner had stated, workers were few, and they were dispersed. There was not even a Canadian ornithological association. Instead, as Rowan was to find out, Canadian ornithologists belonged to the various American societies, or to regional associations, such as the Ottawa Field Naturalists Club, the Province of Quebec Society for the Protection of Birds, and the Alberta Natural History Society.[28]

From Taverner, Rowan learned that there was a lack of Canadian bird books, and bird collections, those indispensable aids for serious study, were few and widely scattered across the country. Only J.H. Fleming (Toronto), W.E. Saunders (London), and Allan Brooks (Okanagan Landing) had extensive collections.[29] Exchanging specimens was a widespread activity, and the best way to obtain study material for systematics and geographic variations. Even Taverner had to borrow from American natural-history collections.[30]

Taverner soon became Rowan's mentor. He was knowledgeable, helpful, had a wide network of correspondents and collectors, and was able to provide Rowan with a list of useful American and Canadian publications and contacts. He offered to identify specimens for him. The initial exchange of letters, in November 1919, was the beginning of a long and fruitful friendship that only ceased with Taverner's death in 1947. On Taverner's advice, armed with a collecting pistol or a slingshot, Rowan began to secure specimens for a study collection of prairie birds. The Winnipeg area was home to a variety of species, but Rowan, attracted by the idea of going to Hudson Bay, wrote to Hewitt for information concerning grants for such a venture.

Rowan was woefully ignorant about the history of explorations in the Hudson Bay region. He knew nothing about the roles that the Royal Society of England, the Hudson's Bay Company, and the Smithsonian Institution played in fostering natural-history collections in the Canadian north, and there is no evidence he ever read any books on the subject. He was soon to share the frustration of Canadian scientists who, because they lacked funds, had to sit back and watch while the well-equipped, well-funded Carnegie Museum expeditions beat them to the Canadian Arctic.[31]

Though Rowan was uninformed about these things, he was certainly prepared to learn. Since he had become a professional scientist in his late twenties, he was aware of lost time and had no intention of repeating someone else's work. To find out what was or was not possible in Arctic ornithology, he asked Hewitt if any competent scientists had been to Hudson Bay. Rowan also told Hewitt that, if he received a substantial grant he would take Reta along. She had the artistic training to sketch specimens and scenery, and was still free from family obligations.[32]

Hewitt sent Rowan's letter, along with a covering note, to Taverner,[33] but for once the kindly Taverner, always willing to help others, remained ambivalent. Taverner also wanted to explore the Arctic, but museum duties plus a shortage of funds had so far prevented him from doing this. Although he could neither provide Rowan with a grant nor hire him for Arctic fieldwork,[34] Taverner sent a bibliography of Arctic ornithology and even offered to buy the specimens that Rowan would obtain.[35] This was a valuable first lesson for Rowan in the realities of funding and research in Canada.

Without sufficient funding, Rowan had to devise an alternative to the Hudson Bay trip. Taverner suggested a study of Shoal Lake, west of Winnipeg. The place had inherent biological interest, Taverner explained, because rising water levels could cause "alterations in its biota as it changes from alkaline to fresh" water.[36] But Rowan wanted to explore Lake Winnipeg from a fishing boat. He had hoped to photograph birds in the district of Moose Lake, where, at a bird reserve whooping cranes were reputed to nest (collecting birds was forbidden).[37] At the same time, Rowan planned to study Canadian birds (shorebirds, gulls, and merlins) also found in Britain, and was eager to collect clutches of birds' eggs. This resurgence of interest in eggs was prompted by the publication in *Biometrika* of the second part of his 1914 cooperative study on the tern eggs at Blakeney Point.[38]

His initial enthusiasm was diminished by mid-April, however, when he discovered the Manitoba government was unable to fund this trip. Characteristically, he was discouraged but soon rallied when he realized that all was not lost. There were good chances for fieldwork at the University of Manitoba's biological field station, recently established east of the city at Indian Bay, (east) Shoal Lake, Lake of the Woods. Although Rowan had abandoned his original plans with great regret, he was soon filled with excitement at the prospect of spending a summer at this spot, unknown to most ornithologists.[39]

Bad luck, this time in the form of illness, continued to plague Rowan, upsetting his carefully laid plans. Though Bill escaped with an inflamed throat, painful but not dangerous, Reta developed scarlet fever, and, at the end of April, had to be hospitalized. She was two months pregnant at the time, and worry about her health was exacerbated by concern about a possible miscarriage. Rowan was depressed as — after the initial euphoria at being back in Winnipeg, teaching at the university, and exploring the bird life of Manitoba — obstacles seemed to spring up in all directions. First there was the lack of funds for his research trip, and then Reta's illness. The Indian Bay trip had to be postponed. Rowan was, as so often before, fed up to the teeth.

When Reta began to improve, Rowan regained his optimism. With university duties out of the way, he began to enjoy a spell of freedom and spent his mornings observing wildlife around Winnipeg — at Crescent Wood, St. Vital, and Headingly. He visited Reta (in hospital, but improving rapidly) every day, accompanied Darbey to an "Old Timer's Dinner" in the Board of Trade Hall, and celebrated the first of May by attending a luncheon at which the Natural History Society of Manitoba was organized. Rowan became a charter member of the society. He was elected secretary of the zoology section, while his friend Alex Lawrence became secretary of the ornithology section.[40]

By the end of May, Reta was well enough to encourage her husband to spend a weekend near the Icelandic settlement of Gimli, where the Darbeys had a shack. This was Rowan's first introduction to the spectacular spring migration of New World warblers, for many ornithologists the highlight of the year in the eastern half of North America. These small passerine birds, so much more colourful than the European wood warblers, winter in South America. From there they set off on their annual spring migration to their North American breeding grounds, which, for most species, are in the boreal forest belt north of the forty-ninth parallel. As an undergraduate in England, Rowan was impressed by the spectacular autumn migration of waders and waterfowl, but bushes "simply alive with warblers" were a novelty.[41] No wonder that the sights and sounds of these colourful small birds rekindled his interest in migration.

It was during this period that Rowan's eldest sister, Nellie Portway, on her way to China with her husband Arthur and their two young children, visited Winnipeg. The Portways brought news, letters, and presents from the Rowan and Bush families. They took brief excursions with Bill and Reta, who was now out of hospital. Nellie was a trained soprano, and to hear her singing (sometimes solo, at other times with Bill and Reta) was an unforgettable experience for all of them.[42]

On 15 June 1920, the Rowans set off from Winnipeg on an all-day train trip through the muskeg to Waugh, the railway station nearest to Indian Bay. The biological station was part of a small settlement overlooking (east) Shoal Lake, and Bill found it a delightful area for fieldwork. Rowan examined seven well-defined faunal habitats around the station: the lake, the forest, the muskeg beyond the forest, several small marshes, a gravel pit, islands, and the scrub.[43] He studied the quaking muskeg, explored the interconnecting lakes by canoe, and spent many hours in the mosquito-ridden marsh, "hidden in the bottom of a reed-covered canoe, to obtain notes on the habits of its birds." Rowan originally planned to spend a night in the marsh. He soon found, as did the early explorers, that without mosquito repellent, or even netting, "no man could have stood it and remain[ed] sane."[44]

Having banded and photographed near St. Albans the tiny, brilliantly coloured European kingfisher, Rowan became intrigued by its larger, duller, shaggy-crested North American relative. He erected his canvas observation blind, but in spite of the intense summer heat he had to wear both a mosquito net and gloves as protection. Despite the discomfort, he spent many hours watching the feeding schedule of the young kingfishers.[45]

At Indian Bay, Reta encountered Native North Americans for the first time. She visited the village, the Cecilia Jeffries School (built in 1908), and the deserted "old treaty and pow-wow ground."[46] She was impressed by the calm dignity of the elders and the beauty and skill of some of the young women. As a young wife living in poorer circumstances than she ever had before, Reta was appalled at the Natives' living conditions, though this village was much better off than many others she was to see in Alberta.

In spite of her genuine interest in Indians, during the summer of 1920, Reta Rowan had more immediate concerns than their rights and living conditions. For someone reading Rowan's field notes and trying to reconstruct his career, the late June entry, "got wire to say I had been appointed to Chair of Zoology at Edmonton," would have come as a total surprise.[47] The notebooks in which he had recorded his experiences at the biological station in great detail ignore the significant events leading to their move further west. These events can only be pieced together from Rowan's correspondence with family, friends, and officials at the University of Alberta.

What was behind the message, "This wire offers you appointment as agreed to in Winnipeg, wire acceptance," which reached Rowan at Indian Bay?[48] When and where did Henry Marshall Tory, president of the University of Alberta, meet Rowan, and what led to the discussion of such an appointment?

During the summer of 1919, H.M. Tory embarked on a wide-ranging search for new faculty members for the expanding university. His position was hardly unique. Other Canadian universities were also faced with the problem of accommodating the large numbers of veterans returning from the war in a steady stream. Scholars were solicited in a variety of disciplines, and the need for more space led to new jobs in the construction industry. The University of Manitoba had to build a new campus. The University of Alberta began constructing a new medical building, which was to house both the existing science departments (chemistry and entomology), and a new department of zoology.

Tory began his search hopefully, but he soon found that competent people were in great demand. As McGill and the other Eastern Canadian universities offered very high salaries, they could attract the best European, Canadian, and American scholars. The University of Alberta could not compete with these older, better-funded institutions, but Tory wanted the best and refused to compromise his own standards. His task was not easy. With an enrollment of 1,106 students in 1919–1920, an increase of 79 percent over the previous academic year, the situation at the university was truly serious. By the summer of 1920, Tory was desperate, as he urgently needed a zoologist to build up a new department. His search eventually led him to Rowan.[49]

In a 1956 CBC Television interview, Rowan recollected that he received a telegram from an unknown person about the professorship of zoology becoming available. This was W.A. Kerr, at the time acting president of the University of Alberta. Rowan thought the whole thing was a joke, and threw out the telegram. When another wire arrived, this time from an H.M. Tory, Rowan took it to the registrar of the University of Manitoba, who advised the sceptical Rowan to take it seriously, but he was on his way to Gimli with Reta and did not bother to reply. Rowan eventually managed to meet with Tory in Winnipeg, and took along his "beautiful wife, dressed in her Sunday best" to the interview.[50] Rowan later joked that it was Reta who was responsible for his having secured the appointment. It is likely that Tory had thought the charming Reta would be a welcome addition to the small university community, but it was Rowan, on his best behaviour, who convinced the exacting Tory to offer him the post.

There is no doubt that Rowan could impress the most discerning of university presidents. At twenty-nine, he exuded energy and purpose. With his pleasant baritone voice, superb vocabulary, and clear diction, he was an excellent speaker. He could, at will, be serious or amusing. He was knowledgeable, had graduated from a prestigious British university, and had a respectable list of publications. Rowan told Tory that he had already lived in Alberta, and was eager to return there. He was happy to accept the opportunity to go, on one year's probation, to the University of Alberta, to lecture to medical students as assistant professor in the Department of Biology. Tory became convinced the younger man was ambitious enough to want to become, when the probationary period was over, full professor and head of the new department. Though somewhat individualistic, he could probably be molded to fit Tory's idea of a zoology professor.

When Tory's telegram finally arrived, Rowan was relieved. No matter how much he enjoyed the summer at Indian Bay, he and Reta, with their first child expected in November, needed a better income. Tory's letter, dated 20 July 1920, confirmed the arrangement:

> You will come to us as Assistant Professor in the Dept. of Biology at a salary of $2,800 per annum with the understanding that if mutual satisfaction is given, you will receive

> promotion to the Chair of Zoology, your fitness for the higher post to be determined as a result of your year's work.

The change in salary was indeed considerable, the opportunity for advancement golden. Rowan's income would be increased by twelve hundred dollars; instead of remaining a lecturer, he would start at the rank of assistant professor, and within the year advance to that of associate professor. Rowan was confident, and did not worry about the probation. Lawrence and O'Donoghue, though sorry to lose Rowan's companionship, encouraged him to accept.[51]

Rowan's delight about his improved prospects was somewhat tempered by the fact that he had to leave Indian Bay earlier than intended. Although classes were to start only on 28 September, Tory recommended that Rowan be in Edmonton by 1 September to prepare for the academic year. The president promised Rowan sufficient working space, but had to admit that "there may be a little crowding up to the first of January."[52]

A more careful reading of Tory's letter would have alerted Rowan to the true state of affairs at the University of Alberta, but Rowan, in his enthusiasm, either did not perceive the letter's hidden meaning or, as usual, disregarded facts with which he did not want to deal. Trying to pack as much fieldwork as possible into the few remaining weeks of the summer, Rowan was disinclined to worry about practical matters such as the high cost of living, the difficulty of finding a flat near the university, or the lack of laboratory assistants. Instead, he lived in the present, photographed birds, and also Reta in the company of Native women.[53] He took copious notes on bird song and bird distribution and battled the mosquitoes. He wrote of his good fortune to family and friends.

During this happy period Rowan made a new friend. This was Darbey's new assistant, British naturalist-collector Cyril George Harrold,[54] who arrived one fine August day on the excursion train. Rowan had already heard about this young man (reputed to be a crack shot) from Lawrence, and immediately liked what he saw. Harrold was slight and wiry, with prominent ears that were accentuated by the flat cloth cap he pulled low over his forehead. He seemed good-natured. His grin was infectious and his eyes, behind steel-rimmed glasses, sparkled with humour. The two men were drawn to each other. Harrold proved to be a field companion par excellence, and Rowan, instead of preparing for his impending move to Edmonton, could not resist a last fling at Indian Bay. So he took Harrold canoeing and introduced him to the bird life of the area. They had a wonderful time, and it was the first of many such happy field experiences. It was with some regret that Bill and Reta returned to Winnipeg.

The following week was a nightmare; their days were filled with planning, packing, and saying goodbye to friends.[55] Soon, like so many other new Canadians, the Rowans headed west — again. Destination: Edmonton. Rowan was happy. His luck had improved, and his prospects seemed excellent. After only ten months in Canada, the chance of a lifetime, the much-coveted break, had arrived. He had been offered the opportunity to build a department of zoology at the University of Alberta.

6

To Build a Department of Zoology

"THE UNIVERSITY is very attractive, and remarkably fine for such a juvenile institution," noted William Rowan with satisfaction at the end of his first day in Edmonton. The Rowans arrived from Calgary on the overnight train, breakfasted at the McDonald (a typically ornate Canadian Pacific hotel), were picked up by H.M. Tory in his car, and were taken to visit the university.[1] Edmonton was new to both Bill and Reta. They were impressed by the winding North Saskatchewan River, the verdant ravines and the University of Alberta, its red-brick buildings, Rowan noted, "carefully planned and laid out in their own grounds."[2] Used to the crowded urban premises of University College, London and the University of Manitoba, Rowan greatly appreciated the space surrounding the buildings and the proximity of the university farms. He soon wrote to an acquaintance that he was "well pleased with Edmonton, and with the University."[3]

Once their household goods arrived from Winnipeg, the Rowans rented a large, unfurnished place at 11017 80th Avenue, in the Garneau district, which was the heart of the small university community. They soon became friendly with several professors and their families with whom they had common interests. On 4 September 1920, Rowan noted that he "had his first bird tramp," and he bought a "good Belgian gun, 12 bore, double barrel, second hand for $27.50."[4] Not long after arriving in the city, he visited William Wolfe and Ashley Hine, the owners of Edmonton's main taxidermy establishment (on 102d Street), who provided him with contacts and a wealth of information on local areas favoured by other naturalists. They told Rowan about Francis Point (an excellent staging area for shorebirds, and a place preferred by hunters), located at the southern end of Beaverhills Lake, seventy-two kilometres east of the city.[5]

Good times with congenial new acquaintances and the prospect of having access to fine collecting grounds somewhat cushioned the shock Rowan received on his first visit to the university's zoological laboratory in Athabasca Hall. Although zoology had been taught for years to medical students as part of the biology course, space, equipment, and library facilities were practically nonexistent. Rowan was challenged by the task of creating a new department. As a first step, he set out to obtain laboratory equipment from A.E. Baird and Company, a supplier he knew near University College, London. Rowan ordered one hundred sets of good quality English dissecting instruments, and soon found that even the purchase of this basic equipment exhausted the new department's meagre financial resources.[6]

Rowan had never been so busy in his life. He lectured to medical students and, at the same time, prepared a "scheme of lectures for next and future years for approval by the powers that be." He was on probation, and determined to make good. Rowan confessed to Canadian government entomologist Norman Criddle that he felt it a

> great responsibility to found a department, with its many advantages and drawbacks, including the fact that I shall more or less have to forget birds for a year or two, till I have the thing on its feet. There simply is not the time to give to them, and I have to nurse a reputation as a zoologist and not an ornithologist.[7]

He could no more give up ornithology than he could give up breathing, though he continued to pay lip service to this desire to concentrate exclusively on zoology.

The distinction Rowan made, at this stage in his life, between ornithology and zoology is interesting. Although ornithologists *are* zoologists, in 1920, zoologists concentrated on the laboratory study of lower animals, such as invertebrates, fish, and amphibians, rather than birds and mammals. In contrast, ornithology remained largely a museum- and field-oriented science rather than a laboratory-oriented one. But things were changing on both sides of the Atlantic, and ornithology had begun to shed its image as a study of birds at the end of a shotgun or in smelly natural-history museums. Although the scientific collection of specimens and study of comparative material remained important, other scientific aims and methods were developed. Rowan did much to contribute to this transformation, of the descriptive nineteenth-century natural history of birds into avian biology. In fact, Rowan was a pioneer of avian ecology with his studies of the breeding biology of birds in relation to environmental factors.[8] Though most of his important research had not yet been done, by the time Rowan arrived to teach zoology in Edmonton, he had already made significant contributions to the new ornithology.

The distinction between ornithology and zoology was to crop up in Rowan's thinking for years to come, and he would unconsciously echo H.M. Tory's beliefs on the subject. It was to cause considerable difficulties and frustrations for Rowan throughout the 1920s. Ironically, though he was to play a large part in changing ornithology into a science in which field study, laboratory work, observation, and experiment all played important roles, at the time Rowan had no conscious research program to effect such changes. The outcome was a byproduct of his own research, rather than the result of a deliberate plan. The atmosphere in the early 1920s, at the University of Alberta, was simply not conducive to the formulation of a research program in the modern sense.

From the time of his arrival at the University of Alberta, Rowan began to establish useful contacts, collect information on prairie ornithology, and acquire reprints and data on North American ornithological subjects. He wrote to American ornithologist T.S. Palmer of his "ambition to get in touch with all I can and to try and keep in my department careful records of all birds obtained by collectors, migration dates, etc." He added that while the volume of the work to be done in Alberta was "quite staggering to contemplate," he was determined to build a scientific library and a study collection. To finance this Gargantuan task, he let it be known to other collectors, he would use bird skins instead of cash, of which he had little. Rowan reiterated, to Palmer, as he did to others, "I am wondering how the University here will appreciate having its Zoo department run by a bird maniac. No one here seems to know anything about birds and I think they care less. They will have to have careful handling."[9]

These early expressions of doubt are significant in view of Rowan's later experiences at the university. Was it intuition or foresight? Rowan certainly had no time to worry about university politics or the best way to handle Dr. Tory and other members of the administration. It may not even have occurred to him that the president himself, who had seemed so friendly and encouraging, needed "careful handling." Rowan was caught up in a never-ending round of teaching, preparing study aids and, time permitting, writing letters (he would usually do this late at night). He had to do everything himself. There were no secretaries, or even typewriters, and there was certainly no time during working hours to write requests for information, government publications, and reprints. The fact that he acquired journals such as the *Auk*, the *Journal of Mammalogy*, and the *American Journal of Ecology* is indicative of his interest in the emerging field of ecology, which was wider than his interest in pure laboratory zoology.

In spite of his initial difficulties, Rowan felt lucky to be at the University of Alberta. At least the facilities, such as they were, were housed under one roof while awaiting the construction of the new medical building. At the University of Manitoba, various departments, including that of zoology, were split up between old and new buildings, and, as botany lecturer Charles W. Lowe wrote Rowan, material and apparatus were "so distributed that no one knows where to look for anything."[10] Edmonton also had its disadvantages, however. The cost of living was high, but Rowan, though he complained to Lawrence, also emphasized the scientific opportunities that arose from the fact that the Edmonton area was unexplored by ornithologists.

Lawrence, as usual, was supportive and encouraged and chided his friend in turn. He warned Rowan about the dangers of being too critical in a new environment, but his advice, "Always boost, Son, don't be a knocker," Rowan found increasingly difficult to follow. He took more notice of Lawrence's comments concerning the need for migration data for Edmonton and indeed the whole of Alberta.[11] This was to have important implications for Rowan's future.

The highlight of Rowan's first busy month was an unexpected

meeting with Hoyes Lloyd and Percy A. Taverner, whom Rowan had only known through correspondence. The two men were returning to Ottawa from fieldwork in British Columbia and stopped at Edmonton to meet Rowan, who rushed to their hotel for, what he called, a late-night "pow-wow." He found both the hirsute Taverner and the clean-shaven Lloyd to be lean and strong, their pale, bald pates contrasting markedly with their tanned, leathery faces and necks. As Taverner unfolded his long frame to greet Rowan, he towered over everyone. Taverner's pronounced stutter surprised Rowan, but this impediment did not seem to bother anyone, and certainly did not prevent him from engaging in a lively conversation.

Taverner invited Rowan to accompany him to some lakes at about 110 kilometres south of Edmonton, but the promised expedition did not materialize, and only the opportunity to travel, with physiology professor A.W. Downs, to Francis Point, a famous duck-hunting area on Beaverhills Lake, alleviated Rowan's disappointment. On Saturday 2 October, Rowan and Downs took a train to the village of Tofield. The distance from the station to Francis Point was six kilometres, and on the way the two men called in at the Francis homestead to have a rest and obtain permission for duck hunting. The point was paradise, indeed, and, with the permission of Mrs. Francis, the two men scared up hundreds of ducks, mostly mallards. Rowan shot eight.[12]

Rowan's enjoyable field activities, carried out mostly as university business, soon brought undesirable repercussions. In fact, within a month of his arrival in Edmonton, Rowan had his first disagreement with Dr. Tory. The university president told him to "lay off birds." Rowan, inwardly seething but outwardly meek, promised to cooperate. What prompted this set-to is not known. It is possible that Rowan, with characteristic generosity, gave some of the ducks he shot at Beaverhills Lake to either Tory or someone close to the president. If so, this was a kindhearted gesture that backfired. It is also possible that Rowan's ornithological activities, carried out in the company of other faculty members, were more visible than his attempts to acquire specimens other than birds for the zoology department. Whatever the reasons, the first clash, in October 1920, was the beginning of a long-standing feud between two volatile, determined people, the administrator, who had long ago given up scientific work, and the new assistant professor, who was at the beginning of his career as teacher, scientist, and innovative researcher.

Rowan soon informed his friends of this new development. To Taverner he wrote:

> [M]y enthusiasm for birds may lead me into trouble with the university authorities. In fact I have been confidentially warned by someone concerned with my appointment here that it is to my best interest if I let birds lie low for a time. The reason is that they are afraid that they have got hold of an ornithologist and not a zoologist. I hope my winter courses will disprove this, but in the meantime I have no choice but to take the tip. But you can bet that every minute I can conscientiously give to birds will be given even if I have to do it in the dark. But collecting, alas, will be difficult.[13]

Taverner replied, "I quite agree with you that it will be better to be fairly quiet regarding bird matters if that is the way the authorities feel about it. When you are established you will have greater liberty."[14] Lawrence advised Rowan to do as he was told: "You had better collect all forms of animal life and call yourself a Zoologist instead of an Ornithologist."[15]

Rowan did not, however, curb his activities, and he did not equate difficult with impossible. In fact, he acquired birds at every possible opportunity for the university study collection. He also made a point of meeting and entertaining visiting naturalists. One was Major Allan Brooks, Canada's best known bird artist, who arrived in late October to collect and paint on one of the local lakes. Rowan was delighted to meet this famous figure, and to see his original paintings, "all handled with exquisite daintiness and with a wealth of colour evidently lost in the ordinary familiar reproductions."[16]

Brooks was also renowned in naturalist circles. Born in India, and raised in Ontario and British Columbia, he originally made a living as a hunter and collector. By the first decade of the twentieth century, his finely detailed paintings of mammals and birds brought him a number of commissions as an illustrator. His interests were wide; he had an outstanding collection of western birds and was well known as a careful observer of breeding biology and bird behaviour. He was also knowledgeable (and highly opinionated) about systematics, migration, and the detrimental effects of crows and birds of prey on other species.

For Rowan, meeting Brooks was an honour and a surprise. He had expected "something of the Chelsea type, bearded, cravated and hatless, possibly in [a] shapeless pair of trousers." Instead he found a dapper man with a clean-shaven chin, whose "quiet, unassuming manner did anything but suggest artistic genius." Rowan was greatly impressed by Brooks's marksmanship and noted that he was "one of the crack shots of the Dominion who can fetch down a flying Crow with a .22 rifle more certainly than many a passable shot can do it with a 12-bore." Rowan greatly admired the care Brooks lavished on his rifle, but never emulated the older man's example. He also envied Brooks's facility with a pencil, and his ability to "sketch spontaneously characteristic poses and plumage in detail from memory."[17] Later Rowan worked hard to develop similar skills.

Rowan was fortunate to meet Lloyd, Taverner, and Brooks — all three were to become useful connections and lifelong friends. So too was the American naturalist Francis Harper, who was to become his staunch supporter. Harper, who worked for the United States Bureau of Biological Survey, visited Edmonton on his return from the Athabasca Delta, "bringing back with him a mass of freshly gleaned information and material from birds to frogs." Rowan later recollected that "such contacts with the outside world periodically livened up the rather confined existence that we led during our early years in Edmonton without a car."[18]

Closer to home, Rowan found another kindred spirit in Bill MacDonald, a third-year engineering student and keen outdoorsman and naturalist. MacDonald collected bird skins and eggs and could provide useful information on the breeding areas of Alberta birds. The two men soon developed a lasting friendship. Rowan also maintained his contact with Billy Wolfe and Ash Hine, and spent many happy hours in their taxidermy workshop, chatting about the local fauna and sketching fresh bird and mammal specimens. He was to recall, "the entire course of my life would have been different without their advice to go and collect at Francis Point, Beaverhills Lake."[19]

Thus, within a few weeks of his arrival, the pattern of Rowan's life in Edmonton was set: he would teach large classes, but have no money for teaching materials; he would become part of a congenial university community, but have trouble with the administration. Rowan found himself in an area of Canada that was among the most promising for, and least studied by, ornithologists, yet he was advised by the university administration, and even his friends, to ignore birds and concentrate on general zoological matters.

Rowan could not, however, ignore birds. He sketched, photographed, and collected them. He introduced his students to birds, and wrote up the observations he made at Indian Bay, Manitoba, for publication in the *Auk*. At about this time Rowan was elected associate member of the American Ornithologists' Union. Entry-level membership in the union needed only sponsors, and practically anyone who cared about birds and conservation, and was willing to pay three dollars, could become an associate. In contrast, full members were elected on the basis of their publications. Rowan aspired to full membership, but felt if his department continued to keep him "as occupied as hitherto, that day will never come."[20]

Rowan's new routine — he would work long hours at the university, read and write at home until late at night, and spend weekends in the field — seriously affected his home life. In Edmonton, while Bill was fully occupied, Reta (who had spent all her available time with Bill in Winnipeg) had to restrict her outdoor activities. The busy days and weeks that left Rowan with little free time stretched into an interminably slow, bleak period for Reta, pregnant with her first child. Bill finally took time off to celebrate the birth of "a lusty little girl," named Gerdine after her paternal grandmother, who was born on 28 November 1920, at the Misericordia Hospital.[21] The proud father promptly notified family and friends. Collecting, sketching, and photography now had to take a back seat. Rowan's time was divided between his family and his course work, which included setting and correcting examinations for two hundred students.

While Rowan seemed to settle into his new position, the university president remained ambivalent about his suitability as a scientist. In early December, to initiate discreet inquiries about him, Tory wrote to Sir Gregory Foster, provost at University College, London. He told Foster of having discovered Rowan at the University of Manitoba, and added that he had "a good record but made a specialty of Ornithology rather than pure Zoology."[22] Tory omitted to mention his earlier discussion with Rowan concerning fieldwork; instead, as he put it, he decided to "verify," with University College authorities, that Rowan had actually taken his Honours B.Sc. in zoology.

Why did Tory wait until December before requesting an official copy of Rowan's university record "to determine his ability to carry on the headship of Zoology"? He had already found out that as a teacher Rowan was "eminently satisfactory."[23] Did Tory suspect that Rowan had lied to him about his undergraduate degree? He knew Rowan had an M.Sc. Is it possible that Tory, whose experience was in the exact sciences, was simply unsure about which qualities were needed to run the zoology department? Whatever Tory's real motivations, just how Rowan's undergraduate examination record was to prove or disprove his suitability for the post is unclear.

Foster told Tory that Rowan had wide interests, "but he rather splayed himself." Although Foster thought that Rowan "had a good deal of leadership about him," he did not think that Rowan would ever become an eminent scientist; he would, however, "make a good teacher and will generally be an effective member of a staff."[24] Foster's assessment of Rowan's scientific potential is an example of the power administrators can have, unfortunately, over the careers of scientists. Indeed, Foster seemed to have confirmed Tory's opinion of Rowan, which was in direct contrast to those expressed by Rowan's old professors and previous employers. It is evident that Rowan's wide interests and predilection for fieldwork were antithetical to Tory's narrow view of scientific research as conducted by university scientists. Tory had been a mathematics and physics lecturer at McGill University, and never did much actual research. An institution builder since the early twentieth century, he regarded Rowan merely as a satisfactory teacher whose scientific interest and research ability remained suspect. Twelve years later Tory wrote:

> I did not consider him qualified at the time for a senior post, but as I only wished a man to give a course in elementary zoology for the Medical School and as he was the only man available at the time, I gave him the appointment. I found out

> afterwards that his disposition was not toward intensive laboratory work as such, but rather outside work, and especially was he giving his attention to collecting and studying the habits of birds.[25]

Like most people, Tory had a selective memory. It is hardly surprising that he had conveniently forgotten that had he been able to offer pay and working conditions comparable to those of Eastern Canadian universities, he could have attracted an already well-established laboratory zoologist. (Marine biologist A.G. Huntsman, a professor at the University of Toronto, actually considered moving to the University of Alberta, but, for reasons unknown, did not).[26]

Though Tory chose to maintain that he had found out about Rowan's interest in fieldwork later, there is considerable evidence that he had known about it from the outset. When both Kerr and Tory missed Rowan in Winnipeg because the latter was working in the field, Tory asked the botanist Francis Lewis to make inquiries about Rowan at University College. Lewis spoke to J.P. Hill and others who knew Rowan as a student and "heard all details about Rowan."[27] "All details" would have included the fact that, in 1919, he was awarded an M.Sc. Moreover, anyone inquiring about Rowan in London would have heard of his wide-ranging interest in zoology, his enthusiasm for fieldwork, and his thorough grounding in laboratory methods. It is likely, however, that Tory disregarded certain aspects of Rowan's past because he was in a rush to hire a zoology professor. Perhaps he thought that once Rowan was in Alberta, he would give up fieldwork and become Tory's tame laboratory zoologist. It soon became obvious, however, that Tory had misjudged his man.

Unfortunately, Tory's restricted vision of scientific research precluded his acceptance of fieldwork as an integral part of Rowan's work at the university. He failed to appreciate that Rowan did all he *had* to do, and that no one could have created and built a zoology department without acquiring study specimens for teaching and future research. There was no money to buy study materials, and Rowan had to assemble the invertebrate and vertebrate study collections in person and by exchange. This latter method, widely used by zoologists everywhere, enabled scientists to acquire specimens not available in their immediate environments. Rowan later received osteological and other material from Europe, New Zealand, Australia, and Africa in exchange for many of the animals found in the Edmonton district, but the university president, without fully knowing what was involved, condemned this well-established practice.

Though no records remain of the initial exchange, one can imagine both Rowan's total surprise at Tory's attitude, and his subsequent defense of his own field activities. Rowan came from a culture where natural-history fieldwork was a respected pursuit; where his own election to the prestigious British Ornithologists' Union had been a reward for his fieldwork and publications. His diary entries for the 1920–1921 academic year indicate that, despite his earlier promise to curb his activities, Rowan spent all available time in the field. His Saturdays were reserved for tramping through the countryside searching for specimens. Reta often stayed home while her husband took students or faculty members along, including the "Misses Pelluet, Ferguson and Tempest."[28]

Rowan always liked what he often referred to as "sweet young things." Now he was ready to impress his female students, and in their company scoured Whitemud Ravine, the university farms, and the riverfront for specimens. His field notebooks are full of information about meteorological phenomena and exciting discoveries, but not of his personal life. We know very little about how he adjusted to having a "lusty little girl" at home, and a picture of the problems he was having at work can only be pieced together from fragmentary information contained in his correspondence.

Evidently, Rowan was allotted no official time for fieldwork, which had to be done on weekends. As anyone familiar with winters at a latitude of nearly fifty-four degrees north could imagine, collecting mammals, never an easy task, was well-nigh impossible during the long and cold winter months. So Rowan slipped into his weekend ornithological work by inclination and also by default. Birds were not only more visible than mammals, but they were also easier to collect. Collecting constituted only a small part of Rowan's activities, however, and by the spring of 1921 he had begun to pursue a number of new biological interests, such as geographic distribution, trinomial nomenclature, and the anatomy of flying squirrels.[29]

It is interesting to speculate whether Rowan simply ignored Tory's earlier warning to curtail his fieldwork, or considered that what he did on weekends was his own affair. Was Rowan oblivious to the rigidity of Tory's opinion concerning the nature of scientific research? Whatever the case, the university president could not understand that Rowan, quite legitimately, did fieldwork during his own leisure time. Edmonton was still a small city and the university community was closely knit. It was inevitable, that Tory would become aware of Rowan's field excursions, and that he would hold these activities against the new professor.

At about the time Rowan stepped up his fieldwork, he unofficially heard about the Tory-Foster correspondence. How and when Rowan found out about it is unknown. Tory certainly never informed him, but the secret leaked out, and Rowan was not simply hurt — he was furious. Rowan was not used to being doubted. He was sure of his own worth, confident in his own abilities as a teacher and scientist, and disgusted with Tory's attempt to delve into the past before deciding to offer him a permanent position. Whatever he did or did not do as an undergraduate was history — and now, in his thirtieth year, he was ready to settle down and do his best. He was certainly ambitious enough to want to become a full professor and not remain second in command at the University of Manitoba. He had a responsibility to his wife and child. And he had informed everyone in England about his wonderful new position at the University of Alberta. Tory's underhanded behaviour provoked a turmoil of feelings in Rowan, and he found it impossible to know how to act. Rowan was not in the habit of ignoring injustice, particularly when it was directed against him, but was unsure if he should confront the president. With great difficulty Rowan restrained his immediate impulse to do so. Lawrence, to whom he turned, as usual, in difficult times, replied posthaste: "Do not say a word to him. It will not get you anywhere and will do no good."[30] What Reta recommended is not known.

Confrontation was inevitable, though who initiated it and what exactly occurred is unclear. Foster's letters reinforced Tory's positive impression about Rowan's suitability as a teacher. But by now it must have been evident that Rowan was unlikely to give up fieldwork. Although a doctorate was not a requirement for the position at the time, the president demanded that Rowan obtain a

D.Sc. Perhaps he thought preparations for this degree would turn Rowan's mind towards what Tory considered desirable zoological research and force him to concentrate on laboratory work.

In mid-February 1921, Rowan wrote to Taverner about an impending trip to England to work on his doctorate. "This is so urgent that I really think I have to do it, though heaven knows I begrudge a summer away from the wild and wooly [sic] west more than I can say."[31] Rowan also told Lawrence about his decision to do graduate work in England.[32] Actually, Rowan was in no financial position to go to England to pursue such research, but he was willing to humour Tory. The president's ultimatum provided a welcome chance to show off Gerdine to the Rowan and Bush families, but with no money for their passage, Rowan had to borrow from his mother against his future inheritance.

Reta went along with the plan. The trip would further Bill's career by appeasing Dr. Tory, and allow her to see her own family. Poor Reta! In a strange city, with only her infant daughter for company, she was confined to her rented home by cold and snow. She only saw her husband at odd times, and saw her new friends only at weekend musical gatherings. Reta felt isolated, but she never complained. Maybe she considered her isolation a necessary part of settling into life in a new land. Brought up in a prosperous household with servants, she now cleaned, cooked, and cared for her child alone. Like many other women at the time who found themselves in similar circumstances, Reta rose to the occasion. Although a kind and loving mother, she never became an enthusiastic homemaker. She simply cared more about people, art, and music, than about spotless windows and dust-free furniture.

Rowan was too busy, and possibly too insensitive, to worry much about his wife's feelings; perhaps he was not even aware of her loneliness. He must have known, however, that her days were filled with unaccustomed drudgery, but he had neither the time, nor the inclination to worry about how Reta filled her hours. In contrast to Reta's narrowly circumscribed day-to-day existence, Bill's life, though always hectic and often frustrating, was more satisfying, because he met a variety of people and followed his own interests.

How did Rowan regard the prospect of engaging in the kind of work necessary to acquire a higher degree? He was proud of being one of those original thinkers who find most academic lectures boring. He often spoke scathingly about book learning and formal schooling. His recognized ability to think creatively, together with his rather indifferent academic record, led him to scorn the "standardised ruts of academic philosophy and dogma on which the more mediocre are nurtured."[33] But in 1921, in order to stay on at the University of Alberta where he had congenial colleagues, the chance of advancement, and the promise of an ornithological paradise to explore, Rowan was still willing to conform to the rules of the academic game that produced doctorates in science. When Tory "recommended" he obtain a D.Sc., Rowan was quick to realize that such a degree would act to legitimize him as a zoologist, increase his stature in Tory's eyes, and help "cinch the chair" of zoology.

Rowan asked his old professors, Oliver and Hill, about working on his doctorate at University College, London during the summer. Oliver's friendly reply reinforced Rowan's decision;[34] Hill not only promised to squeeze Rowan into his laboratory, but also arranged with the provost that Rowan be charged only a minimal fee for the summer session. He warned Rowan, however, that "you may calculate taking a couple of years or so [for] the preparation of a D.Sc. thesis that will carry you through."

What Rowan actually proposed to work on is unclear. Hill wrote: "I gather brown bears are as numerous as sparrows in parts of Canada and if you can strike the breeding season they are worth going after. For years I've wanted a bear placenta."[35] But bear placentas were not readily available in Edmonton and Rowan was far too busy to go looking for bears. There is some evidence, however, that he considered doing his D.Sc. research on the embryology of the emu.[36]

The academic year was drawing to a close. Rowan left it to Reta to pack for the four-month trip to England, while he alternately corrected exams and covered the district on foot, in farmers' wagons, or in a colleague's car. He certainly enjoyed his first Edmonton spring. Melting snow and mud had given way to warm weather and an abundance of singing birds. Accompanied by Bill MacDonald and Dixie Pelluet, Rowan roamed the district searching for zoological material.[37] In mid-April the ice had melted on the river, the swans were migrating, and Rowan camped for two days on Francis Point. The ninety kilometre trip to Beaverhills

Lake, via Bonnie Doon, Cooking Lake, and Tofield, took Rowan and three companions nearly five hours by car over the ubiquitous, slippery Alberta mud called "gumbo." At one point, presaging many such occasions, they had "to put the chains on after much skidding and side slipping and a short rest in a mud hole."[38]

The Rowans left Edmonton for England on 30 April, and three days later, in Montreal, boarded a Canadian Pacific liner bound for Liverpool.[39] Unfortunately, the ship ran into an ice floe and lost a blade from its turbine propeller, which slowed their progress. The trip took nine days instead of the customary six, and passengers had to put up with the ship's constant vibration. Rowan remained unconcerned. While others fretted, he watched a profusion of puffins, guillemots, and razorbills.

Liverpool, often grimy and dull, was bathed in sunshine when the liner with its chilled passengers finally anchored on 15 May 1921. It was an auspicious beginning for the trip to West Yorkshire, Rowan's favourite birding spot in England. "The weather is glorious and the moors look very beautiful and home-like," he noted at Skipton. They walked all over the moors looking for birds. All too soon, Reta and Gerdine were left on their own, while Rowan spent a week observing merlins from a hide, taking photos and copious notes of a nesting pair for a series of articles for *British Birds*.[40]

Characteristically, Rowan's diaries are filled with detailed notes of his Yorkshire field activities, but do not describe the summer's laboratory research. He later wrote to Taverner that it was "no particular delight to me to spend a perfectly glorious summer in the stuffiness of a lab in London."[41] It is evident from his letters that he did not neglect his duties towards the University of Alberta: he continued to look for teaching material. In his spare time, Rowan met old friends, and attended the annual conference of the British Ornithologists' Union, where he was impressed with many scientific papers, including one by Frank M. Chapman, on bird song.

The Rowans returned to Edmonton in mid-September, just before the official opening of the new medical building, which housed the departments of chemistry, physiology, entomology, and zoology as well as the Provincial Laboratory of Public Health. Ivy has long covered its red-brick exterior, tens of thousands of tramping feet have worn away the edges of its marble stairs, and its original offices, lecture halls, and laboratories have been refurbished and reorganized. The well-equipped Rowan Memorial Laboratory and zoology offices in the new, featureless biological sciences building bear no relation to Rowan's early, simply furnished labs, and his unique den in the tower of the medical building is gone. Rowan's old students and friends still recall with amusement, and a certain amount of nostalgia, the "stiff in a tank" one had to pass while climbing the spiral staircase leading to Rowan's spacious office, a room cluttered with books, charts, and specimens. Prominent among its furnishings were a coffee urn and a bearskin rug. It was widely known at the university that all day long Doc Rowan brewed and drank strong coffee and rolled and smoked his vile-smelling cigarettes. Later, there was student lore and general gossip about the various uses of the rug.[42]

At the end of September 1921, the zoology department finally became a reality, and William Rowan (B.Sc., M.Sc., member of the British Ornithologists' Union, and so on) was its acting head. Soon things began to deteriorate, and within a few months Rowan wrote to Taverner about his dissatisfaction with his situation: "I have the heaviest time table of any one on the university staff and the responsibility of running a new department as well, but I still have to be content with the rank of Associate Prof. This may or may not be rectified next session."[43]

Rowan's main problem was he *was* the entire zoology department. He had to write and present lectures, organize and supervise laboratory experiments, prepare study aids, acquire a departmental library, and set and correct examinations. As if all this would not keep him fully occupied, he was also expected to carry on with his own research towards a D.Sc. For once, even the energetic Rowan was feeling overwhelmed, tired, and dejected. Reta, expecting a second child and stuck in a tiny house with Gerdine, could offer little help. Finally Rowan persuaded the administration that he needed a part-time laboratory assistant. As zoology graduates, particularly male ones, were unavailable for such low-paying posts, he hired the botanist Dixie Pelluet.

Pelluet, who was to become one of Canada's outstanding biologists, was at the time waiting for a scholarship to study in England. Though some women did work as assistants and demonstrators at the University of Alberta, there had been no openings for Pelluet. She may have approached Tory for a position and been turned down. She certainly remembered him as "an awful person, a ruthless man, but with remarkable organizing ability."[44] Under the circumstances, she was delighted to earn some money. Her presence freed Rowan from the supervision of all the afternoon zoology laboratories, and she even substituted for him, albeit unofficially, so that he could go duck hunting. While Pelluet silently resented Rowan's occasional disappearances (leaving her in sole charge of the labs), playing hookey acted as a safety valve for Rowan. These escapes (and the odd weekend camping trip) — the fresh air, the exercise, and the opportunity to witness the beauty of the northern lights — relaxed and restored him. He had to get away from the university to keep his sanity. Like many other Canadian academics at the time, Rowan had to contend with large classes, inadequate facilities, and no money. Yet, Tory expected him to build a first-class, research-based department. Rowan was still keen to do so. It is a testimony to his skill and determination that he managed to fulfil his mandate.

Although no records exist of the zoology department's original appropriation, Rowan's 1921 list of expenditures and his 1922 departmental estimates provide some insight into his problems. The department's running expenses included such items as "Frogs, etc. for class use" ($640); stains, fixatives, and preservatives ($350); and slides, dishes, and six glass cases for the proposed invertebrate and vertebrate collections ($720). There was a need for light fixtures and an incubator, which should have been built into the laboratories. Rowan did not even have a worktable and lamps for his own office.[45]

It is possible that Rowan just accepted that fact that he would have to order everything. Although he did not complain to the university authorities, he certainly complained to his friends. Rowan badly needed their sympathy. His original enthusiasm waned, and he temporarily lost sight of the challenge, the career possibilities inherent in the task of building a new department. He toyed with the idea of finding other employment. This was the beginning of a long series of periodic, mostly halfhearted attempts to find such work that lasted until his retirement from the University of Alberta thirty-five years later.

7

The Widening Sphere

RETURNING, in 1921, from a summer of work in England, Rowan plunged into supervising the zoology department's move to new quarters, equipping the laboratory, and teaching even more students. Within a few months, his usually abundant energy deserted him, and he found the cold, grey days too short for all he had to do.[1] He became depressed. His mood improved after the family moved to the Bonnie Doon district. In the relatively spacious cottage at 9121 84th Avenue Rowan had a study. There was room for Bertha, a German immigrant girl hired to help Reta, plenty of space for Gerdine, now a toddler, and for William Oliver (named after F.W. Oliver), born on 17 December 1921. Living in Bonnie Doon had its drawbacks. It was a long streetcar ride away from downtown and the university; this trip was time-consuming and costly, and so Reta became even more isolated.

While his home situation had improved, Rowan was still not satisfied with his progress at the University of Alberta. Although he was promoted to associate professor, Rowan remained impatient, his quick mind frustrated by the cumbersome ways of the university administration. With a certain naïvety, he hoped that, having conformed to some of Tory's wishes, he would immediately advance to the rank of full professor. Rowan was ambitious, and it is not surprising that he gave no serious consideration to the offer to return as zoology assistant to University College, London. He always preferred running things to being an assistant, and despite overwork, a lack of funds, and Tory's peculiar ideas concerning research, Rowan fully expected to have a good career at the

University of Alberta. Though he had to concentrate on teaching rather than on research, Rowan remained confident that sooner or later he would make his mark on science.

During these difficult times, the Alberta countryside became a source of artistic inspiration for him. While Rowan often stated that he found drawing a chore, he spent many relaxing hours depicting both scenery and animals.[2] He derived so much satisfaction from his drawing and painting that he sometimes wondered if he should give up science for art. The science-versus-art dilemma was a Victorian one, and Rowan, despite rebelling in his youth against his strict Victorian upbringing, remained more of a Victorian than he ever realized.[3] Among the intellectual baggage he carried around was the notion that science and art should be separated, and like many of his contemporaries he continued to regard these two areas as incompatible, and pictured his own scientific and artistic inclinations to be at odds with each other. In 1910–1911, his scientific inclination won over his artistic one. For the following decade, he relegated art, to a place of secondary importance. In 1921, when he saw that his scientific career was slow to unfold, despite its promise, art reemerged as a creative activity, a path to a new career.

At a time when teaching was onerous and scientific research a thing of the future, Rowan found the process of artistic creation both soothing and exciting. The product was visible and brought him instant acclaim. As he improved his skill with pencil, pen, and brush, he began to feel immense gratification. Mammal heads, provided by his taxidermist friends seemed to come alive in Rowan's drawings. Bird feathers, so often drab and lifeless on stuffed specimens, regained their softness; the intricacies of their barbs and vanes conveyed a lifelike quality that was to become a Rowan hallmark.

His new friends were enthusiastic about his sketches. Allan Brooks even offered Rowan work as an illustrator.[4] The encouragement of such a well-respected artist spurred Rowan to improve his technique, but he also sought criticism, and Lawrence, in his inimitable style, affectionately teased him: "I cannot imagine how any chap can think that your drawings are of any use whatever — sheer waste of paper . . . . Will this please you?"[5] In a more serious vein Lawrence wrote, "I bet that after a real art training, with lots of backwoods nature study, you would turn into a nature artist of the first water — you excel in detail work which is so necessary for feathers."[6]

During 1921–1922, Rowan explored three different avenues for his future. He considered obtaining his doctorate in zoology; becoming an artist; and somehow combining his scientific and artistic talents. Rowan asked two of his British mentors, curator G.E. Bullen and professor F.W. Oliver, for their opinions on his making art his profession. They both discouraged him.[7] Oliver even suggested to Rowan that before taking up drawing he "should read the life of Audubon . . . . Financially he had a rotten time."[8] But Rowan had no wish to listen to his friends' warnings and have confirmed what he had already feared — that art does not pay. He wanted advice about making a living and asked Taverner if there was "any chance in the near future of getting a post in Ottawa on the Museum Staff."[9] Taverner acquainted Rowan with the realities of life and work in a Canadian government institution: few assistants, fieldwork once a year, a "staff of taxidermists but no work for them for there are no cases to put their work in when completed."[10]

Rowan's concern about his future intensified in early 1922. Spending several summers in England working towards his doctorate would be impractical and very expensive. When Rowan heard of the Ph.D. program at Johns Hopkins University from a visiting scientist, he contacted H.S. Jennings, head of the zoology department at Johns Hopkins, and told him the situation at the University of Alberta was likely to hinder his career. Rowan hoped to utilize his field experience towards a doctorate at Johns Hopkins, "to put in a certain period of residence and to be allowed to escape a certain amount on the grounds of doing field work."[11] Jennings regretfully replied, however, that "no practicable arrangements" could be made for the doctorate, as the university required at least one full year of residency.[12] Things seemed to conspire against Rowan. He could find neither the time nor the money he needed to spend his summers away from Edmonton. Broke and temporarily discouraged, he abandoned the idea of doing graduate work, while hanging on to his dream of studying art.

Rowan may have known that nature artists such as Seton and Brooks had derived most of their commissions from the United

States, but he knew little else about the arts in Canada. He was quite unaware of the new trend, a novel way of looking at nature, developed by Tom Thompson, A.Y. Jackson, and other relatively unknown Canadian artists. Their vividly coloured paintings would, within a few years, create a great furor at home and attract considerable interest at the Wembley Exposition in England. Canadian art, like that other major aspect of our culture, science, was more appreciated abroad than at home. In fact, much of Canadian art, and an increasing amount of Canadian scientific research, were financed by English and American individuals and agencies.

The prevailing Canadian attitude towards the land and its natural resources, and towards life in general, was utilitarian. This attitude had survived, virtually unchanged, from the time of the early Scottish settlers. Henry Marshall Tory embodied this utilitarianism, which provided no scope for artists or scientists who wanted to study but not to master, to enjoy but not to despoil nature. As funds remained scarce, Rowan, like many other Canadians with an artistic bent, eventually turned to the United States for support.

His American mentors, Francis Harper and Owen Bryant (a naturalist with both Canadian and American connections), were practical as well as enthusiastic. They wrote to Rowan about the possibility of finding employment as a naturalist-illustrator in the Boston area. The letters Rowan wrote to family and friends during the winter of 1921–1922, contain numerous cryptic references to a new post in the United States. Whether or not Rowan, with his quick logical mind and ever-broadening set of scientific interests would have been satisfied with the position of naturalist-illustrator cannot be known. He could impose rigid discipline upon himself — to do what *he* wanted to do. But to take orders? For that, the pay would have to have been far more than Rowan could possibly command at the time.

While waiting for an opportunity to materialize in the United States, Rowan sold some illustrations of Alberta game heads to *Country Life*.[13] And although he pretended to be bored with repetitious pencil drawings, he was delighted with his success. The money was useful, and engaging in the process of artistic creation provided a pleasant contrast to administering his department.

Rowan was pleased to hear that Harper had met with Ernest Thompson Seton, and that Seton was "visibly impressed" by

Rowan's sketch of a buffalo. Seton encouraged Rowan in the pursuit of this new profession by believing (as Bullen and Oliver clearly did not) that there was a future in animal illustration. Harper, in his turn, dangled the enticement of a rent-free home on a new bird reservation, near Boston, in front of Rowan.[14]

Rowan, by no means convinced he had a future as an artist in the United States, still wanted to go to Europe, and wrote to both Oliver and the commissioner-general for Canada in France about studying in Paris. Oliver warned Rowan that his success as an artist would depend on "a lot of luck, fashion, and the propaganda methods of the people who 'discover' your talent."[15] The commissioner-general politely informed Rowan that life was expensive in France. Rowan then contacted W.C. James, an old friend and financial adviser to the Rowan family. While Rowan's letter of 15 March 1922 did not survive, from James's reply it is clear that Rowan had asked for an advance of two hundred pounds sterling (or about one thousand dollars) against his future inheritance to study art. The disapproving James turned down his request, and felt obliged to point out that "a man who makes science his 'gagne-pain' lives a more or less unstable existence as far as finances are concerned."[16]

Rowan had no intention of giving up the attractive notion of going to live in Paris quite as easily as James had hoped. His next letter must have been full of practical inquiries, because James first informed Rowan that Paris was the most expensive city to live in, and then asked, "do I understand that your wife would live away from you and that you wish to risk living in such a City as Paris *alone* with all its temptations?" To soften the blow, James encouraged Rowan to make art a "side-show" rather than a career: "work the Exhibition business etc. at Boston for all it is worth and try to unite it with your present professorship."[17] Eventually, Rowan came to accept that studying art in Europe was not feasible. By early 1923, Reta was again pregnant, and with their third child on the way, giving up a steady income was obviously out of the question. Rowan continued to do wildlife drawings, and as his reputation spread, more commissions came his way. This lucrative sideline was to continue for most of his life.

Alberta's abundant wildlife provided Rowan with a never-ending source of artistic inspiration. Amphibians, reptiles, birds, and mammals were the subjects of the Rowan family Christmas cards and of the numerous sketches which he sold or gave to friends. He later exhibited many of his works, which brought him praise and led to further sales. He also began to sculpt. One of his first efforts was a bird bath; the figure that adorned it was modelled on Gerdine, five or six years old at the time. Later he was to sculpt birds and mammals, especially bears.

Throughout the 1920s and 1930s Rowan illustrated numerous popular articles in *Country Life* and other magazines, and continued to send samples of his work to his American friends. Harper remained hopeful that Rowan would move to Boston and, in the mid-1920s, even tried to interest a couple of millionaires in the project. He arranged to have Rowan's drawings exhibited at a meeting of the Nuttall Ornithological Club, and while the drawings were widely admired, the millionaires were loath to part with their money to fund Rowan. "If the fairy godmother fails to materialize," asked Harper, "what else can we do in the meantime?"[18]

There was no definite answer to this question. Art remained one of Rowan's favourite pastimes, but it never became his central occupation. It was one of the best ways of making extra money. There were others: the sale of specimens and writing popular articles helped him to provide for his family and finance his scientific interests. Though fairy godmothers were in short supply, and none appeared to fund a lifetime of artistic activity, Rowan eventually did acquire financial support for his scientific work. So, despite periodic attempts to break away from science, it was ultimately science that provided the focus for his imagination and creative energies.

Like other Canadian naturalists, Rowan needed a provincial collecting permit to shoot birds and mammals. He also required a Canadian banding permit, although he had probably banded young birds in England without a licence. Alberta permits were granted by the provincial game guardian, Benjamin Lawton, federal banding permits by the dominion ornithologist, Hoyes Lloyd. With the necessary permits Rowan could not only collect scientific specimens, but also hunt for pleasure. Rowan was a keen hunter as well as a scientist, an all-round naturalist, and a conservationist. It was not considered hypocritical in his time to be a hunter while active in the latter three roles. Lawton, for instance, was a game guardian and, like most other members of the Northern Alberta Fish and Game Protective League (established in March 1920 and later renamed the Alberta Fish and Game Association), a hunter and naturalist.[19]

Rowan joined the league in 1921, and was soon elected chairman of the Song Bird Committee.[20] From the very beginning, his relationship with Lawton and other members of the league was uneven. He needed the game guardian's help in securing permits and was, in fact, fond of both Mr. and Mrs. Lawton. Rowan was very critical, and with good reason, of those league members who could not even identify the most common species of ducks. Rowan's establishment of the scientific section of the league, in early 1925, "for the purpose of investigating game conditions of the province," was among the measures he undertook to remedy this situation.[21]

Rowan, as always, was full of ideas for scientific investigations. Wherever he looked, he could see exciting scientific problems needing clarification. In early 1922, although he was then actually considering giving up science for art, he embarked on a new study: the examination of the stomach contents of birds. In the United States, economic entomologists and ornithologists had long analyzed stomach contents to ascertain whether or not certain birds were detrimental to agriculture. As Rowan was to find out, there had been practically no such work done in Canada. Taverner sent all stomach material to the Bureau of Biological Survey in Washington, and there was no substantial stomach-contents analysis done at Canadian universities.[22]

Rowan was fired up and willing to collaborate with the Alberta Department of Agriculture on studying species of particular interest to that department. Professor E.H. Strickland, the University of Alberta's new entomologist, greeted the idea with enthusiasm, and offered to help Rowan with the identification of "entomological relics."[23] Lack of time eventually forced Rowan to give up this line of inquiry.

Concurrently, Rowan began to investigate the status of birds introduced into North America. He first became intrigued by the dispersal of the Hungarian partridge, and with typical overstatement informed the chief of the Bureau of Biological Survey, "I am at the moment engaged in studying the spread of birds liberated in 1908 and 1909 at Calgary."[24] He asked Taverner for information about the status of introduced birds, such as the ring-necked pheasant and partridge, in Canada. Rowan devised a questionnaire, to be circulated among two hundred people in Alberta, to establish the exact limits of the territory occupied by the partridge. He planned to keep a systematic check on the bird's "further movements and to map the rate of progress during the next few years." Rowan was convinced that he would gain valuable information from this study that would have more than a "provincial interest."[25]

Supplied with the appropriate permits, Rowan increased the frequency of the trips he took to areas outside Edmonton. He collected at Camrose with naturalist Frank Farley. He frequented Beaverhills Lake with various colleagues, and with visiting scientists such as H.B. Conover of the Chicago Field Museum. During an eleven-day period in Conover's company, for instance, Rowan collected ducks of more than a dozen species, and obtained more than eighty skins of shorebirds such as avocets, marbled and Hudsonian godwits, greater and lesser yellowlegs, and several species of sandpipers and plovers.[26] The excess stock of specimens he acquired on these forays was later used as currency, either in straight sales or in exchange for other specimens.

Rowan was to study shorebirds over a period of years. As comparative material at the University of Alberta was practically nonexistent, he had to acquire (or borrow) skins of dowitchers and other shorebirds. Taverner warned Rowan that the "Dowitcher is a difficult problem,"[27] but Rowan was challenged by "difficult problems." Shorebirds were to form the topic of many of his scientific papers, and provide him with the data that led to his later experimental work.

The new academic year, 1922–1923, brought Rowan some relief from his previous chores. For the first time, he had a full-time demonstrator, John Knox Harkness (B.A.), who had arrived in Edmonton from Toronto in early September. Rowan taught three courses at the time: general elementary zoology for arts students, and general elementary zoology and elementary embryology, for first and second year medical students, respectively. He earned three thousand dollars per year as associate professor, while Harkness received one thousand dollars. As the departmental budget included another $960 for a laboratory assistant, Rowan looked for other help. Early in 1923, Robert Lister joined the department as "lab. boy" and collector. [28] An intelligent, cheerful young man from Norfolk, he became Rowan's sidekick for more than thirty years. Lister worked hard in the lab and the field, and apparently did everything but complain and cook. He was indeed the ideal factotum for someone with Rowan's manifold activities.

The presence of Harkness and Lister freed Rowan from routine chores in the laboratory. He used the time saved to engage in more scientific investigations. Now, he could work on the numerous eared-grebe embryos he had accumulated while planning his doctoral thesis. He could contemplate writing a series of papers on the shorebirds of Alberta for *British Birds*, and dream about an excursion to the North with Bill MacDonald. In 1921, MacDonald spent the summer in the Great Slave Lake region. On his return, he regaled Rowan with tales of gulls, terns and shorebirds in every tree. Rowan had always wanted to go north and, in 1920, in Winnipeg, had been most upset that he could not raise funds for such a venture. The spectre of Arctic terns and yellowlegs was still irresistible in 1922, and the idea of collecting eggs and specimens fuelled his longing to take the trip. But departmental appropriations did not include funds for northern expeditions, and it was unlikely that Tory would support one.

Rowan wrote freely and in great detail to his correspondents about the great collecting possibilities in the North. He also intimated that the administration would frown upon funding any attempt on his part to explore those possibilities. By the end of 1922, Rowan informed Taverner that a trip north with MacDonald "depends chiefly on my ability to wangle cash out of other people, a rotten job."[29] He was so confident of his success, however, that he turned down Taverner's attractive offer of a summer job in Banff.[30]

Rowan had good reason to be hopeful about obtaining money. American collector A.C. Bent, editor of the Life Histories of North American Birds series, encouraged him and volunteered to buy any shorebird eggs Rowan found in the North.[31] Thomas Barbour of the Museum of Comparative Zoology at Harvard University offered direct financial assistance, because of the "great promise of biological results, of interest not only to scientists in the United States but Canada also."[32] Rowan knew that the University of Alberta administration would not take a favourable view of his disappearing into the field for a whole summer. He wrote about his misgivings, but his American contacts could not even imagine the obstacles Rowan encountered at his University. A somewhat non-plussed Barbour asked:

> Can you not see how much it is to the interest of your University as well as to your own interests that [you take] this chance to do a valuable piece of field exploration and research [? It] may bring to both you and the Institution for which you are working a very sure and credible renown.[33]

With Barbour's support, Rowan was determined to mount the expedition, to be undertaken in any case during his summer holiday. He approached the Dominion Cartridge Company and obtained a promise of free ammunition for Bill MacDonald and himself. He then contacted the Alberta and Arctic Transportation Company to ask about fees and schedules for travel from Edmonton to Aklavik, a six-thousand kilometre round trip, of which one thousand kilometres was by rail, and the rest by boat. The cost (accommodation and meals included) was about four hundred dollars. Rowan could not even contemplate finding this amount in Edmonton, but with Barbour's offer of two hundred dollars towards expenses and an extensive and varied list of specimens that he could sell to his American contacts (bats to G.M. Allen, mammals and batrachians to Barbour, shorebird eggs to Bent), Rowan could look forward to a successful summer in Canada's North.[34] But for reasons that are still unclear, his plans fell through.

Rowan's correspondence with family and friends seems to indicate that his decision to stay in town was prompted by a variety of reasons. Reta's unplanned pregnancy was a major factor. She was already run-down and painfully thin, and needed help to look after Gerdine and Oliver. Members of the Rowan family reacted to the news of a third pregnancy in four years in characteristically different ways. Rowan's mother offered to send Bill's unmarried sister Agnes, a trained nurse, to Edmonton so she could help with the children, and Agnes was delighted at the idea of going to Canada

9. C.G. Harold at Beaverhills Lake, Alberta, 1923.
Photograph by William Rowan. Courtesy of Herb Copeland.

and of making herself useful.[35] Arthur, Bill's eldest brother, wrote facetiously that he felt duty bound to draw Bill's attention to the German contraceptive called "Spermaton . . . A Pill," actually a spermicide preparation. As a joke, he even offered to send a year's supply.[37] But contraception was no joking matter in Canada. As of 1892, birth control was legally prohibited.[37]

It is certain that Rowan's situation at the University of Alberta could not alone account for the cancellation of his northern trip. As there were no summer courses, Rowan was not actually obliged to stay in Edmonton between early May and late September. There was much to be done in the laboratory, however, such as preparing specimens and wall charts, and working on the invertebrate and vertebrate collections. In fact, as soon as the snow was gone, Rowan, with the help of Harkness and Lister, trapped mammals at Whitemud Ravine and elsewhere, and visited Beaverhills Lake searching for frog eggs.[38] While teaching was over by early April, correcting exams and collecting specimens took up so much time that Rowan also worked on Sundays, "the blessed day of rest, in which I got all my work for the week done."[39]

It was during this busy period that C.G. Harrold, with whom Rowan had corresponded since the fall of 1920, decided to spend several weeks at Francis Point. The prospect of being with Harrold during the spring bird migration in such a promising area, and at the same time possibly appeasing Tory, may have contributed to Rowan's decision to forego the northern trip. He would derive vicarious pleasure from MacDonald's accounts of birds and mammals. He would hear all about the Eastern Arctic from J. Dewey Soper, one of his zoology students, who was heading north as naturalist on the ship *Arctic* under the command of Captain J.E. Bernier. Soper was to become one of Canada's best-known modern-day explorers.[40]

Whatever prompted Rowan's decision to cancel his trip, he certainly was unhappy about it. With his usual exaggeration, he informed Taverner that he was "fed up to the teeth, and completely sick of life, for the trip north has been scratched. The lateness of coming to final arrangements is to blame for the collapse in the main though there were other factors that proved obstacles."[41] Two days after recording this outburst he went to stay with Harrold on Francis Point, and there speedily recovered.[42] Lister soon joined them, and during the following two weeks Rowan, Harrold, and Lister collected thirty-one species of shorebirds. This was bliss indeed, and the whole experience reminded Rowan of his often-recurring childhood dream of finding himself on a large estate, with a nest in every bush, except this time "it was waders, however, instead of eggs."[43]

The excellent opportunities for biological work found at Beaverhills Lake, and his fond memories of the Blakeney Point and Indian Bay stations, prompted Rowan to think of establishing a university biological station at Francis Point. The advantages of spending extended periods of time at such institutions were well known in the scientific community, and Rowan was convinced that the proximity of such a research station to the university would make the whole idea of fieldwork more acceptable to Tory.

So, sometime in May 1923, Rowan discussed his idea with Tory. Throughout the summer he worked out various plans, submitting a detailed proposal with a list of equipment, projected costs, and even a useful bibliography "of the essential literature that would be needed for the foundation of a library in conjunction with a possible biological station."[44] Rowan sent a copy to Professor Oliver, who considered the "general idea of Francis Point . . . splendid," and suggested only one improvement: the construction of a permanent building, instead of the temporary canvas-and-wood structures, like those used at Blakeney Point.[45]

Tory was less enthusiastic, and it is hard to know if he seriously considered Rowan's proposal. When Rowan declared he wanted to discuss the scheme at the November 1923 meeting of the University of Alberta Scientific Association, Tory wrote him an angry letter: "you have no authority . . . to make public any plan for a biological station nor shall I consider myself in any way committed to any public utterance you may make."[46] Rowan's proposal was subsequently shelved, and like many other good ideas that would have improved research conditions at the University of Alberta, the biological station at Francis Point never materialized.

By the time Reta gave birth to Sylvia (later known also as "Rabbit" or "Pudding") on 28 July 1923, the family had already moved from the house at Bonnie Doon to a three-storey frame house at 11142 86th Avenue. The house had numerous advantages. It was near to

10. Agnes, Reta and William Rowan with Oliver, Gerdine and Sylvia, Edmonton, Alberta, 1923. *Courtesy of the Rowan family.*

the university and downtown, it had central (coal) heating and a very long, fenced-in garden. There was room in the garden for flowers and vegetables, which Reta cultivated with great success. Beginning in the fall of 1924, the garden would also serve as Rowan's outdoor laboratory.

It was a comfortable home, with separate rooms for all members of the family and the live-in maid, and a guest room. Agnes Rowan came to help Reta in 1923, and stayed for a whole year. Later, Reta's sister, Deeda, was to spend time with the family as well. Agnes and Deeda not only helped with the "Rowanberries" (as Taverner referred to the Rowan children), but provided Reta with much-needed companionship. Rowan, absorbed by his ever-widening sphere of activities, was happy with his comfortable, but soon-cluttered study on the second floor, and spent most of his time there. The family hardly saw him. He was always busy, always in a hurry, and was regularly late for meals. After dinner, he played solitaire while reclining on the living-room sofa; then he disappeared into his study. He often typed well into the small hours of the morning, in an attempt to keep up with his correspondence. He was to write his most famous scientific articles in that den, where the aroma of strong coffee mingled with blue smoke from his hand-rolled cigarettes.[47]

Teaching, fieldwork, and writing scientific and popular articles kept Rowan busy throughout the early 1920s. During this period he formed lasting friendships with biochemist J.B. Collip (of insulin fame), and chemistry professor O.J. Walker and his wife Ella May, a talented painter. He also developed an informal network of Alberta naturalists, including Elsie Cassels, Frank Farley, A.D. Henderson, and Tom Randall — all valued correspondents and good field companions. They visited Rowan in Edmonton, and he, in turn, spent time with them: Cassels lived in Red Deer and Sylvan Lake, Farley in Camrose, Henderson in Belvedere, and Randall in Castor.

His fieldwork, easier now because his assistants Harkness and Lister helped with the collecting, sorting, and preserving of biological material, had expanded to include all forms of wildlife. Hydras, frog eggs, birds, and mammals, and everything else available, fell prey to his collecting nets or gun. Rowan conducted fieldwork in all types of habitats: woods and open prairie, coulees and ravines, mountains, lakeshores, sloughs, and marshes. Through this, he developed an awareness of the ecological systems found in different parts of Alberta. He studied game birds, shorebirds, and mammals, investigated water levels, and salinity, and their effects on waterfowl food supply. He was interested in bird migration, and the anatomy, embryology, and taxonomy of birds and mammals. These strands, all intersecting and interweaving in numerous ways, formed the foundation of much of Rowan's future scientific work. Surreptitiously conducted fieldwork provided him with information on shorebirds and biological cycles. It also supplied data for the hypothesis that led to his pioneering experiments.

8

Experiments in Bird Migration: Juncos

ROWAN, interested in bird migration since early childhood, began to collect data on the subject soon after he moved to Edmonton. Taking his cue from Alex Lawrence's remark that "Alberta was very poorly represented" in W.W. Cooke's late-nineteenth-century study on bird migration, Rowan set out to remedy this situation.[1] He began an ambitious project: he would make the University of Alberta a centre of a "migration scheme." He wrote to all reputable Alberta naturalists that "migration records will be kept by competent ornithologists and sent in annually to the University to be filed and collated."[2] Convinced the Prairie provinces constituted "one of the finest fields for this study in the world," Rowan proposed to involve naturalists and university scientists in Saskatchewan and Manitoba.[3]

During the same period Rowan offered to contribute migration records to the United States Bureau of Biological Survey. Canada was already part of this large-scale investigation originally organized by the American Ornithologists' Union and taken over by the Division of Economic Ornithology and Mammalogy of the United States Government in 1886. Naturalists, settlers (including many women), and visitors reported their observations but, because of the settlement patterns of the West, the coverage was uneven. There was more information available on bird migration in Manitoba and the southern part of the Prairie provinces than in central and northern Saskatchewan and Alberta.

As a student in England, Rowan had read about the pioneering studies on bird migration done in the late nineteenth century by

Gätke in Germany, Cordeaux in England, and Hermann in Hungary.[4] As a professional scientist in Canada, he could not keep up with the scientific literature. The University of Alberta lacked a good science library, and Rowan had to buy and borrow books and journals relevant to North American bird migration. This process was slow, and, busy with his other activities, it is unlikely that Rowan managed to read and reflect on the migration literature he accumulated in the early 1920s.

Like many ornithologists of the period, Rowan considered migration to be a part of the life history, the annual breeding cycle, of a bird. In "Observations on the Breeding Habits of the Merlin," published in four installments in *British Birds* in 1921, he discussed the dispersal and breeding locality of this small falcon in West Yorkshire. Rowan pointed out the possibility that one particular district was attracting birds from other areas where the species was disappearing. He added, "To follow up the argument without deducing further evidence would probably be futile, but one cannot help imagining that such a theory would adapt itself to the elucidation of several unsolved problems in connection with migration."[5]

It is evident from his correspondence that during the winter of 1921–1922, Rowan was working on a migration paper. The exact topic is unclear, as the article was never published, but it appears that he planned to obtain more data on the merlin in Canada, by observation and experiment. He told Taverner, however, that "experiments will be rather difficult to control as it means being on the same spot for several years, a thing that is unlikely to happen to me for some time yet."[6] In the end, Rowan never pursued the important questions he raised in the merlin paper, even when conditions improved at the University of Alberta. Instead, at Beaverhills Lake, he began field studies on migrating shorebirds.

In 1922 Rowan wrote to Taverner, "The reason why I am particularly interested in migration here is that the Biological Survey are [sic] very short of Alberta material." He added, "while I have to trace the movements of the birds here it is only a step towards the ascertaining of principles to be derived from facts."[7] To Dr. Joseph Grinnell, a well-known California ornithologist and editor of the *Condor*, Rowan wrote that he was studying the migration of plovers. Grinnell, who would become one of his staunchest supporters, was keen to hear about Rowan's work because "Major Brooks, in whom we here recognize a foremost authority on Canadian birds," had already told him about Rowan's activities.[8]

Rowan's encounters with migrating shorebirds at Beaverhills Lake convinced him that juvenile lesser golden plovers go south in the fall by a different route from the adults. Although this was at variance with all other migration theories, Rowan told Grinnell that the accepted theories were "probably incorrect in their entirety." To test this hypothesis, Rowan had to obtain further data (dates and locality, sex and age, and conditions of plumage) on adult lesser golden plovers collected both near the Atlantic coast and in the interior of the continent. He requested the loan of specimens from all major North American natural-history museums and from several private collections. The well-labelled specimens provided information on the actual date a bird was collected in a certain locality and also documented the proportion of adult to juvenile birds.[9]

"Migrations of the Golden and Black-Bellied Plovers in Alberta" appeared in the January 1923 issue of the *Condor*. It was well received by ornithologists and generated a lively correspondence. Among those who were intrigued by Rowan's theory was A.C. Bent, who "always held the same view that others have published regarding the migration of this species," that golden plovers would go north through the interior of North America and "that all of the birds migrated in the fall along the Atlantic coast."[10] Rowan wrote to Taverner about the "controversy," and Taverner teased him in his usual fashion:

> You have bumped up against the memory of W.W. Cooke, peace to his soul, but he was not quite as big a man as the public thought. He was accepted as gospel and here you come and show him up . . . . If the Golden Plover don't fly as they ought to I think it is bad taste to notice it.[11]

By the winter of 1923–1924, Rowan was convinced he could prove that young golden plovers have an entirely different migration route from the adult birds. His firsthand experience, together with data culled from major ornithological collections, supported

Rowan's original argument that "old birds go south by some route on which they escape general observation." He felt that such a theory may be "revolutionary, and if it turns out to be more fact than fiction, it will be of more theoretical value to the topic of migration than any other observation made up to the present time."[12] Rowan's revolutionary work was indeed in the making, but it was not on the plover.

As an offshoot of his extensive collecting, Rowan correlated migration data with information obtained from specimens at Beaverhills Lake. No part of the birds was wasted: the skins were prepared for the study collection, the innards were preserved for laboratory use, and much of the meat found its way into the stewing pot. Observing over several seasons, Rowan had the opportunity to see the differences in age, plumage, and sex of spring and fall migrants. He noted the gonad size differences between birds migrating north, and others, of the same species, migrating south. He began to think about the factors that could influence migration, but serious work on this topic was, like that on the embryology of the grebes, to be dealt with in the future. Then, during the summer of 1924, several things arose that precipitated his pioneering migration experiments.

For the first time since his arrival in Alberta, Rowan had time to think and talk about scientific problems. His assistant, John Harkness, left and Winnifred Hughes (B.A., M.A.), a recent graduate of the University of Saskatchewan, was hired as an instructor in zoology at fifteen hundred dollars per year, to do mainly "elementary work."[13] Hughes was born in Wales (around 1900) and came to Canada sometime during the war. In 1918 she obtained an entrance scholarship to the University of Saskatchewan, and became one of Professor A.E. Cameron's best zoology students. Hughes was a good scientist and a competent artist. She helped Rowan with the preparation of teaching wall charts, took over some of the laboratory chores, and thereby freed him to think creatively about migration experiments.

The story of how Rowan came to formulate his original hypothesis can be pieced together from his correspondence, publications, notebooks, and the recollections of other scientists. Apparently Rowan sought an external stimulus, an "environmental timing mechanism" of periodic nature, and in a series of logical steps eliminated temperature and barometric pressure, previously thought to be the most likely stimuli. Instead, Rowan decided that day length, which changes at the same rate every year, was the only unvarying environmental factor.[14] Daylight, as such, had already been considered by others as important in plant growth and bird migration. But Rowan had no access to, or time to read, the work of others, and came to the same conclusion independently.

In a 1946 address to the Royal Society of Canada, Rowan recalled:

> In view of theories then current with reference to interstitial cells, sex hormones, and sex behaviour, one only had to suppose that the migratory journey was itself a particular phase of sexual behaviour, as much dependent on the development of the gonads as the characteristic spring antics in which most birds indulge, to establish a practical working hypothesis for an experimental start. If one could artificially stimulate the gonads to spring activity in the fall, one might thereby induce the owners, when released to go north, instead of south in the autumn.[15]

It seems that during the summer of 1924, Rowan's fine logical mind began to sort the information received during the previous four or five years in the field. He later wrote to J.P. Hill that at the time he had done nothing "but analyze data collected over a period of years."[16] Rowan may have remained content to keep collecting evidence and thinking about the various factors involved in migration, but a publication by Gustave Eifrig in the July 1924 issue of the *Auk* galvanized him into action. A letter that Rowan wrote to Grinnell describes what happened:

> I was interested and also disappointed to see the note in the "Auk" by G. Eifrig on "Photoperiodism in migration." I have been collecting data in reference to this topic for 5 years, and thought I had struck something original. The conditions up here however, have prevented me either from carrying out experiments that I have in mind or from sitting down to the job long enough to get it into shape for publication. I am quite convinced however that therein lies the explanation for the

> whole phenomenon of the annual migration of birds. I do not mean of course that it explains why they migrate, but I mean that it is the physiological stimulus that sets the impulse into motion every year. Eifrig talks as though it were a very simple matter. I wish it were. I should have published long ago.[17]

Determined to refute Eifrig's doubts that spring migrant birds were influenced by physiological stimuli such as the enlargement of the gonads, Rowan began writing an answer. He wanted to disprove Eifrig, and at the same time test his own hypothesis that migratory readiness can be experimentally induced by artificially lengthened daylight in autumn. He told Grinnell that "given the time and cash and library facilities for serious research, the migration of birds need not remain forever 'the greatest puzzle in the field of Zoology' as Newton and Owen described it." Rowan believed that "Eifrig has made a very good shot in the dark as a result of reading Garner and Allard's work, but except for his belief that photoperiodism probably is a factor in bird migration . . . he is wrong in every other contention."[18]

Rowan often wrote about his isolation from contemporary scientific research at the University of Alberta. He would also, typically, exaggerate the problem. While much of his intellectual exchange was by correspondence, Rowan could talk about his ideas with J.B. Collip in person. The head of the Department of Biochemistry at the University of Alberta was now a friend as well as a colleague, and Collip's knowledge of sex hormones, and discussions with him concerning the effect of such hormones on breeding biology, influenced Rowan's thinking. During the summer of 1924, he could also clarify his ideas concerning gonadal activity with Winnifred Hughes, whose main interest was embryology, and even discuss his plans with eminent scientists from England.

Rowan declared that 23 August 1924 was "The best day in our Edmonton history." Delegates to the British Association for the Advancement of Science meeting in Vancouver, including D.M.S. Watson and D'Arcy Thompson, visited the University of Alberta. Though time was short, Rowan managed to discuss with Watson his proposed migration experiments.[19] Watson strongly supported Rowan's plans, and Rowan now shelved his paper, begun in haste, on the importance of photoperiodism in migration. Hesitant to publish only on theory, he informed Grinnell that he would test his theories with "a couple of very simple preliminary experiments . . . . If they work, I have a long list of further experiments to try out."[20]

Rowan began his historic experiments in September 1924. Preparatory work was done before the beginning of the academic year, while the actual experimental work was conducted in his "spare time, in evenings and on weekends."[21] In order to obtain live birds, Rowan hired a workman to construct a sparrow trap of the type used by the United States government.[22] This was to be placed near his house, and was intended to catch a large number of migrating juncos. The slate-coloured (now called dark-eyed) junco, was a good choice. A widespread North American member of the sparrow family, the junco winters in the southern United States. It is a hardy little bird, and one of the first spring migrants to reach Canada.

Rowan built two large aviaries to house his captive birds. Because of the perpetual shortage of funds, he had to rely on used materials, such as mosquito netting and packing cases, to construct them. Rowan placed the aviaries in the north end of his own garden: A on the east, to house the experimental birds and B on the west, to contain all control birds. By placing the cages at the far end of his garden, Rowan ensured that they would be away from all artificial sources of heat, and also hidden from the eyes of the university president, who continued to disapprove of Rowan's ornithological work. Both aviaries contained food and water; and the experimental aviary was also fitted with a light fixture, while the control aviary was lit only by natural light.

Rowan's diaries, which provide a considerable amount of detail concerning his fieldwork, only sporadically refer to his groundbreaking experiments. The logs that contain the details of his pioneering research (not found in his published papers) are small, ten-cent exercise books with soft black covers: the junco notebooks. From these we know that Rowan began trapping birds on 20 September, a Saturday. He soon found he was too late to obtain a sufficient number of birds of either sex. In fact, as female juncos migrate south ahead of the males, Rowan managed to trap only one female to about two dozen (adult and juvenile) male juncos in 1924. But he obtained Lincoln's, fox, and white-throated sparrows.

In the junco notebooks there is information about the amounts and types of food given to the birds and, here and there, details of the birds' behaviour. There were also daily weather reports (cut from the *Edmonton Journal* and pasted into the notebooks), which provided the times of sunrise and sunset, and the daily high and low temperatures. Rowan also recorded the exact time the artificial light was turned on and off in the experimental aviary. The actual photoperiodism experiments on one dozen juncos and three white-throated sparrows began on 1 October 1924. Light in aviary A was provided by one seventy-five-watt blue bulb. It was turned on at 6:05 p.m. (or six minutes before actual sunset), and turned off at 7:15 p.m., giving the birds sixty-four minutes of extra light. In the control aviary (B), nine juncos, four white-throated sparrows, and one fox sparrow were allowed to roost in natural light.

The experimental birds continued to receive artificial daylight after sunset, which was augmented by daily increments of five extra minutes. By the middle of October they were exposed to 172 minutes of additional illumination. On 4 October, Rowan noted that "birds [were] going to roost soon after dark in spite of the light." He suspected that the seventy-five-watt blue bulb was insufficient, and first replaced it with a single sixty-watt white bulb and later with two fifty-watt frosted white ones. The latter were to provide illumination throughout the 1924 experiments.

Rowan was acutely interested in observing the reaction of the experimental birds. He remarked that the "Juncos in the experimental cage have now become reconciled to the light and keep wide awake till it goes out. They seem to find their perches without trouble, but there is a moon at present."[23] He also noted their reaction to food. Both controls and experimentals were fed the same mixture of hemp, millet, rape, and canary seed.[24] Later he added buckwheat to their diet. The birds were "not eating the hemp much. Lively most of the evening but going to roost before lights out."[25] A few weeks later he changed the timing of the "main meal from morning to evening in the hopes of keeping them awake and scratching."[26]

The fact that Rowan could conduct experiments in a place accessible with relative ease — his own garden — did not mean that problems and frustrations wouldn't arise. Experiment means controlled manipulation, but Rowan could only work in the evenings, mornings, and on weekends. He could regulate the food and light supply, but had no control over weather conditions, mischievous children, and cat-loving neighbours. He blamed one such neighbour for opening his control aviary during the night or early hours of 6 October. As all the birds escaped, he had to start trapping again.[27] On 18 October, four-year-old Gerdine, nicknamed "Jiggy," opened the same cage and all the control juncos got away again. While Rowan soon replaced his first loss with new juncos, he now had to accept that by mid-October practically all migrating juncos were gone.[28] He still had some of his control sparrows, however, and later transferred a few juncos and sparrows from cage A to cage B.[29] Finally, on 22 November, Rowan banded all experimental and control birds.

Rowan killed his first experimental bird, a juvenile male junco (labelled X), on 15 October. It "was in good shape except for an injury above the bill, considerably swollen." Later he was to find similar injuries on other birds, and concluded that they were caused by the sharp wire edges of the sparrow trap.[30] For comparison's sake, he also killed and preserved a wild junco (labelled C), another juvenile male collected in the neighbourhood. Two weeks later (on 29 October) Rowan took his second set of samples consisting of one adult (X-2) and one juvenile male junco (X-3). He noted they were both "extremely fat and in good shape. Testes minute." He fixed the testes for histological study.[31] After this, he took further samples at two-week intervals.

On 13 November he killed one sparrow (X-4) and one junco (X-5), and noted that although the sparrow had larger testes than previously examined ones, there was no noticeable difference in junco's testes.[23] On 26 November he killed experimental X-6 and found that its "testes [were] smaller than any yet I think!"[33] On 11 December he noted, "killed last white-throat today. X7. Testes apparently larger than any yet. Junco, adult, X8 killed. Testes larger than any yet, both sides about equally developed. Both birds were in good shape, but not very fat."[34] In spite of their lack of body fat, the birds, though often miserable looking, withstood rain, blowing snow, and extremely cold temperatures. One even had ice on his wings.[35] One day Rowan took pity on them. It was so bitterly cold in the house that he "did not hang around long in pyjamas to watch." He took the birds inside for the night and returned them to the cages in the morning. Once indoors, the birds soon began to sing, the adult male "warbling very softly and sweetly this afternoon for a long time while I was quietly drawing."[36] By 22 December both males were singing, before dawn and again in the evening.

Because of the Christmas holiday, Rowan had to wait until 27 December to kill his last experimental birds. These were X-9, the juvenile male; X-10, the only female; and X-11, an adult male. Pleased with the results, he noted:

> My juncos [were] killed today. The [female] has a well developed ovary (fixed Bouin). The juv. male had large testes, about the size of early spring. The ad. male had much smaller ones, but better apparently than the minimum. They were all in excellent shape, and in spite of frozen feet during the arctic spell have no signs of frost bite or missing toes. They have scarcely any vestige of fat on them.[37]

The following day the temperature was "40 below Fahrenheit." Rowan took in his control birds and found them in fine shape. On 5 January 1925 he picked one at random and killed it. "Examination proved the testes to be about equally developed — the right possibly the larger — and both minute."[38]

After he had lost control juncos from cage B, Rowan had to obtain comparative material elsewhere. He asked Grinnell to have someone in California secure the testes and ovaries of wintering juncos and sparrows at two-week intervals during November, December, and January. "My most urgent need is gonads collected about a month after the chosen species has arrived and settled down as a winter resident." These gonads were to be used as rough controls, in Rowan's attempt to justify "drawing conclusions of sorts with reference to the photoperiodism question."[39] The obliging Grinnell sent to Rowan six west-coast (sierra) junco and two golden-crowned sparrow gonads. This enabled Rowan to maintain the view that "if the waxing and waning of the days are instrumental in keeping the migratory movements in time, they must operate through the gonads. My first object was therefore to demonstrate that these organs are affected by light."[40]

And affected by light they were. Rowan's investigations proved that juncos and sparrows receiving daily increments of artificial daylight in autumn experienced a decrease in gonad size for the first few weeks. After the middle of November the birds' gonads began to grow, and continued to do so until the end of December, when they were found to be larger than the gonads of the first spring migrants to reach Edmonton. It is hardly surprising that Rowan wrote to Taverner in a jubilant mood:

> I have succeeded in experimentally inducing Juncos to develop spring fever at Christmas in large aviaries in the garden with temperatures running down to 52 below zero. They were singing all day long and all that sort of thing and on dissection proved to have large spring testicles . . . . I kept [the only female] till the end, when she had well developed ovaries in about the same condition as they have them normally in the spring.[41]

Rowan described the gist of his experiments in "Relation of Light to Bird Migration and Developmental Changes," published in the British journal *Nature* in April 1925.[42] In this short paper Rowan placed emphasis upon his observation that "whatever effect daily increases of illumination may or may not have on migration, they *are* conducive to developmental changes in the sexual organs."[43] The longer paper, which Rowan had started in haste after he had read Eifrig's, was to include the experimental evidence. As he told Taverner:

> I believe that this bit of work of mine is the first attempt in history to prove any of the migration theories experimentally . . . . If I had the cash next fall I believe that I could prove that together with the change in the gonads develops the desire to migrate. I am now doing detailed histological work on my material to try to prove or disprove the existence of a testicular hormone, that might be connected with the migratory impulse.[44]

The 1925 experiments "absolutely corroborated the findings of the previous season."[45] They were different in a few respects from the 1924 experiments, however. Rowan originally intended to liberate experimental juncos, in groups of ten "at regular intervals and to record their behaviour, killing samples for examination of the condition of the gonads at the time of each release."[46] To ensure a good supply of birds, trapping was started earlier than in 1924. This was done by Lister, because Rowan went north to collect wood buffalo, but dozens of juncos died, "apparently as a result of wrong food before I came home."[47] In the end, there were not enough juncos to conduct the planned experiments. By mid-October there were only about fifteen juncos in the experimental cage and half that many in the control aviary.[48]

Because Rowan was in the field until 25 September, and because the academic year with its onerous teaching commitments was beginning, the actual light experiments did not start until mid-October. Artificial illumination was provided by three (instead of the previous two) fifty-watt frosted bulbs.[49]

Details of the 1925 experiments can be found in Rowan's long answer to Eifrig. From this paper, "On Photoperiodism, Reproductive Periodicity, and the Annual Migrations of Birds and Certain Fishes," published in the *Proceedings of the Boston Society of Natural History* in 1926, as well as from the junco notebooks, we know the following: on 22 November, after more than five weeks of daily increments of artificial illumination, the gonads of experimental birds were still at their winter minimum size.

On that date Rowan released two experimental birds. They did not fly off, however, but stayed around the cages all day long and were eventually recaptured. Two weeks later on 6 December, there was a noticeable enlargement of the gonads of the experimental juncos. At that time five birds were liberated. Of this group all but one, an injured bird whose testes were found to be of the minimum size, departed. The following release of birds took place on Sunday 20 December, in poor weather conditions. Because of a two-day snowfall, all natural food supplies were covered by rime, and both controls and experimentals returned to the trap within hours. On 30 December, by which time the gonads of experimental birds were *larger than those of wild spring arrivals*, four birds were liberated. Only one of these disappeared, however, the other three stayed around the aviaries. Rowan noted,

> even when male Juncos settle down on their territories in the spring, their gonads have not yet reached full development.

> There is therefore a stage during enlargement when the migratory impulse ceases. The exact stage I have not determined, but it is very likely that the birds involved in this release had reached it.[50]

Rowan kept taking further samples of control birds, as well as liberating them at periodic intervals to observe their behaviour. Towards the end of February 1926, he remarked that "the gonads of controls are still at their winter minimum."[51] None of the twenty controls released between 6 December 1925 and 17 February 1926 "attempted to use his freedom to leave."[52]

Even before the completion of the experiments, Rowan bragged to Taverner: "My juncos are flourishing. I have now reached the stage that I can let out a batch and say 'Go north,' and off they go, within two hours after release. Or I can say 'Go south' and off they go." Rowan had to admit, however, that he could not establish which direction the birds ultimately took, only that they had gone off somewhere.[53] Rowan was justifiably proud of his achievement; he knew he had done pioneering work. Indeed, by successfully combining his expertise as a field naturalist with his training as a laboratory zoologist, he managed to introduce experimentation into ornithology. This was an important development in the history of ornithology because, in spite of the proliferation of experimental work in biology, ornithology lagged behind other branches of zoology in the area of experimental research. Ornithologists in general had "an almost medieval horror of experiment,"[54] and, although some early twentieth-century work on homing (Watson and Lashley, 1907–1913), moult (Beebe, 1907–1908) and nesting behaviour (Mousley, 1911–1916) had been done, until Rowan launched his well-thought-out research program at the University of Alberta, most ornithologists did not use manipulative procedures or conduct rigorous biological experiments.

After two years of research, Rowan established "(1) that the gonads can be artificially stimulated to premature recrudescence by giving daily increases of light regardless of temperature, barometric pressure, etc.; (2) that birds whose gonads are at the winter minimum, will not migrate."[55] As proof was lacking that the particular condition of the gonads caused migration, Rowan proposed further tests on other ductless glands.

Rowan circulated among his friends the theoretical parts of this paper. He wanted frank criticism, he told Grinnell.[56] To Taverner he wrote:

> I have recently got some interesting evidence as to the possible [effect] that some other ductless gland may have on migration. However, it does not affect my main thesis, as these are apparently also controlled by light . . . . I don't think it is the quantity, quality or amount of light that is effective, in the sense that light may control certain diseases. I think it is primarily a matter of keeping birds awake. . . . The other aspect is not to be ignored however, for in view of ultra-violet ray investigations on diseases that are now being carried out so extensively, there may be something in it. It is a matter of scientific experimentation.[57]

Later, Rowan was to experiment with the effects of both enforced exercise and ultraviolet rays on birds. For the time being, he wanted to get enough evidence to refute Eifrig's theories, and explore the different migratory situations of birds that spend their entire life north or south of the equator. He also had to consider species that are equatorial or transequatorial migrants (that is, species that winter on the equator or cross it from the northern to the southern hemisphere in the winter). He discussed these problems in his correspondence with Taverner, Grinnell, Lawrence, and others, including a new friend named Julian Huxley.[58] They, in turn, convinced him to include a section in the paper about the various categories of migrants. Rowan then stated the view that the immediate stimulus causing migration may not be identical for all birds, and that for equatorial and transequatorial migrants in addition to daylight (an environmental factor), there is an internal physiological rhythm supplied by the gonads, "which exhibit a periodicity as striking as the migrations themselves, and the . . . degeneration and recrudescence of the organs coincide with the migratory periods."[59] In conclusion, Rowan reiterated that annual bird migrations depend on two factors: one internal, "supplied by the reproductive organs when in a particular state of development and physiological activity"; and the other an environmental controlling factor, "provided by the varying daylength."[60]

Rowan's paper was of considerable interest to scientists on both sides of the Atlantic, many of whom soon emulated his original experiments. The inherent research potential of his investigations was also instrumental in securing him a research grant from the Royal Society of London. At age thirty-five, William Rowan had achieved the fame he coveted so much. Now he had to fulfil the expectations of his friends and supporters by conducting experiments on a larger scale.

9

Beloved Wilderness

THE DIVERSIFIED TOPOGRAPHY of Alberta was home to a bewildering variety of birds, and Rowan wrote in 1926 that "it must be many years yet before our knowledge becomes adequate to justify even elementary generalizations" concerning bird life.[1] With his strong need to escape from cramped conditions and restrictive family relationships, Rowan loved the wilderness with a passion, and used it as a laboratory where he could escape from the realities of everyday life.

Rowan remained fascinated with the prairies, forests, mountains, and semideserts; with the ponds, rivers, sloughs, and marshes of this vast land. Most of all, he loved the north-country muskegs, with their variety of life-forms that remained hidden from the casual observer, to be revealed only to the true student of nature. There, among the lakes, sand ridges, deadfalls, and springy moss, Rowan studied animal life. In this "beloved wilderness," as he called it, he could escape his mundane problems and come as close to God as his antireligious nature would permit him.

Rowan's interest in shorebirds was born on the shingle beaches of East Anglia and reawakened and strengthened in the Alberta countryside. A few years after his first trip to Francis Point on Beaverhills Lake, Rowan recalled: "The spot proved so extraordinarily fruitful that I have worked but little elsewhere."[2] Francis Point bore a strong resemblance to Blakeney Point on the Norfolk coast where Rowan had done fieldwork as a student, although the former was "but two miles in length and the briny atmosphere and the shingle are of course wanting." The area offered considerable compensation, however, because of the "abundance of many species that one might see but once in a life-time on the British coast, or perhaps never at all."[3]

Although a journey to the point took hours by train or car, with his infectious enthusiasm Rowan persuaded a number of colleagues to accompany him to hunt waterfowl in season, or collect hydras, insects, and migrating shorebirds for the university study collection. While Rowan's dream of having a field station fell through, in 1923 he obtained collecting and hunting rights from Daniel Francis, the farmer who owned the point.[4]

During his 1921 visit to England, Rowan talked nonstop about the superlative merits of Francis Point. He entertained his acquaintances with stories about the hundreds and thousands of ducks, geese, and shorebirds to be found there. H.F. Witherby enjoyed Rowan's tales of Beaverhills Lake and, as editor of *British Birds*, extracted a promise from the not-too-reluctant Rowan to write a series of illustrated articles about Alberta waders that appeared on the British bird-list.[5] Now Rowan had the perfect excuse for visiting Francis Point, and could justify to everyone but H.M. Tory his sporadic absences from the university when he went on field-trips.

C.G. Harrold was a regular visitor between 1923 and 1928. Rowan later recalled that "Harrold was a constant companion in the field. It was far more than knowledge of birds and gunning that I had the privilege of learning from him through the years of intimate friendship that remained to the end unmarred by a single unpleasant memory."[6] Harrold provided Rowan with the undemanding friendship he needed. The two understood each other without words, and were at their happiest away from the city. If they chose to talk in camp over meals or while preparing specimens, there was always much to discuss: the status and behaviour of birds, or what was seen and collected by others. It was a non-threatening masculine companionship, similar to the one Rowan had enjoyed in his youth with his brother Fred. Sadly, it contrasted sharply with his increasingly strained relationship with Reta, whose attempts at communication about anything but the most trivial topics were soon rebuffed by her husband.[7]

There is no doubt that Rowan loved his wife and children and worked hard to provide for them, but adult relationships with women were missing from his life. His fatherless childhood had not prepared him for a family's demands on his time and energy. Rowan's own idea of a father was the Victorian one of the provider, and he may have thought that food and shelter for his family were all that he, in turn, had to provide. He often complained to friends and family that he had no free time whatever, and intimated how much he disliked "wasting" his time on money-making projects. His vociferous complaints were a way of justifying to others, and perhaps to himself as well, the time he spent doing what he actually liked best: collecting birds and doing artwork.[8] So, during the 1920s, Francis Point came to serve a double purpose. The place proved to be one of great scientific interest where, among the multitude of shorebirds, he could study plumage variations, breeding and feeding behaviour, migration, and systematics. Though it at first seemed only an excellent collecting area, it soon became the centre for Rowan's multilayered biological investigations. It also served as a refuge from overcrowded classrooms, troublesome administrative duties, and a deteriorating family life.

By 1922 Rowan was deeply interested in golden and black-bellied plovers, and short-billed and long-billed dowitchers. For the next ten years, with the help of ornithologists, naturalists, and egg collectors, he studied these species at every available opportunity. While Rowan's plover investigations helped him to refine his ideas concerning bird migration, his dowitcher studies eventually resulted in his making an important contribution to avian systematics.

The status of the long-billed and short-billed birds "across the length and breadth of the North American continent [had] been a matter of dispute" since the early nineteenth century.[9] Early in their correspondence, Taverner informed Rowan that the "Dowitcher is a difficult problem.... As far as measurements go we certainly get typical birds of both forms clear across the prairies .... [unfortunately] we have practically no knowledge of separate breeding areas of the two."[10]

In the following years, "as regards to dowitchers" became a recurrent phrase in Rowan's correspondence. The search for dowitchers took Rowan to many different areas in Alberta, and to several natural-history collections across North America. When fieldwork was impossible, he spent hours in his cluttered tower room atop the medical building, measuring and comparing dowitcher skins lent to him by curators and collectors. Rowan soon found that the bills of the two types varied considerably, and that one could grade the birds according to bill length. He felt, however, that the "splitting of such a variable bird into . . . subspecies [is] the most awful waste of effort and time, and probably a distortion of the real facts."[11]

Rowan was also interested in the greater and lesser yellowlegs, species rare in Britain, though common migrants in Canada. By the 1920s, their nesting area had still not been well defined, and Rowan, always keen to discover new things, longed to find their specific breeding localities. Bill MacDonald, whose geological field trips had taken him to the northern breeding ground of several shorebirds, frequently recounted tales of the North, thereby fuelling Rowan's desire to see the region himself. The Arctic also sounded like an ideal place to discover the breeding grounds of solitary sandpipers, and Pacific and yellow-billed loons.

For a number of years Rowan had to curb his impatience; lack of time and money prevented him from going to the Arctic, and he was mostly confined to investigating birds in the Edmonton area. In 1924, he ventured further afield, often accompanied by a number of keen naturalists and collectors. Among them were Frank Farley, the real-estate agent from Camrose, who discovered several good collecting grounds while travelling on business; Tom (T.E.) Randall, a farmer from Castor; and A.D. Henderson from Belvedere, northwest of Edmonton.[12]

At the end of June 1924, Rowan noted that "Henderson from Belvedere came in for lunch today and spent the afternoon here."[13] Rowan had already enjoyed a brief holiday with Reta in May on Francis Point, and had a short trip with Randall, collecting the birds of the semidesert. Henderson described for Rowan the shorebirds nesting in the muskeg near his home, and invited Rowan to visit him. Rowan accepted with such alacrity that by the first of July he was back in Edmonton, after having had a "glorious trip." He thoroughly enjoyed himself, despite the weather — the heat exacerbated by the lack of shade, "thanks to the caterpillars" — and his having to carry a heavy Graflex camera (with a "half ton lens"), field glasses, and his twelve-bore collecting gun.[14]

Rowan's next extended field excursion was to Lac la Biche with

J.A. Munro, a federal migratory bird officer for the four western provinces, and Mrs. Munro, to examine "some of the Alberta lakes with a view to establishing public shooting grounds."[15] During the fall of 1924, while conducting migration experiments, Rowan had little time to spend out-of-doors. But Harrold was happy to camp on the point, and Rowan, "by a fluke," as he recalled with tongue-in-cheek, took one of his "rare" visits to the place when the "main Golden Plover migration was on . . . . There were hundreds of them this time with flocks running up to 80 birds and no Black-bellies amongst them. Of a long series collected, *all* were juveniles." The only adult was caught by Harrold.[16]

The following winter, Rowan confidently wrote to J.H. Fleming to say that "if the two supposed races [of dowitchers] are really good — an item that cannot be demonstrated until the breeding ground of *griseus* are [sic] found and skins procured there — a third race is easily separable."[17] Eventually, Rowan was to prove the existence of a "third race" but, in the meantime, other tasks took precedence over shorebird investigations.

Rowan discovered another part of Alberta in 1925, when he took the family for a brief vacation to Sylvan Lake. They went as guests of the Cassels, who had a summer home there. Elsie Cassels, vice president of the Alberta Natural History Association, had been observing Alberta wildlife since the late 1880s. Like many other settlers, she had little time, but, by stealing moments from the daily routine and jealously guarding them for nature study, she turned herself into a respected naturalist. A slight, strong woman, then in her sixties, she had already visited Rowan at the university. They carried on a lengthy correspondence concerning the birds and mammals of Alberta, and developed a friendship based on their common interest in nature.[18]

Set among poplars, cottonwoods, and birches, the Cassels's log house, named the Ark, on the north shore of Sylvan Lake, was a perfect vacation spot for Rowan. Before a noisy amusement park and a public beach ruined the south shore, the Ark overlooked a lake of pristine beauty. The older children could play happily on the shore, while Reta, eight months pregnant, watched them with Sylvia toddling at her side. Rowan and Elsie Cassels observed birds from a canoe, or tramped around the countryside. It was a delightful holiday — but all too brief. The family had to return to

Edmonton before the birth of their next child.

Rowan was delighted with the vigorous, sturdy little boy (born on 16 July 1925), named Frederick Julian after his favourite brother and his friend J.S. Huxley.[19] Now, more than ever, he wanted to ensure a comfortable life for his family, possibly by obtaining a better position. Rowan wanted more pay, and the opportunity to openly pursue fieldwork, which he still had to do, he told Grinnell, "surreptitiously, at my own expense and in my own time."[20] Rowan's correspondence with Grinnell includes a number of letters about the possibility of finding a post that would allow him more time for fieldwork. Rowan listed "items on which I am working at the moment with a view to publication," such as migration, the periodic cycles of rabbits and other vertebrates, the "taxonomic status of the Wood Bison," the early development of the eared grebe (for his proposed D.Sc. thesis), the birds of Alberta, and histogenesis "in a giant and undescribed species of hydra."[21] To Harry Swarth, another California ornithologist, Rowan wrote about his plans to study the habits and life history of the cowbird.[22]

In spite of what Rowan told his correspondents about official strictures, nothing could stop his field activities. His summer vacation was his own, and, in 1925, Rowan certainly took advantage of his free time. When Henderson wrote, as Rowan reported to Taverner, that he had taken the "eggs and skin of Dowitcher, 50 miles out of Edmonton,"[23] Rowan felt he *must* collect these dowitchers and add them to his already-extensive series of skins, and so he raced off to visit Henderson. Rowan was greatly excited by the dowitcher eggs and skins. He informed Taverner that the birds were a new, undescribed race of the short-billed dowitcher, and even warned his friend that it would carry the subspecific name "pati," based on Taverner's initials (P.A.T.)[24]

In his spare moments during 1925, Rowan organized his information on Alberta shorebirds for the long-overdue articles for *British Birds*. He began writing in early 1926, and illustrated the papers with the photos he had taken in the field, and with his own pen-and-ink sketches and watercolours, drawn from life or from fresh specimens at the actual collecting sites. The first six "Notes on Alberta Waders Included in the British List" appeared in volume 20 of *British Birds* (1926). Twenty-one figures and eight colour plates depicted habitat, nests and eggs, downy young, and characteristic behaviour (such as the injury feigning of the killdeer), as well as the heads and feet of certain species.The notes themselves, of varying lengths, described abundance, migration, feeding and breeding behaviour, and various field marks, including vocalizations. Not satisfied with publishing them in Britain alone, Rowan also sent copies to Bent for use in his *Life Histories*.[25]

With these papers out of the way, Rowan continued to investigate the "dowitcher problem." The work included innumerable measurements. While Rowan preferred chasing dowitchers in the field to measuring their skins in his office, their status intrigued him sufficiently that for nearly a decade he spent many hours on indoor study. In his tower room, Rowan compared items in his own collection with those borrowed from private sources (Louis Bishop, A.C. Bent, and J.H. Fleming). Museum curators (Taverner in Ottawa, Conover at the Chicago Field Museum, and Grinnell at the Museum of Vertebrate Zoology, Berkeley) also lent him specimens. Finally, in 1932, "The Status of the Dowitchers with a Description of a New Subspecies from Alberta and Manitoba" appeared in the *Auk*. Notwithstanding what he'd said to Taverner, Rowan named the bird after Henderson. It is still referred to as "*Limnodromus griseus hendersoni* Rowan," commemorating its discoverer and describer.

But Rowan did indoor work only if and when he had to, and going after shorebirds, hydras, mammals, spiders, or anything else he was interested in, provided him with a multitude of excuses to get out-of-doors. He longed for these excursions. By the mid-to-late 1920s, his love for the outdoors became so strong, that he put up with adverse weather conditions, insect pests, hunger, and thirst. He endured constant rain, thunderstorms, and blizzards, extremes of heat and cold, and even dust storms. Neither the weather, nor ticks, mosquitoes, and horseflies ever deterred him from dossing down on the ground, in a lean-to or flimsy tent, or even in a haystack. Despite the physical hardships, the pleasure of being in the field was so great that Rowan continued to brave Tory's displeasure to experience it.

Tory continued to oppose Rowan's fieldwork, although how far this opposition extended and what form it took are not exactly known. Rowan's contemporary letters and later recollections, and some of Reta's letters (written after Rowan's death) refer to his

11. Bison, Wood Buffalo Park, Christmas Card, 1925.
Pencil drawing by William Rowan. University of Alberta Archives.

difficulties with Tory. The university president himself wrote to several people, in a disparaging way, about Rowan's predilection for fieldwork.[26] Rowan often used evidence selected to colour the truth when it suited his purpose, and Tory was inclined to do the same. Letters and other evidence make it clear, however, that after several years of relative calm, during which Rowan pursued fieldwork and Tory ignored what Rowan did, field studies became, once again, officially taboo. Things came to a head over the buffalo controversy of 1925.

In "The Passing of the Wood Bison," published in the *Canadian Forum* in 1925, "A Canadian Zoologist" wrote:

> At no period has the herd of wood bison still roaming free in its original home between the Peace River and Great Slave Lake received as much attention as at present. Zoologists in every corner of the continent, and even outside of it are marvelling that these magnificent animals, after passing through many vicissitudes and being provided at long last with a real haven of refuge, should now be doomed to rapid, certain, and complete extinction.[27]

Indeed, by the time this was written, by none other than Rowan himself, the fate of the wood bison was an issue of much concern among zoologists. This was because the Canadian government, against all scientific advice, proposed to mix herds of the large wood bison (or buffalo) and the much smaller plains bison. The latter species was at the time housed at Wainwright Park, an area of 410 square kilometres (160 square miles), east of Edmonton. In this protected environment, the plains bison multiplied rapidly. Soon they depleted the natural forage and overcrowding brought disease which attacked thousands of animals.

Space was not as readily available in central Alberta as it was in the Northwest Territories, where the newly created Wood Buffalo Park was situated (around Fort Smith). The park had an abundance of wild areas and food for many thousands of beasts of both kinds. The government's plan to move the plains buffalo was the brainchild of civil servants who worked under Minister of the Interior Charles Stewart. Though the plan received approval from nature artist and writer Ernest Thompson Seton, it created a great furor among zoologists in universities and natural-history museums.

Rowan threw himself wholeheartedly into the fray. He objected to the transfer of the Wainwright herd on scientific grounds. For him, the buffalo were more than yet another species threatened with disease, diminishing habitat, and eventual extinction. While he most certainly was worried about all these threats, and proposed to do everything in his power to prevent the demise of the magnificent beasts, Rowan was most concerned about losing the buffalo as a potent symbol, one that had the power to evoke the unspoiled wilderness and bygone days. In a later, popular article he wrote of

> a rolling prairie brown with herds of buffalo, of thousands of miles of continuous trails, worn smooth and deep by the passing of millions of feet; of fertile valleys and expansive plains resounding to the thud of hoofs and the hue and cry of the Indian chase or the full-throated hunting song of the wolf pack.[28]

Rowan first heard about the buffalo at Bedford School when Seton, there as a visiting speaker, described endless herds galloping over the prairies, chased by Indians or wolf packs. His schoolboy's imagination was set afire by images of "fertile valleys and expansive plains." When he went west, in 1908, Rowan found that he would only be able to see the free-roaming buffalo in his own imagination. The only bison he actually saw, were captive ones in Winnipeg in 1911. After he moved to Edmonton in 1920, Rowan visited the herd of thousands of bison in Wainwright Park, and revelled in the sight.[29] He admired their large, shaggy bodies and massive heads, sketched individuals and groups, and observed their behaviour.

Rowan's interest in the bison, originally romantic, later artistic and scientific, turned into something of an obsession when, in the December 1924 issue of the *Canadian Field-Naturalist*, he read Maxwell Graham's note concerning the proposed bison transfer. Allan Brooks, H.M. Laing, and Francis Harper also deplored the mixing of the two herds, and sent letters of protest to the Canadian government.[30] Laing, who had a syndicated nature column that appeared in Canadian newspapers, came out strongly against the proposed mix of two distinct bison herds. Rowan, for reasons of his own (such as his fear of losing his collecting permit and even his position at the University of Alberta), tried to work behind the scenes. He stirred up interest in the scientific community, incited other scientists to write letters of protest, and began negotiations with the Museum of Comparative Zoology at Harvard. It was possible that the museum would defray part of a trip to collect wood buffalo by purchasing specimens from Rowan.

Rowan's motives were mixed, and it is hard to separate the various strands of interest that contributed to his violent opposition to the government's proposed plan. He wanted to go and secure specimens in case the species became extinct, to prove to other scientists and to the government that *he* was right in thinking the two herds were distinct enough to be full species. He feared that mixing the two herds would threaten the very existence of the healthy, but less numerous wood buffalo. Worried about the possible extinction of these striking animals, Rowan gave scientific support (his own expertise and that of many others) to his opposition. Rowan also saw that the buffalo would constitute the loss of his childhood dream of the Canadian West.

Rowan received a firsthand account of the wood buffalo and its territory from ex-ranger F.C. Bennett, who told Rowan that there were about fifteen hundred wood bison in two distinct areas in the park, both consisting of enormous muskegs. Rowan avidly listened to Bennett's descriptions of buffalo wallows, vegetation, and wildlife in general.[31] Everything Bennett told him made him long more than ever to go to Wood Buffalo Park and see for himself the area that promised to be a naturalist's paradise. Rowan also genuinely wanted to see if his suspicion that the proposed transfer was detrimental to the wood buffalo was well founded. He practically went on the warpath against the government's plan. In this highly excited frame of mind he told Taverner that "never before in history as far as I know has an animal been deliberately exterminated, wiped right off the map, completely and deliberately effaced by a body supposed to be there for the protection and preservation of wild life."[32]

In 1925, before modern techniques became available to detect genetic differences, Rowan thought the two bison were different species (certainly not an accepted fact at the time) because there were easily observable differences in height, size of teeth, morphological features of the cranium, and so on. He longed to visit the northern range, and collect animals for a comparative study. Rowan knew, of course, that Tory and the University of Alberta administration would never consider funding a northern field trip. While such a trip would have yielded considerable material for the university's vertebrate collection, Rowan did not even bother to ask the university for funds. He expected to obtain the full support of Harper and Barbour, and Barbour had promised to pay him two thousand dollars for two wood-buffalo skeletons.

A note Rowan wrote at the end of August — "have decided to go north and get the Wood Bison with Bill MacDonald" — is misleading. The reader could be forgiven for thinking that the decision came out of the blue, when in fact Rowan had planned and plotted for several months. That the hoped-for trip materialized just when he was due to begin the second year of his junco experiments did not deter Rowan. He instructed Lister about trapping migrant juncos, told Reta that he was going to seize this wonderful opportunity to obtain scientific facts concerning the threatened wood buffalo, and rushed around getting ready for the journey.[33] Whatever Reta may have thought about being left in Edmonton, with four young children, including six-week-old Julian, she dutifully turned up at the railway station to see her husband off.

When Rowan first visited Lac la Biche, in 1924, he did not record his experiences. On the 1925 trip, longer and more leisurely, Rowan had numerous opportunities to write down his impressions. He noted that "100 miles" northeast of Edmonton, the "lakes were getting abundant, cultivation scattered and the dry muskegs getting frequent." At Lac la Biche he saw "the most beautiful northern lights . . . a great curtain of many colours from overhead to the horizon."[34] The party travelled by train, boat, and occasionally on foot, through settlements such as Waterways, Fort McMurray, and Fort Chipewyan.

As usual, Rowan was interested in everything. At Fort McMurray he talked to shopkeepers, trappers, hunters, even a local fire ranger. He listened to local yarns about the abundance of wildlife. On board ship, he chatted to the captain and learned that navigation on the Athabasca River was "no joke" because of the sandbars.[35] Rowan later noted that the boat moved with "many groans and creaks, periodically giving an uneasy lurch and wiggle as she slides over some particularly large bump." Because of the engine vibration, he could not sketch or take photos, but used the slow journey to observe lakes, lagoons, and mossy banks, and to watch for wildlife. He saw large flocks of migrant juncos, robins, and other birds, including "whiskey jacks galore." At Fort Smith, Rowan "talked buffalo" to inspectors, the "wireless man from Ottawa," and the residents. He also collected information on the size of snowshoe-hare and game-bird populations. Fort Smith is the gateway to Wood Buffalo Park, and Rowan wanted to enter the park and go after the large mammals immediately. Instead, he had to take to his bed with a cold.[36]

When the party set off on 8 September, 1925, Rowan, his cold forgotten, rejoiced at the view of parklike meadows and trees. Behind thick glasses, his myopic eyes observed everything.[37] Wet weather and streaming nose notwithstanding, Rowan enjoyed himself immensely. He loved the constantly changing countryside with its closely packed lodgepole pines, its carpets of moss and lichen, its poplars, birches, and spruces, and its "patches of meadow, or willow and grass." The party was spurred on by the idea of the buffalo hunt and the "spectre of buffalo steak for supper," but they saw no large animals, only signs of them: moose and bear dung, and "bear clawings on the poplars." On Pine Lake, they admired ducks and grebes and went out in a canoe for a plankton haul, but the clear, deep lake had none in it.[38]

Two days later, Rowan found the first traces of the Wainwright buffalo. Later, he spotted a huge, sleeping wood bison bull, and "decided to take him, but the tough old beast had to be shot six time before collapsing." Rowan, impressed by the old bull's size and strength, noted that a "howitzer would seem to be the most suitable killer!"[39] He took detailed measurements (standing height, length, "nose to 1st caudal vertebra in a straight line"), then sketched the magnificent head. The party dined on bison liver, a delicacy, and set aside the other parts (ribs, neck, guts, meat, head, and tongue) to be measured and weighed later. Discussions over the campfire inevitably centred on the local wildlife, and it was with great excitement that Rowan listened to stories of the "White Cranes" (that is, whooping cranes), already an endangered species.[40]

Before moving on, they cleaned up the skeleton and dried the buffalo meat. Once en route, Rowan saw a young bull "with large unworn horns," and found plenty of buffalo tracks and skeletal remains. The weather was fine and the northern lights were reflected in the clear lake at night. The following day it rained, it was "blowing half a gale," and Rowan and MacDonald lazed around camp, while listening to Caruso, Galli Curci, and McCormack on the portable gramophone.[41]

On 16 September they shot another old bull. Having collected the two buffalo skeletons Rowan had promised to Harvard, their mission was accomplished. They could return to Fort Smith and home, but Rowan was not particularly keen to rush back to the university. While he was looking forward to seeing his family and continuing his experiments, he was less enthusiastic about beginning a heavy teaching schedule and facing the university president. Rowan was also unwilling to end a trip that could not be easily repeated. Their last night in camp was certainly noisy, "what with minks fighting in the shack, skunks in all the buildings, bats trying to settle on the walls, or catching bugs, horses that wouldn't leave the yard and jangled cowbells half the night."[42] Yet Rowan recorded all this with great good humour.

After the buffalo hunt, Rowan's delight in the north country remained undiminished. As always, his aesthetic enjoyment was intertwined with keen scientific curiosity. On the return trip, he not only observed a variety of birds, but also took a plankton haul from the Salt River. Rowan and MacDonald left Fort Smith in fine weather for Fort McMurray, but couldn't sleep because of the heat and the high winds which later rocked the boat. Rowan did not mind the ever-changing northern climate. He watched the countryside from the slow-moving boat, and listened to the huskies on board howl every time the boat whistle went off. Rowan could contemplate nature for just so long, and soon he was helping the deckhands take on wood.[43]

Rowan's diary presents a vivid picture of the journey. He wrote that the boat

> picked up bags of tarsand [sic] at various spots, flagged on the shore, the broken down fire patrol gas boat and scow and later the Canedusa and barge, all of which we tugged up to McMurray . . . . [A]s we approached McMurray, the river,

> downstream, was extremely beautiful. Smoke from a woodland fire . . . filled the valley with a pale purplish haze and left its characteristic pungent aroma in the nostrils . . . On the east banks the sombre grey cliffs of tar sands sloped away to the sky, here heavy clumps of dark spruces, there splashes of orange, red and yellow — poplar, cottonwood, birch, etc. In the river, giving a perfect reflection, running most of the way across an island, mostly vivid green with fresh vegetation after the recent rains, terminating at one end in a streak of yellow, the ever present sand bar. The heavy timber on the west shore lay in deep shadow, revealing here and there the richest of colours, looking deeper and richer by far in the sombre half-light, than their counterparts on the other, better lit side.[44]

Rowan also listened with fascination on the boat to stories about the northern people, including the skipper's tales about "morals — or their absence" in the region.[45] Much to his surprise, one night Rowan bumped into a "charming young thing who couldn't find a light to get to her cabin." This was Louise Rourke (also known as Dimps Dawson), wife of the Hudson's Bay Company accountant at Fort Chipewyan. A recent arrival from England, she knew Reta's friends from the Slade, and was delighted to meet someone from her own background.[46] She was to become a family friend.

Rowan arrived home on 25 September, took off to see Harrold (who was camping at Francis Point), and told him about his trip to the fabulous North. Although the duck hunting was poor, Rowan enjoyed himself. As long as he could justify his presence at the point by examining Harrold's recent collection, a large part of which would become part of the university study collection, Rowan could delay, albeit only for a few days, resuming his everyday life. He soon had to return to reality, to a noisy, growing family of four children, to a gruelling teaching schedule — and to his exciting experimental work.

Although it took place before the beginning of the academic year and was financed by external sources, Rowan's jaunt to the North highly displeased Tory, who still insisted that fieldwork was not science. And though, during Rowan's first years at the university, Tory's main objection was to field ornithology, it soon became obvious that he opposed everything — from a one-day collecting trip to a lengthy expedition — that would take Rowan into the field. Of course Rowan did not bother to ask the president's permission to go north, and this may have upset Tory, but Rowan did not actually need his consent to go to Wood Buffalo Park on his own time, and he well knew that Tory would never have given his official sanction to any such venture. In fact, Rowan tried to keep the whole plan secret, even from his wife, until he had obtained the financial guarantee from Harvard and had the government hunting permit in his pocket.

By talking to native hunters and guides, and to Hudson's Bay Company personnel, Rowan amassed a considerable amount of information he planned to use as ammunition against the federal government. First he had to face the music, though, because Tory peremptorily ordered Rowan to his office to account for his "delinquent" behaviour. Reta, more than thirty years later remarked, that Rowan was often tongue-tied when facing the president. But he stood his ground this time, and did not compromise his integrity, as we see from Tory's own version of the event, recorded some time later:

> To my surprise I found that he had made an arrangement with Harvard university to go to Northern Alberta and shoot wood buffalo, and I had to tell him frankly that if that was the work he intended to follow he might dismiss from his head any idea of becoming head of a department in any university over which I preside. He stated in reply that he preferred to follow his bent and take second place and there the matter stood.[47]

Apparently, by 1925 Rowan was secure enough as a scientist to follow his own path. His early experiments on the junco were successful, and the brief note he wrote on it for *Nature* was mentioned in other journals. He was receiving praise and extra income for his art work, and had established a network of collectors and prospective buyers for his specimens. Tongue-tied or not, Rowan could and did stand up to the president. Tory's threat of keeping Rowan in second place rang empty, because there was no one to usurp Rowan's position. Whether or not he was made full professor, Rowan *was* the senior scientist in the department.[48] As the pay difference between full and associate professors was negligible, Rowan, already earning money on the side, could easily make up the difference. If becoming full professor meant sacrificing his interests to conform to Tory's narrow view of scientific research, it was simply not worth it. Rowan was ambitious, and an independent thinker. He was also stubborn. He would not comply with Tory's wishes because such compliance would go against the grain of his personality. It would also mean that he would have to curtail his research, which the international scientific community considered to be pioneering.

So it was a stalemate between Tory and Rowan, one that remained in effect from 1925 until Tory left the University of Alberta in 1928. During this period, Rowan continued to teach huge classes, prepare teaching material, conduct experimental work on birds in his garden, and spend his spare time in the field. The Alberta countryside maintained its powerful attractions for Rowan. It was a source of scientific interest and artistic inspiration, and offered him periodic escape from humdrum reality.

Rowan's collecting for Harvard University later landed him in hot water with the federal government as well, because he had sent Canadian specimens to the United States without a permit. How the bureaucrats found out is unclear; it is likely Canadian customs officials notified them of a suspicious shipment. Ironically, members of the Department of the Interior, who originally ignored scientists' concerns about the proposed transfer, and whose pigheadedness threatened the very existence of the wood buffalo, complained about losing important Canadian skeletal material to an American institution. As a consequence, in the fall of 1926, Taverner had to convince them that "it was a jolly good thing that representatives of the Wood Buffalo went to institutions where they would be safe in deposit."[49] The Department of the Interior continued to disregard what scientists thought of the matter, however, and kept on transferring the diseased animals from Wainwright Park to Wood Buffalo Park. Rowan was among the scientists who were neither silenced nor convinced of the advantages of such a move.[50]

The wilderness experience Rowan enjoyed on the trip to Wood Buffalo Park remained with him for a long time. During the following years, his teaching duties, experimental work, and doctoral studies precluded lengthy expeditions. Rowan was determined, however, to escape from his day-to-day chores at every opportunity. However, the brief excursions Rowan took in the vicinity of Edmonton and in the English countryside could not satisfy his deep longing for the wilderness.

Rowan did manage a two-week visit to the muskegs west of Belvedere in 1926, though, with Henderson and Taverner, and it was a marvellous introduction to the type of land that was to become his "beloved wilderness." The party walked and rode across country to Klondike City and Fort Assiniboine, and slept in traders' cabins. They enjoyed the easy companionship of naturalists in the field. The land was so wet that some of the time the horses would not cross the muskeg and "had to go around it."[51] They found greater yellowlegs, and numerous other birds, the weather was fine, though cool, and there were hardly any mosquitoes. Rowan, as usual, did not mind the hard walking. He only regretted that this fruitful area was so far from Edmonton.

10

Further Experiments and Graduate Research

AT THE END OF TWO YEARS of experimental work, in early 1926, it was clear that Rowan could not carry out large-scale investigations in the original aviaries. He needed extra space to house at least one hundred experimental and one hundred control birds, and had to raise funds for the aviaries, bird food, and other material used in histological work on the gonads. In view of Tory's continued opposition to bird studies, however, Rowan had to seek grants anywhere but at the University of Alberta.

Julian Huxley had already suggested that Rowan apply to a non-Canadian organization, such as the Rockefeller Foundation or the Royal Society (of London).[1] D.M.S. Watson, who believed that Rowan's theory was worth putting to a larger test, also recommended the Royal Society. Following their advice, in the spring of 1926, Rowan wrote to the latter institution enclosing a proposal for an extensive research project on the American crow. He chose this species because crows are conspicuous, noisy birds well known to farmers, who have long despised and hunted them. Unlike juncos, crows were not protected by the Migratory Bird Convention Act. Rowan's new research plans included shooting crows; the species seemed an ideal experimental subject.

Rowan asked the Royal Society for $748 to test his original hypothesis that

> the migration of certain classes of birds not wintering in, or south of, the tropical zone [is] instigated by the condition of

> the gonads; . . . [T]he maturing of these organs is dependent upon *increasing* daylight, the attainment of a certain stage of development inaugurating the spring (northward) movements, while the autumn degeneration of the organs, including the southward migration, is initiated by the *decreasing* days following the summer solstice.[2]

He sent the proposal to Watson to be passed on to other members of the Royal Society. Then, confident of a favourable response, he got on with other work. Huxley's letter of 3 June 1926 shook Rowan out of his complacency. Apparently, J.P. Hill, a member of the Royal Society Council (which dealt with emergency grants), told Huxley the application must have gone astray and Rowan should immediately send another one. While Rowan feverishly worked on this, the original application reached Watson. He now suggested Rowan apply for a regular Royal Society grant, because the funds needed were too large to be considered emergency.

In the meantime, Rowan discovered his original estimate of the costs was too low. He needed about fifteen hundred dollars, and could not even start "on the scheme without being absolutely certain" the grant would be available.[3] So he temporarily shelved the large-scale crow project and applied for an emergency grant to complete another stage of the junco experiments. His colleagues convinced him, that the "results would materially increase" his chances of obtaining a larger sum the following year.[4]

Rowan asked for thirty-two pounds sterling (or about one hundred and fifty Canadian dollars) "to erect a large aviary fitted with electric light for the housing of Juncos" during the September to December 1926 period. The estimate included materials for the aviary (seventy dollars), two new bird traps (fourteen dollars), bird food (sixty dollars for four months, low because of a 40 percent reduction on wholesale purchases), and lighting and wiring (seven dollars). He explained that Dr. J.B. Collip, "of insulin fame," promised to cooperate and "make periodic blood analyses of controls and experimentals."[5]

By 1926, Collip had become an internationally known hormone researcher, investigating the blood chemistry of animals. Discussions with him persuaded Rowan that through his experiments he could demonstrate the presence of a gonadal hormone.

Sept. 10th 1926.

Traps (2) put out yesterday afternoon. Nothing in the evening. There are few Juncos about yet anywhere. Pipits were about in large flocks yesterday.

Today produced one White-crowned & one Song Sp. These are in the remodelled old aviaries, now knocked into one, to be used for controls.

We had the first frost (2 degrees) two nights ago. The wet weather, which has been practically continuous since the 25th Aug, seems to be over & the roads are just getting usable again. The Canaries, in the new aviary, have done well. The young of the old hen are fine birds. Her eggs are much larger than those of the second hen. She had apparently quit nesting for good after her last batch, but immediately on transference to the bright, whitewashed, new aviary began again & on the 7th laid a 4th & last egg. These were apparently infertile.

11th The song sparrow is badly hurt on the head. This morning's catch – a juvenile White-crowned – was similarly injured. Before lunch lined the lower half of the traps with mosquito netting, an awful sweat. The sunflowers are being cut down & have moved both traps, one to the west wall of the football grounds & the other to the South wall. Juncos about at both places, but not plentiful. Flocks of Pipits again. Also Tree Sparrows.

12. Extract from the "Junco and Canary Experiments Research Notebooks," 1926.

University of Alberta Archives, William Rowan Papers, 69-16-901.

Liberations.

Experimentals				Controls			
out	in	out	in	out	in	out	in
15.XI.26		29.XII.26		18.XI.26. 40310 ♀	18.XI.26	29.XII.26	
♂ (number not noted)		3 40220 ♀	31.XII.26	40311 ♀	18.XI.26	2 40308 ♀	30.XII.26
These two escaped by accident. ♀ (unbanded)	17.XI.26	1 40210 ♀		40300 ♂	Shrike?	5 40331 ♂	30.XII.26
16.XI.26. 40251 ♀ 4	16.XI.26	7 40249 ♀		40313 ♂	18.XI.26	11 40354 ♂	30.XII.26
40261 ♀ 5		11 40267 ♀		40350 ♂	18.XI.26	4 40327 ♂	29.XII.26
40213 ♂ 1	17.XI.26	4 40231 ♀	31.XII.26	30.XI.26 40310 ♀	30.XI.26	3 40321 ♂	30.XII.26
40223 ♂ 2		9 40263 ♀		40332 ♂	30.XI.26	10 40348 ♂	29.XII.26
40250 ♂ 3	17.XI.26	15 40290 ♀		40234 ♂	30.XI.26	6 40334 ♂	1.I.27
40386 ♂ 6		14 40285 ♂	29.XII.26	40336 ♂	30.XI.26	8 40344 ♂	30.XII.26
40297 ♂ 7		8 40252 ♂		40353 ♂	30.XI.26	1 40305 ♂	30.XII.26
40298 ♂ 8		13 40288 ♂	29.XII.26	8.XII.26 3 40318 ♂	8.XII.26	7 40338 ♂	30.XII.26
19.XII.26 40216 ♂ 4		5 40245 ♂		2 40315 ♂	8.XII.26	9 40347 ♂	30.XII.26
40240 ♀ 5	19.XII.26	2 40222 ♂		10 40293 ♂	8.XII.26	29.I.27 40305 ♂	30.I.27
40215 ♂ 3	19.XII.26	10 40264 ♀	30.XII.26	9 40359 ♂	8.XII.26	40334 ♂	29.I.27
40283 ♂ 8	20.XII.26	17 40337 ♂		5 40325 ♂	8.XII.26	40338 ♂	29.I.27
40352 ♂ 9		18 40269 ♂	29.XII.26	4 40319 ♀	8.XII.26	40340 ♂	29.I.27
40258 ♂ 7				6 40334 ♂	9.XII.26	40344 ♂	30.I.27
40199 ♂ 1	19.XII.26			8 40344 ♂	8.XII.26	40348 ♂	29.I.27
40209 ♂ 2	19.XII.26			1 40313 ♀	17.XII.26 dead		
—— (escaped)				7 40338 ♂	8.XII.26		
29.XII.26 Tree Sparrows							
6 40247							
16 40343	30.XII.26						

13. Extract from the "Junco and Canary Experiments Research Notebooks," 1926.
University of Alberta Archives, William Rowan Papers, 69-16-901.

With the support of Hill, Huxley, and Watson, Rowan's second application was approved. He was awarded the thirty-two pounds "to assist in experimental work in connection with the migration of birds."[6] As it turned out, Rowan had again underestimated the cost of research,[7] but the error was not serious enough to hold him back. With his customary zeal, Rowan threw himself into constructing an aviary "built of shiplap and two-by-fours."[8] By the second week of September he was ready to trap juncos.

As this period coincided with the beginning of a new academic year, Rowan was extremely busy. Every day he greeted the rising sun at the traps he had placed at the experimental farms near a manure pile. By 1 October he had the projected one hundred birds in the experimental aviary. He was ready to administer artificial light.

From his junco notebooks we learn that within a week Rowan was killing sample juncos. In the zoology laboratory he dissected their testes, and fixed them in Bouin's fluid. Evidently, this was acceptable laboratory work. By the middle of November (when the lights went on at 4:40 p.m. and turned off at 10:55 p.m.) he found that the testes of the experimentals had become considerably enlarged, while the testes of the controls remained very small.[9] Beginning in mid-November, Rowan periodically released some experimental and control birds, while others, from both groups, were killed for blood analyses, which were performed by Collip in the biochemistry laboratory. In early January 1927, Rowan noted that he had "killed off all the experimentals (to get injection material for controls) except a few females as most of these were in developing condition."[10] He promptly informed local radio stations and newspapers of his successful experiments.[11] At the end of January, Rowan and Collip injected the last six control juncos with a solution made by grinding "down the frozen testes and ovaries" of the experimental birds, preparing an emulsion and centrifuging it. Two days later Rowan liberated the injected birds and noted that "In less than 1/2 hour . . . all were in, very different behaviour from ordinary controls."[12]

Rowan had earlier admitted to Grinnell that "the evidence is not *conclusive*, but I hope to make it so yet. In the meantime, it is so suggestive, and so in agreement with theoretical forecasts, that I think I may be forgiven for elation (even if a bit undue in other eyes) at the heat of the moment."[13]In addition to his experimental work,

Rowan was writing two papers. One was on the aviary itself, and was to be published in the *Condor*; the other, "Migration and Reproductive Rhythm in Birds," appeared in the 5 March 1927 issue of *Nature*. Rowan's plans included a more detailed article "with the cytology thoroughly worked out. This should be a real contribution to ornithology as well as to [other] branches of science for so little is known of the reproductive organs of birds, and nothing at all of their relation to migration."[14]

With 1,050 copies of his first long paper, "On Photoperiodism," hot off the press in December 1926, followed by the note in *Nature* in March 1927, Rowan's experiments began to create considerable interest on both sides of the Atlantic. The American zoologist Oscar Riddle (at the Cold Spring Harbour Station for Experimental Evolution) was among those who commented on the pioneering nature and inherent scientific interest of Rowan's research. Riddle asked Rowan for reprints of his publications.[15] A. Landsborough Thomson, whose own book on migration had just been published in England, wrote, "Had your experimental evidence then been available I should probably have stressed light and reproductive rhythm more strongly .... As regards your experiments, I need say only that they seem to me to be of great interest. It is definitely a new line of attack."[16]

Migration research occupied much of Rowan's time and energy during the September 1924 to March 1927 period, but he had not entirely given up on his doctorate. Rowan's correspondence with Julian Huxley and discussions with Winnie Hughes, who was just starting her own Ph.D. in embryology at the University of Chicago, reawakened the idea of doctoral research in him. Actually, Rowan had been collecting eared-grebe embryos for a number of years, and by 1926 he considered this species in particular (and embryology in general) as a suitable subject for graduate research. Rowan was conservative in many ways, and because of his training at University College, London, he continued to view embryology as a promising research area for a D.Sc. and had hoped that his old zoology professor, J.P. Hill, would become his thesis adviser. In a letter to Hill, Rowan somewhat optimistically remarked:

> I hope to send you my thesis in outline at the end of September. There are several points that have me stumped still, particu-

> larly the extra-embryonal structures that I think must be unique to the grebe, but if you don't mind being bothered with the thing, I will send it along with drawings and probably a few slides. The lack of literature here is extremely trying. We can get all kinds of material, but literature and references are continual stumbling blocks. If I get anything really worthwhile out of this grebe, I shall proceed to another species and subsequently two more, eggs of all of which are easily procurable here.[17]

Rowan also intimated that, given the chance to go north, he might work on loons, whose embryology was incompletely known and whose systematic position "should prove of exceptional interest."[18] The ever-supportive Hill invited Rowan to work at University College; he even arranged to have him register for a minimal fee.

Although there is no evidence that he ever sent the promised thesis outline to Hill, by the spring of 1927 Rowan was ready to go to England. In his letters to Fleming, Grinnell, Taverner and others, he made frequent references to the impending trip, the need to use a good reference library, and the advantages of working with Hill.[19] From this correspondence we learn that Rowan was frantically busy correcting exams and finishing up odd jobs, while waiting for the eared grebes to lay eggs around the middle of May. He was in luck. The grebes laid early, and Rowan left Edmonton on 19 May. In Winnipeg he had a quick powwow with Alex Lawrence. In Toronto he met Harkness, lunched with Fleming, and measured dowitchers. The kindly Fleming, a wealthy man, persuaded him to accept a gift of cash towards the purchase of important books in England. Rowan then went to Ottawa, to meet Lloyd and Taverner and measure more dowitchers. The *Empress of Scotland* sailed from Quebec City on 25 May. On board Rowan ran into his old friend and colleague, Charles O'Donoghue.

Enrolled in the graduate program at University College, London, Rowan was soon immersed in histological and library work connected with his junco experiments. It is unknown when and why he decided to abandon the idea of embryological investigations, and there are no references in Rowan's letters or diaries to the change of research topic. Evidently, Rowan carried preserved junco organs, in addition to eared-grebe embryos, in his luggage. Perhaps he meant to show them to Hill.

It is unlikely that Rowan discussed his research plans with Fleming, Lloyd, or Taverner. They had no biological training, and Rowan was too busy inspecting collections and measuring specimens to have the time or inclination to talk about anything else. His conversations with O'Donoghue on board the ocean liner must have persuaded Rowan of the suitability of his migration experiments for doctoral research. Back in England, away from Tory's influence, Rowan rediscovered that both ornithological fieldwork and migration research were perfectly acceptable areas of science. Discussions with his old professors, and with new friends such as Huxley and Landsborough Thomson, further reinforced this idea.

It is no wonder that Rowan had a "most delightful trip to the old country" and "a perfectly wonderful time."[20] This was his first visit home since 1921. He was very busy, but there is evidence that he was exaggerating, as usual, when he wrote, "I had to keep my nose to the grindstone without intermission, working at the college by day and earning my bread and cheese at night."[21] His double shift apparently consisted of doing scientific work during the day and "making cash to live on at nights with the pencil." He bragged to H.M. Laing, "I paid my entire expenses both ways and while over there by drawing."[22] In fact, in London he lived with his younger brother Harry, now a prosperous society physician, and mixed the business of science with fun. He visited with his mother, and other members of his own and Reta's families; he went to concerts and art exhibits with Harry and Kitty. He socialized with Huxley and the Watsons, saw his old friend Witherby, and spent time at the Blakeney Point field station with his beloved Professor Oliver. He lectured to the Zoological Society of London on his migration theory,

> with all the big pots of the biological world over there present. I was guest of honour at a dinner after the meeting and met some of them to talk to. The discussion after the address was worth going over for alone . . . . [I]t was quite a surprise to find that my name was well on the map over there.[23]

In mid-August, Reta arrived, having left the children in Edmonton with Deeda. The trip, by rail and ship (the SS *Minnedosa*), gave her a much-needed break from child rearing on a shoestring. She spent one month enjoying the luxury of the family home; the fact that she spent the weekends with Bill added to her pleasure. The Rowans sailed home from Southampton on 17 September, arriving in Edmonton ten days later. There, much to their relief, they found their children had escaped a polio epidemic. Some of their friends did not fare so well.

Rowan delved into his 1927–1928 experiments with renewed vigour. The encouragement of his British colleagues, and the promise of a forty-five-pound grant from the Royal Society, meant he could expand the junco research and deal with issues he had not been able to address before. So, once again, Rowan trapped migrating juncos. He caught 120 between 21 September and 6 October, and placed most of them in the large experimental aviary. Originally Rowan planned to use arc lights, ordered from Germany. They were to provide "real light, ultra violet and all," but did not arrive by the start of the experiments.[24] As an alternative, he decided to use "frosted electric bulbs of the ordinary kind, but totalling 1,050 watts in the place of the former 400 watts."[25] The experiments were conducted from 2 November 1927 to 9 January 1928 and were similar to the earlier ones. More intense illumination resulted, however, in more uniform gonadal development than had been observed in previous years.

With a larger number of birds, Rowan was able to do additional experiments. In January 1928, two groups of experimentals, with gonads artificially enlarged during the fall, were subjected to light deprivation. By using wooden shutters, Rowan was able to restrict the light of one group gradually, the other group was subjected to a sudden reduction of light — from fifteen to nine hours. Rowan found that while the gonads (in both groups) decreased significantly, they did not reach the winter minimum as the control birds did. Then Rowan took two other groups of juncos to cages housed on the top floor of his home at 11142 86th Avenue and exposed them to dim artificial light (a two-candle-power electric bulb) after sunset. One group was allowed to roost in peace, while the other was compelled to exercise at dusk by means of a motor-powered travelling bar "that swept the single perch, food and watertroughs, and floor at intervals of twenty seconds."[26]

The gradually lengthened exercise periods noticeably increased the size of the birds' gonads. Rowan compared the results to those achieved by more powerful artificial light in his previous experiments. He concluded that the important factor in gonad recrudescence was not simply the direct action of "light *qua* light," but the "activity in which the light induced the birds to engage." Moreover, the histological examination of the testes, ovaries, thyroids, parathyroids, and suprarenals proved, that artificial recrudescence in the late fall not only enlarged the testes, but also induced sperm formation. Rowan noted that there was no observable correlation between changes in the glands other than the gonads and the migration period,[27] but for reasons that are unclear, he neglected to study the pituitary gland.

There are no entries in Rowan's diary-cum-field notebook between 5 November 1927 and 2 April 1928. During this period Rowan was conducting his experiments and writing parts of his doctoral thesis. Immersed as he was in his work, he rejoiced to hear of Tory's resignation from the university to become full-time president of the National Research Council of Canada. There was optimism in the air — promise of an improvement in university affairs, and the prospect of advancement, pay increase, and recognition of hard work. In 1927 Rowan was elected, no doubt on the basis of his recent publications, into the "sacred rank of membership of the [American Ornithologists' Union]."[28]

By the spring of 1928, Rowan had written up most of the results of his experiments, and contemplated another quick trip to England to finish his histologic work. The D.Sc. was decidedly within reach. Setting off from Edmonton for a second summer's work at University College on 5 May 1928, Rowan took a different route than he had in the past. He planned to sail from New York City instead of Quebec City, hoping to convince some American scientists to fund part of his research. En route, he stopped in Winnipeg for a visit with Lawrence, as usual. He spent a day talking about hormones and ultraviolet light with John Beatty at McGill University, and arrived in Boston on 10 May. There Rowan met Harper, Barbour, and Bent, spent a day with Colonel John Thayer, a famous naturalist, and visited Fred Kennard, a wealthy collector. The visits paid off; Kennard apparently covered some of the cost of Rowan's trip to England, and others offered to help finance his research.[29] Then Rowan went on to New York to meet with T.H.

Morgan, F.M. Chapman, and R.C. Murphy.

Rowan later recalled that he had a "heck of a time in England . . . I had hardly time to breathe and got no fun out of life at all."[30] This was typical Rowan overstatement. While he struggled to finish his thesis work (which included doing laboratory research, illustrations, and the literature review), he most certainly had some fun. His correspondence indicates that he visited with family, friends, and colleagues, attended private luncheons and dinners, and participated in the social and scientific activities of a number of British ornithological organizations.

Greatly relieved to be rid of the thesis work, Rowan returned to Edmonton for the birth on 27 August, of Josephine, who would be the Rowan's last child. During the fall of 1928, Rowan was daily expecting news from University College, London, but was too busy to fret about the delay. He complained, "I never go out in the evening and am at it till 1 and 2 in the morning night after night. My Sundays go the same way as my week days."[31] As always, he stretched the truth for dramatic effect. Reta was even busier. After the birth of Josephine, both Bill and Reta decided the family was now complete. Although Gerdine and Oliver were at school, the house seemed permanently full of children and Reta, painfully thin again, needed rest, help, and adult companionship.

Rowan was too occupied with teaching, administration, and research to be of much use around the house, though he provided food for some of the meals. Neighbours on 86th Avenue often saw Rowan triumphantly carrying ducks home after a good day at Beaverhills Lake. Rowan gutted the birds in the little pantry off the kitchen, examining them for specimen interest. Sometimes they were cooked immediately by Reta, or Bill when he was so inclined, but most of the ducks and other game birds were hung for the winter from the second-floor balcony, outside Gerdine's room, to be fetched down for a special evening meal. Rowan could rise to the occasion and concoct a wild-bird feast for special visitors. Some guests even received a hand-illustrated menu describing the Alberta fare they would be served. Members of the Rowan family still recall Rowan sitting at the head of the table, carving up jackrabbit, buffalo, or game birds.[32]

With Tory's departure from Edmonton, things finally improved at the university. President R.C. Wallace, "a real scientist as well as a gentleman," was now at the helm, and Rowan hoped to initiate long-term changes in the zoology department.[33] In the meantime, short-term changes worked against him. Winnie Hughes was completing her compulsory residency at the University of Chicago, and Rowan had to carry the full teaching load of four courses including laboratory instruction.

Despite a hectic home life and teaching schedule, Rowan was feeling well, charged with energy. He was conducting a minor study of the vitamin D content of the junco's feathers, and planning major work on the American crow. Now, he could sit back, enjoy talking about his research, and receive news of work done by other scientists. In fact, his correspondence during the winter of 1928–1929 reveals that Rowan spent more time discussing scientific research than actually doing it. After the publication of his paper on photoperiodism in 1926, Rowan received letters of praise from American, British, and other European scientists. These included zoologist Frank R. Lillie, ecologist W.C. Allee, and F.C. Koch, chairman of the Department of Physiological Chemistry and Pharmacology, all of the University of Chicago; geneticist Leon J. Cole of the University of Wisconsin; F.A.E. Crew of the animal-breeding research department at the University of Edinburgh; and G.J. Van Oordt from Rijks University, Utrecht, Holland. In years to come, these scientists were to be Rowan's staunch supporters.

Other scientists who took their cue from Rowan's pioneering research soon joined the rank of Rowan's correspondents, including Canadian-born Thomas H. Bissonnette, then at Trinity College, Hartford, Connecticut. Later there would be considerable competition between the two scientists, and Bissonnette would maintain that he had started working on the effect of light on gonads before Rowan had. A letter from Hughes to Rowan dispels any such claims, however. In early January 1929, after a trip to New York, Hughes wrote, "met a fellow [Bissonnette] in New York who was working with effect of light on bird gonads — getting his idea from you."[34]

Rowan also received the recognition of his Alberta colleagues. He was elected president of the University Science Association, an organization originally established by Tory. In his Presidential Address, given in October 1928, Rowan discussed his ideas concerning the future of zoology at the University of Alberta.

Summarizing some of the major changes in zoology in the 1920s, he discussed particular difficulties at the university, just then entering "a new epoch in its history."[35]

Rowan was vocal in his condemnation of the modern approach of presenting a "smattering of many allied topics and without a firm foundation in any. Such a course might be . . . suitable where students have lots of time on their hands for accessory reading [as they did in Britain] and can be examined on this as well as the set course." It was obviously not useful for Canadian students who, in the absence of government grants, had to spend their five months of vacation making money to subsidize their studies. Instead, according to the old system, Rowan proposed to give them a "sound foundation in the fundamentals" of morphology and histology.[36] Rowan was farsighted enough to see that in general courses there are inevitable overlaps, and some students "get dosed with chromosomes in three different departments and they get virtually the same doses and of similar dilution." He called for a reevaluation of the curriculum, for improvements in the science library, and stressed the need for a good university museum.[37]

In mid-December 1928, Julian Huxley and A. Landsborough Thomson (who, with J.P. Hill, constituted Rowan's doctoral examination committee), unofficially informed Rowan that he had been recommended for the D.Sc. According to the rules of the University of London, however, the doctoral degree could not be conferred on a candidate until the thesis had been published, in whole or in part, to the satisfaction of the examiners.[38] Rowan chose to publish in *Proceedings of the Boston Society of Natural History*, the journal that had published his 1926 paper on photoperiodism. The editors agreed to publish the thesis without delay.[39]

"Experiments in Bird Migration I: Manipulation of the Reproductive Cycle: Seasonal Histological Changes in the Gonads. (Thesis approved for the degree of Doctor of Science in the University of London) by William Rowan," appeared in October 1929. It firmly established Rowan as an original thinker and a pioneer of experimental ornithology. Taverner called it an "epoch making paper as it opens up a whole new field of investigation and throws light upon the obscure motivating mechanics of the development of migratory instinct." Rowan's paper was even mentioned in the *Saturday Evening Post*, and "so achieved considerable advertisement for

Canadian scientists and increased scientific prestige in the popular as well as scientific world."[40] Harrison F. Lewis, who reviewed it in the *Canadian Field-Naturalist*, praised Rowan "for the production of a most useful, stimulating and outstanding paper."[41]

The 1928–1929 academic year was an auspicious one for charting the future course of the University of Alberta zoology department. Rowan was confident that the new president would support advanced teaching and research, and provide funds for the departmental library. Rowan hoped for promotion and better pay. With his D.Sc. expected any day, he could consolidate his position at the university and in the scientific community. The future seemed full of promise in early 1929, but on 4 February a badly shaken Rowan wrote: "Poor old Harrold died this morning in the Flower Hospital, New York, of Meningitis, following a mastoid, itself an outcome of flu. What a rotten place the old Point will be after this."[42]

In the weeks following the bad news, he carried on with his teaching and research. He lectured on wildlife and its protection at Calgary, Lethbridge, and Medicine Hat. He may have undertaken these trips to take his mind of the loss of Harrold, but every bird he collected on the way reminded Rowan of his friend. Francis Point at Beaverhills Lake also changed physically at this time. Rising water levels altered the shoreline. Birds still stopped there in large numbers, but it was no longer the wonderful place it had been.

Rowan's home life was to change as well. Having five children had taken its toll on Reta, who was frankly afraid of becoming pregnant again. This created a new tension in a relationship already strained by an increasing lack of communication. Night after night, long before Bill finished his reading and writing in the smoke-filled second-floor study, Reta collapsed into exhausted sleep. When she wanted to talk, Rowan would jokingly tell her that she had the brains of a chipmunk, then escape into the field or his study.[43] In contrast to Bill, who continued to engage in many enjoyable activities, Reta had little time for herself. Though she had exhibited artistic talent at a young age, was nurtured in her artistic pursuits by loving parents, and had trained with private tutors and teachers, she had practically no chance for self-expression.

In 1929, Rowan planned other experiments. Hughes had returned to work as assistant professor of zoology, and this meant that he no longer had to deal with all the routine jobs and could devote more time to fieldwork. This was a blessing, as at this time Rowan was introduced to a new area: the extensive muskegs west of the Pembina River. In years to come, the region was to be a new refuge from his hardworking daily existence.

Rowan's previous encounters with muskegs (near Lake of the Woods, Lac la Biche, Fort Smith, and Belvedere) paled in comparison to his post-1929 encounters. Neither the difficult walking, the extremes of heat or cold, nor the ever-present insects would ever deter Rowan from frequenting the muskegs. He dismissed the arduous walking with a facetious remark ("as a cure for obesity it is without a rival"), and began to love this uneven, soggy land which felt "like a spring mattress" with "plants growing over ground from which there is practically no drainage." Rowan admitted that the country could be dangerous, and "one never ceases to be obsessed with the idea that one may at any moment fall through." He respected the muskegs, where familiarity bred no contempt.[44]

Rowan was introduced to the new region by Frank Farley who had, Lister recalled, "investigated the muskegs between the Pembina and Athabasca rivers just west of Fawcett, Alberta and had found the terrain and avifauna much the same as that beyond the Athabasca," further west.[45] Relieved to find an area where nothing reminded him of the loss of Harrold, Rowan was keen to go, ostensibly "after eggs of the loon (for embryology) and [of the] greater yellowlegs."[46] At the end of May 1929, with a collecting permit in hand, Rowan, Farley, and young Arthur Twomey, boarded the train for Fawcett.[47]

Rowan noted that the east bank of the Pembina, "good grain country, interspersed with small muskegs," had been settled, but there were few farms to the west of the river, an area of lakes, ridges, and extensive muskegs. Rowan, Farley, and Twomey followed the wagon trail meandering north, west, and then south to the Athabasca River. By midday they had set up camp beside a lake.[48] They saw Bonaparte gulls nesting on trees and loons on small islands in the lakes. Greater yellowlegs, yapping at the intruders, rose from the trees. Sandhill cranes called in flight; their buglelike cries drawing attention to their deep wing beats and extended necks. The cranes could also be seen on their nests on the soaking muskeg.[49]

Migrating birds appeared daily, settling into their nesting territory. Mosquitoes were thick, the muskeg water so icy that it made "one's feet quite numb after a few minutes."[50] There were also deadfalls, a "terrible tangle to navigate on foot."[51] The difficulties notwithstanding (they were not to stop Rowan in any case), there were numerous first-class opportunities to collect and take photographs. Rowan even enjoyed the "high adventure" of attempting to find the nests of the greater yellowlegs.[52]

Rowan soon informed Taverner, "My craze for loon embryos is because I believe I have discovered tooth vestiges in this fowl. If correct, it will be a wonderful discovery, a real thriller, so many embryologists having hunted for them without success."[53] Though bird teeth remained scarce, he later remarked, "we have found an attractive spot, the best of company and unlimited opportunities to observe the habits of birds for ourselves." Looking back, Rowan admitted that he would never have "followed this path with much persistence had it not been for a certain Alberta ferryman, of the name of Joe Dawkins."[54] The English-born Dawkins was a short, stocky, unassuming fellow, with a friendly face and a trace of a British accent. In the years to come, Joe's company, good cooking, sensible observations and comments on people, politics, and life in general were to become part of the attraction of a trip to the muskeg country. Rowan was simply delighted with the initial productive expedition, with the discovery of a new wilderness.

In a happy frame of mind, he returned home to spend some weeks with the family at Seba Beach, Lake Wabamun, a pleasant holiday spot consisting of "a string of cottages about a mile long on the shore and a few stores on the hill."[55] This was an area frequented by members of the university faculty. There were friends for Reta and the children, and for Rowan, coots, grebes, bitterns, ducks, and common terns. The lake was full of jackfish and they were biting well. While Rowan studied birds, collected spiders, or hunted for leeches, minnows, and perch, the children played on the sandy shore.

The family was to return to Seba Beach, but the area was tame compared to the muskegs. Rowan escaped whenever he could and returned to Fawcett on his own, or with his son Julian, or Lister, to observe nature, feast on Joe's cooking, and write and think. The muskegs, with their inherent biological interest, drew Rowan the scientist, but Rowan the man and the artist also learned to love the muskegs for their variety and beauty. In periods of personal crisis, or during and after the dark days of the war, he came to appreciate the fact that human intruders were rare, and "one may spend weeks in complete solitude and uninterrupted peace." It was a "world within a world," he wrote, that exerted a "constant and undescribable fascination for certain curious specimens of humanity . . . a lasting lure."[56]

11

As the Crow Flies

IN A BOOK MANUSCRIPT written for his children in 1936–1937, Rowan set out to tell "the entire story of the Crows from A to Z. Except, that in Science there is no Z. Nothing in Science ever reaches finality and I am sure the Crows haven't."[1] After having spent seven years researching this species, Rowan was well qualified to write about it, and, as he suspected, the crow experiments never reached their projected "finality." Rowan's work on crows was in turn challenging, frustrating, and amusing. It was also time-consuming and costly. There were, however, many compensations. Rowan was able to prove certain aspects of his original hypothesis (by inducing reverse migration), publicize scientific research in Western Canada, and foster cooperation among scientists and the general public.

The story for the "Juvenile Rowans," Rowan recalled, was "one of adventure born of a youthful fancy" at Blakeney Point. After his discharge from the Royal Scottish Regiment, while "recuperating in the sunshine and breezes of the seashore," he watched migrating shorebirds "going by in a continuous stream." The birds were "bound from the north pole to the south . . . for no good reason as far as anyone could tell." Nobody could explain what made them "wear out their constitutions and plumages merely to pass the winter in some spot probably just like Norfolk only thousands of miles away." While he could provide no answer at the time, Rowan had a recurring thought "that it would be an inordinately good joke if one could make these misguided little zealots travel the wrong way and go back to the north for the winter, instead of proceeding south."[2]

A decade later, in Alberta, thousands of kilometres west of Norfolk, Rowan completed his migration research on the junco, and was ready to experiment on the more conspicuous American crow. Housing and feeding hundreds of large, hungry birds was expensive, and in 1926 Rowan applied to the Royal Society for a substantial grant to support this research. In his detailed proposal Rowan explained that he planned to trap nearly one thousand crows "so as to have from 400 to 500 survivors for examination and periodic release." To keep his work out of H.M. Tory's sight, Rowan had decided to rent a barn for the birds at Camrose, instead of constructing a new aviary. Rowan hoped to keep the location secret until he could advertise (in the newspapers, on the radio, and in the bulletin of the university's Department of Extension) the impending release of the crows, and invite the public to shoot the birds. As an inducement, he would offer a reward "for the return of the banded crows killed furthest from the point of liberation on a day to be stated." Rowan planned to schedule the official crow shoot two days after the actual release to give the birds time to travel. He would then wait for the information, map the capture points, and "get a definite idea as to the direction taken by them. If the results come up to expectation we should then have tangible evidence that these birds, at least travel north under stimulation of appropriate light conditions."[3]

Obtaining funds was difficult, and Rowan postponed the project. In early 1928, he inquired once again about major funding. Laid up after having driven a spike through his own foot, Rowan sent applications to the Royal Society and to American organizations such as the Joseph Henry Fund, the Elizabeth Thompson Science Fund, and the Bache Fund. While the Royal Society and the Joseph Henry Fund turned down Rowan's requests, he obtained three hundred dollars from the Thompson Fund and five hundred dollars from the Bache Fund. He also received unspecified amounts of private funding from Boston-area naturalists John Thayer and John Phillips.[4]

As Rowan wrote facetiously to Grinnell, he originally hoped to raise $2,500 "to make a flock of these black jokers go north in November when all good crows should be going south."[5] In 1929, however, without adequate funding, he had to modify his plans. Instead of keeping the crows in Camrose and paying someone else to carry out the experiment, Rowan would do the research in Edmonton. With Tory gone, Rowan did not have to keep the birds in his backyard, and housed them in huge cages along the North Saskatchewan River, west of the High Level Bridge.[6]

In his amusing and popular account of the crow chases, Lister recalled:

> The site chosen for the experiments again showed Professor Rowan's flair for the dramatic. In those days the street cars as well as trains crossed over the top deck of the bridge while other traffic and pedestrians used the lower deck still very high above the aviary. There was much comment from the time the first crows arrived and when lighting started there were few people in this city who were not aware of Professor Rowan and his birds. The crows were fed on cats and dogs from the city pound supplemented by fish scraps from the fish stores and stale bread from the bakeries.[7]

Rowan's choice of location was, indeed, a clever one. The large, noisy crows in their illuminated cages, provided people with free entertainment and increased their awareness of scientific research. This worked in Rowan's favour when it came time to recruit volunteers to round up and trap crows; the "crow drives" were held as far away as Beaverhills Lake. Moreover, by requesting food scraps, he involved large companies and individual citizens in promoting research. So, Doc Rowan's crow experiments became a community affair, and rumours of his adventures with the wily crows reached far beyond the university community. It is impossible to estimate how many Alberta youngsters first became curious about science upon hearing about the crow research. Some of these children are known to have become biologists in later years.[9]

By modifying his original research plans, Rowan saved time, energy, and enough money to buy his first car. It was a secondhand Model T Ford, referred to affectionately (though the nicknames were not very original) as the Tin Lizzie or the Crow Ford. Where Rowan learned to drive is not known. Perhaps one of his colleagues showed him how to shift gears. On 14 August 1929, Rowan and Lister ventured by car to Beaverhills Lake; it was the first of their countless car trips on slippery, poorly graded roads all over Alberta. Lister recalled that in the beginning neither he nor Rowan knew that cars needed oil in addition to gasoline. With admirable British understatement he also wrote, "we were sometimes stranded. The radiator seemed to be forever boiling, "and was often refilled with "soupy water" from a nearby ditch.[9] During the following decades, stories of Doc Rowan and his driving escapades circulated beyond the boundaries of Edmonton. Rowan remained an erratic driver all his life, and his succession of Tin Lizzies were maltreated, neglected, and driven on rough roads in all sorts of weather. It's no wonder that Rowan, and a variety of companions, became acquainted with ditches throughout Alberta, as the car often got mired and had to be abandoned and pulled out later by a farmer's horse. Rowan accepted the difficulties encountered on his driving trips with amazingly good grace. Most of the time he only had himself to blame.

It has long been known by anyone familiar with the species, that crows are intelligent birds. Rowan and Lister soon learned that catching them was a difficult undertaking. Crows tend to roost in large numbers at certain favourite locations. They are omnivorous, curious, and adept at escaping from unlikely places. Rowan had been cautioned by farmers and scientists about trying to capture "the brute" (that is, the crow), but he dismissed their warning until his first crow-catching trip. After having identified a number of potentially good areas for capturing crows in nets and traps, Rowan and Lister found that in fact there was neither an ideal location in which to trap these birds, nor an ideal food with which to bait them. In places where thousands of crows were known to roost, only a few were caught. Others ate the bait in the traps and departed unharmed. Sometimes the crows got injured or, for no apparent reason, died. Undaunted, Rowan and Lister went after the crows with the sporadic help of relatives, colleagues, and friends. The crow catchers had to have strong stomachs to stand the stench of the bait (consisting of animal carcasses, rotten eggs, and bread soaked in alcohol), and enough energy to keep up with Rowan. Edmonton-area farmers were often entertained by the sight of the professor (in a pair of shorts or an old suit), stalking across the stubble on his short, muscular legs, followed by a motley crowd of children and adults.

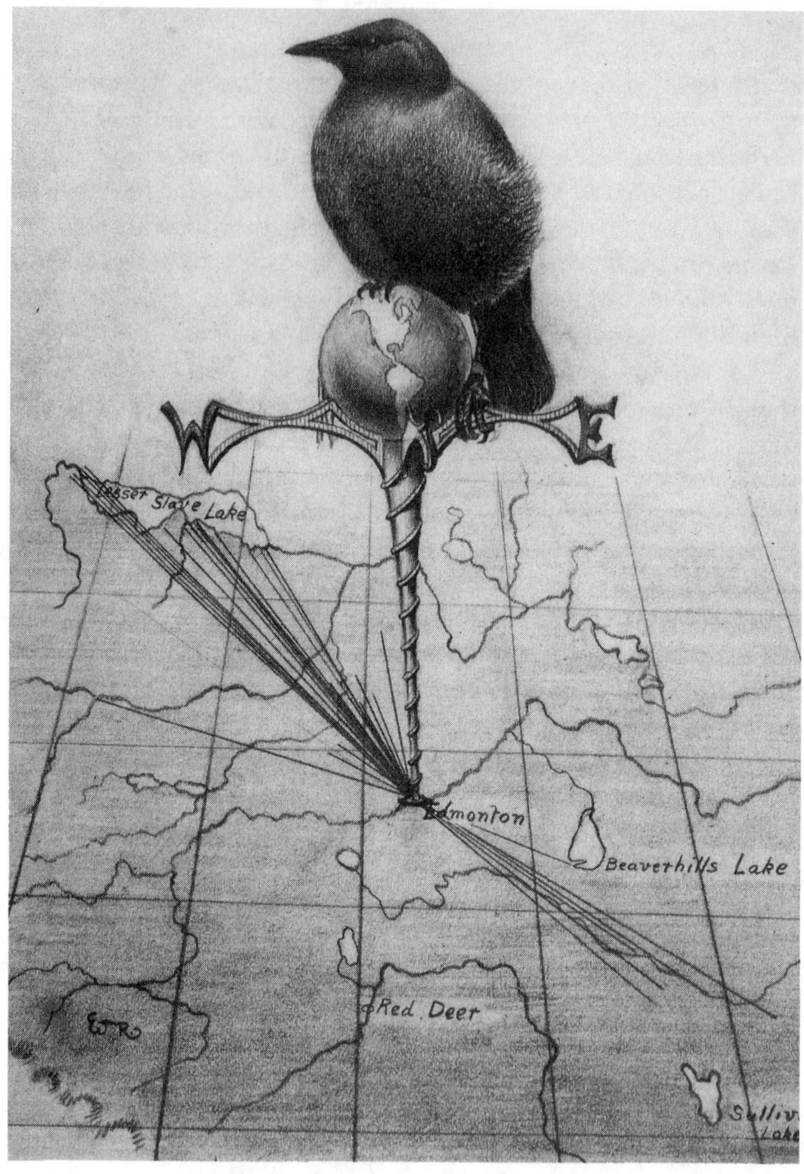

14. "On Top of the World," Christmas, 1929. This drawing depicts the centre of Rowan's first migration experiments with crows in 1929. *Drawing by William Rowan. University of Alberta Archives.*

In spite of Rowan's persistent efforts, the crafty crows did not flock to the traps in huge numbers. Trapping crows may have seemed amusing in retrospect, but it was not much fun and certainly Rowan was far from successful at it. What was he to make of crows that would eat the bait, but somehow manage to leave the traps? Or of the thousands of crows that would roost within 150 metres of the well-baited traps, but fly off without investigating the bait? The city crows were no better. A few hardy ones even resisted asphyxiation. Once, trying a new method of capture, Rowan and Lister carried "half a dozen buckets and a couple of pounds of sulphur and glowing coal" to the base of a crow roost near the university medical building. Lister even held "one dish of sulphur within 18 inches of [a crow] for ten minutes and all it did was to cough periodically. It showed no signs of dropping." It is hardly surprising that Rowan noted, "Don't know what to make of the situation."[10] This was a phrase that was to recur in his notes and letters with monotonous frequency. While crows seemed to avoid the traps, a variety of other species (such as magpies, merlins, and long-eared owls), did not.

Rowan hoped to catch about four hundred crows in 1929 to "castrate, inject, etc.," but, foiled in most of his attempts, had to settle for a smaller sample. In a press bulletin, issued in early November by the University of Alberta Department of Extension, Rowan stated that 140 crows "were successfully taken by various means .... They are in first class condition and are keeping fit."[11] The information was misleading. Rowan started off with 140 crows, but ten birds escaped, a few died from injuries, and others were sacrificed to periodic sampling. At the end of the experiments, only eighty-three crows (fourteen controls and sixty-nine experimentals) remained in good condition. The crow investigations followed the model of the basic junco ones, conducted from 1924 to 1928. The birds were kept in separate, large flying cages, "100 feet long, 15 feet wide and 6 feet high." Experimental crows received artificial illumination from twenty-five five-hundred-watt bulbs (a total of 12,500 watts) during the 28 September to 9 November period. Initially seven and a half minutes of extra light was provided for the birds, but after 20 October this was reduced to daily increments of five minutes of extra light.

Rowan decided to release the crows prior to the Thanksgiving holiday (11 November 1929). Then, in the press bulletin, he asked the public, two days later, to "join in the crow hunt," and gave detailed instructions concerning the packaging and mailing of crow carcasses. He even promised a five-dollar prize for every five United States government bird bands returned.[12] Less than a week after the release, Rowan wrote to a friend,

> We are just getting in the first records and they are very interesting as far as they go .... Apparently all experimentals have stuck to the usual migration line of the crow, N–W + S–E. One has been shot 50 miles S–E, and what the explanation of this anomaly is, heaven only knows.[13]

In another eight weeks, a dejected Rowan wrote, "The Crow news is not so good." Because of the extensive muskeg northwest of Edmonton, he had received few records of sightings or specimens.[14] Just the same, Rowan discussed his results in "Experiments in Bird Migration II: Reversed Migration," published in the *Proceedings of the National Academy of Sciences* in 1930.

Rowan was never one to admit defeat, or even negative results, and now used the available statistics to the best effect. He wrote that upon release, fifty-four of the experimental crows left the vicinity of the aviaries. Of these, twenty-eight birds were killed, and twenty-six remained unaccounted for in mid-May 1930. Some of the fourteen controls stayed around Edmonton, while others departed for the southeast. Rowan was convinced that the geographic location of Edmonton, too near the muskegs, contributed to the low returns. But, as the preliminary results confirmed his original hypothesis, he was confident that by further modifying his research plan he could achieve statistically more significant results. Rowan had intended to trap large numbers of crows all along. While it was not practical to conduct the experiments south of Edmonton, he saw no reason why he could not release the birds, after the experiments, from a location southeast of Edmonton.

In early 1930, Rowan applied for a grant to the National Research Council of Canada (NRC). It is not known who persuaded him to apply. It was the wrong agency to fund Rowan's type of research for a number of reasons; the chief ones were that the NRC was dedicated to promoting utilitarian research, and his old enemy,

Henry Marshall Tory, was its president. While Rowan was well aware of this, he may have underestimated Tory's power. Perhaps having received new grants (from the Royal Society, and American organizations concerned with basic research), he felt more confident and this led him to disregard Tory's animosity and influence. So Rowan submitted a major application to the NRC, but applied nowhere else. This was an error that he soon came to regret.

After a decade of teaching and working under adverse conditions, Rowan must have realized that in Canada money for all but practical research was always scarce. He may not have known, however, that this was because Canadian science had been "guided by an entrepreneurial scientific ideology," brought to this country by the original Scottish settlers.[15] In the late 1920s, this "entrepreneurial ideology" still influenced the funding of Canadian science. Rowan often mentioned the lack of government money for basic biological research in his correspondence with Taverner, but, in his enthusiasm and naïvety, Rowan paid no heed to the well-known fact that *all* the scientific departments of the federal government (the Geological Survey, Experimental Farms, and the Biological Board) had been established with practical aims in mind. In Canada, utilitarian science was supreme, and the NRC was no exception.[16]

In early 1930, Rowan joined the ranks of Canadian scientists who continued to encounter discouragements and difficulties and even indifference to pure research. Tory's presidency of the NRC further exacerbated the already difficult situation many scientists faced across the country. Tory was renowned as a vocal advocate of applied research, a firm believer in the usefulness of science. He was later described as a man who "tended to favour the practical short-term problems that would make a noise; among the long-term projects, he favoured those with a staggering pay-off, preferably in tens of millions of dollars."[17] Tory's attitude towards science exemplified the prevailing Canadian one. Unfortunately for Rowan, Tory was in a powerful position where he could prevent the funding of basic research and promote the projects of his choice, mostly those that involved applied research. A careful perusal of the list of projects funded by the NRC from 1920 to 1935 shows, however, that some basic research *was* funded, particularly in Tory's area, the physical sciences.[18]

Because Tory sat ex officio on practically all committees of the

NRC, he could exert pressure on committee members and influence their choice of grant recipients. Tory also heartily disliked Rowan, who was naïve enough to imagine that, after his move from Edmonton to Ottawa, Tory would forgive and forget Rowan's stubbornness in pursuing his own ideas. That he neither forgave nor forgot Rowan's intransigence is evident from a letter Tory wrote in 1932: "during the last two or three years I was in Alberta I gave very little attention to Rowan due to the fact that only elementary work was done in the department."[19] In fact, Tory's last years in Edmonton (1925 to 1928) coincided with those of Rowan's most intense research activity. And while Rowan carried out his early experiments during his spare time in his own backyard, nothing could long remain a secret in a small, closed, university community. Ironically, it was during this period that Rowan's research on the effect of daylight on the reproductive organs of birds put the University of Alberta on the scientific world map. From Tory's letter it is evident, however, that he continued to consider only laboratory work as real science, and chose to disregard Rowan's pioneering investigations and subsequent fame. By ignoring Rowan's ornithological research and the enthusiastic recognition given it by members of the larger scientific community, Tory could maintain that "only elementary work was done" in the university's zoology department. For Tory, Rowan "had reached his limit" as both teacher and researcher.[20] By taking this attitude, Tory could with a clear conscience prevent Rowan from being funded by the NRC, and later destroy the younger man's chances for academic advancement.

In ignorance, Rowan applied to the NRC. He stressed the theoretical importance of his research, and mentioned his previous grants from the Royal Society and several American associations. He pointed out that, as a result of his original work, various universities in North America and in Europe were "actively repeating the experiments." He emphasized that this work, "which was entirely conceived and started in Canada, and which has already been productive of various results entirely new to science, should be continued in the Dominion." Rowan also stated that the experimental work for his proposed investigations would be carried out in the zoology laboratory of the University of Alberta, which, he added, no doubt for Tory's benefit, "is adequately equipped for all the usual types of zoological research work." Rowan did not mention what the useful outcome of his research would be. The fundamental importance of his proposed investigations could not possibly impress Tory. Rowan only asked for $1,905 but he received nothing.[21]

The NRC kept no detailed records of the actual discussions concerning grant applications. The committee meeting minutes reveal only that the committee "agreed that his application be not granted."[22] Reasons for the refusal were not given. At the same time, another proposal, by Professor O.S. Gibbs of Dalhousie University requesting $1,500 "to assist an investigation on uric acid secretion of the bird," was also rejected.[23] By contrast, a proposal by R.C. Dearle, a physicist at the University of Western Ontario, to investigate the "indirect ultra-violet solar radiation and its distribution," received $1,080. Dearle's research was in an area that Tory understood and supported.

Rowan was dejected and fed up and complained volubly about his misfortune to all and sundry. He was further incensed because the late arrival of the letter of refusal caused him to miss the application deadlines of other granting agencies. So Rowan did no research on crows in 1930. Instead, he concentrated on other topics, such as shorebird breeding biology and taxonomy, the egg tooth in the loon, hydras, mammals, and biological cycles. He also wrote numerous letters, several articles, and his first book. Rowan's publications on his migration experiments had already reached scientists in all parts of the world and, as a result, in 1930 his correspondence became more varied, and this permitted him some important exchanges of ideas. Answering the letters could at times be onerous, however. The zoology department still did not have its own secretary, although by this time it shared one with the physiology and entomology departments. Rowan therefore typed most of his own letters in his increasingly cluttered study at home. The clicking keys of his antiquated machine became a steady background noise during all family activities, and was heard, late into most nights, by the children in the nurseries on the floor above.

But life was not all work. In fact, Rowan realized that if he did not spend time doing experiments he could go on collecting trips. He took another holiday with Reta and their five growing children at a rented cottage at Seba Beach. Runtie, as Josephine was known, was by now a toddler. The water was clean, and Rowan could take his older children fishing, or teach them to swim and dive. The children helped him sail the *Reta*, the model boat he had made. The Rowans' friends already included Osman J. and Ella May (Jacoby) Walker, field companions Bill and John MacDonald, and professors E.H. Strickland, A.W. Downs, and W. Hughes. With the 1929 expansion of the university faculty, their circle of friends widened. Ted (E.H.) Gowan, a brilliant Rhodes Scholar from Alberta with a Ph.D. in meteorology from Oxford and his ebullient fiancée Elsie Park (who was to become a successful playwright), joined the group. So did mathematician Frank (E.S.) Keeping, botanist E. Silver Dowding (the future Mrs. Keeping), and biochemist George Hunter and his wife Mary Elizabeth Wyllie (an arts and medicine graduate from Glasgow). O.J. Walker (everyone called him by his initials) and Ted Gowan were enthusiastic outdoorsmen. Hunter, who had an angelic face but, due to a bad hip, was physically handicapped, soon became a friend to both Bill and Reta. He was an outspoken, left-wing radical with a passionate love for literature. Hunter's varied interests made him an ideal companion. He read poetry or discussed world events with Reta, and hunted ducks with Rowan.[24]

On his return from Seba Beach, Rowan found a letter waiting for him from British naturalist Reginald E. Moreau, a botanist by profession and a keen ornithologist by avocation, at the time working at an agricultural research station in East Africa. Moreau asked Rowan to send him reprints of his migration papers and the two began a regular correspondence.[25] Rowan soon informed Moreau that he was primarily interested in "dealing with general principles," and would welcome information on the birds of the equatorial regions. He related his tale of woe about the NRC, and explained, "Being a problem of pure science I suppose it was really foredoomed in such a quarter there being no promise of money making anywhere in it."[26]

Rowan had already discovered that he was more likely to obtain research grants from American than Canadian sources. While he was planning his strategy for raising funds to support his future research, a new opportunity for acquiring fame and for making money presented itself. He would write *The Riddle of Migration*. Earlier that year, in the spring, a British publisher had asked Rowan to write a book on bird migration.[27] Rowan was flattered. He replied that he had already half committed himself to writing a long book for Oxford University Press (this cannot be substantiated, however), but was interested in writing a shorter book "dealing with the possible mechanisms of migration." Always keen to be a pioneer, he believed that such a book would "cover entirely new ground." The project appealed to Rowan, because he felt it could be done with relatively little effort, and the class of reader

> to which the book would cater to would be primarily bird fanatics, since they constitute in themselves quite an extensive market, but it would also aim to rope in the more general reader who might be interested in a straightforward exposition in simple English of the biology of migration.[28]

The attractive offer notwithstanding, Rowan eventually decided to publish a small "dollar book," dealing with the *biology* of migration, with Williams and Wilkins, an American publisher. He proposed to illustrate the book, in pencil or ink, himself.[29]

The timing was perfect. For the first time in over five years, Rowan was not actually engaged in time-consuming research. To his publisher he explained:

> In view of the fact that parts of my experiments, or points arising directly out of them, are being repeated or elaborated by over a dozen departments of physiology, biochemistry, and zoology the book might conceivably have an added sale in strictly scientific in addition to popular circles.[30]

By mid-January 1931 Rowan had a contract promising him ten-percent royalties for *The Riddle of Migration*. In the end, warming to the subject, he could not restrict the text to the dollar-book length of thirty thousand words, and the resulting volume had to be priced at two dollars in the United States and Canada. The book was favourably reviewed in both the popular and scientific presses. It made Rowan practically a household name in Canada, and famous in naturalist circles around the world.

By the time the manuscript was sent to the publisher in May 1931, Rowan knew he would be awarded the necessary funds for large-scale crow investigations (four hundred dollars from the Elizabeth Thompson Fund and one thousand dollars from the United States National Research Council). He wrote to Moreau,

> I shall be castrating and injecting bunches of [crows] and doing various other things. Crew (the geneticist) in Edinburgh, Koch at Chicago (Prof. of physiology) and Oscar Riddle, the Cold Springs Harbor pigeon fellow, biochemist and geneticist, are all having a finger in the pie and providing me with some of their own pet extracts, so I ought to be well fixed. I am afraid my efforts are threatening to become too highbrow for ornithology. I see Witmer Stone didn't even bother to notice my attempt with crows in the Auk. I should have thought it might have been of some interest to bird people even if not a success for certain.[31]

Moreau's reply is particularly interesting because, like self-trained ornithologists in all parts of the world, Moreau felt he was "devoid of biological training." Determined to remedy this, he read a wide range of scientific texts. As a result he became "painfully conscious of the narrowness and amateurishness of so much ornithological work." He deplored the fact that hardly "any workers on birds have even at intervals turned their eyes to biology as a whole or even to the wider implications of their own studies." Witmer Stone was at the time editor of the *Auk*, and his neglect of Rowan's experiments was an excellent example of this attitude.[32]

Rowan seized every available opportunity to publicize his research. While attending an international conference on biological cycles in July 1931, he gave an interview to a *New York Times* journalist. The resulting article carried the following title: "TO USE 1,000 CROWS IN EVOLUTION TEST." Subtitles informed the reader, "Alberta Scientist Hopes to Prove Acquired Characteristics Are Transmittable and Habits Altered by Light," "Dr. Rowan Finds Artificial Sun Baths Lead Birds to Fly North in Winter," and "Gland Seen as Cause." The article reported "Professor Rowan must have the crows early this Fall. With them in hand, he hopes that he may be able to adduce some evidence in support of the Lamarckian concept of evolution."[33]

That Rowan wanted to "adduce some evidence in support of the

Lamarckian concept" must have come as a surprise to most of his friends. It is true that in some of his early correspondence with Taverner and others he mentioned the subject of evolution, even the Lamarckian hypothesis (the inheritance of acquired characteristics), but this was always in a general sense, and never in connection with his experimental work. Certainly his early papers offered no proof of his interest in the subject. In fact, the first clear evidence of it can be found in *The Riddle of Migration*, where Rowan focused on the immediate stimulus for migration, and, by using the example of the Lapland longspur, also provided "a scenario" for the evolution of migration. This scenario indicates that Rowan made certain assumptions derived from the Lamarckian view of evolution.

Rowan was not alone in reconsidering the Lamarckian hypothesis. In the 1920s, many field naturalists and experimental biologists were still Lamarckian in orientation because of their incomplete understanding of the mechanisms of evolutionary biology.[34] Undercurrents of Lamarckism remained so common that migration theories developed as late as the 1940s revealed a certain ignorance of how natural selection operates, and vestiges of Lamarckism were still present in university biology courses in the mid-1960s.[35] Perhaps Rowan only toyed with the idea of Lamarckism. There is no evidence he believed in it seriously. His son Julian and some of his former students are still convinced that, in discussing the hypothesis, Rowan often played the devil's advocate. Perhaps so. It is highly likely, then, that in his interview with the *New York Times* journalist, Rowan simply referred to the Lamarckian hypothesis to grab the reader's attention.

As one reads Rowan's crow notebooks, field notes, and correspondence with other scientists, it becomes evident that crow catching (using gopher traps, Jack Miner traps, and large nets) continued to be an erratic and onerous undertaking. From 1 August to 8 September 1931, only 403 birds were caught at Beaverhills Lake. Kept at a farmhouse before their transfer to the cages in Edmonton, the birds were fed a variety of scraps. By the middle of September, 101 of the trapped crows were dead, and Rowan noted with consternation that the post mortems indicated nothing was organically wrong: "the fault has probably been in the food supply being inadequate earlier on."[36] It soon became obvious that Rowan would have to expand his crow catching activities in order to reach his goal of trapping one thousand crows. He located crow roosts around the university and in the Bonnie Doon district. He involved friends, relatives, and colleagues in crow catching, but the crows eluded them.[37] On 8 September, a disappointed Rowan noted, "this finishes the crow season. It is a waste of time and effort to try for more."[38]

So, in spite of a concerted effort, only half the projected number of crows were trapped, but Rowan still went ahead with the experiments. From his crow notebooks in which he recorded details of the experiments, and which were never published, we know that he divided the birds into eight groups: (1) controls, to receive no lighting and no treatment; (2) controls "A.P.L. 1–40," to receive no lighting but to be given 1 cc of placenta extract (supplied by Collip) every second day starting 11 November 1931; (3) "C. Controls U II-4," a group of crows to be castrated and given 0.5 cc of male urine extract daily (supplied by Koch), no lighting; (4) "C. Controls U II-3," to be castrated and given 0.5 cc of male urine extract daily (supplied by Koch), starting 11 November 1931, no lighting; (5) "C. Controls," to be castrated but receive no lighting and no treatment; (6) "Con. U" controls, to be housed at the university (instead of the crow cages near the High Level Bridge), and to receive daily doses of 0.5 cc of pituitary extract (prepared in the university's biochemistry laboratory), starting 16 November 1931; (7) "C. ex.," that is, "experimental birds (that received light treatment) to be castrated. Not to receive any other treatment"; and (8) "Ex. y.," experimental birds to be castrated, but to receive no other treatment. Experimental birds were to be "Ducoed" — that is they were to have their tails painted yellow with Duco automobile paint.[39]

Rowan obtained the experimental hormone solutions from a variety of sources. F.C. Koch of the University of Chicago sent him the male urine extracts in two different strengths.[40] Rowan's old friend and colleague, J.B. Collip, now at McGill University, sent the placenta extracts, while the pituitary extracts were prepared by two different methods at the University of Alberta biochemistry department. The actual illumination of the experimental crows was done with twenty-two five hundred watt bulbs, beginning 15 October 1931. Two days later Rowan installed a "glimmer light" — a single bulb to be left on for ten minutes after the "main lights" were turned off.[41] Jim Thompson, a local youth, was hired "for feeding, lighting, cleaning and generally attending the crows."[42] On 27 October, after only twelve days of light treatment, some of the experimental crows were removed from the illuminated cages, and castrated by "Mr. Cormie from the government poultry department." Castrating live crows proved to be difficult, but Rowan and Cormie persisted, and with a special instrument made at the university's machine shop, successfully operated on more than two dozen crows during the following week.

Hormone treatment of the control birds began on 11 November. In the Crow Notebooks Rowan wrote: "The castrated birds are receiving .5 cc [Koch's extract] per day; the non-castrated, 1 cc [Collip's extract] every second day. The castrates are in two groups, one of 5, the other of 10, receiving the 2 different extracts." Injecting birds was easy, but catching them turned out to be a time-consuming and tiring occupation. Rowan planned to liberate the birds after two weeks of hormone treatment, and on 23 November, in good weather, began to get ready to crate the crows prior to flying them by rented plane to Medicine Hat. First he killed sample birds and examined their gonads. As expected, the experimental males had "huge testes," the female "a large ovary with well developed follicle," and the capon "was in excellent shape without any vestige of gonad and all traces of the [castration] wound gone." Later in the day, the tails of all the experimental birds were painted yellow, and Rowan noted that the "colour shows up well even in electric light."

All was ready for the 24 November flight when Rowan learned that Captain Burbridge, the pilot, was ill, and the weather became too foggy to fly. Thoroughly upset, Rowan made an arrangement with the airport to be phoned "the instant the weather looks possible, when the crows will be packed at top speed and we shall be off." Rowan also noted that he had been offered a four-seater Fokker "at the same figure, that would carry two passengers and three crates of crows." The crates contained 262 crows and were labelled A, B, and C. Crate A contained 152 experimentals, crate B the 55 controls, and crate C 55 others. This latter group was made up of 22 experimental capons, 15 control capons treated with Koch's extract, 3 control capons given no extract, 7 controls given pituitary extract, and 8 controls treated with placenta extract — all to be liberated at different locations.43

The story of the crow flight is of special interest, because it turned out to be an important stage in Rowan's crow experiments. It was also the first commercial flight undertaken by Grant McConachie, who later became president of Canadian Pacific Airlines. Apparently McConachie purchased the blue Fokker monoplane with $2,500 borrowed from his uncle only a short while before this historic flight, and the transportation of Rowan and his crows was the first commission McConachie's company, Independent Airways, received. Ironically, while McConachie's first customer was impatiently waiting to take off with his precious cargo, the young pilot was "circling the Edmonton airport putting in the last twenty-five minutes of his mandatory fifty hours" of flight time to obtain his licence.[44]

Rowan's own notes do not refer to his having to wait for the pilot, but do mention the upset stomach that kept him in bed on 25 November. As had happened so often before, the stressfulness of the situation had caused Rowan to become physically ill. After all, the anxiously anticipated flight would help Rowan prove or disprove his original experimental hypothesis concerning bird migration. By the time the sky cleared on 26 November and Rowan received the go-ahead from the airport, he was in fine fettle. He rounded up his helpers (Strickland, Lister, and Thompson), crated the crows, kissed his wife goodbye, and drove to the airdrome. There Rowan and McConachie had their photographs taken for publicity, loaded the plane, and, with Professor Strickland, took off.[45]

Rowan had originally hoped to get to Medicine Hat with the experimental crows, but by the time the plane approached the small railway station at Hackett, about 160 kilometres southeast of Edmonton, it was mid-afternoon. The three men were freezing in the unheated plane (also Rowan had apparently eaten nothing for over forty-eight hours), and they had to return to Edmonton before nightfall "as the plane had no night equipment." Rowan asked the pilot to land so they could release "all the birds together to avoid further stops." The birds, observed Rowan, "looked very dishevelled and sick," but soon recovered and scattered "into the northwest quadrant." Rowan, McConachie, and Strickland stayed only

15. Releasing experimental crows at Hackett, Alberta, November 26, 1931. This was the first commercial flight undertaken by pilot Grant McConachie, who later became president of Canadian Pacific Airlines. *University of Alberta Archives.*

EXPERIMENTS IN MIGRATION
1931
Loading crows at Edmonton for the southward flight, Nov. 26, 1931
(Pilot McConachie and Dr. Rowan)

With many thanks for your interest and assistance

16. Crow research "thank you" card, 1931.
University of Alberta Archives.

long enough to drink coffee and warm themselves in a nearby farmhouse before taking off for Edmonton. Due to the prevailing tail winds, the return to Edmonton was much faster than Rowan expected and, in fact, he could have well afforded "at least a second stop in order to turn all the experimentals out by themselves."[46] By then it was too late. From the circling plane, Rowan and Strickland watched as the crows settled on straw piles, their tails shining "proudly like burnished gold in the evening sunlight."[47]

Now that the crows were freed, news of their release could be broadcast, but to prevent immediate hunting, the exact locality was not disclosed. The jubilant Rowan then celebrated the crow release with a dinner, paid for with money from his research grant, at the MacDonald Hotel. But Rowan had been chilled to the bone on the airplane, and was soon in bed with pleurisy. "Perhaps it was as well," he recalled: it "gave me something other than Crow returns to think about and doubtless made me tolerable at home."[48]

During Rowan's convalescence, Thompson and Lister cleaned and dismantled the famous crow cages under the High Level Bridge. The experiment site that had provided free entertainment for Edmontonians of all ages for over three years disappeared overnight. For those still interested, the crow hunt had to serve as a substitute. Rowan knew the importance of widespread publicity and, as he had in 1929, advertised the release of the crows in newspapers and on the radio across western Canada and the northern United States. Anxious to have the cooperation of a large variety of people, he aimed to involve university scientists, students, bird banders, farmers, hunters, and the general public in the crow chase. Areas to the southeast and northwest of Medicine Hat, the original release point, were of particular interest, because crows migrate from the southeast to the northwest in the spring, and reverse this pattern during the fall. Rowan had predicted that experimental birds would fly to the northwest and the controls to the southeast. During the fall of 1931, he wrote numerous letters and sent announcements to radio stations in Montana, South Dakota, Oklahoma, Manitoba, Saskatchewan, and Alberta. He must have been persuasive, because he received promises of cooperation from many radio stations, and also from the staffs of agricultural colleges and universities in the provinces and states likely to be traversed by the crows. He even had the Canadian

General Electric Company mention the treated crows in their sunlamp advertisements. If the publicity Rowan generated was adequately widespread, he could, presumably, get on with his other work while waiting for his army of volunteers to send the crows they had killed. The early results did not meet with his expectations, however, and the impatient Rowan, still recuperating from his illness, fretted and fumed. In this mood he wrote to Taverner, damning all crows:

> After treating them like princes, feeding them to repletion . . . removing the testicles from many of them and thus relieving them of life's biggest burden and the root of all evil . . . after injecting them with extracts specially made by the famous in various parts of the world for their particular delectation; after giving them a royal treat to finish with in the form of a $125 aeroplane ride to the sunny south; damn my soul if they aren't continuing the trip south under their own steam . . . .[49]

As he had been so often in similar circumstances, he was now fed up with the project. But in March 1932, having received a sufficient number of returns, he drew a distribution map of the released crows and wrote up his results. "Experiments in Bird Migration III: The Effects of Artificial Light, Castration and Certain Extracts on the Autumn Movement of the American Crow (*Corvus brachyrhynchos*)" was published in the *Proceedings of the National Academy of Sciences* in late 1932. The article included data from the experiments, and had nine maps showing the directions taken, and extent of dispersal, of the various group of crows.

To Rowan's dismay, many of the experimental birds were never retrieved. Of the 152 birds released in 1931, only 35 were found to the northwest of the release point. Evidently, in "both years the north-bound birds were heading into sparsely settled territory with very poor chances of recovery. In both cases the percentage of returns was much below that of other groups."[50] Like it or not, he had to admit that, although reversed migration had been "successfully induced in at least a percentage of our experimental birds . . . The low percentage of reversed birds may be due to some misadjustment in our scheme of manipulation or perhaps to some missing factor."[51]

Rowan's results showed that castrated birds exposed to light travelled south, proving that "as far as the southward trek is concerned . . . the fall condition of the gonads is not concerned in the story."[52] As the control capons also flew south, Rowan concluded that "These two groups seem to have settled one point. Whatever may be the case with the northward migration, the southward is evidently not associated with the state of the reproductive organs. The movement must depend on some other, at present undetermined, factor." Of the other three groups, capons receiving male urine extracts proved to be sedentary, the placental controls were doubtful, and the pituitary controls "commit themselves to no verdict at this stage."[53]

Rowan knew the results did not support a clear-cut conclusion, and he would have to revise his original hypothesis.[54] He observed, however, that "A remarkable 'sense of direction' was exhibited" by the birds.[55] This was to play a significant part in Rowan's later experiments with crows. While migration and artificial illumination continued to interest him, for the time being Rowan put plans for large-scale migration experiments aside. He developed other concerns, personal and professional. His state of mind was not conducive to extended experimental work.

12

Depression and Light

ROWAN BECAME FULL PROFESSOR in the fall of 1931. Preoccupied with the crow experiments, the fact that he did not receive a salary increase with the promotion did not even disturb him.[1] He simply read the letter that informed him of this development without worrying about its full implication and carried on with his research, satisfied to have received his overdue promotion at a time when many people were losing their jobs and others were suffering pay cuts.[2] In late November, after the historic flight to Hackett with the yellow-tailed crows, Rowan's euphoria evaporated. Confined to his bed with pleurisy, he was feeling miserable. With too much time to mope, he brooded about his financial situation. As was his custom from time to time, Rowan reviewed his future at the University of Alberta, and began to survey job opportunities at other institutions.

On the mend after a good rest, Rowan promptly recovered when he was advised by Collip to contact Sir Arthur Currie, Principal of McGill University, about the post of chair of the zoology department. Rowan had already heard about the post from Charles Elton who, in September 1931, talked to Currie about Rowan's research and his long, drawn-out feud with Tory. Elton recommended that Currie consult scientists at Harvard about Rowan, and Currie promised he would "not take Tory's opinion without question." Elton also remarked that he thought Tory was still unsure about Rowan's potential because he thought Rowan was "a Freudian."[3]

Rowan learned he could pay for the trip by lecturing to the Sigma

Xi Society at McGill University.[4] He briefly visited Montreal after Christmas, entertained scientists with tales of the "thrilling work" he had been doing on juncos and crows, and talked to Currie.[5] So while Rowan did not send a letter of application until March 1932, he stated his interest in the McGill position in person. In the meantime, Currie inquired about the suitability of various scientists for a number of McGill posts. Tory replied: "With regard to Rowan, I find it a little difficult to write about him because I am afraid that what I have to say will not be of any great help to him in securing an appointment at McGill." Tory wrote, Rowan "got a B.Sc. from the University of London . . . on a semi-war basis," and informed Currie that he, Tory, had not been impressed with Rowan as a scientist, because Rowan "would not stick to the laboratory." Tory recalled he had told Rowan that "his only hope of becoming a competent zoologist and of proving his right to the headship of the department . . . would be by taking up some special line of work and sticking to it until he had proved his position as zoologist." Tory added, "Unless Rowan has completely changed since I knew him I would not consider him at all capable of ever organizing such a department or of drawing to it men who would be zealous for work."[6]

Unaware that his chances of a future at McGill were already ruined, Rowan requested testimonials from British, American, and Canadian scientists. In his quests for grants and positions, Rowan could always rely on the support of certain eminent people, who came through time after time with impressive letters of recommendation. This time, F.A.E. Crew stressed "the manifest interest in him and his work which is exhibited by zoologists in Great Britain." He stated that Rowan's investigations "relating to bird migration . . . which concern the interaction of light, pituitary and gonad activity, are regarded by experimental biologists here as being full of magnificent promise." McGill's facilities would "enable Dr. Rowan to make contributions to biological knowledge that would attract further renown. He is exceedingly keen and competent and stands at the beginning of what can be, given the opportunity, a brilliant career."[7] Julian Huxley emphasized that Rowan was "a rare combination of fieldworker, systematist, general zoologist and experimentalist," and would make an excellent chairman of zoology.[8]

Rowan's actual application to McGill included details of his education and previous research, a history of the Department of Zoology at the University of Alberta, and a list of his goals, interests, publications, and current research.[9] All this was to no avail. In spite of the glowing references, Grinnell's pessimistic forecast, "it would be an almost unexpectable throw of good fortune, if the appointment came your way — no matter what your scholarly merits stack up to," came true.[10] Indeed, for reasons that now cannot be ascertained, instead of the highly recommended Rowan or the much-praised McGill lecturer N.J. Berrill, Dr. Harold B. Fantham, a South African zoologist, got the post.[11]

Rowan's reaction to the unwelcome news of Fantham's appointment is not known. The letter bearing the news must have arrived while Rowan was doing fieldwork — studying loon nests in the Pembina-Athabasca muskegs. His field notes make it evident, however, that Rowan did not spend the summer in Edmonton brooding on this turn of events. Instead, he immediately returned to the field. Just when he had practically resigned himself to the fact that he would remain at the University of Alberta, a visitor told him about a vacancy: Queen's University needed to replace the recently deceased A.B. Klugh. While unsure whether the upcoming position was for a senior or a junior zoologist, Rowan sent a letter of inquiry to professor W.T. MacClement who, in turn, informed him that the Queen's financial office "will press for accepting a young man, who will be glad to come at a comparatively small salary."[12] Though his attempt to win this post was unsuccessful, that summer, Rowan enjoyed his first journey across the Rockies, Selkirks, and Cascades. The trip began as a holiday, and remained one for the rest of the family, but Rowan, scientist to his core, could not forego the opportunity to visit the University of British Columbia and inspect its zoology department. He spent a morning with Professor McLean Fraser, a marine biologist, who urged Rowan to visit the Pacific Biological Station, and Rowan, easily persuaded when it suited him, took the ferry to Vancouver Island; the station was situated near Nanaimo. It was housed in a low building with a wonderful view of Departure Bay. Rowan was entertained there by the director, Dr. W.A. Clemens, who introduced him to a number of visiting scientists. Among these was R.A. Wardle from the University of Manitoba, who boosted Rowan's morale by telling him that it had been "generally expected" that he would get the McGill zoology chair.[13]

Rowan's seemingly sudden desire in late 1931 to change employment had complex roots. Although he later stated that "serious research was impossible" at the University of Alberta, this was no longer true.[14] In any case, by 1931 Rowan had achieved considerable fame for the research he had conducted there under difficult conditions. He was recognized by a large number of scientists, and zoologists in many countries began to emulate his research. Numerous lay people were also familiar with Rowan's scientific and popular articles and nature art. This included European and American naturalists, readers of *Country Life*, listeners of Western Canadian and American radio programs, hunters, conservationists, railway personnel, and farmers. The general public in Western North America followed with great interest the story of Doc Rowan and his yellow-tailed crows. By late 1931, William Rowan was a household name.

Under President R.C. Wallace, the situation at the university had improved, and Rowan had more opportunities than ever to do fieldwork and spend time in his beloved wilderness. Moreover, he had just completed a major research project and, twelve years after setting up the zoology department, he finally became full professor. While this promotion was not, as previously mentioned, accompanied by a pay increase, given the economic situation it was highly unlikely that Rowan could have commanded a much better salary at any other Canadian university.[15]

How then can we explain the restlessness that induced Rowan to seek a new position? Why would he want to go to McGill, a large, established institution that had the type of rigid structure he had always despised? Rowan always found it hard to conform to guidelines imposed upon him by institutional administration, but he knew that McGill had its compensations. Among these were the Blacker-Wood Library (where W. Henry Mousley presided over a priceless collection of ornithology books and rare journals), the proximity of his old friend Collip, and the interest shown in his work by other McGill scientists. He must have heard from Collip and others, however, that research conditions at McGill were only slightly better than those at the University of Alberta, that the science departments were understaffed, and even lacked basic instruments such as microscopes.[16] The reasons for Rowan's sudden desire to escape from the district he loved cannot be pinned down to working conditions at the University of Alberta, particularly as he planned to pursue research on loon embryos and biological cycles. He needed the large tracts of land that only parts of the western provinces could provide. Why would he then plan to give up his outdoor laboratory of forests, lakes, and muskegs, for the more restricted field opportunities available in southwestern Quebec?

Rowan possibly did not even admit to himself that his chief reason was personal and not professional. While he justified his wish to depart from the university with well reasoned arguments, it was not his own position but a certain member of the university community he wanted to leave behind. Rowan first became aware of the extent of Reta's involvement in community affairs while he was recovering from pleurisy. He also realized that his wife often attended meetings in the company of Professor George Hunter. Rowan had always considered Hunter his own friend and hunting companion. Now he discovered that the biochemist had become Reta's friend. This was a blow to Rowan's self-esteem. By all accounts, the friendship between Reta Rowan and George Hunter was a platonic one that blossomed over the years to become an important part of Reta's life. The two shared the same philosophy and world outlook; they were both interested in international affairs, and each had a passionate desire to work for those less fortunate. Reta certainly had more in common with Hunter than with her own husband.

Rowan was not pleased to share his wife's attention with one of his own friends or with anyone else. During the years of intense scientific investigations, Rowan was caught up in his own work, absorbed in his own interests. Attempting to advance his career and, at the same time, improve the family's financial situation, he had no time to worry about the state of the world. Reta helped him whenever possible,[17] but she was emotionally isolated and excluded from her husband's concerns — he was totally unaware of her feelings. There is no doubt that Rowan loved his wife and was proud of her artistic ability. Had he been more honest with himself, though, he would have admitted that, after more than a decade of married life, they had little in common. He preferred the companionship of his colleagues, students, and friends to that of his wife. Reta was often lonely, and felt cut off from a large portion of her husband's life. It is hardly surprising that like many other intelligent women she became increasingly interested in social issues. It was at this time that Hunter became important to her. He provided her with the intellectual stimulation and adult companionship she missed in her married life.

Reta, like her husband, was in many ways naïve. She never imagined that not only her husband but also others in Edmonton might misconstrue the friendship. Later she remarked that perhaps she became "too fond" of Hunter; she admired his "manly qualities" and his ability to rise above the confines of his disabled body. She respected his high principles, appreciated his sensitivity to her feelings, but she would never have knowingly jeopardized her family life. She simply did not see why her love for her husband and children should preclude close friendships with other people.

After Rowan's death, Reta recalled that during the first ten years of their marriage "there was always something lacking — the communion of two minds — no evenings spent together at home. I grew only in knowledge of the animal world, which I loved, but not of [Bill's] inner thought or philosophy."[18] Indeed, Rowan never shared his plans, thoughts, or interests with his wife, only with other scientists and artists. While he sporadically complained about his recurring problems with Tory, he remained unable to communicate his inner feelings. By the early 1930s, Reta had realized that another war would pose an "awful danger to my little ones," and joined the Women's International League for Peace and Freedom.[19] Later she joined other associations, including the Friends of Indians. By a series of chance events, her life became richer, more purposeful, at a time when Rowan was ill, dejected, and increasingly depressed.

In 1958, nearly thirty years after the Rowans met the Hunters, Reta would recall that she had hoped that the congenial Hunters would be adopted by the Rowan children as "an uncle and aunt as so often [was done] in the old country." The two families spent time together even during the summer vacations, but this further emphasized the differences between what Reta perceived as her husband's selfishness — "he never joined any associations except scientific ones" — and Hunter's "high devotion to the philosophy of socialism and his willingness to participate in community organizations of an idealistic nature."[20]

It is apparent that the continuous lack of communication between the Rowans was detrimental to Reta's personal growth. Once she joined peace groups and national programs she made new friends who challenged her mind, and she remained grateful to Hunter for having helped her to grow "to maturity of mind and person." Rowan felt neglected, since, according to Reta, he "expected a wife who would devote her entire thoughts and life to his needs."[21] Forty years old in 1931, Rowan was perhaps beginning to experience what is now referred to as mid-life crisis.

When Rowan's initial attempt to break away from Edmonton failed, he threw himself into new experiences, his restless mind forever seeking new fields to conquer. During the summer of 1932 he planned experiments on the effect of daylight on ducks, to be carried out at Delta, Manitoba. As we shall see, this was the beginning of a long association with American industrialist James Ford Bell, and with waterfowl research at Delta. Rowan also initiated serious investigations of biological cycles for which he had been collecting information for the better part of a decade. He also continued his research on the effects of light and exercise on the seasonal reproduction of animals.

Besides all this, Rowan taught five courses, three of them with Winnifred Hughes. How the work was divided up is unknown. There were two junior courses — animal biology for arts students and general elementary zoology for medical students — a senior course on embryology, and two advanced courses — the comparative anatomy of chordates and that of invertebrates. Rowan was also preparing a new course, "Zoo 55," which was to become the first Canadian university course on ornithology.[22] Rowan's energy seemed on the wane, however. He often came home tired and dejected, and he became moody and depressed. During the summer of 1932, he developed stomach pains, his typical reaction to stress. This time, though, his doctor diagnosed the pains as gall-bladder trouble, which surprised no one, since Rowan had a fondness for rich food and consumed large quantities of coffee every day. Another doctor, consulted during the family vacation in British Columbia, actually thought Rowan was suffering from a nervous

17. William Rowan, early 1930s.
Photograph by Reta Rowan. University of Alberta Archives.

breakdown, but after the holiday Rowan felt fine and saw no need to see a doctor until the spring of 1933, when the pains recurred.

The severe pains alarmed the whole family, and Rowan promptly received the attention he craved. But even Reta's concern did not alleviate his symptoms. Finally, Rowan agreed to go to England and undergo a thorough medical examination. If possible, he was also to enjoy an entirely work-free holiday, but, when he learned in April that his salary had been reduced by 15 percent, he changed his mind and called off the trip.[23] Although the reduction had long been expected by members of the university community, the news did nothing to improve Rowan's depression. He was no longer able to work at night to raise extra cash, which he certainly needed to support his family.

Reta had a hard time inducing her husband to go to England, but Rowan did not need much persuading to go to the muskeg country and rest in the company of Joe Dawkins. This trip cost so little, that Rowan was no doubt happy to comply. Since he still half believed that he had gall-bladder trouble, he kept to a diet of chicken, but did not rest. For a few days he tramped all over the muskegs, ridges, and fields searching for breeding birds, and then, on 22 May 1933, still worried about his health and finances, Rowan boarded a Canadian Pacific train for the first part of the journey to spend the summer in England.

On the eastbound train he began to enjoy himself. As usual, Rowan stopped in Winnipeg to talk to Lawrence, and in Ottawa to see the National Museum and visit with the Taverners. There, the initial euphoria over, he began to feel tired and dispirited, and suffered from violent abdominal pains. He again began to doubt that it was wise to spend the much-needed money on a journey to England. After a lot of dithering, he finally went to Montreal where he had an appointment with a Dr. Elder, "a good belly specialist," who saw Rowan at midnight, examined him till 2:30 a.m., and informed him that his pains were caused by nerves. The doctor advised Rowan to postpone his trip, and, to have a good rest in Montreal before sailing.[24] Much to everyone's surprise, this was precisely what Rowan did. He remained in Montreal for another fortnight, staying at the Ford Hotel, and finally sailed on the *Empress of Britain* from Quebec City on 10 June.

Whatever the reasons, Rowan looked ill. Taverner wrote to their mutual friends Fred Kennard and J.D. Soper of Rowan's poor health. The response was sympathetic. Kennard wrote: "He certainly is a 'wild Irishman,' and just as certainly has many attractive qualities. But no one of his physique and temperament could possibly treat himself as he does and continue to live."[25]

In London, under orders from his brother Harry, now a successful physician, Rowan "spent several days in bed and was x-rayed umpteen times at the cancer hospital. Nothing organically wrong — gall bladder perfect — and verdict again nervous breakdown." Reta was greatly relieved, and wrote touchingly childish, loving letters to her husband. She constantly urged him to take it easy, because she was convinced the illness was caused by overwork, and all he needed was a good rest. Coming from the reticent Reta, the letters are surprisingly demonstrative. She freely praised her husband's accomplishments and even his vigour by saying, "there are times, mostly bed-times, when I think that youthfulness with you is a habit!"[26] This was indeed a forward thing to say for someone who, after having five children in eight years, feared pregnancy and, in any case, preferred kindness and affection to sexual passion.

Reta's letters, combined with the love and concern he received from the Rowan and Bush families in England, did much to restore Rowan's health. Within a few weeks he noted, "My appetite is still colossal and I have regained my weight."[27] No wonder. In Edmonton he rushed his meals, rarely taking time to talk to his family. In England Rowan relaxed and talked at the table. He regularly lunched with Huxley, had tea with J.P. Hill, and went to the D.M.S. Watsons' for dinner. He visited with scientists in Oxford, Cambridge, and Edinburgh, and finally met his correspondent R.E. Moreau, on leave from his post in Africa.[28] He spent time in libraries, laboratories, and zoological gardens, lectured at schools and to scientific associations, and spent time in art galleries and at the theatre. Rowan even went to BBC House "for a trial of voice."[29] On another occasion he "shook hands with the great R.B. Bennett at a Canada House reception."[30]

With his health and self-confidence restored, Rowan returned to Canada in mid-August, sailing once again on the *Empress of Britain*. In the fall of 1933, Rowan was in good form and for a while work went well. He was happy teaching several courses, including the new one on ornithology. He began a new series of light experiments on juncos and canaries, which involved weighing their food and waste; he also wrote a review article on bird migration for the American Ornithologists' Union fiftieth anniversary. Rowan was delighted to receive a grant of fifty pounds from the Gunning Fund of the Royal Society for his proposed research "on the Canadian rabbit cycle."[31] This was particularly important, because earlier in the year the United States National Research Council had turned down his application for such a grant.[32] Finally, a significant honour came his way. He was asked to "consent" to be nominated for fellowship in the Royal Society of Canada.[33]

Within a few weeks, though, Rowan was unable to continue his research, lost interest in teaching, and could not even enjoy the fellowship nomination. Plagued with ill health, by early December he was unable to walk. He suffered from leg pains that came with sudden and frightening intensity. There are no records of his movements and experiences between 27 November 1933 and 3 February 1934, so we cannot determine what provoked the excruciating pains. We do know, however, that he was incapacitated and unable to get out of bed to cope with everyday life.[34] Although he later referred to this ailment as a nervous breakdown, perhaps Rowan, like many scientists before him, had simply forced himself to a point of exhaustion with his puritanical propensity for overwork.[35]

Rowan's medical records show that he was admitted to the University of Alberta Hospital on 22 January "under the care of Dr. Kenneth Hamilton, for the purpose of diagnostic testing." This consisted of a spinal puncture, ordered because of Rowan's complaint of "boring pains in the legs." No physical reasons were found for the pains, however, and Rowan was discharged from the hospital with a prescription for painkillers.[36] Relieved that in spite of the agonizing pains there was nothing organically wrong with him, Rowan spent a few peaceful days resting (with the help of the medication) at Fawcett. In the amiable company of Dawkins, with whom Rowan had developed another nonthreatening relationship (Dawkins continued to address him as Doctor, or Professor), Rowan was able to indulge in "glorious walking with the [snow] flakes falling quietly and steadily with practically no wind." He shot rabbits for food, tried ice fishing for greyling, and talked to the "very hard up" local residents.[37]

In the spring, he did fieldwork in the muskegs, where walking on the uneven, spongy terrain is difficult for even a healthy person. He had to agree with Conover that there was no better test for the "legs than the muskegs. If they hold out there, they ought to last . . . anywhere."[38] In his beloved wilderness Rowan felt almost his old self again as he observed the breeding activities of a multitude of organisms, such as waders, loons, and "thousands of dragonflies . . . of many different species" copulating on the wing.[39]

After a day in the field, Rowan relaxed in Joe Dawkins's small but well-equipped shack listening to Dawkins tell stories, or discussing "local gossip, relief graft, dirty work at the Post Office . . . local morals, weather, road work and how the homes of M.P.s have accounted for gravel roads into useless corners of Alberta."[40] At other times he strolled along the river, took photographs or, accompanied by Lister, drove around the district. Once, the car got stuck in the quagmire "up to the axles." The two men slept "excellently in the car, in the mud-hole, in the centre of the King's highway!"[41]

In 1934, the Rowans were introduced to the Jasper area of Alberta; their friends the Walkers had a summer cottage there at Lake Edith. The cold, green water of the lake, the warm scent of pine rosin wafting from tall conifers, and the simplicity of the log cabin were delightful. The whole of the Jasper region was theirs to discover. Maligne Canyon, Medicine Lake, the Angel Glacier on Mount Edith Cavell, and the Athabasca and Sunwapta falls were still largely free of the hordes of tourists that were to invade the area in the years to come. Most of the roads were still under construction, and there was little traffic. This was a new type of wilderness for Rowan, and the family would spend much time there.

It is clear that Rowan made a serious effort to relax, sleep, and spend time with his family. He gave more attention to his hobbies of sketching and photographing animals, and began to draw the human form, most notably the female form of Joan, daughter of their artist friend Florence Mortimer. More than half a century after she first posed for Rowan, Joan Gregg (née Mortimer) recalled that as a teenager she used to babysit Sylvia, Julian, and Josephine Rowan. Joan was talented, like her mother, and studied art, but during the Depression positions remained scarce, and she was glad to earn some money as a model. Rowan enjoyed Joan's charm and wit and soon employed her as his assistant to illustrate the insides of specimens.[42] The company of a pretty, lively, and artistic young woman cheered Rowan at a time when his relationship with Reta was undergoing a transformation. He used Joan as a sounding board for his ideas concerning the differences between male and female sexuality.

Rowan's views on this topic were far from original; they echoed the Victorian idea that women were unwilling partners in sexual encounters. No doubt, like many of his contemporaries, he imbibed such notions as a young man in England.

The lives of Bill and Reta began to take different directions. Rowan occupied himself less frequently with research and, feeling well once again, devoted more time and energy to other interests; Reta became more involved with social issues, developed friends of her own, and had less time and inclination for sex with her husband. Perhaps it is hardly surprising that Reta's behaviour, reasonable as far as she was concerned, reinforced her husband's ingrained notions concerning male and female sexuality. A decade or so later, he was to discuss these ideas with his son Julian, and recount them, together with an increasingly pessimistic world view, in an unpublished manuscript entitled "The Last Chapter." In 1934, he simply flirted with Joan and others, and while he talked a lot about women, it seems as though there was more talk than action.[43]

During this period, his health and energy restored, Rowan began yet another hobby. It may have been his family's connections with railways that prompted his desire to build a set of miniature railway tracks for his children's steam engines. In August 1934, he was already hard at work on the first set of railway tracks in the garden of the rented cottage at Seba Beach.[44]

During the summer of 1934, Huxley informed Rowan that he would be coming to Canada in 1935 to give a series of lectures.[45] The two men had known each other for over a decade, had carried on a long and varied correspondence, and had spent many enjoyable hours together during Rowan's infrequent visits to England. Finally, it was Rowan's turn to receive Huxley. Huxley planned to arrive from Vancouver in late January, stay with the Rowans and spend time in the field. But his train was stuck for five days in a snowdrift, his lectures in British Columbia had to be cancelled, and by the time he turned up in Edmonton, inadequately clothed, his throat was inflamed and his long, red nose was dripping. Although he felt miserable, Huxley delivered an exciting lecture to a large crowd in Convocation Hall, University of Alberta. Afterwards Rowan hosted a buffet for the famous visitor and a select group of friends and Alberta luminaries. He fed his guests, he later claimed, "on a selection of native game as illustrated on the menue [sic]. There were nearly twenty birds to cook. We had them done at the university kitchens."[46] In addition to wild duck and partridge, grouse and prairie chicken, there were also mule deer, supplied by the obliging Dawkins. Fifty years after the event, Rowan's game buffet with its hand-illustrated menu were still talked about with admiration.[47] The guests were entertained with music, singing, and lively conversation. Huxley and Rowan talked late into the night, arguing over the respective merits of Lamarckian and Darwinian evolutions.[48]

During his visit, Huxley advised his friend to apply to the Carnegie Foundation for a British Empire Fellowship, that would finance a sabbatical year in England. As always, Huxley offered to write letters of recommendation on Rowan's behalf, and on board the train from Edmonton to Winnipeg penned a testimonial to the Canadian secretary of the fellowship, Dr. W.A. MacIntosh of Queen's University.[49]

Rowan was excited by the prospect of working for an entire year in England, "untrammeled by teaching and departmental duties." It was the opportunity of a lifetime, and he began to muster help to realize it. He wrote to a number of friends and supporters about "applying for one of the Carnegie Corporation grants." He explained that two such grants were given annually to applicants from each of the "Dominions but out of these ten names only two will be picked by the final Selection Committee in England." Rowan was confident that, once his name was selected by the Canadian committee, his chances in England would be "first class[.] Huxley, Marshall, Crew, J.P. Hill, D'Arcy Thompson and a whole flock of British luminaries would be glad to see me get over."[50]

Rowan asked Collip to "stress the broader aspects" of his experimental work, and "to emphasize the fact that it has led to a tremendous amount of research work in America and Europe." He added, "you know, old lad, what such an opportunity will mean to me after the years of climbing over incessant obstacles that have hung like a mill stone round my neck."[51]

In his actual application, sent on 31 January 1935, Rowan proposed to do a year's research "into the mechanism of migration and the effects of artificial illumination on birds and other animals." He planned two working stages. In the first stage he proposed to complete work on the "histology of the ductless glands available from the 1931 experiments with crows and the histology of the gonads of migrating birds collected for the applicant by other investigators from several corners of the world." In the second stage, Rowan was to carry out further experiments with light, and stressed in his application that the "importance of the work is perhaps best indicated by references to the volume of university research" in North America and Europe that had grown out of his own original experiments "with artificial light on birds." He added that his research had often been referred to in the "physiological and biochemical literature."[52]

In spite of the strong support he received from Collip, Huxley, and others, Rowan did not get the grant. He was not even nominated. What exactly happened is still unclear. According to Huxley, Rowan's application had been "knocked out on the Canadian side." Huxley deplored the fact that "some curious influences [were] at work in Canada .... It really is a shame ... a scandal with your record and all the backing you had."[53] As the records of the Canadian committee cannot be located, it is only possible to speculate that Tory's long tentacles had reached the committee and prevented Rowan's nomination. Whatever the reasons, Huxley was incensed, and wrote to President Wallace of the University of Alberta to tell him that Rowan's name "had been turned down in Canada." He added,

> I thought that you might like to know that Professor J.P. Hill, FRS, on hearing that Rowan hadn't been nominated became almost violent! Indeed it does seem to me that something has gone agley somewhere when there *is* a really good Canadian candidate, not to let his name go forward to the Central Committee and only submit weak names — *inter alia* it is bad for the reputation of Canadian science.[54]

Although nothing could be done for Rowan at this time, he could reapply during the following year. Huxley's letter *did* have some result — at least Rowan told Huxley he had noticed a change in Wallace's attitude.[55] This may have been only a figment of his overactive imagination, however. In fact, Wallace had always been rather friendly to Rowan, and it was not Wallace, but Acting President W.A. Kerr who wrote the letter of recommendation, or condemnation, to the committee in 1935.[56]

Wallace began an active campaign to support Rowan. In the letter of recommendation he wrote for Rowan when Rowan applied for the grant again the next year, he praised him as an authority on bird migration who "has won a reputation which has extended far beyond the bounds of Canada . . . . [his] work is held in very high regard by outstanding biologists in the British Isles."[57] With Wallace's support the scale tipped in Rowan's favour. On 16 May 1936, the Executive Council, Universities Bureau of the British Empire notified Rowan by telegram that he had been "selected for Carnegie Corporation Grant 1936–37." After sixteen years of intensive work, Rowan was finally able to spend a whole year on scientific research. He would have time to think and work without undue pressure. The attraction of escaping from university duties and family commitments was so great that Rowan even reconciled himself to leaving Reta to her social concerns and increased involvement with world affairs. Despite his disapproval of his wife's friendships with others, including the one she had with Hunter, Rowan could not forfeit the chance to spend a year of freedom in England.

Rowan had three months before his departure from Canada. These were busy, happy months filled with field activities at Francis Point and the Pembina-Athabasca muskegs, preparations for the sabbatical year, and a long family vacation at Lake Edith where, in 1935, the Rowans bought a log cabin next to the Walkers.[58] There Rowan began to construct the "Lake Edith Railway" on 12 July 1936, an elaborate affair that was to consist of a system of single tracks, carts, signals, tunnels, and mountains. Rowan wanted to incorporate "in miniature, as many as possible of the typical features of Canadian mountain railroading." Family and friends helped Rowan with his "surveying, track-laying, tunneling and bridge building." The work took about six weeks to complete, and cost only fifteen dollars because inexpensive materials were used.[59] Later Rowan created a landscape for the railway to journey through, and named prominent features of it after family members. The work went on for a number of years. Mount Oliver was finished in 1938, "complete with lake, precipice and beetling crags, rock tunnel and waterfall (Josephine Falls) [fed by a] 30-gallon reservoir built into the back of the 'mountain.' "[60]

When not playing with his railway, Rowan enjoyed the outdoors. He hiked and watched animals, sketched a dipper feeding its family, and studied the beavers. He took his children fishing and visited the summit of the new road that travelled near the Athabasca Glacier. He admired the impressive scenery. Rowan was intrigued by the motley work crews he met at the road-maintenance camps, and by the pikas, chipmunks, rabbits, and an enormous bull moose that "galloped beside the car for a quarter of a mile." There were numerous bears around, both black and grizzly, and Rowan, utterly fearless, photographed them at every available opportunity. On 16 September 1936, Rowan left for a year's sabbatical in England. No doubt it was an emotional leave-taking, but he only noted that "Runtie [was] in tears for an hour."[61]

13

Light and Seasonal Reproduction in Animals

ROWAN DID NOT KEEP a diary during his sabbatical leave, which took place between 16 September 1936 and 1 August 1937, but as he wrote numerous letters, research proposals, scientific papers, and even a popular book (never published), his activities during this period can be pieced together with reasonable accuracy. From these sources it is evident that in London Rowan lived with his brother Harry at fashionable Onslow Square, participated in the scientific and artistic life of London, and visited many parts of the British Isles. He spent time in Cheltenham with his old friend Oswald MacOustra, now a physician for the so-called horsey set, and had many discussions with Charles Elton, Dr. John R. Baker, Dr. Solly Zuckerman in Oxford, F.H.A. Marshall in Cambridge, and F.E.A. Crew in Edinburgh. He also made two trips to the Continent.

During this period, Rowan enrolled at the Slade School of Art and attended exhibitions. In early May, he was a guest at a luncheon reception given by the Duke of Kent for "Artists of the British Empire Overseas." Rowan's silver-point drawing of Josephine, which he had submitted with trepidation and in great secrecy — only Reta knew about his plan to do so — hung in the exhibit and was much admired by the other artists and the public. In his spare time, Rowan worked on a popular account of his crow investigations.

Officially, Rowan was a research associate working on previously accumulated histological material in J.P. Hill's laboratory at the

Department of Anatomy and Embryology, University College, London.[1] The appointment gave him some useful privileges, such as a free library card, a reduced tuition fee at the Slade, and a private laboratory with "the most comfortable armchair in the world."[2] This was a great help, because the leg pains that practically paralyzed him in Canada recurred during his first few months in England, when Rowan was still anxious about things at home.

Rowan expressed deep-seated worries about his own situation at the University of Alberta in a letter he wrote in October 1936 to Dr. W.A. Kerr, the university's newly appointed president. Rowan told Kerr that "some of the injustices that [Tory] left behind him are still in existence and among them, pre-eminently is my own department." He asked Kerr for a pay increase, pointing out that for many years he had been "receiving a salary far below the responsibilities of the headship." Rowan also requested an increase for "Dr. Hughes who has suffered with me without complaint. She has been an integral factor in the success of the department but both her rank and salary are far below what they should be." In the letter, Rowan cites more personal grievances and practically blames the university for his illness; it occurred, he wrote, because he had to make "ends meet by earning additional money with night work." This, in turn, led to his nervous breakdown in 1933: the breakdown was "an outcome of the handicaps imposed upon me by circumstances and consistent overwork over a period of years."[3]

Kerr replied that he could not offer Rowan a raise for the coming year. The situations was further exacerbated when a colleague informed Rowan that the provincial Social Credit government planned "to produce their own currency and will make all other currency illegal in Alberta."[4] Because of governmental restrictions, Rowan could not even obtain money due to him from an already established research fund at the University of Alberta.[5] Since he was at a distance of several thousand kilometres from Alberta, he could do little about the situation, and soon turned his mind to raising research funds in England. By early 1937 he had managed to obtain forty pounds from the Royal Society, thirty pounds from the University Bureaus of the British Empire, and twenty pounds from the Institute of Animal Behaviour.[6]

Soon his active, satisfying life (he spent happy hours with his family and friends, and basked in the appreciation of his scientific peers), helped heal his body and mind. By the end of his year's leave Rowan's health was much improved.[7] Rowan was ready to do research at the beginning of 1937. He had already obtained live juncos from Western Canada for a repeat of his 1928 experiments on the effects of enforced wakefulness on the sexual organs of birds. This time he started the experiments in January, when the days were much shorter than they had been in March (the month during which the original experiments were conducted), and found that the results substantiated his earlier findings, which had been published in *Nature* in 1928.

Rowan also began two entirely new projects: the first to determine whether birds respond to barometric pressure; and the second to study the effects of light and enforced wakefulness on London starlings. For the first project, Rowan kept an ordinary barnyard cock in a large glass cage equipped with a vacuum pump, but it proved impossible to control the pressure, and he soon abandoned the project.[8] He was more successful with his starling investigations which, in any case, fit into his larger oeuvre on the effects of daylight on the reproductive organs of birds.

The story of the London starlings was amusing at the time and it is still so in retrospect. Rowan, fond of a good story, embroidered it in several ways, until its central players included himself; British ornithologist James Fisher; the London police chief; a few London bobbies, and Kenneth Clark, director of the National Gallery.[9] Stripping the accounts of all subsequent embellishments, it is likely that the following happened. Around midnight in early 1937, Rowan, on his way home from the theatre, noticed starlings fidgeting, instead of sleeping, on large buildings around Trafalgar Square. He thought the late-night illumination and constant traffic noise had kept the birds awake, long past their usual roosting time. Here was a prime opportunity to test one of his earlier experimental findings. Initially, Rowan requested permission to fire a collecting gun in the Borough of London. The London police chief replied, understandably, "certainly not!" But later a highly amused Kenneth Clark authorized Rowan and two friends "to enter the National Gallery and catch Starlings on the roof." Clark stipulated, however, that the National Gallery would not be held responsible if Rowan or either of his companions fell off the roof.[10]

There was another reason for Rowan to undertake this investigation. For a number of years he had been annoyed by T.H. Bissonnette, and was delighted to have the opportunity to refute the other scientist's findings on the starling. One must remember that Bissonnette first heard about Rowan's junco experiments from Winnie Hughes, and then proceeded to repeat some of Rowan's investigations with the starling.[11] According to Rowan's correspondence, Bissonnette, in his articles on his own starling research, deliberately neglected to refer to Rowan's pioneering work on the juncos. Rowan, in haste, misinterpreted Bissonnette, who actually had referred to Rowan's junco experiments, but did not agree with Rowan's conclusions about the connection between enforced exercise and the enlargement of the gonads. Despite this misunderstanding, Rowan, who by this time had been acknowledged as *the* pioneer researcher in the area of light and seasonal reproduction in animals, remained hurt that Bissonnette had failed to give him credit.

There were good reasons why the two scientists had come to different conclusions concerning the effect of exercise on gonadal activity. Bissonnette failed to substantiate Rowan's findings precisely because he had worked with starlings (a nonmigratory species with a nervous temperament) instead of juncos.[12] Rowan had recognized this fact, in principle at least, by the early 1930s, but had neither the time nor the opportunity to refute Bissonnette's conclusions. Finally, in 1937, he could repeat his own early experiments on juncos in a cage fitted with a mechanical device. He could also study wild starlings kept in a state of enforced wakefulness both by traffic noise and late-night illumination, and have a control group of country starlings that went to roost in peace at sundown.

Rowan's work in England on juncos and starlings resulted in several publications. As a first step, on 5 March 1937 Rowan sent an article to *Nature*. "Effects of Traffic Disturbance and Night Illumination on London Starlings," was published in the 17 April issue of the journal.[13] In the longer "London Starlings and Seasonal Reproduction in Birds" Rowan detailed his own earlier experiments and all others that followed his initial investigations.[14] He discussed the gonad-pituitary relationship (first suggested by F.H.A. Marshall in the mid-1930s), the effects of artificial illumination (including methods of administration, and wavelength and light intensity), and "mode of action of light," that is, both increased day length and the eye as a receptor.[15] On the basis of new evidence, including his current work in London, Rowan reinterpreted his 1928 conclusions concerning juncos and enforced activity. He was now convinced "that extended daily activity, induced by means of light or compulsory exercise, induces also changes in the physiology and metabolism of the animals concerned." He stressed, however, that the biological means by which sexual responses to light changes are "achieved cannot be expected to show uniformity from species to species or class to class."[16]

During his sabbatical, Rowan had numerous opportunities to discover the extent of the research that grew out of his early experiments. The well-stocked British science libraries contained periodicals with many articles on light and reproduction. The time was obviously ripe for Rowan to sum up problems and investigations in this growing research area. In "Light and Seasonal Reproduction in Animals," published in *Biological Reviews of the Cambridge Philosophical Society* in 1938, Rowan set out to "review the history and consider the present status of the subject."[17] He discussed photoperiodism in plants; light, migration, and reproduction in birds; experiments in migration, and other light experiments on more than fifty species of animals (birds, mammals, reptiles, amphibians, fish, and invertebrates). Most of the animals used were "species with short breeding seasons restricted to the spring in the northern hemisphere."[18] The review article, one of the most important products of Rowan's sabbatical year, included information culled from 117 scientific papers by 95 authors and coauthors. Rowan's own output of one dozen papers — two of which were with other authors — formed a significant part of this impressive list.

During this productive period, encouraged by fellow scientists, friends, and publishers, Rowan even contemplated writing another book on migration. First he talked about updating his 1931 *Riddle of Migration*, and publishing the new version in England with his old friend Witherby.[19] When the Sidgwick and Jackson publishing company persuaded him to do a major work on the biology of migration instead, Rowan wrote to Reta to say that, this was to be "the first serious thing of my life in book form." He soon realized, however, that writing such a book was more time-consuming and required more energy than he had originally envisaged. Nevertheless, he hoped to "make it the standard work on the subject. It is going to have some original features, but will be as careful a bit of conscientious work as I am capable of producing." He remarked that he was "beginning to feel jolly glad that I have stuck to my guns throughout."[20] This promising work was never completed, however. Rowan became involved in other projects, including a study of the gonads of the migrant European passerines that Moreau had collected for him in East Africa.[21]

Amidst all this research and writing, Rowan took two trips to the Continent, the first in late March and the second in early July 1937. Actually, because of his strained financial situation, Rowan almost cancelled the first trip, but an invitation from the famed Konrad Lorenz, together with the forty-pound Royal Society grant, helped to change his mind.[22] The visit to Altenberg, near Vienna, where Lorenz experimented with jackdaws and ducks, was fascinating for Rowan, and the two scientists soon discovered that they shared an interest not only in scientific topics, but also in model railroads.[23]

Rowan's second European trip took place in July, when he attended part of the annual conference of the Deutsche Ornithologen-Gesellschaft (German Society of Ornithologists). As always, he was greatly stimulated by meeting other scientists, and joined the group on a sightseeing trip to Saxony. Amid glorious scenery, Rowan discussed ornithology with Erwin Stresemann of Germany, Jean Delacour of France, and King Ferdinand of Bulgaria. Then he went to Berlin, Königsberg, and Kranbeck, where he took a ferry to the famous Rossitten bird observatory. Arriving after a rough eight-hour crossing, Rowan had little time to inspect the observatory and talk to the resident ornithologist. He learned, however, that the "light question is only just taking on in Germany but all kinds of people are planning to start and my visit has given them a good deal of extra enthusiasm."[24] Returning to Berlin, Rowan spent time at the zoo, drank beer with the zookeeper, visited several art galleries, and shopped for toys with Lorenz. Then he took the train to Holland to visit G.J. Van Oordt's laboratory at Utrecht.

The German trip was useful from a scientific point of view, but more important perhaps, it gave Rowan a glimpse of Nazi Germany. During parts of the trip when he travelled alone, Rowan was able to observe the economic situation (high prices but a general lack of goods), watch clean young men marching in uniforms, and note the excellent roads but dearth of privately owned automobiles. This unmediated view gave Rowan a different impression of Germany from the one he had received in the company of internationally known scientists. For the first time he realized war was practically inevitable, and began to understand Reta's concerns. Rowan knew information about Germany would greatly interest his wife. For once he had something to share with her. After the long separation Rowan began to look forward to an improved relationship.[25] He had already written to Reta that after the "events of the past years, a sort of new start in life would be the loveliest thing in the world I could dream of. Perhaps we could come to understand each other in a way that would last the rest of our lives."[26] So, in spite of having witnessed an increasingly complicated and depressing political situation in Europe, Rowan could see the light for his own future. He had regained his health and was looking forward to his return to Canada; he hoped that Reta would find him "a more cheerful person to live with than [he had been] for the past few years."[27]

On 21 August 1937, full of optimism that his family life as well as his working conditions at the university would now improve, Rowan left for home on the *Empress of Britain*. But the Rowans only had a brief time together at Lake Edith before Bill returned to his old lifestyle — long hours of work at the university and most of his spare time spent in the field. Rowan resumed keeping a diary. The detailed entries give a good account of his numerous outings but, as before, there is scant information on his research. By contrast, his experimental notebooks are more detailed than before. These, together with his correspondence, provide a good picture of the elaborate, sophisticated investigations Rowan pursued after his return from sabbatical. As historical records the notebooks and correspondence are particularly valuable because the results of these investigations were never written up for publication.

On his return to Edmonton Rowan was charged with energy, his self-confidence bolstered by the worldwide interest accorded his original research. His mind was challenged by scientific colloquia, by informal discussions with peers, and by reading up-to-date scientific literature. Rowan was full of ideas. He planned to test the effects on animals of light directed through a variety of colour filters; he wanted to study the results of controlled exposure to x-rays and to ultraviolet rays using sunlamps, and to investigate the effects on birds and frogs of the surgical removal of their thyroid and pituitary glands. Rowan was keen to do new research, but in his old surrounding the old problems persisted. There was no money available at the university, and in September it was too late to apply elsewhere for a grant. Rowan was determined, however, to raise the necessary cash. As a first step he offered to sell his collection of prairie birds to Grinnell. Rowan told Grinnell that after his productive year in England it was harder than ever for him to face "this wretched government of ours . . . and [found] even our research funds tied up and out of reach [and] none of our salary cuts restored."[28] Grinnell replied: "We are exceedingly weak on northern collected stuff and the fact that you are the collector adds something, though intangible, to the value in my eyes."[29] Grinnell offered, and Rowan gratefully accepted, $350 for the collection.[30]

At about the time Rowan planned to sell his collection he was unsettled further by a letter from Collip. Apparently, on his way from London to Edmonton, Rowan had stopped in Montreal to see his old friend and learned that Fantham had died and the chair of the McGill zoology department was again vacant. Collip thought Rowan had a very good chance of being hired, and advised him to get letters "from Julian Huxley and a number of other outstanding men who . . . would be only too glad to give you the 'boost.'"[31] Rowan soon learned, however, that McGill zoologist N.J. Berrill had already asked Huxley for a letter of support. Huxley was willing to write a letter on Rowan's behalf as well, but McGill had postponed appointing Fantham's successor.[32]

Whatever his hopes for a McGill position, Rowan had to carry on with his day-to-day activities. Fortunately, he managed to obtain a grant through Dr. Carl Moore of the University of Chicago, and could carry out his proposed research.[33] This was a good development indeed, and by early October Rowan started trapping juncos, his original experimental species, which were easier to trap than crows. He also planned to use sparrows and frogs, in addition to juncos, to test the connection between the eye and the pituitary gland.

During the winter of 1937–1938 Rowan conducted a varied and sophisticated series of experiments. He thought he was refuting

18. The Rowan's cottage at Lake Edith, near
Jasper, Alberta, late 1930s.
Courtesy of the Rowan family.

19. In characteristic pose — William and Reta, Edmonton, Alberta, 1938.
Courtesy of the Rowan family.

Bissonnette and other investigators who maintained that wakefulness and exercise without light could not induce gonadal development. There are no publications detailing his research and conclusions, however. In fact, the only published notice of all this work was a half-page addendum to his 1938 review paper in *Biological Reviews* in which Rowan summarized his recent work. There he intimated that when the "histological examination has been completed, confirmation and full details will be published elsewhere."[34] However, other projects precluded the continuation of this project. Rowan worked instead on mammals, ducks, and gamebirds, and became increasingly preoccupied by concerns about the war, and the scientist's role in war and peace.

It is not known who recommended that Rowan apply, in 1938, to the National Research Council of Canada for a grant to test his theories on the effect of light on the seasonal reproduction of the mink. Rowan spent most of the summer at Lake Edith, working on the model railway, and enjoying a family vacation. Perhaps his daily observations of mammals turned his active mind to applying his theories to more practical ends than bird migration. Quite likely he was influenced by dentist L.A. Smith, a former student, who had a mink farm near Calgary. In any case, Rowan was convinced that mink ranches could benefit greatly if birth rates were increased through the use of artificial light. It is also possible that he wanted to use the mink, an easily accessible member of the weasel family, to repeat Bissonnette's and Marshall's work on the ferret.

In his detailed grant application to the NRC, Rowan stressed that the investigation would deal with "one of the basic problems of organisms of the northern hemisphere — reproductive periodicity." He added parenthetically, that the experiments "may also be of practical value to the fur-trade since two crops of young per annum would be possible." As he had done in the case of birds before, Rowan hoped to prove that "the brief spring breeding season of the mink depends essentially on daylength rather than temperatures or quality of light and that it can be shifted to the winter months by experimental control of the salient factor — daylength." Rowan also proposed to use x-rays to "elucidate the associated function of the pituitary gland."[35] Because practically all the equipment needed, except the mink cages, was already available at the University of Alberta, Rowan only requested four hundred dollars. This included funds to purchase ten pairs of mink (at ten dollars per mink), and to cover the cost of cages, food, light, and "care for 4 months" including five dollars per month for an assistant. The gamble paid off and Rowan was awarded the full four hundred dollars. The Standing Committee on Assisted Researches stated, "After considerable discussion of the possible economic and scientific value of this work, it was agreed that Dr. Rowan be granted the sum requested."[36] The existing correspondence makes it clear that Rowan actually did the work on the breeding of the mink, but he never published the results, and his notes on the subject are missing.

As far as can be ascertained, this was the last major light experiment that Rowan completed. He remained interested in, and did some work on, migration, orientation, and gonad cycles. He did a histological study of the gonads of three species of African breeding birds. These were collected in East Africa and shipped, packed carefully in long tubes, by Moreau, who supplied additional notes on the "moulting stages of specimens," as well as all the pertinent ecological data.[37] The actual laboratory work was done at the University of Alberta by Albert Wilk, one of Rowan's senior students in ornithology. "The Moult and Gonad Cycles of Three Species of Birds at Five Degrees South of the Equator" (1946) was coauthored by Moreau, Wilk, and Rowan. It shed light on the "breeding seasons of tropical birds and their possible timing factors."[38]

Rowan had no time or inclination to perform further experiments. Many factors worked against him continuing his research. The major one was the war. Rowan originally planned to expand his investigations of the effect of traffic disturbance on London starlings. Now the project had to be abandoned. Starlings could not be secured in London because of the blackouts, and in any case British scientists, though in principle willing to collect for Rowan, had other duties and concerns.[39] Other problems surfaced at home and at the university, and Rowan may simply have lost heart. Ironically, at a time when he questioned even the point of conducting fundamental research, Rowan was able to obtain a large grant from a new source: the Rockefeller Foundation.

The year 1939 was a bad one in many respects. War was inevitable, but even before Hitler walked into Poland Rowan's world had changed. Although his diaries do not mention the death of his mother during the summer, Rowan was deeply affected by it. Regular commercial flights between North America and Europe were still a thing of the future, and he could not even go to the funeral. Rowan mourned his mother deeply, but he was glad she did not live to see another war. Characteristically, Rowan threw himself into work and play. He taught summer school in July, then joined the family in Jasper where, as usual, he watched and sketched animals and worked on the model railway. He observed that bears were numerous, and that "the Brewster Chalet at the Athabasca glacier . . . is beautifully finished . . . and already well patronized."[40] The prospect of a large number of tourists flooding into the area turned his mind to a new way of capitalizing on his talents. He had already started modelling clay animals for fun and now, with Oliver planning to go to university, Rowan decided this would be a lucrative sideline. By the following spring he was hard at work creating plaster bears. These, and later a number of other plaster animals, were sold to hotels in the Banff-Jasper region. The extra income they brought was much needed, because the salary reductions instituted at the University of Alberta in the early 1930s were still in effect. Rowan now earned $4,125 annually instead of $4,500, and part of his salary came in the form of vouchers from Alberta's Social Credit government.

"In the peace and quiet of the Rockies . . . . that war can occur in 1939 seems too fantastic to be true!" noted Rowan on 3 September.[41] In the pine-scented mountain air, war seemed unreal. Rowan could accept death as part of the natural world, but not armies, cruelty, famine, bombs, and destruction. He became depressed and worried about the future of humanity. He began to develop a pessimistic world view. He even decided to add a serious last chapter to his lighthearted manuscript "As the Crow Flies." Rowan spent a week on Smith's mink ranch working on the manuscript, enjoying the magnificent view of the Rockies, visiting the nearby Blackfoot Indian reservation. The kindness and thoughtfulness of the Natives temporarily restored his equilibrium. Trips to see Dawkins at Fawcett and hunt ducks on Francis Point also helped him to carry on. It was at this time that his old hero Ernest Thompson Seton, accompanied by his wife and young child, visited Edmonton. The eighty-year-old artist-naturalist impressed everyone with his energy. At his lectures there was standing room only, and Rowan, cheered by the Setons' presence, entertained them with gourmet meals, music, and good conversation.

Despite his worry about the state of the world, Rowan, as usual, remained active on a variety of levels. He continued to draw and sculpt, maintained his interest in research that was being carried out elsewhere, and advised young researchers. No wonder Moreau, who always admired Rowan's versatility and industry, wrote, "Some men get four lives into a lifetime and others are not half alive."[42] After Rowan finished "As the Crow Flies" and sent it to a publisher, he began several other writing projects. In early 1940, encouraged by Huxley, Rowan made plans to expand his research on biological cycles. This was especially important at the time, because, due to the war, British researchers were unable to work on fundamental research. Huxley also urged Rowan to carry on the "migration and reproduction work."[43] He had already discussed Rowan's scientific work with Dr. Warren Weaver, director of natural sciences for the Rockefeller Foundation. Huxley encouraged Rowan to apply for a grant; he wrote, "I am not unhopeful that [Weaver] will do something for you, if you play your cards right."[44]

Rowan followed the advice. He requested and received fifteen hundred dollars from the Rockefeller Foundation to investigate the pituitary-hormonal relation as well as the inheritance of the migratory instinct in crows.[45] In his application, sent in April 1940, he gave a concise history of his previous research on light, and listed the four major problems he would investigate: the migration of birds, the effects of light on the avian gonad, neo-Lamarckism and migration, and the pituitary-gonad relationship. He wanted to increase the number of castrated birds he would use to elaborate and extend the "previous use of hormones . . . with special reference to the function of the pituitary and gonads."[46]

During the summer of 1940, Rowan and Lister, searching for breeding crows, travelled hundreds of kilometres in all directions without much success. The hot, dry August weather, following unseasonable July rains, resulted in a "marked scarcity of crows" across the Prairie provinces. In fact, Rowan noted, all that "travelling and unremitting labour" netted only 250 crows. The experience made Rowan cautious, and he kept the crows' location secret. They were housed in a large building rented from the Edmonton Exhibition Association, but, after some boys broke into the building on 29 September, nearly two hundred of the crows escaped. Attempts to trap additional birds resulted mainly in exhaustion and frustration, and at the end Rowan ended up with only seventy-five crows.

Rowan faced a serious problem. Much as he hated to report negative results, he had to advise the Rockefeller Foundation of the mishap and possibly return the rest of the grant. As he had already invested much time, energy, and a large portion of the grant in catching and feeding crows, Rowan was reluctant to admit defeat. With some exaggeration he wrote: "I find it difficult . . . to admit the first failure of my career to fulfil the terms of a research grant, but circumstances have been unrelentingly against us."[47] Rowan had an alternative plan for the grant. He wanted to investigate the direction taken by the immature captive crows, which had received no treatment of any kind, and see whether or not these inexperienced crows would follow the usual northwest to southeast migration route. With the permission of the foundation, Rowan carried out this experiment. On 9 November 1940, Rowan released fifty-four crows, 60 percent of which were subsequently recaptured.

Rowan was also allowed to keep the rest of the grant for another year because his teaching load had been increased due to "the reconstitution of our medical curriculum,"[48] but by the summer of 1942, he had serious doubts about spending money on fundamental research. The United States was at war, and Rowan expected that there, as it had in England, basic research would cease. He wrote, "Experiments in migration are so far removed from the war effort, that I am wondering whether to drop the matter or proceed with it."[49] The Rockefeller Foundation assured him, however, that they were glad to see "basic research continue provided this did not interfere with essential war effort."[50] So Rowan began to trap crows once again, and to carry out the proposed light and hormone experiments. For reasons that cannot be ascertained, he abandoned the project before its completion.[51] After the war Rowan attempted to trap crows again, hoping to use different kinds of extracts on them, but once more he was unlucky and caught no crows. In 1946 he ruefully admitted to a young scientist that the "matter still rests in abeyance."[52]

Rowan had practically given up on light experiments, but others continued with the research. His correspondence on the subject, with peers, students, and younger scientists, remained an important part of his life. J.S. Huxley, R.E. Moreau, J.G. Van Oordt, Niko Tinbergen, Emil Witschi, W.S. Bullough, D.S. Farner, and Albert Wolfson were among them, and their varying approaches and conclusions challenged his mind.[53] Wolfson, who with D.S. Farner carried Rowan's original work to new heights after World War II, later wrote of the indebtedness of many scientists to Rowan "for introducing the experimental approach to bird migration."[54] Although Rowan's other concerns took him away from experimental work, he enjoyed being called a pioneer. His ground-breaking research was valued by scientists who built their own research on it. In 1946, Rowan was also honoured by the Royal Society of Canada, which awarded him the Flavelle Medal for his outstanding research work.[55] This recognition was the best he could possibly achieve in Canada.

The award citation was read at the official presentation on 20 May in Toronto. It praised Rowan for opening up "this whole field of inquiry which includes some of the most vexed problems of animal behaviour." It mentioned that numerous other scientists followed in Rowan's footsteps and "added greatly to our knowledge of the effect of light and other ecological factors on migration, the seasonal reproduction in animals and related phenomena." The citation emphasized the fact that Rowan not only made the first important contribution to this area of investigation, and built "a sound Department of Zoology at the University of Alberta, but has brought distinction to it through his researches."[56]

In addition to the address Rowan gave at the presentation ceremony, entitled "Experiments in Bird Migration," he gave another talk: "The Inception of Human Speech," — a topic that became part of a book-length manuscript, "The Last Chapter," which was "a pessimist's view of the 20th century looked at from the standpoint of human biology."[57] Though most of the eminent Canadian biologists who listened to Rowan's invitation address were already familiar with his previous investigations, they enjoyed the opportunity to hear his views on the connection between fact and theory in scientific research. For, in "Experiments in Bird Migration," Rowan not only reviewed his pioneering investigations but he also stated his research philosophy:

The establishment of simple facts of this sort, that have in the past been considered untenable myths, seems to me to be one of the most useful functions of experimental biology. Facts will always be facts, concrete and tangible, and they will undoubtedly always give rise to further theories . . . . Out of such theories there arises that further type of experimental work that sifts and analyses, that probes into causes and effects, that eliminates and establishes, and which, if one happens to be lucky, may bring to light some unexpected generalization that may further our understanding of life at large.[57]

14

Population Cycles

ALTHOUGH ROWAN DEVELOPED into an ardent conservationist during the 1920s and 1930s, we can easily see from his field notes that he had long been aware that wildlife populations were diminishing in Western Canada. He later recalled that his interest in fluctuating animal numbers, or cycles, originated in 1908.[1] Under Professor Oliver's direction at Blakeney Point, Rowan had studied the relationship of the rabbit to its food supply, an animal-ecology topic. After he moved to Edmonton, Rowan once again became concerned with certain aspects of animal ecology, particularly the four-and ten-year fluctuations of game birds and furbearing animals. On his hunting and collecting trips in the Edmonton district and in his casual chats with trappers, settlers, and other hunters, Rowan first learned about the periodic disappearance of game. He heard that this unexplained shortage of grouse, rabbit, and other animals seriously affected the inhabitants of remote areas. In Canada, a country with a dispersed population, hunting and trapping had always had considerable economic value. Since the late nineteenth century American hunters had flocked to the north country, and so hunting also became a lucrative part of the new tourist industry.

Rowan was a keen hunter who thoroughly enjoyed shooting for sport. Like other hunters, he also wanted to ensure a continuity in animal populations. In contrast to most contemporary North American conservationists, however, Rowan did not believe that hunting regulations would solve all conservation problems. For Rowan, field naturalist and trained scientist, the best approach to conservation was a thorough investigation of all the factors responsible for the periodic or permanent disappearance of wildlife. At the University of Alberta, Rowan was in an excellent position to study wildlife cycles. When collecting data about the animals of the Edmonton district, he observed their occurrence, numbers, and habitats, and noted changes in water levels and natural food supplies. Later he obtained comparative information (both historical and geographical) from old-time naturalists, as well as from farmers, hunters, and trappers.

In 1924 Rowan decided to study the cycles of the "chicken" or (sharp-tailed grouse) and the "rabbit" (the varying or snowshoe hare), at the same time. Though busy with teaching, sketching, fieldwork, and migration experiments, Rowan began a long-term study of what he later termed "Canada's premier problem of conservation."[2] His plan was supported by Julian Huxley, and one of Huxley's students, the ecologist Charles Elton, who had studied the vole cycle on the Spitsbergen Islands, and whose *Animal Ecology* (1924) had initiated a new orientation in the study of animals.

Rowan began corresponding with Elton in 1925. The British ecologist lacked firsthand experience with rabbit population cycles. He was eager to hear from Rowan "on the subject of fluctuation in animals" because he realized there was "a good deal of work to be done by correlating other people's facts."[3] Rowan, in turn, wished to keep in touch with Elton, who had access to scientific literature that was, Rowan later remarked, "entirely out of reach of an institution like ours with a limited library."[4] Elton's literature search soon revealed that fur traders of the Hudson's Bay Company and members of the Moravian Mission in Labrador had recorded cyclic phenomena. Their historical records, which pertain to areas between thirty and sixty degrees north of the equator, became an important part of the twentieth-century scientific study of population cycles.

In Canada, J.H. Fleming used the early ornithological literature to document, in 1907, the population fluctuations in snowy owls, birds of prey that feed on small rodents in the Arctic. Later, Ernest Thompson Seton searched the Hudson's Bay Company records to plot the numbers of furbearing animals.[5] His graphs were incorporated into Gordon Hewitt's *Conservation of the Wild Life in Canada* (1921).

By the early years of the twentieth century field studies were being carried out by scientists in Britain, the United States, the Scandinavian countries, and Russia. Following the British red-grouse inquiry, and the ruffed-grouse studies in New York State and Minnesota, Taverner encouraged Fred Bradshaw to study the ruffed-grouse cycle in Saskatchewan.[6] During the same period Norman Criddle started to investigate the fluctuations of grasshoppers in Manitoba. Rowan was thus one of many scientists who began to question the how and why of changes in game-bird and mammal populations. His ecological studies had broad implications: population fluctuations were a conservation problem affecting animals of the north temperate zone and had fundamental scientific importance. But Rowan's views were regarded sceptically by hunters, and his 1924 prediction of a game-bird "crash" in 1927 apparently scandalized the Alberta Game League. Rowan later remembered that because the prairie chicken was "just beginning to get really thick again throughout central Alberta, all thought that I was cracked."[7]

As part of his larger study, Rowan looked for local phenomena, such as maximum and minimum numbers in rabbit and grouse populations.[8] As he could not carry out this investigation singlehandedly, in March 1925 he approached the Hudson's Bay Company, asking them to distribute "a number of small parcels of one and two ounce bottles containing some suitable fixative," such as formalin, to the various trading posts. The instructions explained the general purpose of the study. Trappers on their winter rounds were asked to note the general condition of the skinned animals and examine the internal organs of those found in poor condition. Rowan wanted the collected samples of diseased internal parts to be put in bottles, labelled appropriately, and mailed to him at the university. He stressed that evidence of disease, together with other data, "might lead to highly important results."[9]

Like many of the good ideas that grew out of Rowan's wide range of interests, this one fizzled out. Even though the district manager of the Hudson's Bay Company was interested in "solving the mystery of the law of periodicity existing among fur bearing animals," the plan was thought unworkable because the "Indians would laugh" at it and the "white trappers would not do it without remuneration."[10] He suggested that Rowan address his inquiries directly to hunters and trappers. They might then provide him with the information at no cost. Rowan at this point began what was to become three decades of sporadic data gathering in Alberta. Elton encouraged him to publish his findings in the *Journal of Ecology*,[11] but Rowan was too involved in various other projects to take the time to do so. While his work on biological cycles took a back seat to his other research interests, Rowan corresponded with a number of scientists about this topic. He finally met these colleagues during the summer of 1931, at the First International Congress on Biological Cycles in Matamek, Quebec.

In the 1930s, Matamek was an isolated village just east of Sept Iles on the north shore of the St. Lawrence River, and could only be reached by boat. In good years it was a naturalist's dream area, as well as a paradise for hunters and fishermen. In good years, the cold waters of the Gulf of St. Lawrence held food for numerous whales, porpoises, and seabirds. There were salmon in the rivers, and deer, moose, and game birds on the inland muskegs. In bad years, the food supply decreased and the natives lived in poverty and hunger.

Because he spent summers at his hunting lodge in Matamek, American conservationist Copley Amory knew about the plight of the local inhabitants, and wanted to do something to improve their lot. By 1930, he had realized that both the locals and the various fur-trading companies "would benefit in economy and efficiency by conducting their trade with more knowledge of the phenomena of cycles."[12] Amory discussed the wildlife situation with American conservationists and scientists. He talked to officials of the Royal Danish Trading Company and the Hudson's Bay Company and, at Oxford, to Elton who, since 1925, had been working as a consultant for the Hudson's Bay Company. Elton persuaded Amory to organize a conference and invite researchers from various backgrounds to exchange their ideas.[13]

Typically, the Canadian Matamek conference materialized because of American initiative and funding. As the moving force behind the scheme, Amory hoped the conference would help scientists to coordinate their future research and perhaps even lead to the establishment of a permanent centre for research on biological cycles. He raised funds, invited scientists, government representatives, and officials of the forestry, fishing, and transportation industries. He publicized the conference, played host at his hunting lodge, and financed the travel of various contributors. Although Rowan was occupied with plans for his extensive crow research, he prepared enthusiastically for the meeting. He anticipated a lively scientific exchange, and also hoped to benefit from the occasion by persuading government officials to finance his research projects. But the journey from Edmonton to Matamek was prohibitively expensive. Fortunately not everyone was affected by the Depression, and an unidentified friend offered Amory ten thousand dollars for conference expenses.[14] Then Amory invited Rowan to help the organizing committee, arranged a free pass for him on the Canadian National Railway train from Edmonton to Quebec City, and obtained free passage for him on the Clarke Steamship Line boat from Quebec City to Matamek. He even sent Rowan a small cheque to "help provide some comforts on the journey."[15]

Rowan left Edmonton on 11 July 1931 for Toronto, Montreal, and Quebec City. He spent 14 July in Quebec City as a "temporary member of the Garrison Club [which had a] lovely old building and magnificent grounds." Rowan was the "guest of [club member] Colonel Stanton of the Clarke Steamship Company." The colonel's hospitality and the luxurious surroundings were a welcome change for Rowan, but on board the *North Voyager*, later in the day, he had no cabin and even had a hard time finding a quiet corner.[16] Used to sleeping in haystacks, tents, and on hard railway seats, Rowan took all this in stride. Up at dawn, he watched the heavily forested coastline, so familiar from his cross-Atlantic voyages, but looking larger and more imposing from the smaller ship than it had from the deck of an ocean liner. A fifteen-kilometre railway trip inland from Clarke City took the passengers to a factory that prepared pulp for the London *Times*. Rowan did not comment on the stench of the pulp mill or on the polluted streams. He only remarked on the "most magnificent rugged site."[17] At Matamek, Rowan explored the countryside with Elton and Amory. He found the coast biologically "poor. The rockpools contain practically nothing." He noted, however, that there were winkles, chitons, urchins, whelks, and mussels on the island, Beluga whales and dolphins in the St. Lawrence, and salmon in the Matamek River.[18]

Because the Matamek conference aimed to stimulate government as well as scientific interest in the cyclic fluctuations of plants and animals, the participants included Dr. Charles Camsell (president of the Royal Society of Canada and deputy minister of mines), the Honourable T.G. Murphy (minister of the interior), and J.B. Harkin (commissioner of the National Parks Branch). The federal government also provided some funds for the conference. Quebec representatives included ministers Hector La Ferté (Department of Game and Fisheries) and Honoré Mercier (Department of Lands and Forests). The Canadian scientific community was well represented by R.E. De Lury (astronomer and assistant director of the Dominion Observatory), who wished to promote research on the influence of sunspots on cycles; Harrison F. Lewis (ornithologist at the National Parks Branch); J.R. Dymond (zoologist at the Royal Ontario Museum); R.M. Anderson (zoologist at the National Museum of Canada); and A.G. Huntsman (marine biologist at the University of Toronto). Several European and American scientists, conservationists, businessmen, and government representatives participated in the paper sessions and round-table discussions. There were even a few journalists present. The Montreal *Gazette* and the *New York Times* covered the entire conference, and *Le Soleil* (Quebec City), *La Presse* (Montreal), and the *Montreal Daily Star* reported on the opening sessions.

The conference began on 24 July 1931. Elton described the worldwide nature of wildlife fluctuations. He reported that in the late 1920s, Vito Volterra, an Italian mathematician working on theoretical formulations of the population problem, could not obtain sufficient biological data for his work. In view of the later importance of Volterra's equation for population biology, his complaint was an indication of the elementary state of research on the subject in that period.[19] Rowan introduced the novel idea that ducks may have cycles of about thirty-four years, and emphasized the influence of water shortages on duck production.[20] He discussed the fluctuation of bird life in Western Canada, and the possible effects of ultraviolet radiation, vitamin D, and various parasites on animals.[21] Harrison F. Lewis used census data collected by the National Parks Branch to show that weather influenced the size of seabird colonies in the Gulf of St. Lawrence, while R.M. Anderson stressed the importance of surveys and life-history studies in obtaining information on population numbers. J.R. Dymond spoke about turning museums into repositories for research material, which would be made "readily available for other researchers."[22] American scientists gave papers on their investigations of game-bird cycles, snowy-owl invasions, and diseases of wild animals.

The conference also became a forum for discussions on how to best train and finance researchers. The problems Canadians faced were highlighted when comparison were made between the financial support available in Britain and the United States and that available in Canada. At Oxford University, with the financial aid of the Hudson's Bay Company and other agencies, preparations were under way to establish the Bureau of Animal Populations under Elton's direction. In the United States, game-management expert Aldo Leopold explained, various industries proposed to underwrite fellowships in agricultural colleges to aid cooperation on cycles research. By contrast, in Canada, Dymond pointed out, there were no private sources to fund research, and government agencies were unable or unwilling to provide support in their stead. Ichthyology was relatively well funded because of its economic importance to the fishery, but graduate work in other areas of zoology went unsupported. The gloomy fiscal prognosis for Canadian research clouded discussion of the future study of population fluctuations. While American scientists proposed to continue their regional and statewide studies, and their British counterparts pinned their hopes on Elton's Bureau of Animal Populations, Canadian scientists, at best, could remain optimistic.

After the paper sessions and round-table discussion, members of the conference relaxed. They made field excursions into the treeless muskegs, "firm but very springy."[23] Rowan had a great time talking with noted scientists and government officials in a congenial environment. They all enjoyed the good food, wine, whiskey, and conversation. Rowan celebrated his fortieth birthday at Matamek, and the thoughtful Amory hosted a party for him. Amory had supplied a "magnificent cake made with candles and all and I had to sit beside him for dinner." Rowan was toasted by members of this international assembly, and remarked with uncharacteristic, and probably false, modesty that he was "quite overcome by such unmerited adulation."[24] The writer-naturalist Thornton W. Burgess recited "The Perfect Cycle," a poem he had written for the occasion. It began:

What is a birthday? Just a cycle
That's completed once a year
There's no crash, no fluctuation
Sunspots never interfere.

Seven stanzas later, it ended with:

What's a birthday? Just a marker
In the whirling of the spheres
To remind us life eternal
Is not measured by the years.

Burgess then raised his glass and said "And now ladies and gentlemen, I ask you to drink to this Toast: May Rowan's birthdays attain their peak only when all the crows fly north." He dedicated the poem to "William Rowan to celebrate a birthday far from home on July 29, 1931, at Matamek on the Labrador."[25] At the beginning of August, Rowan left Matamek by boat for Rimouski, and there transferred to the Maritime Express for Montreal. In Montreal he took the CNR train to Alberta, and upon arriving home joined his vacationing family at Seba Beach. Rowan had little time to ponder the outcome of the Matamek conference, as he was kept busy correcting proofs of *The Riddle of Migration*. Later, the crow research took over his life.

It often happened that Canada provided the natural setting for research supported and conducted by non-Canadians. During the 1930s and 1940s, with the administrative backing of the National Parks Branch (Canada), members of the Bureau of Animal Populations conducted extensive investigations on the lynx and snowshoe hare in Canada. The work, by Elton, Mary Nicholson, and Helen and Dennis Chitty, was based mostly on questionnaires. Later, they compared their data with Hudson's Bay Company records. Although the large-scale "snowshoe rabbit inquiry" was a project originally envisaged by Rowan, he never had the resources to send questionnaires to naturalists, hunters, and trappers across the country, or the time to evaluate the data. In the past, with their minuscule government appropriation, the National Parks Branch could only fund small-scale studies. Now they were delighted to reap the benefits of Elton's long-term research.

During the following years, several universities, including the University Toronto and University of Minnesota, developed research projects that involved the study of cycles. Rowan could find no money to initiate similar projects in Alberta, and it would have been futile to turn to the National Research Council of Canada. As long as Tory was at its helm, Rowan had no chance of obtaining funding from this source. In fact, Elton's application, backed by the Hudson's Bay Company, was also rejected by Tory. Apparently, after the conference, Elton had approached Tory and explained to him the economic benefits of research on furbearing animal cycles. Tory promised to bring Elton's proposal to the council for evaluation, but, according to Charles Camsell, Tory did nothing of the sort, and the proposal was never even seen by council members.[26]

Rowan knew he had to look elsewhere for funds, but he was too busy to conduct a search. Pursuing the crow investigations, looking for other positions, and travelling with his family to the West Coast left him little time to devote to raising funds. Finally, in the fall of 1932, he began to think about applying to the United States National Research Council. Rowan's correspondence on the subject with American ecologist F.E. Clements reveals that he felt somewhat hesitant about approaching the American organization. The letters also describe the difficulties Rowan and other Canadian scientists faced in the early 1930s. Rowan told Clements that the provincial government in Alberta had reduced the

> University Grant by the rather staggering sum of $150.000.00 [for 1933]. Research of any kind means absolutely nothing to our farmer government, but hitherto we have managed to squeeze little items here and there out of our departments to help things along. Now we shall be extremely fortunate if we can buy the bare materials for our students.[27]

Rowan also explained that he was reluctant to apply to an American agency because he was convinced that "the cycle problem is one of vital interest to Canada and Canadians," and it should therefore be the Canadian government that supported such research — "unhesitatingly."[28] However, the money was unavailable in Canada and despite his strong sentiments about Canadian support for Canadian conservation and economic problems, Rowan did send a plan for a cooperative research project to the United States National Research Council. He proposed an investigation of population cycles in Western Canada, "with special reference to the Edmonton, Alberta, district."

Rowan maintained that "the usual approach to the cycle problem, the collecting of statistics from far and near and their subsequent examination, will never bring fruitful results for the simple reason that facts so collected are not the crucial ones." The facts only demonstrated the existence of fluctuations. Rowan's alternative approach was "a concentrated local investigation, seeking to probe the problem from every suggestive angle" to obtain different data. For this he initiated a multidisciplinary investigation, and planned to involve specialists from a variety of disciplines to "handle each separate item and the whole will finally be co-ordinated and critically sifted." Rowan stressed the suitability of Edmonton as the centre for this research. Apart from the fact that he was based there, the city was "far enough north to get cycles on an impressive scale, within easy reach of the unsettled wilderness and yet possessing men and equipment fitted for such an undertaking." Rowan also proposed to cooperate with Elton, who, being at Oxford, was "in a position to survey the entire field on both sides of the Atlantic."[29]

At a time when multidisciplinary research was rare, Rowan's plan was highly innovative. It included a study of tree rings, particularly those of the white spruce, to be conducted by Professor Moss of the university's botany department. Meteorological phenomena (such as the ozone content of the atmosphere and ultraviolet radiation) were to be investigated by physics professors Nichols and Gowan. Rowan, Hughes, and Lister were to carry out the "biological side" of the investigation. They were to collect and weigh animals, do post mortems, analyze stomach contents, count embryos in rabbits, and clutch-size variations in grouse. Other observers were to contribute data on the feeding habits of the animals concerned. Rowan wrote that he expected the peak of the rabbit cycle to occur in 1935, and that the years between 1932 and 1935 were "the crucial ones with all the animals involved fast reaching their maximum numbers."[30]

Rowan envisaged pathological and biochemical studies as integral parts of the investigations. Cultures deriving from the post mortems, "that could be handled on the spot" were to be studied by the university's pathology department, while the diseased grouse material was to be sent to Professor A.O. Gross at Bowdoin College, and the rabbit material to Professor E.G. Green at the University of Minnesota. Rowan was convinced that the biochemical aspects of the cycle would prove of primary importance. Through his long associations with Collip, Hunter, and a number of American biochemists who supplied him with hormonal extracts for his migration studies, Rowan was made well aware of the growing importance of biochemistry.[31] He co-opted professors Hunter from biochemistry and Climenko from physiology to investigate the general biochemistry and physiology of rabbits, as well as blood changes, which were an important means of assessing the rabbits' health. Strickland, the entomologist, was to study the ticks that were the carriers of turalemia and other diseases.

Rowan's estimated research cost was only $2,220 for a three-year period. Although this was a modest amount and Rowan had good supporters for his proposal, including Ellsworth Huntington of Yale, the United States National Research Council was unable to fund the request. Rowan heard the bad news just before he set out for England in May 1933, but he was too sick to fret about the refusal. Once in Britain, and feeling better, he applied to the Royal Society's Gunning Fund and received a grant of fifty pounds to do research on the Canadian rabbit cycle.[32] As this was far from enough for the proposed multidisciplinary investigation, Rowan curtailed his research plan. His nervous breakdown in December 1933 temporarily disrupted all his activities, including a series of "national network" radio broadcasts on cycles, which he began during the winter of 1932–1933. These popular talks reached a wide circle of listeners, some from as far away as Winnipeg, who faithfully tuned in every week.[33]

By the mid-1930s, Rowan was forced to revert to his original investigation of nearly a decade before, circulating letters of inquiry to farmers, trappers, and settlers. He devised several questionnaires on game birds and furbearing animals, such as the Hungarian (now gray) partridge (introduced into the region in the early twentieth century and beginning to show signs of cyclic fluctuations), the ruffed grouse, sharp-tailed grouse, lynx, coyote, fox, mouse, snowshoe hare, squirrel, groundhog, and gopher.[34] There were questions about current and past abundance of the various species, sudden changes in animal populations, and diseased and dying animals. Prospective respondents were asked to fill out the questionnaire but, Rowan added, "If you cannot yourself fill in the answers, please hand the questionnaires to someone who can, but PLEASE do NOT ignore it."[35] The response was not only enthusiastic, it was practically overwhelming. Rowan received numerous replies from old-timers — settlers who remembered the presence, or absence, of animals in the late nineteenth and early twentieth centuries. Guides, trappers, and game wardens wrote of their long-standing interest in the problem of animal fluctuation, interest that intensified after Rowan's radio talks.

In 1934, Rowan managed to obtain further funds. He received a $420 grant from the Carnegie Foundation to pay for the technical assistance of Dr. Winnifred Hughes and two research fellows, and also $700 to hire a graduate student to do research on cycles. This student was to be J.D. Gregson, who had done his B.Sc. research on ticks at the University of British Columbia, and who hoped to pursue graduate studies on the rabbit tick and conduct experiments "in the physiology of their feeding."[36] Gregson arrived in Edmonton in late September 1934, and was soon immersed in the study of rabbits and ticks. Within a few months Rowan and Gregson had made an exciting discovery.[37]

As Rowan described it, Gregson was trying to get the ticks to feed on the rabbit (the host animal) in the laboratory, but the ticks would not even attach themselves to the rabbits. Based on his own previous work on the effect of artificial illumination on juncos and crows, Rowan recommended in November (he told J.B. Collip) that Gregson "try the lighting business on a rabbit for six or seven weeks and then cage one or two ticks on it and watch the results." Gregson followed the advice and in early January, put a tick on the animal. "It immediately attached itself and engorged at the usual summer rate." Rowan wrote to Collip, "As far as I know this is the first time in history that anyone has gotten the indirect effect of this discovery in which one animal, the tick, has shown immediate response to the changed physiology of a second animal, the rabbit."[38] A report on the discovery, coauthored by Rowan and Gregson, was published in *Nature* in 1935.

Although the proposed multidisciplinary investigation on cycles had to be abandoned, Rowan, by means of questionnaires and actual field observations, managed to accumulate much useful information. The fieldwork, which often included trips to all sorts of habitats in southern and eastern Alberta, also provided a perfect excuse for Rowan to spend time outdoors. On his travels Rowan talked to a great variety of people. He enjoyed meeting old-timers, many of whom were already familiar with the "Doctor" through his radio broadcasts and newspaper articles. Much of the information they gave him reminded Rowan of the stories he had listened to so avidly as a young man on the Canadian Prairies. Instead of the wolves and buffalos of the old days, he now heard about the prairie chicken, which "used to sit on the fence posts in great numbers, and one could shoot a dozen with one shot."[39] One of Rowan's casual informants was a tramp he had picked up on his travels who told him that the rabbit and grouse "had practically gone, many [rabbits] failed to turn white and were apparently the ones to die in the fall."[40] Another contact, a parson interested in animal cycles, told Rowan about finding cysts on various parts of snowshoe hares.

The cross-country trips helped Rowan to form a general impression of the current state of the population fluctuations. In December 1934, after an exhausting five-day car trip that took him back to the Dorothy area of southeastern Alberta, Rowan noted that he only saw a few rabbits and even their tracks were "not plentiful." In contrast to mammals, ruffed grouse were numerous in the northern parts, but partridge populations had decreased everywhere. By early September 1935, Rowan found that there were few Hungarian partridges, and that rabbit and prairie chicken numbers had also dwindled. The problem was obviously widespread. There was a "natural vacuum of rabbits and all the species of grouse."[41] Rowan was in a good position to study the factors involved in the crash of wildlife, but could not convince the Alberta Game League to cooperate in the investigations.[42] As so often before, Rowan had to carry out his investigations on his own, and on a shoestring.

During the 1920s, while trying to save the threatened buffalo, Rowan had also collected some information on the whooping crane. By 1930 he had become one of the people who supplied data to Fred Bradshaw, director of the Saskatchewan Natural History Museum, who, prompted by Taverner, had initiated an investigation and an education program. Bradshaw sent fifteen hundred circulars and questionnaires to correspondents from Alaska to South America to solicit information "regarding the migration, occurrence, nesting and breeding grounds of the Whooping Crane."[43] Interested in the status of this species in Alberta, Rowan wrote to Bradshaw that he had heard whooping cranes in the Pembina-Athabasca muskegs but could find no evidence of nesting. Bradshaw assured him that these birds show "their cunning in hiding from any intruders . . . this is possibly one reason why little is known of the Whooping Cranes in their breeding grounds." He also told Rowan that although three nests had been found in a well-settled district, few of the residents had any idea "these magnificent birds" were nesting there.[44] The chief migration route was through Saskatchewan, but what happened to the birds north of the settled region was still unclear. Rowan's help in unravelling this mystery was much needed, particularly because Bradshaw suspected the best information concerning the cranes in Alberta would come from the region north of Edmonton.[45] On his subsequent trips to the muskegs Rowan never ceased to listen and watch for whooping cranes, but he never actually saw the birds.[46]

Rowan's work on wildlife and conservation, like that of Taverner, Brooks, Laing, and other Canadians, complemented similar studies carried out in the United States. The disappearance of wildlife was a North American concern, but the principles of game management advocated by American President Teddy Roosevelt, American forestry expert Clifford Pinchot, and others, were only aimed at the species of wildlife that were of great interest to hunters. Game animals and certain other species (those either spectacular in appearance or existing in very large numbers) were more likely to be noticed and protected than other, more obscure ones.

In his attitude towards game animals, Rowan was more sophisticated that most conservationists of his time. For Rowan there were no bad birds, no pests, no varmints, and he was highly critical of others (including Allan Brooks) who maintained that the only good hawk or owl was a dead one. He saw nothing contradictory in hunting ducks and other game species while trying to conserve them, killing breeding birds and collecting their nests and eggs for biological investigations, or using specimens for his artwork, while trying to preserve habitats. He was a "wise-use" conservationist.[47] Unlike many of his contemporaries, Rowan could fully appreciate the artistic, educational, and recreational uses of the wilderness. Through his innumerable popular articles, letters to editors, radio broadcasts, and public lectures, he worked hard to instill in the Canadian public an interest in wildlife and conservation.

Rowan's ideas on conservation were developed in detail in a book manuscript aptly named "Beloved Wilderness." It was never published, but in a brief talk given in Winnipeg in 1957, Rowan summarized more than thirty years of experience with Canadian wildlife and conservation. It is evident that he deplored the "rabid anti-predator breed" of sportsmen who blamed the fact that game populations were declining on wolves, foxes, owls, and hawks rather than on humans or unknown biological factors. During his long association with Canadian and American hunters, Rowan became convinced that the "function of predators seems to be misunderstood by the average sportsman." He did not deny that predators "if abundant can make a sizable dent in the population of prey species, "but stressed that the human predator, irresponsible hunter and poacher, can do incomparably more harm.[48]

15

Conservation Problems

ROWAN'S CONSERVATION CONCERNS could not be separated from his interest in basic biological principles. The species that provided him with the information needed for his work were protected by various laws: the junco by the Migratory Bird Convention Act; game birds, ducks, and hares, to some extent, by provincial hunting regulations. Rowan came to see, however, that "the steady encroachment of man and what we euphemistically call progress . . . on the wildlife domain" was one of the major problems of modern conservation and intelligent management was a key to its solution.[1] This was a philosophy expounded in the United States by Aldo Leopold. Rowan began corresponding with Leopold in the early 1930s, and within a few years the two were working hard to ensure that wild ducks and their habitat would be preserved on the Canadian Prairies.

During the 1930s, when extreme drought across the western provinces and states caused much personal suffering, the lakes were reduced to mere sloughs, and the "sloughs to nothing." Without water there were no ducks. This created serious problems for Canadians, and Americans, for whom duck hunting on the Canadian Prairies had become a favourite pastime.[2] As the drought coincided with a widespread economic depression, the loss of revenue from hunting licenses and tourism further exacerbated already serious economic problems. Rowan's original interest in ducks was closely tied to his love of shooting, as was his interest in other forms of wildlife. Throughout the 1920s he observed the changing patterns of duck populations. Decreasing water levels had resulted in the shift of favoured staging areas for waterfowl at Beaverhills Lake and elsewhere.

In Canada, waterfowl research was either government funded or conducted privately by individual naturalist-ornithologists. In the United States, the Bureau of Biological Survey was responsible for such studies, but the economic importance of this research area also led to the establishment of private conservation organizations, such as Ducks Unlimited, and the Delta Research Station in Manitoba. It was inevitable that Rowan, with his varied interest in wildlife, become one of the scientific advisers of the Delta Research Station. It is unclear how Rowan and the station's benefactor, American industrialist James Ford Bell of Minnesota, first established contact. Bell may have heard about Rowan's light experiments or read *The Riddle of Migration.*

Bell had been hunting ducks for a number of years around Delta Marsh at the southern end of Lake Manitoba. He owned a hunting lodge there and often invited friends and colleagues for duck shoots in the fall. In the early 1930s, Bell watched the decrease of waterfowl with dismay. He observed that declining water levels, together with increased hunting pressures, resulted in the drastic reduction of the numbers of breeding ducks. Like many farsighted hunters who were also "wise-use" conservationists, Bell was convinced that waterfowl were a renewable resource. He decided to raise ducks in a hatchery and return them to the marsh. In the summer of 1932 he began corresponding with Rowan and invited him to hunt at Delta.

Rowan was excited at the prospect and took the train on 26 September 1932 to Portage la Prairie. At the station he was met by "Mr. Ward, Bell's head man, a very decent fellow." Together they drove on rutted, slippery roads to the hunting lodge, where Rowan finally met Bell, "a tall, pleasant man of 53." A good host and an enthusiastic hunter, Bell showed Rowan the marshes and the tidy, carefully planned hatchery, then took him by canoe "for a real shooting over decoys with 2 guides." Because he was known around Edmonton as a crack shot, Rowan was surprised that he could not hit the birds from the canoe. He noted that it is "curious — and absurd — that a duck, momentarily standing still in the air, should be difficult to hit, but as soon as they come overhead with the wind doing anything up to 80 miles an hour, they prove most satisfactory targets."[3]

Rowan and Bell had much in common. They both loved the outdoors and hunting, and were deeply interested in wildlife, conservation, and art. Rowan hoped Bell would become a financial backer for his proposed light and cycle research. Bell, in turn, wanted to benefit from Rowan's scientific advise about breeding ducks in a hatchery under artificial light. Their association proved fruitful for waterfowl research. Their correspondence indicates that Bell lent Rowan money. As Rowan was always in need of a "spot of cash," the loans continued; theoretically, the money was to be paid back at some future date, in practice, most of it wasn't. Bell also became a concerned friend. When Rowan complained about his ailments, the older man wrote: "you are young; you have a vast amount of knowledge and all the prospects of a very constructive life; it therefore behooves you to take care of yourself."[4]

Bell pledged his support for the duck-breeding program, as long as he was able to finance it. To make it all work, he attempted to involve other sportsmen, as well as a number of American and Canadian government, and private, organizations. As hunting in Manitoba provided revenue for the provincial government, in 1933–1934 the government offered Bell's duck hatchery the services of their pathologist, who could determine botulism and other possible diseases.[5] There were many other unknown factors contributing to the duck problem. Bell was particularly puzzled by the abundance of ducks in some areas, and their scarcity in others. He worried that "the duck was doomed."[6]

In 1935 things improved. Water levels were again rising. This increased the natural food supply. It also encouraged the growth of plants, which were used as nesting cover by breeding ducks. During this period the hatchery was functioning reasonably well, even though it lacked scientific and technical direction.[7] Prior to his sabbatical, Rowan discussed with Bell the need to encourage research on canvasback-breeding biology. Once in England, Rowan looked for a suitable scientist to do the work. As a result of his search, he asked F. Fraser-Darling to work at Delta. Although the scientific work involved was challenging to Fraser-Darling, the pay (about three hundred pounds) was not enough to support his family. He declined but suggested that Rowan recruit a "younger fellow . . . someone recently graduated and with a little research experience."[8] The man who eventually took the position was H. Albert Hochbaum. Born in Colorado in 1911, Hochbaum studied ornithology at Cornell University under Arthur A. Allen, and game management at the University of Wisconsin under Aldo Leopold. A big, strapping fellow, Hochbaum was a keen hunter, outdoorsman, and a budding artist. He was ideal for the job.

So in 1938, the Delta duck hatchery became the Delta Research Station, and Rowan became part of the august group that advised it on research in duck-breeding biology and conservation. There were three scientists on the advisory board. Two were Americans: Aldo Leopold and Miles Pirnie; one was a Canadian: William Rowan. They planned the duck-breeding program and served as Hochbaum's advisers on canvasback research, itself financed jointly by Bell and the American Wildlife Institute. Rowan was a scientific adviser par excellence, and invested considerable time in supporting duck research at Delta Station. Nearly fifty years later Hochbaum recalled that Rowan had brought scientific rigour into waterfowl research and was always helpful, conscientious, and ready to encourage and offer helpful criticism. Just the same, to a young man, such as Hochbaum, just beginning his first major scientific investigation, Rowan's clear intellect, wide scientific knowledge, great field experience, and sardonic humour, seemed "a bit awesome."[9]

Rowan was always willing to correspond with Hochbaum, to chide, and to recommend yet another revision; he would also suggest important new lines of investigation. Hochbaum, in turn, encouraged Rowan in his many interests, and boosted his ego, praising his art, his writing, and his scientific research. "Every second year zoology student is familiar with your work in bird migration," he wrote to his mentor in 1943, "but very few ornithologists are familiar with your other talents."[10] Because the two men got on so well, it is hardly surprising that Rowan visited Delta at every available opportunity. Hochbaum was bright, considerate, and somewhat deferential. A sound scientist, excellent artist, and keen outdoorsman, he was a man after Rowan's own heart.[11]

Rowan's involvement with the Delta Research Station came at a providential time. The roles of mentor and adviser were perhaps more important to him than they were to Pirnie and Leopold, because at the University of Alberta Rowan had few graduate students and assistants. Hochbaum was older than most of Rowan's students, and the two became good companions and friends. They soon developed an affectionate bond that was beyond that of mentor and student. They were to spend much time in each other's company, at conferences and during Rowan's periodic visits to Delta. The obvious disparity in their physical appearances — the tall, blond Hochbaum towered over the short, balding professor — disguised numerous similarities of interest, and Hochbaum's use of the formal address "Doctor" when speaking to Rowan masked the real affection between the two. With Hochbaum Rowan was always in good spirits, and never complained about anything but his salary, but during their nearly twenty years of friendship Hochbaum learned that Rowan was a man working "far beyond his tether . . . [and was] extended beyond his personal resources."[12]

Delta Marsh, "a wilderness in a land of wheat fields"[13] was to become another of Rowan's favoured retreats, one where he could find solitude or companionship, a place of artistic and scientific inspiration. When problems confronted him at home and at the university, when he was depressed by the spectre of warring humanity and concerned about the future of the world, Delta and Al Hochbaum were to provide a haven, a respite, a retreat from the complexities and problems of everyday life.

During the summer of 1942, Rowan spent an increasing amount of time talking to farmers, conservationists, and other scientists about the need to investigate the coming peak of the ten-year cycle. His light and reproduction research stagnated, and the investigation of biological cycles assumed new importance. He once again circulated questionnaires about game abundance. He also obtained important statistical records on size, weight, and disease from an unexpected source — the illegal game that was killed after the legal bag-limit had been reached. Rowan discovered this source on his frequent visits to farmers and trappers.

He had ample field data on cycles but, as usual, needed funds for more sophisticated investigations. His hopes for a grant from the new Society for the Study of Cycles (established in New York to carry on the work discussed at the Matamek conference a decade before) fell through with America's entry into World War II. Rowan was not alone in being frustrated by the lack of funds. The peak of the next population cycle was expected in 1943–1944, and Canadian and American scientists fumed, unable to embark on the large-scale studies that would have helped them to understand the underlying reasons, the complex biological factors, that created this widespread phenomenon. In the meantime, Elton, at Oxford, gave up his work on biological cycles to study rat control for the British Government.[14]

The enterprising Rowan then launched a new scheme in early 1942: he hit upon the idea of selling game stamps of his own design to raise money for conservation. In the United States the sale of duck stamps to hunters had been a successful source of revenue for wildlife habitat preservation, and a similar project augured well for Canada. Rowan's idea was enthusiastically supported by members of the Alberta Fish and Game Association, while the University of Alberta Science Association agreed to distribute the stamps and administer the funds. The stamps (five different designs at twenty-five cents each, or five for a dollar) were subsequently sold throughout the Prairie provinces to hunters, stamp collectors, schoolchildren, and people interested in natural history. Hunting-licence vendors received a 10 percent commission to sell the stamps, while personal friends helped to promote the project without remuneration.

Unfortunately, there was no money for widespread publicity. Instead, a printed notice, a set of sample stamps, and a letter were sent to hunting-licence vendors to be displayed in conspicuous locations. The letter explained to vendors that the stamps were issued by the University of Alberta Science Association and approved by the provincial game department to raise funds "for a scientific investigation of certain game problems, such as the ten-year cycle of upland game birds and rabbits." The stamps were to provide funds for research during the war, "when the conservation of animal life, and particularly the question of diseases, takes on an important aspect."[15]

Rowan's stamps of the Canada goose, mallard duck, ring-necked pheasant, Hungarian partridge, and ruffed grouse were appreciated, but not many were bought. By the end of the first year the sale of stamps was far below what had been expected, and it seemed the whole scheme was a failure. He could not hope to sell enough to raise the one thousand dollars needed for research on the grouse cycle, and worried that "if the cycle goes untouched this time, it means waiting another 10 years."[16] Rowan had hoped to raise enough money to start a truly experimental investigation of the cycle problem. He had intended to induce artificially the cycle in captive animals and study the factors responsible for complex population fluctuations. Two years later he still had no money for this project and had to postpone the "experimental cycle" until after the war.[17] The sale of stamps would never bring in the money he envisaged but, eventually, there was enough for the purchase of a precision instrument to record ultraviolet radiation. Unfortunately, the equipment bought in 1944 was not delivered until 1946.

"I would give a lot to be situated . . . in some quiet spot with congenial home life and the chance to really write," wrote Rowan to Hochbaum in late 1945.[18] Life for him had become so "poisonous" that, by the summer of 1946, he seriously considered "leaving the university and abandoning science altogether." As he had so often before, Rowan wanted to change his life, give up teaching, and get into something else. He contemplated a business career in plastics with his son Julian. At other times, Rowan simply wanted complete freedom to do research and "a spot of writing in my leisure time."[19]

Encouraged by Al Hochbaum and Alex Lawrence, Rowan contemplated moving to Delta to work on the game cycle. He hoped for a nonteaching affiliation with some institution, such as the Wildlife Management Institute or the University of Manitoba. An even more attractive plan was to become a consulting biologist with Upland Game Birds Unlimited. This proposed organization was the brainchild of E.B. Pitbaldo, a Winnipeg lawyer, who with other Manitoba hunters hoped to establish a chartered corporation to investigate upland birds. Nothing came of this, however, because the government would not allow donations to such an organization to be tax free. Rowan was disappointed, but soon recovered and submitted a proposal to the Wildlife Management Institute. His project, entitled "Investigation of the Ten-Year Cycle of Upland Game Birds, the Snowshoe Rabbit, and Some Other Resident Animals of the Canadian North," could not be undertaken due to financial reasons. As had many of Rowan's previous pipe dreams, his plans for a business career or a nonteaching research affiliation remained unfulfilled.[20] Rowan was used to disappointments, and persevered with other plans. In 1949, still as keen as ever about drawing and sculpting, Rowan began lecturing on art anatomy.[21] The following year, he devised another scheme to capitalize on his art. He wrote to Hochbaum, that this would be a "new venture in the marketing line — a folder of drawings (pencil) of interest to naturalists and sportsmen," to be sold for five dollars and used on Christmas cards.[22]

Despite the fact that Rowan wanted to give up his academic career, he continued to be a challenging teacher. His colourful style — he delivered lectures from notes scribbled on scraps of papers — continued to stimulate and entertain hundreds of students each year. He now made an effort to involve advanced undergraduate students in his population-cycle investigations. Many of these students became biologists and conservationists, and more than thirty years after Rowan's death they still recalled with amusement and fondness their field excursions with him.[23] Rowan had always encouraged and inspired others to carry out biological research; now he developed a number of mentor-apprentice relationships with a group of selected students. F.A. Oeming, Roy Anderson, David Stelfox, and Lloyd Keith not only learned about science and nature from Rowan, but they also were exposed to his increasingly pessimistic world view, and his musings about the scientist's responsibility to society and about human integrity. In turn, they gave Rowan affection and loyalty, companionship and intellectual challenge, and even the odd argument. In various ways these relationships compensated Rowan for his lack of sympathetic colleagues and a harmonious family environment.

Life at home became happier in 1949, after George Hunter, Reta's friend and ally in political and peace work, left Edmonton. His departure was involuntary and sudden. Rowan noted that "On 29 June George Hunter was up before the Board of Governors and fired within 24 hours . . . . Little sympathy as people have for him, resentment is high . . . [His departure] has left the biochemistry department denuded and research students stranded."[24] Rowan had been hurt by Reta's friendship with Hunter, and considered his erstwhile field companion as the bane of his existence. Although life without Hunter in the background was likely to be more pleasant, Rowan was incensed by the way Hunter was dismissed, and voiced his feelings about it to everyone.[25] Rowan's correspondence about the Hunter case contains tangible proof that Rowan did not just write about integrity as a desirable quality, but that he was, indeed, a man of integrity. He sent letters of protest to the president of the University of Alberta, the principal of Queen's University, and to a number of fellow scientists.

Apparently Hunter had been let go after having had acrimonious relationships with University of Alberta presidents W.A. Kerr and Robert Newton for several years. He was charged with using his lectures to spread his political views. Rowan at the same time was lecturing to his students on warring humanity and the dangers of propaganda, but was not considered to be a Communist. By contrast, Hunter had been known for his leftist sympathies and was believed to be a card-carrying member of the Communist party. While the latter was untrue, Newton finally saw a way to get rid of Hunter, and, as Michiel Horn points out, the "procedures used were a travesty of due process."[26] The case was heatedly debated among faculty members, who felt they needed protection against sudden dismissals.[27]

In the late 1940s, Rowan's life often seemed to consist of a series of unpleasant encounters with colleagues and the university administration. He seriously worried that the world was facing annihilation resulting from the irresponsible use of the atom bomb. Rowan reacted to threats to his authority as department head, and to the general threat to humanity, with periods of depression, during which he questioned the usefulness of scientific research. Between these bouts he was feverishly active, tramping through the countryside, or concocting new fund-raising ideas for his own research on population cycles. At other times he was fully immersed in writing and talking about the evils of propaganda, and pondering solutions to the world's problems.

During these depressing years, Rowan retained his love of the outdoors and never entirely lost his interest in science. In 1946, when he finally received research funds from the Alberta Research Council for experimental investigations of population cycles, he had the perfect justification for spending increasing amounts of time studying the rabbit and game-bird situation in Alberta. The field investigations helped him to tolerate the time spent indoors, setting schedules, reading the scientific and philosophical literature, and writing letters. He also worked on several book manuscripts, numerous newspaper articles, radio talks, and scientific papers — all of which grew out of his long-standing interest in biological cycles.

While internal relations in the biology department were tense, during the 1950s, Rowan had many satisfactory experiences away from the university. He spent enjoyable periods of time at and around Anzac, southeast of Fort McMurray in northern Alberta. Just how Rowan met John Waring, a former mounted policeman, is unclear. Waring apparently knew a great deal about population cycles in the North. On his first visit to Anzac, in August 1950, Rowan noted that he was impressed by Waring's log cabin, which was so "immaculate, so tidy that I felt uncomfortable (but it was a shambles when I left!)." Waring reminded him of Joe Dawkins.[28] During the last few years of his life Rowan visited Waring several times a year. The tidy log cabin at Anzac replaced Joe's shack at Fawcett as a haven where he could rest, meditate, and revel in the undemanding friendship of a relatively uneducated, but genuinely interesting man. Indeed, Rowan's growing friendship with John Waring was a substitute for his friendship with Joe, now old and weak and unable to care for himself.

Depressed by the Korean War, Rowan fell in love with the Peace River country of northwestern Alberta, "with its magic name of human enchantment, the Utopian dream of all men."[29] Rowan left Edmonton by car on 11 May 1952 to accompany William Round, a cinematographer with the Department of Economic Affairs of Alberta, with whom he had been cooperating on an Alberta wildlife film. The two men were to visit the areas north and west of Grand Prairie to see trumpeter swans and other waterfowl. Rowan was enchanted. He found the area "incomparably lovely . . . a veritable artist's dream . . . . A charmed world!"[30] The scientist, the filmmaker, and a local guide found twenty-six pairs of the rare trumpeter swans and many other interesting birds, including nearly fifty pairs of Ross's geese and a few white-fronted geese. In a week they "procured material that could easily have taken years of painstaking effort" to gather. Accompanied by his graduate student Al Oeming, Rowan returned to the Peace River region in August after a Native guide found two whooping cranes in the area, then among the rarest birds in North America. Much to their disappointment, Rowan and Oeming found only tracks.

Rowan's concern about conservation deepened after the war. In a 1949 talk (published in the *Edmonton Journal*) he recalled that Canadians had accepted the nineteenth-century extermination of the buffalo as something that "simply had to be, the inevitable price of civilization." Rowan called for an intelligent management of wildlife and environment; he stressed the need "to finance conservation work on a scientific basis."[31] With his own funding, Rowan hoped to make a concerted effort to do a scientific study of population fluctuations, which, in turn, would lead to more efficient conservation measures. By this time Rowan considered the ten-year cycle a preeminent problem in Canadian conservation. He wrote about the subject for both popular and scientific publications. "The Ten-Year Cycle: Outstanding Problem of Canadian Conservation" was published in early 1948, by the University of Alberta Extension Department, as an illustrated pamphlet for hunters and the general population. In it Rowan discussed rabbit and game-bird cycles in a simple, readable style while introducing the basic biological problems of cycles.[32]

In "The Coming Peak of the Ten-Year Cycle in Alberta," read for Rowan by Dr. Ian McTaggart Cowan at the fifteenth North American Wildlife Conference in Washington, in 1950, Rowan reiterated the need for large-scale investigations of the "intrinsic factors on an experimental, and possibly Dominion, basis. The chief obstacle remains financial." Although Rowan and his students had already compiled valuable data on food plants, embryo counts, and clutch sizes from returned questionnaires, he maintained that the major controlling factor was of "climatic origin." From the discussion that followed the presentation of the paper at the Washington conference, it became apparent that at the time there were two divergent schools of thought: one group believed that "cycles are inherent in animal populations, others believe[d] that they are extraterrestrially controlled."[33]

In yet another paper, written in the late 1940s at the request of Penguin Books for their new journal *New Biology*, Rowan tackled the subject of the climatic influence in more detail. The original title of the paper was "Canada's Greatest Conservation Problem," but, as a result of the comments and criticism of several colleagues, Rowan changed it to "Canada's Premier Problem of Conservation." In this article Rowan reviewed the nature of furbearing-animal and game-bird population fluctuations in northern areas, and discussed the disease theory of population decline. Although he admitted the scientific basis for the ten-year cycle still rested on conjecture, he offered three possible alternative causes: "a) numbers, *per se*; b) weather; c) some hitherto undetected climatic factor." Rowan toyed with the idea that ultraviolet radiation, low in the northern winter, was in some way responsible for population fluctuations. He now noted that "migratory birds, evading the northern winter . . . appear to remain immune from the effects [of population fluctuations]," and at the "time of the crash numerous diseases are on record." These, in turn, may cause "the large scale decimation of the crash . . . due to a deficiency condition of nutritional imbalance."[34]

Elton found the article readable and valuable — a "very good and fair summary of the problem." He wrote, "There is obviously some large field of discovery about the physical universe in relation to animal life that has quite eluded us all so far."[35] But not all scientists agreed with Rowan's views. A.G. Huntsman doubted that the ten-year cycle could "properly be described as Canada's greatest conservation problem." He did concede, however, that it was "a very great biological problem." Although Huntsman considered Rowan's documentation of the pheasant cycle insufficient, he was prepared to support Rowan's application to the National Research Council's committee on wildlife research.[36] But Rowan chose to apply to other organizations.

In May 1949, Rowan, keen to initiate a trans-Canada "assault on the problem," applied to the Department of Indian Affairs for a grant. A few months later he asked the Arctic Institute of America for six thousand dollars and the Department of Mines and Resources for fifteen thousand dollars for a three-year period.[37] The Arctic Institute turned down the proposal, the Department of Indian Affairs transferred Rowan's proposal to the Department of Mines and Resources, and the latter put the request on hold pending the "approval of other eminent scientific specialists in the Canadian wildlife field."[38] Nearly a year later, Rowan was still waiting to hear about the decision.[39] He was eventually notified

20. Drawing of Black-billed magpie by William Rowan which appeared on the cover of *The New Trail*, May 1949.
University of Alberta Archives.

that "a highly qualified and authoritative source" thought it was unnecessary to start immediate work on the cycles.[40] This decision did not make sense to Rowan, but, although he protested vociferously, he had no choice but to work with the small budget provided by the Alberta Research Council.

Rowan and his students carried out investigations on the snowshoe hare in experimental enclosures at Elk Island National Park and at Cooking Lake. The research was assisted by the provincial game department, the provincial veterinary laboratory, and a bush pilot, John Nesbitt, who provided Rowan with records of game birds and rabbits in northern Saskatchewan and Alberta. The Cooking Lake enclosure, a fenced but uncovered "four acre plot," was stocked in late 1950 with about fifty rabbits, most of which were killed by birds of prey during the winter. Another set of experiments, to be carried out in "10′ by 6′ outdoor cages," which were constructed by Oeming, was abandoned because the rabbits, for a variety of reasons, simply did not survive. More successful was the Anzac project, carried out by John Waring, who investigated "rabbit movements, embryo numbers and the general condition of rabbits." Waring kept records of rabbits trapped by local native populations and examined them for signs of pregnancy and disease. Lloyd B. Keith, one of Rowan's senior students, worked during the summer for Alberta Game Commissioner E.S. Huestis, at Brooks, Alberta, "studying pheasant and farming conditions."[41]

Even without substantial funding, Rowan planned to collect all manner of data before the next population crash to identify both diseases and nutritional deficiencies. To keep the rabbits alive under experimental conditions, in 1953, he changed the food rations and installed a sunlamp in the cages to increase the ultraviolet radiation. Rowan planned to hire a graduate student for the summer to "study certain aspects of the ten year cycle program" in the field, and to analyze the "mass of data that has been accumulated over the past number of years on the Biological Cycles Project" for his M.Sc. thesis. Rowan's cost estimate for the project was relatively modest: $1,850 for the year — half of which was for the student's salary (five months at $180 a month).[42] Unfortunately, Rowan's troubles with the captive animals never ceased. He added vitamins to improve the rabbit's diet but they simply did not thrive. Many of them had coccidiosis, which did not respond to sulpha drugs, and the discouraged Rowan temporarily halted his experimental investigations. Instead, he spent time censusing game birds and rabbits.[43] He made several visits to Brooks to visit Lloyd Keith. On a driving trip to the north of Edmonton, he "talked to umpteen farmers, truck drivers and garage men" about the Hungarian partridge population.[44]

In late 1952, Rowan visited Frances and Frederick Hamerstrom who lived in an old, ramshackle farmhouse that served as their headquarters in Plainfield, Wisconsin. The Hamerstroms studied game birds, particularly the sharp-tailed and pinnated grouse. The vivacious Fran was the first American woman to obtain a master's degree in game management (in 1940, from the University of Wisconsin). She was, Rowan noted with approval, also an "A #1 cook."[45] The farmhouse was full of people; Rowan met Wallace Grange, J.J. Hickey, Robert McCabe, and John Emlen, all experts in game management, and a visiting German ornithologist, Gustave Kramer. Fortified by good food and drink, and in pleasant company, Rowan talked about migration experiments, biological cycles, and conservation problems late into the night. One of his favourite topics was the Hungarian partridge. Fascinated by this species's life cycle and status in Alberta, in the early 1950s Rowan began to work on a manuscript about it. Concurrently, he worked on several shorter publications. One was a response to LaMont C. Cole's paper on population fluctuation and random oscillation. Rowan had read Cole's 1951 article with great interest and mounting scepticism. Two years later, Oliver Hewitt, editor of the *Journal of Wildlife Management*, invited several scientists to respond to Cole's paper in a panel on population behaviour.[46] Rowan, gratified to have been asked, enthusiastically agreed.[47] His was one of ten articles in "A Symposium on Cycles in Animal Populations," published in the January 1954 issue of the journal.[48]

As a child, Rowan had been interested in mathematics. Although, as an undergraduate he had conducted biometrical investigations on nesting birds, in adulthood he shied away from statistical investigations and mathematical modelling. Now, in his "Reflections on the Biology of Animal Cycles," he even admitted, albeit facetiously, that he had been "filled with envy at the mathematician's privilege to juggle figures, to smooth curves or to extrapolate them, or to pull rabbits from the bosoms of appropriately devised formulae." Rowan felt that he could not use mathematical formulae because "rabbits are living organisms — erratic, temperamental and independent. In having to deal with them as they are, all chance of enjoying the mathematician's advantage disappears."[49] Rowan criticized Cole for overlooking "the fact that animals are living organisms, readily responsive to environmental changes."[50] He protested Cole's statement that biologists were actually hunting for mysterious explanations for the ten-year cycle. Rowan maintained that if "the 4-, 10-, and 35-year [duck] cycle should all hinge on the single mathematical postulate enunciated by Cole [it] would not only be indeed a mystery, but an insoluble one." He remained confident that existing gaps in understanding cycles could be remedied with "persistent effort, and some ingenuity in the matter of approach." He felt there was "no reason why they should not be finally solved but on a biological, not a mathematical basis."[51] Rowan's criticism and the evident split among the authors studying cycles indicated the growing gulf between mathematical modellings of nature, conducted chiefly in the office and the laboratory, and the biological investigations of scientists who had firsthand experience with the organisms they studied in the field.

Rowan had often, and with great gusto, hunted duck, partridge, and grouse for food. He killed other species of birds, mammals, and amphibians for scientific collections, and used juncos, sparrows, crows, and frogs as experimental animals. As an early animal ecologist, Rowan enjoyed and appreciated the interrelationship of living organisms, and fought for public education and better conservation measures. Understandably, he was upset when, in the early 1950s, the "sportsman's eternal war on hawks and owls" erupted once again. In an address made to the Alberta Fish and Game Association in Calgary on 18 February 1955, he spoke of hunters shooting "birds of prey that sit on telephone poles or fenceposts" from their cars for sport. He reminded his audience that these hunters believed by shooting raptors "they have saved hundreds of upland game birds for posterity," when 95 percent of such hawks "are gopher hawks." Rowan pointed out that by killing them, hunters "deprive the farmer of a faithful ally . . . . and benefit only the shell manufacturers." Rowan explained that the food chain in raptors is tied to the mammal cycle, the fluctuation of voles and gophers and rabbits. He informed his audience, that since

World War II, attitudes had changed even in England, and gamekeepers were paid to preserve rather than exterminate rarer species of birds of prey. Rowan would have liked "nothing better than to see Alberta sufficiently sofisticated [sic] to be in the vanguard of a sane hawk and owl policy."[52]

Rowan and his students had been conducting a systematic owl investigation since 1950. As he had with many previous studies, Rowan aimed with this one to replace fiction with fact. He had evidence, based on large-scale stomach and pellet analyses (which had helped him to determine the food habits of the northern owls), that the birds were "far more innocuous than sportsmen, trappers and poachers."[53] Most sportsmen were uninterested in scientific evidence that countered their own claims, however, and they continued to shoot the "vermin." In fact, the hunters were bent on removing several species of raptors from the list of provincially protected birds and returning them to the predator list. To fight them, the Edmonton Bird Club (inaugurated in 1949) formed a "Predator Committee" in the mid-1950s (consisting of Rowan, E.T. Jones, and C.G. Hampson), and arranged a discussion with members of the Alberta Fish and Game Association to be held in Red Deer in January 1956.

Rowan hoped his scientific arguments, bolstered by his results, would convince those in opposition at the meeting that control measures were unnecessary for most owl species. If needed at all, "they were to be carried out and enforced by a COMPETENT field man able to distinguish the various species in order to prevent indiscriminate slaughter."[54] The meeting turned into a fiasco. Journalists, who were invited to cover the hearing, adjourned to a beer parlour together with many of the "anti-hawk and owl fanatics." Others (mostly hunters) who stayed till the end of the meeting refused to identify the twenty-six hawk skins the predator committee took along as samples. Rowan later maintained that the opposition showed ignorance "of the identity and biology of predators as well as the literature dealing with them."[55]

Rowan complained about the anti-hawk group to the manager of the *Calgary Herald*, and to various friends. He invited the fanatics to the "University Night" (to be held on 2 March 1956 in the convocation hall of the university), an event he organized annually for local hunters. It was attended by about six hundred people, "largely sportsmen," who came to see a film on "wavies" (snow geese) provided by Ducks Unlimited, and to hear Rowan's address, "a critical review of the case of predatory birds in Alberta."[56] Rowan then sent copies of his talk to N.A. Wilmore, minister of lands and forest, and to E.C. Manning, premier of Alberta. He continued to write letters about the hawk and owl problem in Alberta to the provincial newspapers, and even sent one to *Maclean's* (to a new column called "For the Sake of Argument"), but this letter was never published. The annoying controversy used up much of his time and energy, and restricted his involvement in other work. In the end, birds of prey remained protected.

Rowan never finished his monograph on the Hungarian partridge. In 1956, with Lloyd Keith as junior author, he published "Reproductive Potential and Sex Ratios of Snowshoe Hares in Northern Alberta" in the *Canadian Journal of Zoology*. The paper was based on investigations carried out by John Waring at Anzac between 1949 and 1956. The most significant finding was that the annual reproductive potential of hares was "more than 50% greater than that indicated by comparable data from Minnesota" because "of higher peak populations in northern regions."[57]

Keith went on to do graduate work at the University of Madison in Wisconsin, and has continued to investigate the ten-year cycle. He dedicated his monograph *Wildlife's Ten-year Cycle* (1963) "To the memory of Professor William Rowan, a distinguished scientist, my teacher and friend." The copy Keith gave to Reta also bears the hand written inscription, "To Reta Rowan with my deepest affection, Lloyd Keith. I hope that the Professor would have enjoyed reading this." Indeed, Rowan would have enjoyed reading the book, but even more, he would have been proud of the career of his young friend and protégé who has continued to do research, with his own students, on the ten-year cycle.

16

Warring Humanity

ROWAN WAS PRONE to bouts of depression, and during the last twenty years of his life his mood swings increased in frequency. During the same period, he changed in other ways. In the past, his chief interests had been science, art, and conservation, and he had cared more about certain individuals than about humanity as a whole. In the late 1930s, he became a concerned citizen of the world who viewed the changing scenes of World War II and its aftermath with increasing pessimism. This shift in perspective happened in 1937 during Rowan's sabbatical leave and, while it did not take full effect until the 1940s, it eventually altered the course of his life.

Rowan had remained unaffected by the larger political events that occurred after World War I. During his years of intense scientific research he distanced himself from issues of war and peace. After the 1918 Armistice Day celebrations, like many others, Rowan was happy to put all thoughts of war aside and soon his life as a scientist took precedence over concerns about the fate of humanity. In fact, throughout the 1920s and part of the 1930s, Rowan had believed that international issues were the domain of politicians, or simple idealists such as Reta and her friends. Rowan's outlook broadened in the mid-1930s after he began corresponding with Ashley Montague, a British-born anthropologist living in New York City. The two men discussed human sexuality and intellect, and this exchange soon awakened Rowan's interest in these and other issues. In the past he had always found humans considerably less interesting than birds and other animals. Now, he began to develop a philosophical interest in human biology.

In the early months of his sabbatical year, which he spent in England, Rowan wrote to Reta: "I am not interested enough to bother my head about propaganda even in international affairs . . . I would sooner be spending time on hormones and radiation."[1] In late March 1937, he was jolted into awareness of an impending war because of Mussolini's threat to send armies to Spain. At the same time, Rowan could still write playfully, "Maybe I shall be fighting in Spain yet instead of getting on with migration and [then I would find] some of the international feeling on which my dear wife is so keen."[2] That summer he finally realized that war was a serious threat, and found that talking about international affairs was "a delicate matter and politics are best left severely alone in Germany."[3]

The approach of war marked a new direction in Rowan's thinking that ultimately affected all aspects of his life. Back in Edmonton he found he could no longer escape reality by immersing himself in scientific work. War intruded on everyone's life, even at a distance from the battlefields, the bombings, and the deprivations. In the safety of Western Canada, Rowan worried about his family and friends in England. He spent endless hours deploring the selfishness of warmongers. He fretted about the evils of propaganda and the future of the world. Rowan had always been politically conservative, through indifference rather than conviction. In the 1930s this led to many arguments with Reta who had leftist sympathies. While in England, in 1936–37, Rowan had hoped for a permanent reconciliation with Reta. The letters he wrote to his wife dealing with his impressions of Nazi Germany certainly contain indications that he had begun to acknowledge the validity of her concern with international affairs. For the first time, Rowan made a conscious effort to write to Reta about issues that had long been close to her heart. This new awareness was no doubt a direct outcome of their long separation, a yearning to patch things up with Reta and, as always, Rowan simply found it easier to communicate his feelings through letters than in person.

Once he returned, Rowan's good intentions soon evaporated. The Rowan children later recalled that there had been an ongoing argument between Bill and Reta. Minor disagreements on any given topic soon escalated into full-blown clashes over war and peace. They quarrelled in the kitchen, the study, and the bedroom. Reta, with her pacifism and strong socialist sympathies, her long-standing loyalty to the International League for Peace, and her commitment to various League activities, became the target of her husband's tirades, the butt of his verbal attacks.[4]

Rowan had strong opinions, but an incomplete understanding of politics. Increasingly impatient with Reta and other pacifists, including George Hunter, he became more sardonic than ever. In his late forties his physical appearance also changed. He developed a slight stoop, and his expression became increasingly bitter. Work became a chore. While he carried on with teaching and administrative duties as head of the zoology department, he lost some of his zest for scientific research. He even started to question the role of science and scientists in times of war and peace. Not surprisingly, he became interested in groups concerned with these issues, and, in 1940, joined the new Society for Freedom in Science, founded by British scientists who feared government control of scientific research.[5] University of Chicago scientists F.R. Lillie and W.C. Allee were among the members. The latter was to become one of Rowan's faithful correspondents on the subjects of science, war, and peace.

"Warring Humanity: A Biologist's View: Integrity Is Key to World Peace" was the title of a talk Rowan gave to the University of Alberta Philosophical Society in early 1943. An abbreviated and slightly amended version was published in the *Calgary Herald* in two installments (26 June and 3 July 1943).[6] The article contained the kernel of Rowan's evolving philosophy in the context of a number of the issues that dominated his thoughts and writings for the rest of his life. The list included human biology, war, peace, the greed of politicians, natural science versus social science, and the integrity of scientists. Much of the article was marred by Rowan's muddled thinking about human biology, his decidedly elitist tone in discussing the sciences and scientists, and his increasingly pessimistic view of the future of humankind. He later expressed his opinions on these topics in lectures, broadcasts, and newspaper articles; he discussed them with his correspondents, and worked and reworked them in yet another unpublished manuscript, "The Last Chapter."[7]

It was in "Warring Humanity" that Rowan first discussed the immediate and ultimate effects of modern warfare. He bemoaned the fact that in war the fittest are selected for slaughter, and that "such a program actually puts the principles of natural selection in reverse." He explored the "animal nature of man," and his "distinction of standing at the top." In "Warring Humanity," Rowan also dealt with the brain and the nervous system, and with reflex, instinctive, and intelligent behaviours. He talked about human evolution and genetic inheritance. He spoke of how he deplored both Hitler's politics and the attitude of a world that had become "too busy hunting post-war markets to give the Hitlerian powder-keg more than casual attention [and had] failed to take an intelligent interest in the world environment which [it had] itself . . . helped to create."[8]

Integrity became his catchword. Rowan thought science was the only human activity based on integrity, but admitted that not all scientists were honest. For Rowan, and for many of his contemporaries, science meant biology, chemistry, and physics. Like them, Rowan had an incomplete understanding, as well as a deep suspicion, of the social sciences and considered them less important than science proper. Rowan believed that the aims of the social sciences required political propaganda to be realized, and in "Warring Humanity" he warned his readers that sociology, economics, and politics were not based on integrity, and nothing "in human affairs that is not based on integrity can survive." By contrast, Rowan stated, scientists "have achieved an international brotherhood, another of the ultimate ideals of humanity. Racial and economic and political prejudice are not permitted to warp scientific thought . . . even though political control may temporarily contaminate it as in Nazi Germany today."[9]

Rowan even attempted to refute the notion that "brilliant brains" were the result of education, and remarked that some apparent failures, such as Darwin and Mendel, "men of extreme originality . . . have nevertheless become leaders in the world of thought." Was Rowan including himself in this august group? Was he blowing his own trumpet when he wrote that versatile people "can figure things out for themselves and in doing so escape the standardized ruts of academic philosophy and dogma on which the more mediocre are nurtured." He certainly believed that "born original [such people] achieve originality by scorning the path of routine."[10] Rowan's school record and professional experiences indicate that his disdain for mediocrity and his high standards, which he applied both to himself and to others, were anything but objective. To the readers of "Warring Humanity" it was obvious that Rowan never believed that all people were created equal and that he admired those who were exceptional. It was perhaps less evident that he firmly believed himself to be one of them.

Rowan was an original scientist and an admired nature artist, but he wasn't a philosopher. While his scientific work was characterized by a clarity of thinking and a deep knowledge of his subject, the same cannot be said of his philosophical musings. He'd had little training in presenting his philosophical ideas in a clear, consistent manner; his only such training took place during his brief period of participation in the University College, London debating society. He'd had very little time as an adult to read, reflect on, and thoroughly digest different schools of thought. No wonder he found it difficult to get on with the writing of "The Last Chapter"; by early 1944 he had admitted that certain parts of the project, such as the chapter on the environment and its effects on human affairs, and the section on integrity, were causing him difficulty. Rowan wrote to Allee to say that he had tried to assess his own and his friends' behaviour under different conditions, but found that human "motives are so mixed that they are almost impossible to analyze."[11] If we look at his correspondence, it becomes evident that he spent more and more time away from science and the everyday world in attempting to do just that.

During the 1940s, when Rowan was doing less actual scientific work than he had during the past quarter-century of his life, he increasingly pontificated on science and "the scientific method." Rowan knew firsthand that good ideas "occur constantly, but though we honour them with the definition of conceptual thought, they still have to be subjected to trial." By now he firmly believed that scientists were the only likely leaders of the future, as they could be "trusted to point the way of progress," and displayed a "balanced mixture of emotion and reason."[12] In the same period, Rowan also reevaluated his ideas about ethics and religion. He became convinced that ethics were inherently the same as "hunger or the sexual drive," and could legitimately be considered "to be one of, if not *the* highest development of our own cortex." As to religion, Rowan commented to his brother Fred, a very religious man, that there is "not the slightest scientific evidence of the existence of anything that we can term a soul."[13]

If Rowan feared for the future of humanity during the war, this concern deepened after the bombs fell on Hiroshima and Nagasaki. His immediate reaction to the bombing of Hiroshima was "one of resentment, and unqualified disgust that the atomic bomb should have been used without preliminary warning."[14] To Fred, and to others, he criticized Truman and the American government for their secrecy. Admittedly he was a pessimist who feared that war would exist "as long as politics remain politics." He did not even realize that he was echoing Reta's sentiments when he told Fred that the idea of future wars was "unthinkable," and that war was "so utterly incapable of solving anything, that we *must* find another solution."[15] To Allee he wrote that an "international army [should be] in sole charge of atomic materials and the world['s] heavy armaments."[16]

Rowan was not alone in his mistrust of politicians and his fear of the future. Many others, including a number of eminent scientists, were critical of President Harry Truman. Albert Einstein and other physicists circulated petitions, initiated protests, and established the *Bulletin of the Atomic Scientists* in an attempt to influence the American government not to use atomic energy for weapons.[17] Rowan now became despondent about the future. He wrote to Allee, "In the technological sense we can do anything . . . [but] in the spheres of integrity and reason and human decency we are infantile. We have the bomb: from the moral or ethical or rational viewpoints, we haven't the faintest idea what to do with it: we're stumped."[18]

With all this on his mind, Rowan could not finish "The Last Chapter." Each international crisis forced him to rethink the issues, change some of the text, and add or delete passages. The work became a compendium of physical anthropology, biology, and an early form of sociobiology. In it, Rowan strove to relate contemporary opinions and writings on human sexuality, science, and art; he reinterpreted and enlarged on these subjects. The opinions he expressed while doing so he later stated more concisely in a number of talks and shorter publications. Rowan was aware of the difficulties with the complex and growing manuscript, and kept on seeking competent criticism from friends and acquaintances. He needed long periods of uninterrupted time to think and to write, and so he spent his vacations, in 1945 and 1946, in Jasper, working on the book. He rushed to finish so he could enter it in a one-thousand dollar competition held by the Oxford-Crowell publishing company. Because the closing date was 1 July 1946, he had no opportunity to rewrite. He could not even retype the book, but this did not stop him from sending off the manuscript. Not surprisingly, it failed to win the coveted prize.[19]

Rowan always managed to recover his equilibrium and recharge his energies by spending time in his beloved wilderness. Now, more than ever, he needed to escape from everyday life. The times he spent away from Edmonton, in the 1940s, helped him to cope with his worries about the world and, closer to home, with the deteriorating situation in the zoology department. "The country looked lovely in the sunshine with the heavy rime — still increasing — on the trees," noted Rowan at Fawcett in early 1941. He was spending time with his old friend Joe Dawkins. The weather was cold but invigorating, and the two men "fed like Princes with egg and bacon to start the day on, game in the evenings for dinner and light lunch, with tea, coffee and thick cream ad lib whenever wanted."[20]

Rowan also travelled to the East, visiting Chicago, London, Toronto, New York, Albany, Montreal, and Kingston. In early May 1941, he took the train through the Dakotas to St. Paul and Chicago, where he visited the university, the art institute, and the Field Museum, and discussed birds and old times with his former field companion H.B. Conover. At a dinner party held at the University of Chicago by biologist Carl Moore, Rowan finally met his correspondent W.C. Allee, as well as F.R. Lillie, Margaret and Blaine Nice, Sewall Wright, and the staff and senior students of the biology department.

After leaving Chicago, Rowan visited naturalist-ornithologist W.E. Saunders in London, Ontario, and was royally entertained by his former colleague Ned Corbett in Toronto.[21] In New York City, Rowan went to art galleries and the American Museum of Natural History. At Cold Spring Harbour he lunched with Oscar Riddle, another longtime correspondent. On his return trip, Rowan stopped in Montreal to see his friends, then attended the Royal Society meeting in Kingston. By the end of May, Rowan was back at Fawcett.[22] A few weeks later he took a trip to the Rockies to sell his model animals which, he noted, "got an excellent reception."[23] In spite of his deepening depression, Rowan kept busy with a variety of activities.

Since early childhood, Rowan had liked pets. Shy in displaying emotion towards people, he lavished affection on animals. In May 1942, twenty years after he first became interested in the anatomy of the species, he acquired a baby flying squirrel. He fed the small mammal a combination of milk, water, and sugar from a doll's bottle, but in spite of the loving care the animal died.[24] Characteristically, while Rowan spent much time with his new pet at Fawcett, he complained about having to attend Gerdine's graduation from the University of Alberta. In his notebooks Rowan wrote detailed accounts about animals, but the fond father only noted that he "Suffered Convocation for the second time in my life," and soon returned to Fawcett "for some peace, sleep, leisure and writing."[25] There Rowan acquired another young flying squirrel, to be followed by others that became an integral part of the Rowan household. In 1985, old friends and colleagues could still conjure up, with amusement, an image of the absentminded, chain-smoking professor, wearing mismatched socks, with a flying squirrel perched on his shoulder or peeping out of the top pocket of his rumpled suit.

Although Rowan had always had problems with the administration, particularly during Tory's presidency, he had gotten on well with his colleagues. By the 1940s, however, it seemed that war could not be kept at bay in his own department. In fact, the increasingly acrimonious personal relations there contributed to his deepening depression.

When Rowan returned to Edmonton in 1937, he found that the financial cuts that had been instituted in the early 1930s were still in effect. There was no money for expansion. Winnifred Hughes had been acting head of the department in his absence, with only Richard B. Miller, a graduate student from the University of Toronto, to help her with the course work. On Rowan's return, the work had to be carried out (as it had since the mid-1920s) by himself, Hughes, and Lister, with the occasional help of a graduate student. When student enrollment grew during the 1938–1939 academic year, Rowan finally obtained permission to hire another lecturer, and offered the post to Miller, at the time finishing his doctorate in Toronto.[26] Miller had good references and was already familiar with the department.[27]

Miller began at the University of Alberta, in the fall of 1939, by teaching invertebrate zoology. In his spare time he pursued research on whitefish biology. This was important during the war as whitefish constituted a much-needed food source.[28] Miller's presence soon caused problems in a department that had long suffered from lack of office and laboratory space. Now Rowan, Hughes, and Miller had to share the small departmental office where there was no privacy and life was, as Rowan told the dean, "an endless stream of interruptions by telephone, students and staff."[29]

Actually, Rowan still had his office atop the medical building. He had occupied this hot, untidy room for over twenty years, and had no intention of giving it up. The rest of the department had only one small room for the preparation of specimens and other study material, and one of the laboratories had to accommodate sixty students for seven classes per week.[30] This arrangement was not only inconvenient, but the lack of space, equipment, time, and funds also "proved bars to research." Rowan even circulated the rumour that pure research could only be conducted at night, when the laboratories were not occupied by students, and told Acting President Robert Newton that regular hours did not "exist (except on the timetable) . . . [and] we may be in the department more or less continuously by day and night." He, Rowan, had actually "slept on the floor of the lab for a period of weeks and had been woken up by the night watchman on each of his rounds in order to put a fresh ice-pack on a series of aquaria."[31] While Rowan's habit of sleeping in haystacks, automobiles, and other unusual places in the course of doing field research is well documented, this statement is the only reference I have found to Rowan being forced to sleep in the lab in order to do departmental work. In all likelihood he exaggerated the situation in an attempt to convince Newton of the seriousness of the case.

Rowan raked up examples of neglect and mistreatment (both actual and imagined) on the part of the administration that went back for years. In the fall of 1941 he informed Newton about the tremendous amount of work he had done in preparing 140 wall charts, making equipment, ("on the premises," with the aid of Hughes) and building up the "completest vertebrate museum in the Dominion" — largely without funds from the university.[32] This time Rowan did not stretch the truth; he simply pointed out all past injustices. Improvements were necessary, but it was hard to get support for them from the administration, and Rowan was increasingly conscious of the fact that during the war there were job opportunities, at least for junior faculty, at other Canadian universities, and he was in no position to compete for them. He worried that Miller and Hughes would leave for better employment.

So Rowan began to badger the dean for research money and salary adjustments. In letters concerning departmental estimates, he pointed out that Hughes, an excellent teacher, was hired as an assistant professor in 1929 (with a starting salary of $2,500), and since then had been given only one raise. He asked for "fair compensation at this belated date for an injustice of long standing," and recommended that the administration "raise Doctor Hughes to the rank of full professor and give her the salary that goes with the rank." As for Miller, Rowan asked that he have his salary increase maintained, because he

> ranks as one of the ablest and best qualified fish specialists in the Dominion and is at present cooperating with the Provincial government in fisheries work that is of vital interest to the Alberta populace at large. We cannot afford to lose him to the Government or some other post.[33]

Rowan still wished to keep Miller at the university and, in 1942, even offered to teach summer school to free Miller from "chore work." But somewhere, somehow, things began to go wrong between the two men. In the winter of 1942–1943 Rowan began to feel that he was burdened with chores "that should have fallen on Miller's shoulders as junior man in the Department in order to provide him with the time required for reports, scale counts, etc."[34] He resented that time and funds for research came relatively easily to Miller.

Though Rowan complained that the salaries remained unsatisfactory, and Hughes should have long ago become full professor with "the salary that goes with the rank," the status quo remained. Hughes and Miller obtained salary increases of $200, but Rowan's salary remained unchanged at $4,700 for 1942 and 1943.[35] Perhaps Rowan was too ambitious on behalf of his longtime assistant, who also happened to be a woman. In the next round of protests about salaries and advancement he changed tactics. He asked that Hughes be made associate (and not full) professor, and that his own salary be kept the same, while Hughes's be raised to $3,400 and Miller's to $2,600.[36] In spite of his requests, the administration notified Rowan that *he* was to get a raise (though only to $4,800), Hughes was to receive $3,100, and Miller, $2,700. At the same time Lister finally got $1,500, at long last achieving parity with other technicians. There was even an appropriation of $240 for a stenographer. Rowan was also informed that the "Head of each Department is responsible for seeing that the net expenditures during the fiscal year are not in excess of the amount provided."[37] During the following years this became a standard warning.

Rowan's annual letters to the dean asking for advancement for his staff became routine until after the war. Then it became clear that Rowan needed more personnel and funds to deal with the projected student influx. In March 1946, Dean John Macdonald notified Rowan that both Hughes and Miller had become associate professors at annual salaries of $3,500 and $3,400 respectively, and that funds would also be made available for a sessional lecturer. In May 1946 J.E. Moore was hired at a salary of $2,500.[38]

If the administration was satisfied with these changes, Rowan most certainly was not. In fact, he was incensed, and protested Hughes's "loss of seniority."[39] Even though Rowan approved Miller's promotion, he complained to the dean about his "being accorded precedence in rank over Miss Hughes." Rowan stressed that Miller had been given much better opportunities at the University than either Hughes or he, Rowan, ever had, and that the university "advertently or inadvertently, has been the gainer at Dr. Hughes' expense." Rowan showed uncharacteristic sensitivity to a potentially explosive situation when he wrote, "in the interest of my department and its continued smooth functioning in the future, I find myself unable to accept the situation." He then showed the kindness and generosity typical of him and well known to his closest friends, although it was a quality that eluded the casual observer. He asked that Hughes be given a further increase of two hundred dollars, and if that proved to be impossible he wanted the administration "to arrange with the Bursar that $200 of my own salary be diverted to Dr. Hughes' account." He emphasized that this was "a specific request, not merely a suggestion."[40]

University president Robert Newton also wrote to the dean. He praised Rowan's "loyalty to Miss Hughes and his desire that she should not be superseded in his department." He added:

> Notwithstanding Miss Hughes' excellent teaching ability and performance, we could never contemplate appointing head of a scientific department any person who is not actively productive in research . . . . I hope Professor Rowan will be satisfied that we have acted according to our own wisest judgement and cooperate with us in promoting harmonious relations within his Department.[41]

Newton had totally misinterpreted Rowan's letter. Rowan had asked that Hughes be granted a salary higher than that given to the relative newcomer, Miller, but had no intention of giving up the headship of the department. In fact, as we shall see, he was to resist vigorously all attempts to unseat him. As to "harmonious relations within his department," the administration's refusal to advance Hughes most certainly aggravated an already-acrimonious situation.

Without knowing of all the pleading Rowan had done on her behalf, Hughes was harbouring resentment about her own position. The lack of space and extra work due to increased enrollment (there were about seven hundred new students in 1947) were bad enough.[42] Curiously, Hughes later blamed Rowan for the loss of her seniority, though she seemed not to resent Miller's own advancement. There were other factors that soured relationships among members of the department. By early 1947 the situation had deteriorated to such an extent that Winnie Hughes was unable and perhaps unwilling to put up with things any longer, and turned against her former friend and colleague.

In the early 1940s, Rowan's philosophical concerns, periodic crow investigations, and conservation work took time away from administrative duties. Administration for Rowan was always a chore. Its significance paled in comparison with that of his scientific pursuits. After Miller joined the staff, and later still, after returning veterans inflated the student population and Moore became a lecturer, Rowan's lack of interest in administration (and his inaptitude for it) came to the fore. Rowan had always worked in a cluttered space: the fact that he was involved in so many activities, which he carried out in haste and with minimum assistance, meant that his offices — at the university and at home — were never tidy and well organized. He had been known to lose lecture notes, socks, and even specimens, including several of Dr. Louis Bishop's dowitcher skins, which eventually resurfaced after about a decade. By 1946 it was obvious that over the years he had become overly casual in the day-to-day running of an increasingly complicated university department.

Rowan was decidedly more concerned with larger issues than departmental administration. While he worried about external relations and the future of humanity, internal relationships suffered. The infighting was tiring and demoralizing. As always, Rowan tried to cope with his problems by disappearing into the field, doing something creative, or spending time with friends and colleagues. In this dark period, worrying about the state of the world, hassling with the administration and his staff, Rowan went off to Toronto to receive the prestigious Flavelle Medal of the Royal Society. Soon he was back in the West, trying to work on "The Last Chapter."[43]

There is no mention, of course, in Rowan's field notes about a major upset in the zoology department. That there was internal warfare, may be learned from his correspondence with both Hughes and the administration. Hughes was a hard worker and an excellent teacher. A capable scientist, reliable colleague, and pleasant field companion, she was a good friend to both Bill and Reta, and an honorary aunt to the Rowan children. This made the blowup that occurred between Rowan and Hughes in early 1947 even more traumatic. It must have happened as follows: disturbed by the lack of space, and resentful due to various real and imagined slights, Hughes reproached Rowan for not having either the department's or her own welfare at heart. The accusation hit Rowan hard; he felt that it was unjust and vicious. After all, he had been suggesting, asking, and demanding a raise for his second in command for nearly a decade. There is no doubt that crowding causes stress. Rowan had studied animal populations for over twenty years; he was aware of the detrimental effects of crowding, and had often tried to relate biological principles to human behaviour. Somehow, in this case, he was unable to make the connection or read the signs of a brewing strife as accurately as he would have done in the case of an animal sample.

Under his sardonic exterior Rowan was easily hurt, and he was likely to fly off the handle. Not surprisingly, he was unable to stay calm when his old friend Doc Hughes collared him and accused him of selfishness, negligence, and other unspecified vices. Exhausted and already upset about a number of things, Rowan turned up at Hughes's home and blew his top. But as soon as he stormed out of her little house, he repented. Rowan was mad at himself and contrite, and soon apologized in writing: "I can only excuse myself on the ground that the shock of your accusation, so unexpected and so unjustified, in view of the circumstances, completely bowled me over."[44] It was obvious that Rowan had no intention of hurting Hughes, and that he was unaware of her simmering resentment. He was surprised to learn that the assigning of a room to Moore, the new lecturer, upset Hughes, as she wanted the room for herself. Hughes was not in the habit of confronting Rowan, however, and for a long time did not protest. No wonder Rowan was flabbergasted about the whole thing. He told Hughes that private offices would become available next term, and as a temporary measure offered Hughes his own tower office and promised not to disturb her there. He wrote, "If this will in any way compensate for my seeming discourtesy I shall be grateful." He signed the letter "with deepest regrets I have ever expressed in my life."[45]

After the initial fight with Hughes, Rowan retired to a friend's house at Cooking Lake, working once again on the "Last Chapter." Tired and depressed, he didn't "make much useful headway."[46] So, after winding up some university business in what he thought was a satisfactory manner, Rowan left for Eastern Canada. On the way he visited his elder son Oliver in Winnipeg, attended the annual meeting of the Royal Society of Canada in Quebec City, and spent a few enjoyable days with his younger son Julian at Brownsburg, at the western edge of the Laurentian Mountains, before going on to Toronto.[47] There, he learned that Hughes was not easily appeased.

In a brief, rudely worded letter, Hughes informed Rowan that since his departure the department (that is herself, Miller, and Moore) had ordered binocular microscopes and other equipment, and submitted plans for converting space recently vacated by the biochemistry department into offices and labs. She added:

> I thought, when you banged out of my house . . . accusing us all of conspiring behind your back, that it had finally penetrated your mind that we are all fed up with the aimless and shiftless existence of the Department . . . . This is not a personal matter between you and me, nor between you and anyone else. It is between you and the rest of the department.[48]

These were strong words, and serious accusations, and Rowan read the letter with dismay.

He had hoped to do intensive library research in Toronto, but feeling tired and dispirited, he could not concentrate.[49] Hughes's charges hurt, and he found the tone of the letter "beneath contempt." In his reply Rowan offered her two choices, to apologize or resign, because, he wrote, "I certainly do not propose to spend my last years in the department in the atmosphere that has been . . . created behind my back."[50] Then he wrote a letter of protest to the university administration. Apparently, before his trip to the East, Rowan had arranged with the bursar that he, Rowan, would order the microscopes in Toronto.[51] He told the administration that he felt his colleagues had destroyed his authority as head of the zoology department by ordering equipment without his knowledge. But this was not the end of the matter. A letter from the university informed Rowan that the dean had authorized both the order of microscopes and the alterations done to the new space allocated to the department. The letters that were then exchanged by the president, his executive assistant, and Rowan clearly indicate that the department's actions had a galvanizing effect on Rowan. He proceeded to reorder the needed equipment, and obtained better terms (payment and delivery) than had Miller. Rowan then asked that the "order submitted by Dr. Miller be immediately cancelled." He wanted a full explanation, from the dean, "of this incredible episode."[52]

With all this on his mind, Rowan was not at his creative best. Being judged a hopeless administrator and being compelled to struggle with philosophical problems he could not solve were bad enough, but now Rowan could not even concentrate on his reading. He returned home, but continued to feel "extremely punk," physically and mentally exhausted, and remained thoroughly depressed. He wrote that

> "The Last Chapter" gets duller and more uninteresting every time I look at it! Would love to ditch it and forget it forever. The world looks more poisonous and hopeless daily: a commentary on events of the moment will be out of date before it sees publication anyway! The weather is hot and dry and the news always depressing.[53]

Rowan would have been even more depressed had he known that while he was grappling with his writing about the biological aspects of human nature, the Board of Governors of the University had appointed Miller as administrative officer of the zoology department, as of 1 September 1947, with an honorarium of three hundred dollars per annum. He learned of this turn of events from a copy of Newton's letter to Miller, which had been forwarded to him while he was visiting Gerdine in Vancouver. Rowan was incensed. As far as he remembered, he had cleared up "certain misunderstandings" with the dean prior to his departure. That is, he had asked the dean "to intimate officially to Dr. Miller that he would be expected to carry a greater share of departmental duties during the coming year."[54] Evidently Rowan's recollections of the events differed considerably from those of the dean himself, who remembered that they had agreed Miller would assume responsibility for administrative work.[55] Rowan protested. What he had actually requested was that Miller be asked, by either the dean or the president, "to participate more effectively in the routine duties of the department."[56]

Rowan's memory, selective under the best of circumstances, was apparently at fault. At the time of the discussion, he was very upset about departmental hassles, rushed as usual, and more depressed than ever. He may not have taken in the full implications of the discussion, or he may simply have chosen to interpret them in his own way. He certainly had no intention of giving up his seniority to a relative newcomer, or relinquishing control of a department he had built according to his own ideas, with minimum help from the administration. Rowan did not object to Miller "calling periodic meetings of the department to consider routine business[.] I will naturally preside at such meetings." He insisted, however, that "the extent and quality of departmental supplies and equipment will be decided" at meetings, and that all departmental mail requiring "other than [a] routine answer" be turned over to him "for consideration." He also wanted to be consulted about timetables, teaching schedules, and allocation of working space.[57] Clearly, despite the onerous nature of administrative duties, Rowan had no intention of letting anyone usurp his position. While he eventually agreed to Miller taking on new duties, in all probability relieved at not having to do the routine work himself, Rowan maintained a proprietary interest in the department.

Although Rowan must have felt a bit hurt that his subordinates questioned his ability, he had probably never fancied himself to be much of an administrator. The growing animosity between Rowan and Miller could be attributed to the fact that this was a case of a younger man replacing an older one: Rowan was fifty-five in 1946, when all this began to boil over. The situation underlined an already-existing difference in their approaches to science. Rowan was a man of scintillating scientific ideas, of world renown, who, by the 1940s, did not have the patience for the day-to-day minutiae of scientific research. Miller was a bright, hardworking young man, a stickler for detail, but much narrower in his interests. During the following decade their different attitudes towards science and scientific research, administrative duties and the teaching of graduate students, caused innumerable conflicts and emotional upheavals for both of them.

After Winnie Hughes finally resigned, in 1949, Dr. Stewart Clare took her place. R.B. Miller continued his research on whitefish parasites, while J.E. Moore studied the vertebrate fauna of Alberta and helped Rowan with his work on the ten-year cycle.[58] Miller remained responsible for administrative matters, such as annual and library reports, and was promoted to full professor in 1950.[59] Although there was no question of Miller succeeding Rowan as head of the department, other changes were to take place.[60] There were more graduate students, a biological station was established, and in 1951 Miller resigned as administrative officer of the department, not because of the work involved, but because he felt this arrangement was "extremely distasteful" to Rowan. Miller had simply had enough of "the atmosphere of hostility — which my position as administrative officer seemed to engender."[61]

The following year, Moore became secretary, that is, he replaced Miller as administrator, but this did not improve the relationship between Rowan and Miller. Rowan resented that Miller obtained grants without any apparent effort. He was annoyed that Miller seemed to have few problems in establishing a departmental research station at Gorge Creek. We must recall that in the early 1920s Rowan had tried to institute a similar station at Beaverhills Lake, but the plan was vetoed by H.M. Tory. Now, nearly thirty years later, Miller had the administrative backing for a biological research station and Rowan, perhaps without being fully aware of what he was doing, began to block Miller's plans to have all zoology professors and graduate students do research there.

Miller had hoped that his resignation as administrator would restore a "measure of the cordiality" the department had enjoyed in the early 1940s, but neither man was able to put the past behind him. Rowan remained hostile to Miller. The younger scientist remained highly critical of Rowan's methods of conducting science, and often referred to his department head as a "windbag," among other uncomplimentary terms.[62] They continued to subvert each other's efforts. Rowan encouraged graduate student Jack Millar to study moose in the Athabasca Forest, not at the biological station, while Miller supported the grant application of Albert Wilk, Rowan's former graduate student, for fieldwork on birds.[63] Wilk wanted to collect field data to update and complete the late Frank Farley's manuscript on Alberta birds. Rowan had worked, off and on, on a similar manuscript. For years he had heard Miller acerbically remark that field ornithology (as practised by Rowan and others) was not sufficiently rigorous. Indeed, Miller's views were so widely known that it seemed his support of Wilk's fieldwork on birds was meant to annoy Rowan. Perhaps it is hardly surprising that after more than thirty years of scrambling for research funds Rowan resented the ease with which Wilk, with Miller's and President Newton's support, obtained a grant of one thousand dollars in 1951, and another of the same amount in 1953.

Rowan's depression persisted throughout the 1940s. He struggled to finish a manuscript that he carried around with him in his thoughts like a dead weight. His family situation had also changed. Reta was rarely around, perhaps subconsciously avoiding political arguments with her husband. Her sphere of activities widened over the years. In 1942, she became chair of the Council of Canadian Unity in Edmonton, and also played an active part in the Committee of Friends of the Indians.[64] The new house at 10721 86th avenue, which the Rowans bought in 1946, its front door kept unlocked in western fashion, became an overnight sleeping place for Natives who came to discuss important issues with Reta. Rowan often did not feel at home in his own house, the first city home they had ever owned. His loneliness and depression were further exacerbated by the absence of his children: Gerdine and Oliver were married, Sylvia and Julian lived in Toronto, and, in September 1947, Josephine, the youngest Rowan child, also left home. Josephine was a cellist who, having won several scholarships, was going to Baltimore to study at the prestigious Peabody Academy of Music. Rowan wrote, "She is the last of the brood to leave home and what [life] will be like without her, Heaven knows . . . Reta and I are alone again . . . tomorrow is our wedding anniversary. What a priceless farce life can be."[65]

Rowan tried to fight the depression with fieldwork, for which he had a new companion. This was the Swiss-born, British-educated physiologist Dr. Otto Hohn, who had accepted a position at the University of Alberta because he had hoped to benefit from the presence and professional advice of Rowan. No wonder Rowan liked the tall, keen young man whom he considered "an awfully decent fellow."[66] But not even a new field companion could lift his deepening gloom, and by Christmas 1947, he felt abandoned by everyone. Reta was visiting her sister, Deeda, in California, and the children were spread out across the country. Although the younger Rowans plotted to have a Christmas reunion in Winnipeg, and even planned to pay Rowan's fare, they kept their plan a secret, and Rowan, who had no money for such a trip, declined to go. Instead, he went to Jasper, where on Christmas Eve he noted that he was "feeling as lonely as a saint in hell and in the depths of another depression."[67]

17

Science, Ethics, and Peace: "A Biologist Looks Forward"

THROUGHOUT THE 1940S and 1950s Rowan continued to write and talk about science and peace. In 1948, he gave a Sigma Xi lecture at the University of Michigan entitled "The Future of Humanity, from a Biologist's Viewpoint."[1] A month later, he was invited to give another lecture, "Science and World Peace," at the British Columbia Academy of Science. Here Rowan once again explored man's development, and stressed human speech, which "has made possible his science, his religion, his philosophies, his literature, and the rest . . . in brief, his conceptional thinking capacity." For Rowan, these were not typical human achievements but "the product of a relatively small fraction of the human race, a handful of remarkable men, intellectual giants, precocious in their vision, scattered through history from all corners of the globe, geniuses, world leaders."[2] This was undoubtedly an elitist world view, yet there is no evidence that anyone in the audience challenged Rowan's notions. Nor did anyone complain about it after the speech was printed. Rowan became a vocal advocate of such a view because, during the war, he believed that man could control his environment but not himself.[3] Rowan voiced a common fear: nuclear holocaust. His discussions concerning what one could do about avoiding it mesmerized audiences and obfuscated the implications of all other issues explored in his talks.

One of Rowan's major concerns centred on ethical issues in science. He questioned the "relationships of science and scientists to humanity at large. Is their function merely to discover and invent, or is the moral responsibility of control an inseparable phase of the issue?" He explored the dangers of overpopulation, the Cold War, and propaganda. He warned audiences about the after-effects of nuclear blasts, such as mutations in biological organisms. Because of the threat of both nuclear and biological warfares, Rowan emphasized the fact that the very existence of humans depended on a change of thinking, on mental, rather than morphological adaptations. He proclaimed the importance of the survival "of *all* members of a single species, *Homo sapiens*, not just favoured nations." Criticizing politicians' use of propaganda, he asked, "can the present moment be converted from catastrophe to success?"[4]

Rowan believed that science could serve humanity because of its inherent integrity. For him the only way to avoid total annihilation was to fight the forces of destruction. He wrote:

> perhaps I am merely a pessimist: perhaps an irresponsible idealist, a dreamer of dreams, an impractical seeker after Utopia, but I think not. The day must come — it has come — when our thinking must catch up on our changed environment . . . . the final criterion of human success is not the material output of science . . . . It is the sum-total of moral and spiritual values expressed in one simple word — *integrity* — that matters most, and of integrity, science is at least one of the world's outstanding exponents.[5]

In the past Rowan had often given radio talks about nature and animals. In February 1951, he gave two lectures for the Canadian Broadcasting Corporation Department of Talks and Public Affairs. In "A Biologist Looks Back," broadcast on 18 February, Rowan discussed "the new environmental crisis" (as he called the population explosion) threatening the world. He forecast a shortage of food resources, and talked about European rearmament, the hydrogen bomb, and the "horrors of biological warfare."[6]

In "A Biologist Looks Forward," broadcast on 25 February, Rowan claimed that "only in one field of activity has the human intellect consistently proved its worth, in the field of science . . . for in no other profession has a search for truth and integrity been adopted as an inflexible standard." Repeating his previous concerns, he discussed propaganda, war, and rearmament. He stressed that "violence leads only to further violence," and called for North Americans "to take the lead in the construction of peace while there is yet time." Rowan had obviously come a long way from that day in 1914 when, as an enthusiastic young man of twenty-three, he eagerly joined the Royal Scottish Regiment. Perhaps his protracted arguments with Reta about war and peace made more of an impact on him than he would ever have admitted. It is probable that Rowan believed he became a pacifist by reflecting carefully and at length on issues of war and peace, and by corresponding with like-minded scientists, such as Baker and Allee. Whether or not he admitted it to himself, Reta's influence can certainly be detected in Rowan's position concerning the fight against Communism. One "cannot fight an idea of the intellect with arms," he told his audience, but "we could stem the tide by offering the world a better alternative." He recommended "spending our billions on reconstruction in place of . . . devastation."[7]

The talks were a great success, and brought in bags of mail. Rowan expressed the fear felt by many Canadians — but he expressed it better than most others. Delighted with the response of the ordinary people, he also appreciated the money he received from the CBC.[8] Rowan, whose voice was well known to radio listeners in the western provinces and states from the talks about nature and conservation he had broadcast in the region, was beginning to have a considerable following. A different, larger, audience listened to his ideas on human biology, science, war, and peace with rapt attention.

Although Rowan gave up long-term, sophisticated experiments on migration in the early 1940s, he continued to be full of ideas, and occasionally conducted homing experiments on blindfolded birds. He even tested the sense of direction in humans, including himself: on 12 July 1946, he swam blindfolded in the North Saskatchewan River, with his son Julian and some friends. Other human biology experiments were conducted in the zoology lab; they took the form of intelligence testing, and undergraduates served as unwitting experimental subjects. It is on record that in the early 1950s, prior to some of his laboratory sessions, Rowan adjusted the shades on the goosenecked lamps at each student's

21. William Rowan with pet raven, early 1950s.
University of Alberta Archives.

place, so that the light would shine in their faces. Only a small number of the students responded by returning the shades to their usual angle, and Rowan concluded that only these few students, about 5 percent of the class, were really intelligent.[9] Apparently it did not occur to Rowan that some may have been too intimidated to tamper with the laboratory furnishings in front of the professor.

Rowan thought, and talked, about the differences between male and female sexuality — much of it based on his own experiences with Reta. Beginning in the late 1940s he also corresponded with friends and other writers on the differences between male and female intelligence. In his advanced zoology classes he would often shock his female students by stating, in an offhand manner, that "biologically there is no basis for the equality of sexes." He informed the class that males had larger brains, and were therefore more creative than women. As he explained, and he was certainly was not alone in holding this view, the woman's role was to be a partner, to inspire the man with her sympathy and devotion. "Some women take violent issue with this flat-footed statement of a double standard," noted journalist Barbara Moon in a 1952 article about Rowan.[10] His students may not have realized that his views were similar to those held by many other men of his generation and that, in this area, his thinking was far from clear or even consistent.

Although Rowan enjoyed observing human foibles, he was not used to being subjected to close scrutiny by others. During interviews he could always put on an act, talk about selected topics, and thus impress the interviewer. It therefore felt strange to him to be scrutinized by a world-renowned photographer. Nevertheless, being "Karshed" was one of Rowan's most enjoyable experiences. Rowan first met Yousuf Karsh in early 1952, when the famous Armenian-Canadian photographer was in Edmonton.[11] They met again in June 1952, in Ottawa, where Rowan, after having attended the Royal Society and the Conservation Society meetings in Quebec City, was visiting with journalist John Bird and his wife Florence, who wrote under the pseudonym of Anne Francis. As Rowan recalled, he had phoned Karsh "thinking it would be exciting to see a selection of his better portraits and also his studio." During lunch in an expensive restaurant, Rowan was no doubt at his scintillating best trying to impress Karsh, who soon decided to take Rowan's portrait. While delighted to be included in Karsh's "rogue's gallery," Rowan may have wished that he had been better prepared to be photographed. On that day, 6 June, he felt scruffy with his untrimmed moustache, messy hair, and rumpled shirt (the weather was hot and humid), but Karsh was unconcerned by such trivia.[12] He was more interested in Rowan's face, his ever-changing expressions, his characteristic postures. He photographed Rowan with his hands folded in front, his usual cigarette, in its long holder, held in his right hand, and the family signet ring visible on the little finger of his left hand. Karsh's attention was flattering and enjoyable, and Rowan took pleasure in the hours spent with the Birds, both in Ottawa and at their country house. A trip to the National Gallery "to worship at the shrine of Tom Thompson," and the annual Press Gallery Dinner, which Rowan attended as the guest of John Bird, provided even more diversion. He then went on to Toronto for a visit with Julian and his wife, Niva.

Back in Edmonton, after his second Peace River trip, Rowan noted: "Karsh and wife in town today . . . saw proofs of the photos taken in Ottawa."[13] Rowan's reactions to the proofs are interesting:

> [T]hey are good — they cannot be anything else — but possibly too much like me! I have a curious feeling, when looking at myself in print, as in the case of my own writing, or drawing, or sculpture . . . that I am merely sizing up some other person and I don't like the face I have to look at. I can read most of my own weaknesses in my own physiognomy. Truth is, I don't like my own face in this curiously objective examination.[14]

Whether he liked the portrait or not, Rowan bought a copy of it. He must have thought that twenty-five dollars was not too much to pay for a memento of being photographed by Karsh.

Rowan, so often critical of others, was rarely known to cast aspersions on himself. His reaction to the Karsh portrait is one of the few recorded instances of his extreme self-criticism. Perhaps Rowan could see his own weaknesses in the photograph. To other observers (he sent unauthorized copies of the photo to family and friends), the Karsh photograph presented a face totally unlike the one seen in all snapshots of Rowan in this period, or for that matter, in all previous photographs. It shows Rowan in a relaxed, but typical posture. There is no trace of the self-conscious grin seen in earlier snapshots, or of the stiffness seen in the studio portraits taken of the Rowan brothers during World War I. The bitter expression, the deep creases on either side of the mouth, the brooding eyes, all so evident in photos of the middle-aged Rowan, have been transformed under Karsh's hand into a pleasant expression, a charming smile, and eyes that twinkle behind rimless glasses. Here Rowan's face is curiously smooth, devoid of the sardonic expression that was his hallmark. Karsh the artist managed to capture Rowan's essence, transcending unhappiness, strife, and depression. The photo presents a thoughtful, affectionate man, a man rarely glimpsed by anyone beyond a small circle of intimates: his son Julian, his brothers Fred and Harry, and a few devoted students and friends.

Rowan could relax and enjoy himself in a number of ways, but he could rarely put aside the larger issues he had been exploring for more than a decade. He continued to stress the importance of integrity, both in everyday life and in issues concerning the future of humanity. Although in the postwar period he often grumbled about bumping into visiting Native Canadians who were waiting in the Rowans's home to discuss their concerns with Reta, in the early 1950s Rowan came to terms with his wife's interest in Native affairs. He accompanied her to meetings held on various Indian reservations, and learned to like and respect the Natives he encountered. Chief Crowchild from the Sarcee Reserve in southern Alberta was a well-known promoter of Indian sports and a participant in federal discussions concerning the revisions of the Indian Act. When he and his wife were refused accommodation in Edmonton's Leland Hotel because they were Natives, Rowan vigorously protested the "insufferable" insult.[15]

Things seemed to be looking up for Rowan, particularly because in mid-September 1953 he finally met Eric Harvie, the oil millionaire, known for his interest in museums and libraries.[16] Rowan and Harvie had already exchanged letters concerning the establishment of a small natural-history museum in Banff. Unaware of this correspondence, Donald Cameron, director of the Banff School, suggested to Harvie that Rowan could be useful to him with the "collection of museum specimens in Western Canada." Cameron told Rowan that such work would "provide an exciting adventure for you on your retirement."[17]

Rowan's first impression of Harvie was that he was "a difficult chap to read."[18] The two men, the lawyer turned oil magnate and the university professor, were practically the same age. Despite their different circumstances they had common interests and got on well. Rowan occasionally entertained fantasies in which his "tame millionaire" provided funds for his research — but Harvie was unlikely to part with any of his fortune to support Rowan. He was willing, however, to invest in projects for the people of Alberta, and in 1954, upon hearing of Rowan's plans to go to Europe, charged him with the task of obtaining natural history books for his private library, which eventually was to be turned over to the province.

It is not known when Rowan decided to take a busman's holiday with Reta in Europe. No doubt he was keen to see his family in England. He intended to talk to game-management officials, other scientists, and friends in Britain and on the Continent. He intended to visit zoos, because he hoped to establish a zoological garden in Edmonton. In fact, Rowan planned to be away from Edmonton for several months, as he wanted, as well, to attend the annual meeting of the Royal Society of Canada in Winnipeg, and visit his children in Toronto, before going to Europe.

The Korean War was just over and the Cold War still in effect, and Rowan considered the Royal Society meeting the perfect forum for discussions of science, war, and peace. In a telegram sent to the program committee of the society, he suggested three topics: "The responsibility of science in the atomic age"; "Science as a contributor to world peace"; and "Science, the road to world understanding." Rowan was convinced that "such a symposium would enormously enhance the prestige of the Royal Society in the public eye."[19] Because there had been a tremendously encouraging response to his two CBC talks in 1951, Rowan thought that if, in 1954, "the Royal Society could face the issue of science and human survival on its public night, it would unquestionably elicit a similar reaction across the entire Dominion and possibly around the globe. After all, the Royal Society carries some weight and prestige."[20]

In spite of Rowan's hopes, the program committee did not choose to hold a symposium on science and peace. Instead, it scheduled Rowan's own "Intellect and Human Survival" as the third of five papers given in the biological sciences section. So now, in 1954, Rowan had to rehash his 1948 British Columbia Academy speech. He expressed his worries about human affairs being left in the hands of a group of untrained men "elected on an essentially emotional and purely political basis, whose lack of qualifications would not be accepted by any other profession on earth." Rowan talked about the atomic bomb and the more powerful hydrogen bomb, which was tested for the first time on 1 March 1954 in the South Pacific. He warned his audience about further destruction. Although Rowan did not actually suggest that scientists "should run human affairs," he did suggest that they "should be consulted in the management of our 20th century environment which they themselves have created." Because radio had "become the voice of humanity," Canada, through its own radio network, the CBC, "could provide the world leadership to see us through the intellectual revolution that is today stirring all humanity."[21]

Rowan's session was unusually well attended. Visiting scholars, students, and local people waited to hear for Rowan's widely advertised talk.[22] When it was over, R.D. Gibbs, president of the biological section, turned to the dumfounded audience and invited discussion by asking, "Are we too stunned by the impact of this?"[23] Inevitably there was a mixed reaction; some of the scientists agreed with Rowan, while others were disgusted by his views. According to the 1 June 1954 edition of the *Winnipeg Free Press*, Dr. Jean Bruschesi, president of the Royal Society, "personally dissociated himself from what was said."[24] The press had a field day quoting and misquoting Rowan's "most provocative address."[25] Rowan later noted that his talk "either aroused enthusiasm or indignation. The Free Press damned me, the Bulletin was impartial, the Fellowship mostly dubious. Other notices have varied."[26] In fact, the writer of the *Winnipeg Free Press* article, entitled "Rule by Scientists Termed 'Doomed' World's Only Hope," misinterpreted Rowan's main point and quoted him as saying, "humanity is doomed unless objective scientists take over the world's affairs." As Rowan was quick to point out to the newspaper's editor, this was diametrically opposed to what he actually had said.[27]

Rowan's laconic diary notes do not reflect his state of mind. The hostility of some members of the audience surprised and dismayed him. Although Rowan always invited controversy (some people even thought that he thrived on it), he remained sensitive to criticism. Rowan was more wrought up by the events of the day than he would have cared to admit. Dr. Bruce Collier, the biochemist who replaced George Hunter, recalled, in 1985, that after his controversial address Rowan asked him for a sedative because he could not sleep.[28] By the following morning, fortified with coffee, Rowan was his usual critical self; he read the various newspapers and wrote a polite letter to the editor of the *Winnipeg Free Press* to correct the journalist's misconception.

After a hectic week in Toronto, the Rowans left on their European trip. It was the first time Rowan had returned to England since his sabbatical in 1936–1937, and this would be the first vacation Bill and Reta had spent on the other side of "the pond" since 1927. They left on the *Empress of Scotland* from Montreal, arriving in Liverpool on 15 June. They remained in England for a two week-visit, then they sailed for Scandinavia, where they enjoyed the conviviality of Göteborg, and visited the old university town of Lund. Rowan even took a side trip to the famed Falsterbo bird-banding station. Later, Bill and Reta admired Stockholm's many islands and bridges, its medieval Gamla Stan (or old town), and its famous zoo.[29] After visits to Denmark and Finland they went to Germany. Gustave Kramer, now on home territory, took Rowan to his laboratory at the Max Planck Institute and showed him the "classical cage and artificial sun with which he demonstrated the reaction of birds to the angle of the Sun."[30]

In the Austrian Alps, the Rowans saw the chamois. They listened to music in Vienna, and visited the Schönbrun Palace and Zoo. After returning to England, they enjoyed the company of Sir Peter Scott in Slimbridge, Charles Elton in Oxford, and Julian Huxley in London. In London, Rowan also met with William Bullough, who encouraged Rowan to replace him as guest lecturer at the opening session of the fourth International Photobiology Congress in Amsterdam. In fact, Rowan later wrote, "on learning that I was in England [Bullough] insisted that, provided that the Congress Committee agreed, I would take his place and deliver the guest lecture."[31] The committee did agree, and Rowan went to Amsterdam.

In the thirty years since Rowan had begun his pioneering experiments on photoperiodism in birds, photobiology had grown into a separate scientific field. The variety and depth of the congress program must have pleased, and maybe even surprised Rowan, who had not kept pace with recent developments. When Rowan began his experiments on juncos in 1924, there were less than half a dozen papers on photoperiodism in existence, and he had not read most of them as they were published in obscure journals. The 1954 congress program consisted of about 150 papers on the effects of photoperiodism on plants and animals, on the medical implications of photoperiodism, and on the physics, chemistry, and climatology of nonionizing radiation.[32] Rowan felt stimulated but overwhelmed by all the new research. He had been surpassed: photobiology research was now an area to which he, the pioneer, could no longer contribute. He hadn't taken part in it for so long that when he planned his European trip he had been unaware of the congress.

Rowan's actual reactions to the congress are unknown. To the NRC, which funded some of his travel (awarding him six hundred dollars after he had gone to Europe), he simply wrote, "it was extremely interesting and informative."[33] To Moreau, now editor of the *Ibis*, Rowan sent a more detailed account. He remarked that much time was spent on

> the botanical end of the topic . . . the rather limited discussions on photoperiodism in animals brought out the difficulties of comparing one species with another or one group of animals such as insects with another such as birds. The truth is probably that even though responses to daylength may be superficially similar in many living organisms the means by which the ends have been attained must vary with the mechanisms available within the groups of species themselves.[34]

He further explained that photoperiodism "incorporates two separate concepts . . . that while the day-and-night relationship is responsible for establishing *diurnal* rhythms in insects (and, of course, in other animals and plants as well), it also controls *seasonal* phenomena." The short-term and long-term effects of photoperiodism had implications for cross-equatorial migrant birds. He objected, however, to the general application of the term itself "to seasonal effects when used without qualification." He added, to "demonstrate the effects of varying daylength as the biological responses of plants and animals is relatively simple. The problem of the underlying mechanisms is something quite different." Although knowledge of these mechanisms was still insufficient, he thought "the central nervous system itself may prove to be the most important photoreceptor." It is symptomatic of Rowan's integrative approach to science that, stimulated by the conference, he saw a connection between photoperiodism and biological cycles.[35]

The enjoyable summer trip was followed for the Rowans, almost predictably, by sadness, depression, and ill health. On the return trip to Edmonton, Bill and Reta stopped in Toronto to await the arrival of a new grandchild. Rowan was greatly upset to find that the little girl born to Julian and Niva on 13 September had a harelip and a cleft palate. With typical exaggeration he wrote, "Today has been one of the tragedies of Rowan history."[36] Perhaps, with his elitist views, Rowan could not imagine any member of his family having a visible birth defect, and while he attempted to give Julian and Niva the best emotional support that he could, he began to question the power of the medical establishment over life and death. Rowan may have long thought of euthanasia as a viable solution to suffering and terminal illness. Now, the day after his return to Edmonton, he wrote to the editors of British, Canadian, and American medical journals about the topic. The letter he sent to them all was obviously prompted by the "tragedy," which he never mentioned, citing instead several other examples in favour of euthanasia.

The responses of the medical associations varied. William Boyd, a Toronto pathologist, praised Rowan's wonderful letter which "took a lot of courage to write," but "was *most* timely and beautifully expressed."[37] The editor of the *Journal* of the American Medical Association wrote that "the subject at best is a controversial one, and when a journal has not only the national but international coverage . . . it is to our advantage to keep the controversy within its pages to scientific rather than moral and sociological problems."[38] Rowan's letter on euthanasia, with its broader implications concerning politics, decision making, and the consequences of them both for humanity, was eventually published as "A Layman Challenges Medicine" in the May 1957 issue of the *Historical Bulletin of the Calgary Associate Clinic.*

Rowan may have been particularly susceptible to depression at this time. While the European trip was a great success, and there is no indication of his having been ill on the trip, he must have dwelt on the subject of death. What prompted Rowan to update his will during the summer of 1954 is unclear. The death of Joe Dawkins left him sad, although he knew Joe's health had been failing for a number of years. But it meant that another tie with his past was lost, and Rowan genuinely mourned the "genius in the bush" (he used this as the title of his brief article about Joe in the *Edmonton Journal*). The family reunion, in England, after nearly twenty years, forcefully brought home to him the reality of aging and death. There may have been discussions about wills and estates. Whatever the reasons, Rowan revised his will in Finland, on 15 July, two weeks before his sixty-third birthday. He gave specific instructions for the disposal of family heirlooms: he left his signet ring to Oliver, and his cigarette case and lighter, together with his natural history notebooks, to Julian. Various silver and china objects were to be divided among his three daughters, and the house, together with the money from the sale of his books and vertebrate collection, were to be given to Reta. Then came the part that, after his death, caused considerable concern among his colleagues.

Rowan specifically requested that "When I die, my brain is to be extracted and sent to the Royal College of Surgeons, London . . . I would like my skeleton to be cleaned up and left to the Department Vertebrate Collection." Ironically, after Rowan died, it was determined that his skeleton could not be used in the department of zoology; the department was not licenced to have custody of human remains. Because the department of anatomy had such a licence, the skeleton was kept there, but remained unidentified. It could not be ascertained what happened to Rowan's brain. According to Dr. Ray Salt, it was sent to a neurologist in Montreal "as requested" — but Rowan had requested it be sent to England.[39]

Rowan, although still pessimistic about the future of the world, had many satisfactory experiences at about this time. In 1955, Canada Post issued a series of wildlife stamps, including a five-cent one bearing Rowan's new rendering of the whooping crane. He gave a successful talk on CBC Radio on Darwin, for the "Architects of Modern Thought" series. He received many letters from listeners, and so many requests for copies of his talk that it was eventually published as a pamphlet. He remained involved in planning the

Edmonton zoological garden and, in late 1955, gave a series of radio broadcasts and wrote some popular articles for the *Edmonton Journal* on zoos and captive animals.

It was an irony of fate that Rowan, who frequently wanted to abandon teaching for research, art, or even business, thoroughly enjoyed his penultimate year (1955–1956) at the university. As the senior professor in the department, Rowan co-taught an introductory course on taxonomy with Miller and Moore, though what his share of this course was is unknown. He was heavily involved in more advanced courses, and taught both ornithology and land biology (principles of game conservation), each course consisting of three hours of lectures and three hours of laboratory work per week. Field trips were mandatory, and Rowan and his students tramped all over the Alberta countryside observing and collecting bird specimens, and studying mammals in the field or in the various enclosures erected by Rowan and his assistants for the population-cycle study. Rowan also taught graduate courses on animal behaviour, life histories of American birds and mammals, and conservation topics, and, during the summer of 1955, a new field course designed for teachers. The fifteen students in this course, "Zoo 5" enjoyed both the course content and the company of their quirky professor. They expressed their appreciation with a poem entitled "Birthday Ode," written for Rowan's sixty-fourth birthday:

> It became the fate of a favoured few
> To study a subject — abbreviated "Zoo"
> Without the waste of too many words
> They plunged right into the study of birds
> Festooned with cameras-field glasses-waders
> They developed into a party of raiders
>
> . . . .
>
> In course of time many problems arose
> Can the animal breathe, and has it a nose?
> And why do animals whose size is the least
> Have names that exceed the extent of the beast?
> They realised no sin could be half so vile
> As to confuse an amphibian with the class reptile.
> The professor who guides us has made it a pleasure
> And left us all with life-long treasure.[40]

Though teaching was satisfying once again, Rowan planned for his retirement. In 1948, he had approached R.C. Wallace, now principal of Queen's University, about the sale of his vertebrate collection, but Queen's had no more money for such a purchase than had the University of Alberta, and the collection remained in Edmonton.

In early 1955, Rowan reconsidered selling his collection. Apparently he had hoped that "his tame millionaire" would buy it and donate it to the university, but Harvie had other plans, and the university was not in a rush to purchase a collection that was, in any case, housed on its premises and already used by its advanced students. Rowan then wrote a letter to the university authorities describing the importance and extent of this unique study- and research-material collection, and sent them several testimonials from other zoologists. Although details of the protracted negotiations are unavailable, we do know that in August 1956 the Board of Governors of the University of Alberta purchased the collection for five thousand dollars.[41]

During 1955 Rowan continued to work on the manuscript entitled "Beloved Wilderness," which had grown out of a series of radio talks given in the late 1930s and early 1940s. The original talks were aimed at the general public, because Rowan hoped to instil a knowledge of animals and an understanding of conservation concerns in lay people and hunters. In his draft introduction Rowan stated that "Beloved Wilderness . . . was designed to meet the specific requirements of Canadian sportsmen . . . . to provide them with factual and reliable information on subjects they love most."[42] He proposed to include chapters on sanctuaries, game birds, ducks, mammals, the environment, and animal populations. Later he planned additional chapters on the muskegs, the Prairies, and big game; but progress was slow, and the manuscript was never completed.

The original talks were snappy and factual. Delivered in Rowan's rich baritone voice, peppered with humorous asides, they informed and entertained a devoted following across the western half of the continent. In print, the texts of the talks lacked vigour. To anyone familiar with Rowan's evocative writing, "Beloved Wilderness" seems uninspired and dry. But Rowan never embellished the original text, and while he tried sporadically to improve the manuscript, he never invested the time and effort required to produce compelling nature writing. By contrast, in his short paper on the Peace River journey, published in the limited-circulation university paper *New Trail*, he managed to communicate his enthusiasm and love for his beloved wilderness in a way he never could in the long manuscript. So "Beloved Wilderness" remained in his study, with "As the Crow Flies" — a much more lively, entertaining, and, potentially marketable product and with "The Last Chapter," which, despite its timeliness, was disorganized and depressing.

Rowan approached 1955–1956, his last year as a professor, with mixed emotions. On the one hand, his pessimism about the world persisted. He joined the Society for Social Responsibility in Science, an international organization whose council included American and British physicists, chemists, and engineers.[43] On the other hand, Rowan looked forward to a life devoid of departmental hassles and chores, and to having unlimited time for writing and art. He yearned to be involved again in scientific research. In fact, since he had three manuscripts in search of publishers (two of them incomplete), he had become increasingly involved in the Edmonton Zoo, and he had made plans to tramp around the Alberta countryside collecting specimens and hunting ducks for sport and food, it is hard to know just how Rowan envisaged his retirement. To lesser mortals, his proposed schedule would have seemed more like one of forced labour than leisure.

By all accounts, Rowan had retained much of his energy, and in his mid-sixties could still outwalk his younger friends. But he had never looked after himself, and now, increasingly, suffered from periods of fatigue and a variety of illnesses. In 1954 he nearly broke his arm in an accident; the arm became infected and he needed lengthy antibiotic treatment. In September, 1955 on a bird survey in southern Alberta, he caught a severe chill and later noted that he shivered so violently it was "like the ague. My heart was also missing every second beat." But he was, as usual, up early the next morning looking for game birds.[44]

Rowan applied to the National Research Council, and in 1956 received a grant of $2,830 to work on "Experiments in Bird Migration VI: Effects of Castration and Certain Hormones on the Migratory Movements of the Common Crow (*Corvus brachyrhynchos*)." To finish his long-abandoned crow experiments, he planned to determine, whether or not "the migratory impulse is initiated by seasonal changes in the pituitary gland directly via gonadal hormones."[45] He saw this project as a last attempt to "clean up some of the loose threads that nobody has picked up since I started the ball rolling." The NRC funds and the research time that became available to him on his retirement finally enabled him to incorporate research on hormones "of wide biological significance" into his investigations. Rowan still hoped to publish a number of papers on the ten-year cycle.[46] He also struggled with a novel, "This Great Advertisement," a "reflection on the shallowness" of the American way of life, started sometime in the 1920s. To an ex-student he wrote, "This is something of a program for a gentleman (if I am one!) just retired for senility and general decrepitude but if I live long enough, it might still be done."[47]

As Rowan approached retirement he planned a number of trips to the United States and Eastern Canada to visit family and friends. At the end of his last term as zoology professor, two events occurred at the university that provided him with considerable satisfaction. On 2 May 1956, a dinner was organized in his honour at the Men's Faculty Club. The toasts of affection reinforced his belief that despite the problems he'd had with his department he had many friends and admirers within the university. Rowan was also gratified when the administration asked if he would teach one or two courses after retirement, and then, with great pleasure, turned down the request. By contrast, he readily agreed to be interviewed on the CBC television network as part of the program called "Profiles." In his field notes and in a letter written after retirement to his "Dear Kids," he dealt with both the interview (one of his graduate students, the wrestling promoter turned zoologist F.A. Oeming, was the interviewer) and his feelings about retirement. The interview was the week's "great event," and involved flying to Winnipeg and enduring several rehearsals.

Although "glad to be retiring," Rowan complained about insomnia. In the past he had done his best writing in the quiet of the night, at home, in his upstairs study thick with cigarette smoke, over innumerable cups of coffee. Then, after a hard day's work, he slept well. In fact, Rowan had always been proud of being able to sleep anywhere: in haystacks, old shacks, tents, and cars. Now, sleep began to elude him, and on field trips he often had to stop and rest. Characteristically, he continued to engage in his manifold activities.

On 1 September 1956, Rowan wrote to his children: "If dates could be milestones, I expect the above is one, for today I have become a retired gentleman ... We are in very picturesque country, rolling and full of sloughs, all full of ducks . . . and sitting on the hillside . . . I had time to ruminate."[48]

In his field notes he remarked, "Am now retired gentleman. Celebrated by being in the crow field at 4.30 a.m."[49] The crows, those wily brutes that in the past had led him in a merry dance, had not changed in the intervening years. Rowan rediscovered that catching crows was time-consuming, tiring, and highly frustrating. Eventually, during the fall of 1956, he abandoned all attempts to do research on them. He spent little time outdoors during the winter of 1956–1957, but he did hunt ducks and band snowy owls. He worked instead on his manuscripts. In addition to three book-length works, Rowan wrote a number of shorter pieces, including two talks: one for the Golden Jubilee of the Manitoba Game Association, also entitled "Beloved Wilderness," and the other for the Edmonton Unitarian Church, entitled "A Biologist Looks at Ethics" (which was delivered a month before his death). These summed up his two major interests and concerns of the 1945–1957 period: conservation and the future of science, peace, and integrity.

By the early spring of 1957, Rowan was glad to be in the field again. He took several trips with two young friends, naturalist-filmmakers Edgar T. Jones and Cy Hampson. On an excursion to southern Alberta Rowan finally encountered a species that had long eluded him, the magnificent sage grouse. The three men drove south of Medicine Hat across the Cypress Hills to the sagebrush flats near the American border. The historic area straddling the Alberta-Saskatchewan border is now part of Cypress Hills Provincial Park, but in the 1880s, only early western traders, illicit stills, and Fort Walsh, the original home of the Northwest Mounted Police, could be found there. Lodgepole pines grow in the valleys. There are numerous species of western birds and mammals. The rolling hills (their peaks escaped the Ice Age) are populated by pronghorn antelopes, and Swainson's and ferruginous hawks, who prey on small rodents. The flats on the southern slopes of the hills are breeding areas for the sage grouse, and these areas were the destination of Rowan and his companions in late April 1957.

On the drive south they found the nest of a pair of ferruginous hawks and photographed a great horned owl. The pronghorns stirred Rowan's memory of his first Prairie visit. Near the border they finally "walked right into a very tame singleton [sage] cock but had no cameras." Rowan sketched this "veritable aristocrat of the wilds," capturing its "stately strides," and the following morning was delighted to observe "the spectacular display of a small bunch of seven or 8 *cocks* and a couple of *hens*" from a distance of about thirty metres. He was intrigued by the sight and behaviour of these large birds, and was surprised to find that their calls were inaudible to the observers in the quiet morning air, despite "their colossal air sacs and seemingly violent convulsions."[50]

Rowan's delight with the sage grouse was tempered by his painfully stiff back. Although he rested, his condition persisted, but before daybreak he was back in the blind. His copious notes describing both the light conditions and the changing behaviour of birds, show a curious resemblance to the detailed notes he took four decades before on a night watch at Blakeney Point, Norfolk. Sore back notwithstanding, Rowan sketched for well over two hours in a cramped position and made more than a dozen drawings, some of the "wandering hen," others of the much larger, more colourful male birds in resting and display poses and while "sparring."

The hectic pace Rowan had set for himself was beginning to take its toll. He often felt tired and achy, even dispirited. Rest at home was sometimes impossible because of house guests, notably his youngest daughter Josephine who, temporarily separated from her husband, had returned home with her two small boys. To Rowan, the house at 10721 86th Avenue seemed too cramped and, resentful of having to share Reta with others, he frequently fretted about the invasions of his home. At other times, when he felt well and energetic, he considered his grandchildren well behaved and wonderful.

Trips to the muskegs — so enjoyable in the past — still attracted him, and during the spring of 1957 he often went to Fawcett. It was an area where many of his old friends lived, and where the muskegs hid sandhill cranes and shorebirds on the nest. Now, however, wading through the wet spots and climbing over hummocks were an effort. In early May, the weather turned freezing and Rowan, inadequately clothed, as usual, "took six straight hours in the muskeg, wet often to the waist but never dry, alone." The sky was overcast. He lost his bearings, and could foresee "being recorded as an unknown skeleton maybe 20 years from now."[51] In his field notebook he wrote: "I have seldom been colder, especially in the afternoon when my feet and legs were permanently water-logged in iced water."[52] Undaunted, he tramped some twenty-five kilometres under a leaden sky looking for cranes, and finally admitted that "after my strenuous muskeg trip I am so tired that I cannot even write coherent English, or type decently."[53]

A week later, in the early hours of the morning Rowan wrote to his "Dear Kids." "I am once again back from the country, this time from sweltering heat and mosquitoes instead of snow and ice. But it was a good trip."[54] Accompanied by Jones and Hampson, Rowan visited Francis Point at Beaverhills Lake, where he "naturally recalled the old days of Harrold when the lake was falling and sandbars and mudflats were appearing everywhere and the place was a Mecca for shorebirds." In the late 1950s, though, after several years of rising water levels, "there wasn't one shore bird for every hundred we sometimes saw at about this time of the year." Rowan noted that the changing environment had resulted in the total absence of certain species, such as meadowlarks and Sprague's pipits. By contrast, the potholes around Tofield and to the southwest around Miquelon Lake were "covered with ducks," as they had been in the old days, and there was no shortage of mosquitoes. Although Rowan regretted many of the changes, he was interested in comparing "the ecology of a falling lake with a rising one," and made numerous sketches for his "Beloved Wilderness" manuscript. He admitted that it was a "pleasure to be in the open air again and reliving some of the old days."[55] Other excursions left him exhausted.[56] Nevertheless, at the end of May he went to Toronto to attend the annual meeting of the Canadian Audubon Society. While there, he also discussed "Beloved Wilderness" with his publisher. He talked about pheasants, game laws, and game literature with scientists, and planned a new science series with Lister Sinclair at the CBC, before returning home via Delta, Manitoba. On 5 June 1957, Rowan arrived at Delta for what turned out to be the last time. Hochbaum had a premonition a few days later when he overheard his mentor muttering "thank goodness it is not inside my head," while wiping blood off his face (presumably from a nosebleed).[57]

Rowan had apparently complained of headaches and fatigue during the last two years of his life. Always a heavy smoker and coffee drinker, he continued to abuse his body after his retirement. With more time on his hands, and some spare cash, he began to drink heavily, as well. Suffering from increased insomnia, he took sleeping pills.[58]

His last three weeks cannot be traced in detail. There is evidence that he continued to look for sandhill cranes in the muskegs, and worked on "Beloved Wilderness" and on several book reviews for the *Edmonton Journal*.[59] After a mid-June visit with Sylvia in Red Deer, accompanied by Josephine and her boys, Rowan stayed in Edmonton, alone.[60] Reta attended the Western Canada Unitarian Conference in Wynyard, Saskatchewan, while Josephine and the children visited Gerdine in Vancouver.

Rowan enjoyed the peace and quiet of the little house; if he was lonely after a day's work, he could always phone friends. Work on his manuscripts was still slow, and excursions into the muskegs led to exhaustion. After one of these strenuous trips, Rowan suffered a fatal heart attack. Josephine returned from Vancouver on 30 June 1957. She found him slumped on his bed, partially undressed, dead. A record of Dvořák's *New World Symphony* was still spinning, silently, on the gramophone.[61] Though grief stricken, Josephine sent telegrams to members of the family and coped with official matters; Reta, unaware of Bill's death, enjoyed the peace and beauty of the Saskatchewan countryside in the company of close friends.

On the night of Rowan's death, the sky over the Prairies was lit up by a full circle of shifting lights — an unusual and spectacular display of northern lights. Rowan, the scientist, the man who loved nature and tried to interpret its meanings, may not have found enough scientific evidence to demonstrate a connection between the two events.[62] But he would have been thrilled that his own passing had coincided with a dazzling atmospheric display that illuminated his beloved wilderness.

Epilogue

WILLIAM ROWAN was one of the most renowned Canadian scientists of the first half of the twentieth century. A man of many talents and interests, he was a respected biologist, conservationist, and nature artist, a challenging teacher, and a popular writer and radio personality. Although trained in England, Rowan spent practically all of his professional life in Canada. He was a good general biologist whose main interest was in birds, and he began his research during a period when ornithology was undergoing a major transformation: from descriptive natural history to modern biology. Rowan was an intuitive, creative, and highly energetic scientist who favoured an interdisciplinary approach to research. At a time when zoology was becoming an increasingly reductionist experimental science conducted in laboratories, Rowan's pioneering work in ornithology combined the traditions of nineteenth-century British natural history with the laboratory methods of twentieth-century zoology. To these Rowan added an ecological perspective, which he employed in his study of the immediate stimulus of bird migration, his first major research topic.

Rowan also studied hydras, the anatomy of mammals, and the embryology of loons and grebes, and, for over thirty years, conducted wide-ranging investigations of the cyclic fluctuations of the game birds and mammals of the north temperate zone. Rowan's research, beginning with his experiments on a small North American bird in 1924, attracted great interest in the scientific community, and his innovative approach to studying the physiological basis of migration stimulated much experimental work in Europe and North America. During the following two decades, investigations into the effects of daylight on the reproductive cycles of animals were extended by Rowan and others to involve more than fifty species of animals, of all classes of vertebrates. The effects of Rowan's research on various areas of biology are undeniable. Avian physiology, breeding biology, photobiology, migration, biological cycles, and the ecological study of waterfowl owe their present level of advancement to Rowan's pioneering investigations. His work was highly regarded by his contemporaries, and his writings are included in most zoology textbooks, books on avian physiology, and histories of ornithology.

Although Rowan is best remembered for his scientific work, he also made his mark as a teacher. He trained several generations of medical doctors and a number of famous wildlife biologists. He communicated to his students the excitement of scientific research, and taught them the importance of the scientist's responsibility to society. In their turn, they taught new generations of students to conduct their scientific research in an ethical fashion. Rowan's activities also included nature photography and nature art. His pen-and-ink drawings and his sketches have long been valued by naturalists and scientists; his handmade Christmas cards were also treasured by many of his friends and colleagues.

Rowan was a colourful person who had a flare for publicity. By the late 1920s he had discovered the inherent potential of radio as a medium for advertising his own scientific work, and for popularizing science and conservation. Thus, in addition to publishing his popular illustrated articles in journals such as *Country Life*, from the late 1920s on, first locally, and later nationally Rowan broadcast countless talks on nature, animals, conservation, science, war, and ethics. For nearly three decades many thousands of people, from all walks of life, across Canada and the northern United States, tuned in regularly to listen to Doc Rowan's stimulating talks.

Rowan saw the importance of many areas of research and conservation at a time when funding for such work was sporadic, and when university authorities and the federal and provincial governments made little effort to listen to scientists. His concern, in the 1920s, about the threatened wood buffalo is a good case in point. Seventy-five years after Rowan's initial warning about the dangers of mixing healthy and diseased buffalo herds, the problem resurfaced. In the early 1990s there is still controversy in the scientific community over the status of the wood buffalo.

Rowan's scientific impact can be measured by the frequency with which his research is cited in the work of other scientists, and by the number of research programs in all parts of the world that grew out of his original investigations. His influence can be seen in the various kinds of recognition he received posthumously, such as the Rowan Memorial Term held at the University of Alberta in 1975, which marked the fiftieth anniversary of Rowan's first publication in *Nature*. The scientific programs of the 1986 International Ornithological Congress in Ottawa and the 1991 American Ornithologists' Union Conference in Montreal clearly reflect the fact that numerous scientists continue to follow in his footsteps. No scientist could wish for a better tribute. Other areas of his influence are harder to demonstrate. How do we quantify his effect on conservation, on the ethical conduct of scientists, on the enduring commitment of generations of doctors and scientists to issues of science, war, and peace? How do we determine the extent to which his concerns, the preoccupations that increasingly found expression in his lectures, radio talks, and popular writings during the 1940s and 1950s, continue to affect students, scientists, and the general public?

Thirty-five years ago, at Rowan's memorial service in Edmonton, the Reverend Charles Eddis said, William Rowan was a person who "embodied in noble fashion the principles he believed in and stood for — intelligence, integrity, and a world-embracing ethical conscience . . . . Without him, we shall never be the same. Because of him, we shall never be the same, either." No human being could wish for a better accolade.

Notes

Chapter 1: **The Lap of Luxury, 1891–1908**

1. Arthur Rowan to Reta Rowan, 20 July 1959, William Rowan Papers, University of Alberta Archives, Edmonton (hereafter WRP).

2. Arthur Rowan to W.O. Rowan, 21 November 1957. Notable among these family members were Sir William Rowan (1789–1879), field marshall and administrator of the Province of Canada (1849–55), and his brother Sir Charles Rowan (1783–1852), first commissioner of the London police force. See Charles Reith, "Charles Rowan, 1783–1852," copy of a police magazine circa 1952, Rowan family papers (hereafter RFP), *Dictionary of Canadian Biography*, Vol 10, s.v. "Rowan, Sir William."

3. Athalie Abraham, conversation with author.

4. Translation of an undated obituary from a Danish newspaper, in the family's possession.

5. Athalie Abraham, conversation with author.

6. W.R. Rowan bought the Schlössli from its former owner, Rudolf Oppliger, for 54,900 Swiss francs (I. Acherman-Knoepli to author, 18 January 1988).

7. See *Cook's Tourist Handbook of Switzerland* (London: Thomas Cook and Son, 1905) 28–29; or *A Guide through Basel and Environs* (Basel: Hotelkeepers' Union, 1890) 4, 56.

8. Agnes Rowan to Julian Rowan, 1 June 1958. I thank Julian Rowan for lending me this letter.

9. Ibid.

10. Arthur Rowan to Reta Rowan, 20 July 1959, WRP.

11. Ibid.

12. Apparently her sons adored her, and would do anything in their power to avoid hurting, or even upsetting her; in later life she did not get on with Agnes (Athalie Abraham, conversation with author).

13. Quoted in Barbara Moon, "The Acid-Minded Professor," *Maclean's* 15 May 1952, 56.

14. Arthur Rowan to Reta Rowan, 20 July 1959, WRP.

15. Ibid.

16. Athalie Abraham, conversation with author.

17. By this time, the eldest child, Nellie (22), was a missionary in China.

18. Owned by the "Misses Armstrong," Armstrong Cottage is listed as vacant in the 1901 Bedford Directory (p. 90). The listing was no doubt compiled early in the year, or late in the previous year. The Bedford School records for 20 September 1901 give the family's address as 41 St. John Street. The house at 12 Merton Road was built on an 80 by 119 foot (or 24 by 36 metre) lot. I thank N.K. Lutt, from the Bedford County Records Office, for providing me with the builder's blueprints and other information concerning 12 Merton Road. When I visited the town in 1987 the house (renumbered 16 Merton Road) was still intact.

19. "Welcome to North Bedfordshire" [leaflet], Public Relations Office, North Bedfordshire Borough Council, 1985.

20. Arthur Nightall, conversation with author.

21. Agnes Rowan to Julian Rowan, 24 November 1958; Arthur Rowan to W.O. Rowan, 21 November 1957, RFP.

22. Billy possibly substituted natural philosophy for Greek, but as this subject came under classics, there is no evidence that he actually did so (Arthur Nightall, conversation with author).

23. Arthur Rowan to W.O. Rowan, 11 August 1957, RFP.

24. The boarders wore suits (Arthur Nightall to author, 23 July 1987). All the day boys went home for meals.

25. Fred Rowan to Reta Rowan, 1 November 1959, WRP.

26. Agnes Rowan to Julian Rowan, 24 November 1958, RFP.

27. Agnes Rowan to Julian Rowan, 1 June 1958, RFP.

28. Moon, "The Acid-Minded Professor," 56.

29. Agnes Rowan to Julian Rowan, 24 November 1958, RFP.

30. Fred Rowan to Julian Rowan, 1 November 1959, RFP.

31. William Rowan to W.C. Allee, 10 July 1943, WRP.

32. William Rowan to P.A. Taverner, 30 May 1923, P.A. Taverner Papers, Ornithology Division, National Museum of Natural Sciences, Ottawa.

33. "Mr. Kearton's Lecture," Supplement," *Ousel*, 18 November 1905.

34. R. Kearton, *Wild Life at Home: How to Study and Photograph It.* London: Cassell and Co. 1898, 9–11; In the United States, Herbert Job, F.M. Chapman, and F.H. Herrick were among the pioneers of wildlife photography.

35. Kearton, *Wild Life at Home*, 17–18.

36. "Lecture," *Ousel*, 19 February 1906, 19–20.

37. Patrick A. Dunae, "'Making Good': The Canadian West in British Boys' Literature, 1890–1914," *Prairie Forum* 4 (1979): 165.

38. Ibid., 167.

39. Fred Rowan to Julian Rowan, 1 November 1959, RFP.

Chapter 2: **A Life of Adventure, 1908–1911**

1. George Musk, *Canadian Pacific: The Story of a Famous Shipping Line* (London: David and Charles, 1981), 23. The first CPR advertisement in Lloyd's List appeared in 1903, and quoted the following fares for the journey: from Liverpool to Quebec City and Montreal, saloons were available from ten pounds sterling, second-class cabins cost seven and eight pounds sterling, and steerage was five pounds and ten shillings. There were also special fares for settlers going to Winnipeg.

2. Gerdine Rowan McPhee, interview with author, 11 August 1985.

3. Louise Rourke (also known as Dimps Dawson), a friend of Bill and Reta Rowan, eloquently described such a journey in chapter 2 of *The Land of the Frozen Tide* (London: Hutchinson and Co., 1929).

4. Ranch pupils paid for the privilege of working on a ranch; in many cases they were exploited. See J.R. Craig, *Ranching with Lords and Commons: or, Twenty Years on the Range* (Toronto: William Brigg, 1903), 242–43. Remittance men were common in the British colonies of the late nineteenth and early twentieth centuries. There were innumerable jokes about them. Being a remittance man offered a way out of a restrictive Victorian way of life for many young men. See *The Canadian Encyclopedia*, s.v. "remittance man." F.G. Roe, "Remittance Men," *Alberta Historical Review* 2 (1954): 3–12; and M. Ellen Hughes, "Remittance Men," typescript, 1978, Glenbow-Alberta Institute Archives, Calgary (hereafter GAA).

5. See Wilfrid Eggleston, "The Short Grass Prairies of Western Canada," *Canadian Geographical Journal* 50 (1955); Claude Mondor, "The Canadian Plains: The Vanishing Act," *Nature Canada* 5 (1976).

6. See Patrick A. Dunae, "'Making Good': The Canadian West in British Boys' Literature, 1890–1914," *Prairie Forum* 4 (1979).

7. W. Rowan, talk given to the Alberta Fish and Game Association, (hereafter Calgary talk), typescript 18 February 1955, William Rowan Papers, University of Alberta Archives (hereafter WRP).

8. Craig, in *Ranching with Lords*, quotes an early rancher's recollections of the arrival of the Chinook and the subsequent changes in temperature (p. 48).

9. There is an abundance of material on the Canadian Prairies. These range from informal recollections and compilations of local histories to scholarly books and theses. The Glenbow-Alberta Institute Archives, Calgary, has a considerable collection of ranching-history material, which includes manuscripts, photographs, clothing, and equipment. See, for instance: A.A. Allen, the *Gleichen Call* (Gleichen: Gleichen Church Women, 1967–1968), 82; C.J. Christianson, *Early Rangemen* (Lethbridge: Southern Printing Co., 1973); H.B. Roen, comp., *The Grassroots of Dorothy*, 1895–1970 (N.p.: Dorothy Community, 1971); E. George, "Ranching in Southern Alberta," *Alberta Historical Review* 3 (1955). Among the more scholarly works available on the subject, the following are noteworthy: S.M. Evans, "The Passing of a Frontier: Ranching in the Canadian West, 1882–1912," Ph.D. diss., University of Calgary, 1976; D.H. Breen, *The Canadian Prairie West and the Ranching*

Frontier, 1874–1928 (Toronto: University of Toronto Press, 1983); Gerald Friesen, *The Canadian Prairies: A History* (Toronto: University of Toronto Press, 1984). I also benefited from reading Sharon Butala, *The Gates of the Sun* (Saskatoon: Fifth House, 1985), and Maria Nelson's compilation "Glossary of Pioneer Terms," in *Saddles, Sleighs and Sadirons* (N.p.: Chestermere Historical Society, 1971).

10. Rowan, Calgary talk.

11. One section equalled 640 acres; Bunny's ranch (near Dorothy) was relatively small, and he employed only one or two ranch hands. Details of Brooks's life are unavailable, but he is mentioned as a ranch hand in the Eliza Wilson Letters (GAA); there was also a Sergeant Brooks (Eliza Wilson Diaries, GAA), whose identity cannot be established. The two may have been the same. Rowan must have become good friends with him, as after a trip to Gleichen in 1953, he noted with regret, "None of the old timers remembered Erny Brooks" (field notes, 20 May 1953).

12. According to Tom Gooden, curatorial assistant at the Glenbow-Alberta Institute, cowboys and ranchers at the time wore clothes that bore no, or very little, relation to the cowboy clothing popularized by American movies, that is, Levis, modern cowboy hats, big belt buckles, and so on. The original cowboy wore dark, or neutral-coloured work clothes. Many items were bought second hand; English military trousers and jackets were especially favoured, because of the durability of the material of which they were made. Khaki twill or woollen trousers were worn either over or tucked into black-leather, high-heeled, or lace-up boots. Summer shirts were white, with blue and black vertical stripes, and no collar. The cowboy hat of the time was the original Stetson, with a pinched crown and stiff brim (reminiscent of a Boy Scout hat); its leather strap could be worn under the chin, or in the back — British military fashion. Large cotton kerchiefs were pulled over the face to protect it from the dust. In winter the cowboys wore long johns, two pairs of trousers, flannel shirts, pullovers, fur-lined heavy-duck jackets, fur caps, mittens, heavy boots, and chaps. Indoors they wore carpet slippers or moccasins. Accessories were devised to prevent being "hung up" on the saddle, a recurrent fear of cowboys.

13. The ford on rancher Jack Clark's land is still visible, as are the tepee rings and old cart tracks. I am grateful to Doug Clark for having shown these to me. Doug and his brother Roy are Jack Clark's descendants, and live on the working ranch with their families.

14. Rowan, Calgary talk.

15. Bunny ran his ranch operation by the clock, and was not likely to deviate from his routine. All ranchers kept cows for domestic use. (Bob McKnight, interview with author, 16 June 1987; Mr. and Mrs. Hugh Peake, and Mr. and Mrs. Eric Hodgson, interviews with author, 17 June 1987).

16. B.H. Bunny (1880–1964) was the son of an English doctor. He emigrated to Guelph, Ontario in the late 1890s, but soon went to work on a ranch in southern Alberta. After a stint with the Lord Strathcona Light Horse Regiment during the Boer War, Bunny returned to Alberta in 1903 (Isabelle

Bunny Carter, interview with author, 21 June 1987). See also, G.N. Thomas, "Harvey Davies," in Roen, *Grassroots*, "C.H. Bray" and "Bryce Hamilton Bunny," Ibid.

17. Craig, *Ranching with Lords*, 242.

18. Singsongs were an integral part of ranching community socials (Bob McKnight, interview with author, 16 June 1987); See also Sheilagh Jamieson "Women in the Southern Alberta Ranch Community, 1881–1914," in *The Canadian West. Social Change and Economic Development*, ed. H.C. Klassen (Calgary: University of Calgary Press, 1977).

19. William Rowan to Percy A. Taverner, 16 January 1925, P.A. Taverner papers, Ornithology Division, National Museum of Natural Sciences, Ottawa.

20. William Rowan, field notes, 1908–11, 1–4.

21. John O. McHugh, "The Roundup, 1906," typescript, GAA. Rowan's first roundup may have started at the neighbouring ranch owned by Eric Smail. One of his early photographs is entitled "Starting of the Roundup," Smail's, 1908.

22. Frederick Rowan to Reta Rowan, 1 November 1959, WRP.

23. M. Ferrara, *St. Albans — Past and Present* (St. Albans: The Campfield Press, 1982), 52.

24. Details of Rowan's second journey west are from his field notes, 1908–1911, 1–4.

25. *Winnipeg — the Gateway to the Golden West* (Montreal: Valentine and Sons Publishing Co. [1910 ?]) contains numerous photos of the city's parks; another useful source is *The Book of Winnipeg: A Handbook for Investors, Tourists and Immigrants* (Winnipeg: J.L. Anderson Publishers, 1912).

26. Born in Wales of Scottish parents, A.G. Lawrence (1888–1961) was educated in Scotland and England. Although keenly interested in nature, especially birds, plants, and fossils, he trained as a chemist and worked in an English steel mill until, injured in an industrial accident, he partially lost the sight in one eye. The accident prompted Lawrence to leave the steel industry, and also the British Isles. Having read many books about Winnipeg and seen numerous advertisements about the opportunities of the Canadian West, he decided to emigrate to Canada. He worked for the City of Winnipeg (in the health department) as clerk, statistician, and secretary until his retirement (Gerdine Lawrence Crawford, interview with author, 5 July 1985). See also C.S. Houston, "In Memoriam: Alexander George Lawrence, 1888–1961," *Blue Jay* 19 (1961).

27. Gerdine Rowan to William Rowan, 8 July 1911, WRP.

Chapter 3: Science It Is, 1912–1915

1. David Taylor, *The Godless Students of Gower Street* (London: University College London Union, 1968), 9.

2. Athalie Abraham, interview with author, 15 August 1987.

3. H.H. Bellot, *University College London* (London: University of London Press, 1929), 392–93.

4. The total fee for the year, including laboratory costs and student-union membership, was thirty-eight pounds, eighteen shillings and sixpence. All information on courses, timetables, and fees are from University College calendars for the years 1911 to 1918, and from William Rowan's file in the University College records office.

5. The laboratory fee of fifteen shillings per session included "schedules, laboratory note-books, use of microscope, reagents and materials" (UCL calendar, 1911–1912, 71).

6. D.M.S. Watson, "James Peter Hill, 1873–1954," in *Biographical Memoirs of Fellows of the Royal Society* (London: Royal Society, 1955). Oliver was the son of the well-known botanist Daniel Oliver, keeper of the herbarium at Kew gardens (E.J. Salisbury, "Francis Wall Oliver, 1864–1951," in *Obituary Notices of Fellows of the Royal Society of London* [London: The Royal Society, 1952]).

7. Athalie Abraham, interview with author, 15 August 1987.

8. Arthur Nightall to author, 25 September 1987.

9. William Rowan to D.M.S. Watson, 27 March 1956, William Rowan Papers, University of Alberta Archives, Edmonton (hereafter WRP).

10. See Salisbury, "Francis Wall Oliver."

11. Ibid., 230.

12. Ibid., 236–37.

13. F.W. Oliver, "Some Remarks on Blakeney Point, Norfolk," *Journal of Ecology* 1 (1913); S.J.M. Gauntlett, *Where to Watch Birds in Norfolk* (Privately published 1985).

14. E.J. Salisbury, "Arthur George Tansley, 1871–1955," in *Biographical Memoirs of Fellows of the Royal Society* (London: Royal Society, 1955), 234; D. Worster, *Nature's Economy* (San Francisco: Sierra Books, 1977), 205.

15. Field notes, 7 January 1913, WRP.

16. Kitty Marsland to William Rowan, 28 January 1918, WRP.

17. See Sheilagh Jamieson, "Women in the Southern Alberta Ranch Community, 1881–1914," in *The Canadian West: Social Change and Economic Development*, ed. H.C. Klassen (Calgary: University of Calgary Press, 1977). See also the various notices in *Gleichen Call* (1907–1912), and other contemporary Western Canadian newspapers.

18. University College, London first admitted women around 1880. As Oxford and Cambridge would not confer higher degrees on women until the mid-to-late 1940s, aspiring women scientists either had to go abroad, or study at one of the colleges affiliated with the University of London.

19. William Rowan, curriculum vitae, 1928 [?], staff file, University of Alberta Archives, Edmonton, mentions that he could not afford to go to Brazil without a grant; the Royal Society of London Library has no record of the grant application.

20. William Rowan, "Some Observations on a Tern Colony," *Journal of Ecology* 2 (1914): 18.

21. William Rowan et al., "On Homotyposis and Allied Characters in the Eggs of the Common Tern," *Biometrika* 10 (1914): 144–66; William Rowan et al., "On the Nest and Eggs of the Common Tern (*S. fluviatilis*, A Cooperative Study." *Biometrika* 12 (1919): 308–53.

22. Field notes, 13 August 1913.

23. On 2 December 1913 he noted the purchase of *British Birds, with their Nests and Eggs*, 6 vols. [author and publication details unknown], and Thomas Bate, *Crustacea Stalked and Sessile Edged*, 2 vols. n.p., 1863–1868.

24. Field notes, 5 February 1914.

25. Ibid., 16 May 1914.

26. Ibid., 7 July 1914. Autochrome plates were invented in 1907 by Auguste and Louis Jean Lumière.

27. S.A. Lakoff, "Scientists, Technologists, and Political Power," in *Science, Technology and Society — A Cross Disciplinary Perspective* ed. Ina Spiegel-Rosing and Derek de Solla Price (London: Sage Publications, 1977), 358.

28. William Rowan to W.C. Allee, 10 July 1943, WRP.

29. Rowan actually entertained Seton and three of his professors on 2 May 1913. He sold the article to *Knowledge* for two guineas (about ten dollars). This information is provided in a letter from Rowan to A.G. Lawrence, 2 May 1913, which was found in a copy of William Rowan, *The Riddle of Migration* (Baltimore; Williams and Wilkins, 1931) in the Delta Waterfowl and Wetlands Research Station Library.

30. Marjory Rowan to author, [?] July 1985.

31. Field notes, 4 March 1915.

32. Ibid., 8 March 1915.

33. Ibid., 9 March 1915.

34. Ibid., 13 April 1915.

35. Ibid., 25 May 1915.

36. Ibid., 26 June 1915.

37. Ibid., 2 October 1915. See also J.D. Howell, "'Soldier's Heart': The Redefinition of Heart Disease and Specialty Formation in Early Twentieth Century Great Britain," in *The Emergence of Modern Cardiology*, F.W. Bynum et al. (London: Wellcome Institute for the History of Medicine, 1985).

38. Field notes, 9 July 1915.

39. K. Magill to author, 21 January 1988.

40. "Discharge Certificate of a Soldier of the Territorial Force," WRP.

Chapter 4: **In Search of Employment, 1916–1919**

1. See J.D. Howell, "'Soldier's Heart': The Redefinition of Heart Disease and Specialty Formation in Early Twentieth Century Great Britain," in *The Emergence of Modern Cardiology*, ed. F.W. Bynum et al. (London: Wellcome Institute for the History of Medicine, 1985).

2. Field notes, 10 November 1915, William Rowan Papers, University of Alberta Archives, Edmonton (hereafter WRP).

3. Ibid., 15 April 1916.

4. *Union Magazine* 7 (1916): 285.

5. The connection between taxidermy and ornithology has been explored in Paul L. Farber, "The Development of Taxidermy and the History of Ornithology," *Isis* 68 (1978).

6. Marjorie Rowan to author [?] July 1985.

7. Gerald Christy to William Rowan, 17 May 1916, WRP.

8. A.G. Lawrence to William Rowan, 3 May 1916, WRP.

9. Ibid.

10. E.W. Darbey to William Rowan, 18 October 1916, WRP.

11. Field notes, 18 June; 8 July 1916.

12. Rowan had first mentioned ringing in his field notes on 23 July 1916. Bird banding had become widespread in the early twentieth century; see H.B. Wood, "The History of Bird Banding," *Auk* 62 (1945).

13. William Rowan, Curriculum Vitae, 1928 [?], staff file, University of Alberta Archives, Edmonton.

14. P.J. Hartog to William Rowan, 18 January 1917, WRP.

15. From Charles Darwin to Julian Huxley, numerous British scientists became famous as ornithologists, but the instruction of ornithology remained excluded from British universities until well into the 1930s. In the United States the first college course in ornithology was offered in 1895, at Oberlin College.

16. "Certificate," Rowan family papers.

17. William Rowan, "Topical Sketch," typescript of a play, December 1917, WRP.

18. Ibid.

19. See Rowan's "Sex," and "Man" in "The Last Chapter," typescript, WRP.

20. Field notes, 8 June 1917.

21. Thomas Kuhn, *The Structure of Scientific Revolutions*, 2nd ed. (Chicago: The University of Chicago Press 1970), 38.

22. Field notes, 6 June 1917.

23. Ibid., 9 September 1917.

24. Ibid., 11 September 1917.

25. Catherine Arnott to William Rowan, 26 November 1917, WRP.

26. Field notes, 10 December 1917.

27. William Rowan, "Bird Life at Eastby Crag," newspaper cutting [source unknown], WRP.

28. J.H. Badley to William Rowan, 4 January 1918, WRP.

29. Rowan's letter did not survive, but see Kitty Marsland to William Rowan, 28 January 1918, WRP.

30. W.R. Mitchell, "Between Two Wharfedale Bridges: An Exploration of Barden and Bolton," *Dalesman* 32 (1971): 1038.

31. Rowan, "Bird Life."

32. Field notes, 21 March 1918.

33. J.H. Badley to William Rowan, 30 March 1918, WRP.

34. Field notes, 10 April 1918. He gives a poetic description of the moors

in his Field notes, 8 May 1918.

35. Ibid., 6 August 1918.

36. William Rowan to Arthur Rowan, 22 September 1918, WRP.

37. Ibid.

38. Field notes, 21 September 1918.

39. William Rowan to Arthur Rowan, 22 September 1918, WRP.

40. Ibid.

41. William Rowan to Arthur Rowan, 29 September 1918, WRP.

42. Field notes, 29 September 1918.

43. Ibid., 4 November 1918.

44. Ibid., 14 November 1918.

45. A.G. Lawrence to William Rowan, 23 April 1918, WRP. Charles Henry O'Donogue (1885–1961) was an eminent zoologist (anatomist, taxonomist). See obituaries, "Prof. C.H. O'Donogue: Zoology at Reading," *Times* 5 December 1961; *Nature* 193, 13 January 1962, 118–19.

46. J.P. Hill to William Rowan, 1 July 1918, WRP.

47. C.H. O'Donoghue to William Rowan, 27 November 1918, WRP.

48. William Rowan, letter of application, WRP.

50. J.P. Hill, letter of recommendation, 19 December 1918. Copy in WRP.

51. Hoyes Lloyd (1888–1978) became one of the most important persons in twentieth century wildlife conservation in Canada.

52. C.H. O'Donoghue to William Rowan, 11 March 1919, WRP.

53. C.H. O'Donoghue to William Rowan, 19 April 1919, WRP.

54. Ibid.

55. C.H. O'Donogue to William Rowan, 6 June 1919, WRP. In fact, the University of Manitoba sought applicants for four positions: an associate professor of Political Economy, at two thousand dollars per year; a physiology assistant at twelve hundred dollars per year; and lecturers in both botany and zoology at an initial salary of sixteen hundred dollars per year. The lecturers were to assist generally in the work of the respective departments, and carry on research. Copy of announcement by Secretary, University of London, WRP.

56. William Rowan, staff file, WRP.

57. H.W. Falk to William Rowan, 20 June 1919, WRP.

58. William Rowan, curriculum vitae, WRP.

59. Sir G. Foster to William Rowan, 5 August 1919, WRP.

60. The post of Assistant in the Department of Zoology and Comparative Anatomy, University College, London, was actually advertised by the Secretary of University College on 1 July 1919, at 250 pounds sterling. Copy in WRP.

61. Field notes, 9 September 1919.

Chapter 5: Second in Command: The University of Manitoba, 1919–1920

1. William Rowan, application, staff file, University of Alberta Archives, Edmonton (hereafter application).

2. Field notes, 16 September 1919, William Rowan Papers, University of Alberta Archives, Edmonton (hereafter WRP).

3. Ibid., 15 October 1919.
4. Ibid., 21 October 1919.
5. Ibid., 23 October 1919.
6. Ibid., 25 October 1919.
7. Ibid., 26 October 1919.
8. William Rowan, "As the Crow Flies," typescript, WRP.
9. Field notes, 27 October 1919.
10. "As the Crow Flies."
11. *President's Report*, (Winnipeg: University of Manitoba, 1919–1920), 9.
12. Ibid.
13. The North American species was *Rana pipiens*, the European one *Rana temporaria*. Field notes, 4 November 1919.
14. Ibid.
15. Ibid., 4 January 1920.
16. Ibid., 15 November 1919.
17. "As the Crow Flies."
18. William Rowan, application.
19. Field notes, 18 January 1920.
20. Ibid., 31 March 1920.
21. Ibid., 3 April 1920.
22. Ibid., 7 April 1920.
23. Watson (1886–1973) became famous as a zoologist-paleontologist at University College, London. Before his untimely death from pneumonia, Gordon Hewitt (1885–1920) showed great promise as an entomologist and conservationist. Janet Foster, *Working for Wildlife: The Beginning of Preservation in Canada* (Toronto: University of Toronto Press, 1978), 36–37.
24. C.G. Hewitt to William Rowan, 18 November 1919, WRP.
25. By the second decade of the century, university-educated ornithologists taught at some American universities (Arthur A. Allen taught at Cornell University and Joseph Grinnell at the University of California, Berkeley). Percy Algernon Taverner (1875–1947) was a typical self-trained naturalist and an excellent artist, well-known and liked by numerous Canadian and American ornithologists. See M.G. Ainley "From Natural History, to Avian Biology: Canadian Ornithology, 1860–1950," Ph.D. diss., McGill University, 1985.
26. William Rowan to P.A. Taverner, 21 November 1919, P.A. Taverner Papers, Ornithology Division, National Museum of Natural Sciences, Ottawa, (hereafter PATP).
27. P.A. Taverner to William Rowan, 25 November 1919, WRP.
28. Canadian ornithologists Montague Chamberlain (1844–1924) and Thomas McIlwraith (1824–1903) were among the founding members of the American Ornithologists' Union established in 1883. Because ornithological problems were similar in Canada and the United States, and because there were relatively few ornithologists in both countries, the science had developed in a "North American context." The Society of Canadian Ornithologists was finally established in 1981.
29. P.A. Taverner to William Rowan, 25 November 1919, WRP. W.E.

Saunders (1861–1943) was a pharmacist and naturalist; James Henry Fleming (1872–1940) an active avocational ornithologist who, in 1932, became the first Canadian president of the American Ornithologists' Union.

30. The establishment of subspecies was an all-important topic in North American systematics. In the late nineteenth century, American ornithologists advocated the use of trinomial nomenclature, that is the use of generic, specific, and subspecific names to designate each species. By the early twentieth century, ornithologists belonged to either of two camps. They were "splitters," who divided species on the basis of minute differences into numerous subspecies, or they were "lumpers," who advocated the joining of two or more subspecies into one species.

31. See Ainley, "From Natural History," esp. ch. 4 [on exploration].

32. William Rowan to C.G. Hewitt, 15 January 1920, PATP.

33. C.G. Hewitt to P.A. Taverner, 23 January 1920, PATP.

34. P.A. Taverner to C.G. Hewitt, 26 January 1920, PATP.

35. P.A. Taverner to William Rowan, 26 January 1920, WRP.

36. P.A. Taverner to William Rowan, 2 February 1920, WRP.

37. William Rowan to J.H. Fleming, 28 March 1920, J.H. Fleming Papers, Royal Ontario Museum Archives, Toronto (hereafter JHFP).

38. Ibid.

39. William Rowan to J.H. Fleming, 24 May 1920, JHFP. After negotiating with the Greater Winnipeg Water District, in early 1920 the university leased two buildings to be used as a field station. O'Donoghue became its first director. Such field stations were widely used in Europe and the United States. University College, London had two (one at Plymouth for marine biology, and another at Blakeney Point for plant ecology and faunistic studies). In Canada, at the time, there were already two marine-biology stations (at St. Andrews-by-the-Sea and at Nanaimo), but none for general biological studies.

40. Field notes, 1 May 1920.

41. Ibid., 24 May 1920. The Manitoba Audubon Society was established in 1915, and in October 1920, it was amalgamated with the new Natural History Society of Manitoba. I am grateful to Dr. Martin McNicholl for this information.

42. Field notes, 26 May 1920. Mary Portway Brodrick to author, 22 September 1987.

43. William Rowan, "Ecological Note on the Birds Observed at the Biological Station of the University of Manitoba," *Ecology* 3 (1922): 257.

44. Ibid., 258.

45. Field notes, 29 June 1920.

46. Ibid., 9 July 1920.

47. Ibid., 25 June 1920.

48. The telegram, dated 25 June 1920, was sent by H.M. Tory (1864–1947), the president of the University of Alberta, from Guysboro, Nova Scotia, and is now held with the William Rowan Papers.

49. Walter H. Johns, *A History of the University of Alberta*, 1908–1969 (Edmonton: University of Alberta Press, 1981), 70–74.

50. William Rowan, interview with Al Oeming, "Profile," CBC Television, 27 August 1956.

51. A.G. Lawrence to William Rowan, 14 July 1920, WRP.

52. H.M. Tory to William Rowan, 20 July 1920, WRP.

53. Reference to this photo is found in the letter from A.G. Lawrence to William Rowan, 19 July 1920, WRP.

54. The British-born Cyril Guy Harrold (1896–1929) was an excellent field-naturalist and collector (see William Rowan's obituary of Harrold in the *Auk* 46, no. 3 (1929):285–86.

55. Field notes, 26 August 1920.

Chapter 6: To Build a Department of Zoology

1. Field notes, 29 August 1920, William Rowan Papers, University of Alberta Archives, Edmonton (hereafter WRP).

2. "As the Crow Flies." typescript, WRP.

3. William Rowan to Norman Criddle, 7 October 1920, WRP.

4. He likely purchased the gun at William Cottle's gunsmith shop on 102d street (field notes, 4 September 1920).

5. Beaverhills Lake has also been spelled Beaver Hills Lake.

6. William Rowan to A.E. Baird, 17 September 1920, WRP. Each set consisted of one large knife, one small knife, one medium pair of forceps, "one medium pair 5 inch" scissors, one "blunt seeker," and "2 needles mounted in wood." Scalpels cost four shillings; dissecting forceps, two shillings and nine pence; and dissecting scissors four shillings and nine pence.

7. William Rowan to Norman Criddle, 7 October 1920, WRP.

8. M.G. Ainley, "From Natural History to Avian Biology: Canadian Ornithology, 1860–1950," Ph.D. diss., McGill University, 1985. In 1908, in the United States, Charles C. Adams published "The Ecological Succession of Birds." Within a few years, Althea Sherman published a series of pioneering papers on long-term nesting studies, and S. Prentiss Baldwin established a bird-banding laboratory for population studies. In Canada, William Henry Mousley (1865–1949) conducted field experiments on the breeding biology of passerine birds, and worked out the concept of territoriality (1919, 1921) at about the same time that Elliott Howard's *Territory in Bird Life* appeared in Britain.

9. William Rowan to T.S. Palmer, 23 September 1920, WRP.

10. C.W. Lowe to William Rowan, 10 December 1920, WRP.

11. A.G. Lawrence to William Rowan, 28 September 1920, WRP.

12. Field notes, 2 October 1920. Ardrey Whidden Downs (1882–1966) was born and educated in the United States. In 1920 he was "appointed Professor of Physiology and Pharmacology at the University of Alberta" (see *New Trail* 24, no. 1 (Summer 1966). Duck shooting had long been a favourite pastime for many westerners, including a good proportion of the university faculty. For Rowan, it soon became more than a pastime. Hunting was not only a challenge as sport, but also ducks were good to eat, and, throughout

the 1920s and 1930s, increasingly became staple food for the Rowan family. Ducks were also to become important study material.

13. William Rowan to P.A. Taverner, 9 October 1920, P.A. Taverner Papers, Ornithology Division, National Museum of Natural Sciences, Ottawa (hereafter PAPT).

14. P.A. Taverner to William Rowan, 29 October 1920, WRP.

15. A.G. Lawrence to William Rowan, 22 October 1920, WRP.

16. "As the Crow Flies." Allan Cyril Brooks (1869–1946) was an internationally known bird artist and collector. See H.M. Laing, *Allan Brooks: Artist Naturalist* (Victoria: British Columbia Museum Special Publication, no. 3, 1979).

17. "As the Crow Flies."

18. Ibid. Harper (1886–1972), naturalist, author, and editor, a graduate of Cornell University, participated in several northern expeditions.

19. Ibid.

20. William Rowan to P.A. Taverner, 24 November 1920, PAPT.

21. Field notes, 28 November 1920.

22. H.M. Tory to C.G. Foster, 6 December 1920, William Rowan staff file, University of Alberta Archives, Edmonton. Tory came from a Scottish background which instilled in him a strong utilitarianism. By the end of World War I, he had become convinced that Canada would have to emulate other countries that were "rapidly going in for science." For Tory, the path was clear. Scientific research, conducted in numerous university and industrial laboratories, would lead to wealth. For this reason, Tory stressed the importance of short-term projects, and favoured those with potentially lucrative payoffs. For him, fieldwork on birds was unlikely to have one. M.W. Thistle, *The Inner Ring: The Early History of the National Research Council of Canada.* (Toronto: University of Toronto Press, 1966), 206.

23. Ibid.

24. C.G. Foster to H.M. Tory, 30 December 1920, William Rowan staff file.

25. H.M. Tory to Arthur Currie, 11 January 1932, H.M. Tory Papers, National Research Council Archives, Ottawa.

26. A.G. Huntsman to H.M. Tory, telegram, 19 June 1920, H.M. Tory Papers, University of Alberta Archives, Edmonton (hereafter HMTP). Huntsman (1883–1973) had a seemingly good career at the University of Toronto. It is not clear why he wanted to go to Edmonton, and there is no record about this proposed move among the A.G. Huntsman Papers, University of Toronto Archives.

27. Francis Lewis to H.M. Tory, 11 August 1920, HMTP.

28. Field notes, 20 November 1920.

29. Rowan's correspondence with Taverner is full of discussions concerning the distribution and taxonomy of birds; Rowan's original curiosity about mammals was rekindled by a pair of flying-squirrel skins given to him by Ashley Hine. Rowan was immediately fascinated by the animal's adaptations for gliding, rather than flying. Wishing to publish a paper on this species, but

finding the literature on it in his own small library insufficient, Rowan sent one of the skins to Harper for subspecific identification.

30. A.G. Lawrence to William Rowan, 10 February 1921, WRP.

31. William Rowan to P.A. Taverner, 14 February 1921, PATP.

32. A.G. Lawrence to William Rowan, 26 March 1921, WRP.

33. William Rowan, "The Last Chapter." typescript, WRP, 249–50.

34. F.W. Oliver to William Rowan, 1 April 1921, WRP.

35. J.P. Hill to William Rowan, 5 March 1921, WRP.

36. William Rowan to H.S. Jennings, 3 March 1922, WRP.

37. Field notes, 9 April 1921.

38. Ibid., 24 April 1921.

39. Ibid., 8 May 1921.

40. Ibid., 16 May 1921.

41. William Rowan to P.A. Taverner, 27 September 1921, PATP.

42. Elsie Park Gowan, interview with author, 22 July 1985; A.F. Oeming, interview with author, 27 July 1985; Joan Mortimer Gregg, interview with author, 25 September 1985.

43. William Rowan to P.A. Taverner, 26 November 1921, PATP.

44. Dixie Pelluet, interview with author, 16 July 1986. Born and educated in England, Dixie Pelluet (1896–1990) studied science at the University of Alberta. She graduated in 1919 with a B.Sc., and, assisted by a five hundred dollar Fellowship she went to do graduate work at the University of Toronto. But in 1921, with an M.A. in botany, Pelluet was unemployed. At the time, she was expecting a one thousand dollar travelling fellowship, offered annually by the Canadian Federation of University Women, which she did receive.

45. William Rowan, "Department of Zoology, Estimates, 1922," University of Alberta Archives, Edmonton.

Chapter 7: The Widening Sphere

1. William Rowan to P.A. Taverner, 26 November 1921, William Rowan Papers, University of Alberta Archives, Edmonton (hereafter WRP).

2. William Rowan, interview with Al Oeming, "Profile," CBC Television, 27 August 1956.

3. Jacob Bronowski, *The Common Sense of Science* (Harmondsworth, Eng.: Penguin Books, 1962), 9.

4. William Rowan to P.A. Taverner, 23 October 1920, P.A. Taverner Papers, Ornithology Division, National Museum of Natural Sciences, Ottawa (hereafter PATP).

5. A.G. Lawrence to William Rowan, 25 October 1920, WRP.

6. Ibid.

7. G.E. Bullen to William Rowan, 12 March 1921, WRP.

8. F.W. Oliver to William Rowan, 1 April 1921, WRP.

9. William Rowan to P.A. Taverner, 26 November 1921, PATP.

10. P.A. Taverner to William Rowan, 8 December 1921, WRP.

11. William Rowan to H.S. Jennings, 3 March 1922, WRP.

12. H.S. Jennings to William Rowan, 13 March 1922, WRP.
13. William Rowan to P.A. Taverner, 10 February 1922, PATP.
14. Francis Harper to William Rowan, 22 March 1922, WRP.
15. F.W. Oliver to William Rowan, 19 May 1922. In the same letter, Oliver also replied to the news that Dixie Pelluet was on her way to study botany at University College, London: "She can come and work in this lab . . . . The possibility of a job to help out is *nil* . . . . The college fee for a research student is £22=2=0 per session, plus about 4 departmental fee."
16. W.C. James to William Rowan, 31 March 1922, WRP.
17. W.C. James to William Rowan, 25 July 1922, WRP.
18. Francis Harper to William Rowan, 26 December 1925, WRP.
19. Alberta Fish and Game Association, minute books. I am indebted to Dr. Dennis Grover for information, and for the loan of the minute books and other archival material.
20. Ibid. Rowan attended the second meeting on 17 February 1921.
21. Ibid.
22. P.A. Taverner to William Rowan, 13 March 1922, WRP.
23. William Rowan to P.A. Taverner, 13 March 1922, PATP. E.H. Strickland (1889–1962) established the University of Alberta's Entomology Department in 1922.
24. William Rowan to Chief, Bureau Biological Survey, Washington, 10 March 1922, WRP.
25. William Rowan to P.A. Taverner, 8 March 1922, PATP.
26. William Rowan to P.A. Taverner, 22 July 1922, PATP.
27. P.A. Taverner to William Rowan, 23 September 1922, WRP.
28. Robert Lister (1902–1988) came to Canada in 1920. Although he remained a technician in the Department of Zoology, University of Alberta, all his working life, he developed into an excellent naturalist.
29. William Rowan to P.A. Taverner, 27 December 1922, PATP.
30. William Rowan to P.A. Taverner, 5 January 1923, PATP.
31. A.C. Bent to William Rowan, 2 February 1923, WRP.
32. Thomas Barbour to William Rowan, 2 March 1923, WRP.
33. Thomas Barbour to William Rowan, 13 March 1923, WRP.
34. Thomas Barbour to William Rowan, 11 April 1923, WRP.
35. Agnes Rowan to William Rowan, 29 January 1923, and 10 February 1923, WRP.
36. Arthur Rowan to William Rowan, 14 February 1923, WRP.
37. It is possible that Reta and Bill knew of some form of birth control while they were in England. Arthur, in a letter written to Bill on 28 February 1920 (WRP), referred to Reta's first pregnancy and remarked: "Marie Stopes [the British birth-control crusader] does not appear to be infallible, what!" On birth control in Canada, see Diane Dodd, "The Canadian Birth Control Movement: Two Approaches to the Dissemination of Contraceptive Technology," *Scientia Canadensis* 9 (June 1985).
38. William Rowan to P.A. Taverner, 21 April 1923, PATP.
39. William Rowan to P.A. Taverner, 29 April 1923, PATP.

40. P.A. Taverner to William Rowan, 20 April 1923, WRP; W.W. Stevens and G.W. Scotter, "Joseph Dewey Soper, 1893–1982," *Canadian Field-Naturalist* 97 (1983).

41. William Rowan to P.A. Taverner, 12 May 1923, PATP.

42. Field notes, 14 May 1923, WRP.

43. William Rowan to P.A. Taverner, 30 May 1923, PATP.

44. William Rowan to H.M. Tory, 22 November 1923, H.M. Tory Papers, University of Alberta Archives, Edmonton.

45. F.W. Oliver to William Rowan, 25 March 1924, WRP.

46. H.M. Tory to William Rowan, 22 November 1923, WRP.

47. Julian Rowan, conversation with author.

Chapter 8: **Experiments in Bird Migration: Juncos.**

1. W.W. Cooke, *Report on Bird Migration in the Mississippi Valley in the Years 1884 and 1885* (Washington: Government Printing Office, 1915). A.G. Lawrence to William Rowan, 28 September 1920, William Rowan Papers, University of Alberta Archives, Edmonton (hereafter WRP).

2. William Rowan to Don Patton, 8 March 1922, WRP.

3. William Rowan to A.E. Cameron, 5 March 1922, WRP.

4. John Cordeaux established the British Committee for the Migration of Birds in the 1870s; during the following decades, Otto Hermann campaigned for bird-migration studies in Hungary; In 1891 Heinrich Gätke published his justly famous book on the Heligoland bird observatory. See E. Stresemann, *Ornithology: From Aristotle to the Present* (Cambridge: Harvard University Press, 1975), 333–34.

5. "Observations on the Breeding-Habits of the Merlin," *British Birds* 15, no. 6, (1921): 128–29.

6. William Rowan to P.A. Taverner, 27 September 1921, P.A. Taverner Papers, Ornithology Division, National Museum of Natural Sciences, Ottawa (hereafter PATP).

7. William Rowan to P.A. Taverner, 27 December 1922, PATP.

8. William Rowan to Joseph Grinnell, 24 October 1922, Joseph Grinnell Papers, Museum of Vertebrate Zoology, University of California, Berkeley (hereafter JGP); Joseph Grinnell to William Rowan, 30 October 1922, WRP. Grinnell (1877–1939) was a noted American ornithologist (see J.L. Linsdale, "In Memoriam: Joseph Grinnell," *Auk* 59 (1942). Grinnell became one of Rowan's most faithful supporters.

9. William Rowan to Joseph Grinnell, 23 July 1923, JGP; William Rowan to P.A. Taverner, 23 August 1923, PATP.

10. A.C. Bent to William Rowan, 14 June 1923, WRP.

11. P.A. Taverner to William Rowan, 2 August 1923, WRP.

12. William Rowan to J.H. Fleming, 17 February 1924, J.H. Fleming Papers, Royal Ontario Museum Archives, Toronto.

13. A.E. Cameron to H.M. Tory, 30 June 1924; H.M. Tory to Winnifred Hughes, 5 July 1924, Department of Zoology Papers, University of Alberta

Archives, Edmonton.

14. J.J. Hickey, conversation with author.

15. William Rowan, "Experiments in Bird Migration." *Transactions of the Royal Society of Canada* 3rd ser., sec. 5, 40 (1946):123–24.

16. William Rowan to J.P. Hill, 19 June 1926, WRP.

17. William Rowan to Joseph Grinnell, 30 July 1924, JGP.

18. William Rowan to Joseph Grinnell, 8 September 1924, JGP. Rowan was referring to a paper by W.W. Garner and H.A. Allard, "Effect of the Relative Length of Day and Night and Other Factors of the Environment on Growth and Reproduction in Plants," *Journal of Agricultural Research* 18 (1920).

19. Field notes, 23 August 1924, WRP; William Rowan to J.P. Hill, 19 June 1926, WRP.

20. William Rowan to Joseph Grinnell, 8 September 1924, JGP.

21. William Rowan to J.P. Hill, 19 June 1926, WRP.

22. Rowan to the editor, *Auk* 16 November 1924, WRP.

23. Field notes, 11 November 1924.

24. Junco notebooks, 30 September 1924, WRP.

25. Ibid., 13 October 1924.

26. Ibid., 18 November 1924.

27. Ibid., 7 October 1924.

28. Field notes, 18 October 1924.

29. Junco notebooks, 16 November 1924.

30. See, Rowan, letter to the editor.

31. Junco notebooks, 29 October 1924.

32. Ibid., 13 November 1924.

33. Ibid., 26 November 1926.

34. Ibid., 11 December 1924.

35. Ibid., 16 December 1924.

36. Ibid., 19 December 1924.

37. Ibid., 27 December 1924.

38. Ibid., 5 January 1925.

39. William Rowan to Joseph Grinnell, 26 October 1924, JGP.

40. William Rowan to Harry Swarth, 5 January 1925, JGP.

41. William Rowan to P.A. Taverner, 5 January 1925, PATP.

42. He chose this journal because of its prestige, and also because it was there that the British physiologist A.E. Schafer first published his ideas concerning light and bird migration.

43. "Relation of Light to Bird Migration and Developmental Changes," *Nature* 115: 495.

44. William Rowan to P.A. Taverner, 31 January 1925, PATP.

45. William Rowan to J.P. Hill, 19 June 1926, WRP.

46. William Rowan, "On Photoperiodism," *Proceedings of the Boston Society of Natural History* 38 (1926): 176.

47. Junco notebooks, 15 October 1925.

48. Ibid. Rowan also used captive-bred canaries in both cages, and found

that the experimental canaries would start singing around Christmastime. Because these cage-birds lacked the ability to defend themselves, he could not liberate them to test their migratory behaviour, as they would soon have fallen prey to cats.

49. Junco notebooks, 15 October 1925.

50. Rowan, "On Photoperiodism," 177.

51. Ibid., 176.

52. Ibid.

53. William Rowan to P.A. Taverner, 16 December 1925, PATP.

54. Stresemann, *Ornithology*, 354. See also M.G. Ainley, "William Rowan and the Experimental Approach in Ornithology," *Acta Congressus Internationalis Ornithologici* 19 (1988).

55. Rowan, "On Photoperiodism," 177.

56. William Rowan to Joseph Grinnell, 1 February 1925, JGP.

57. William Rowan to P.A. Taverner, 14 February 1925, PATP.

58. Julian Sorrell Huxley (1888–1975) was an eminent evolutionary biologist, ethologist, and a prolific writer. He became the first Director General of UNESCO in 1946 (see A. Landsborough Thomson, "Sir Julian Sorrell Huxley," *Auk* 93, no. 1 [1976]).

59. Rowan, "On Photoperiodism," 182.

60. Ibid. 183.

Chapter 9: **Beloved Wilderness.**

1. William Rowan, "Notes on Alberta Waders Included on the British List, I: Semipalmated and Killdeer Plovers." *British Birds* 20 (1926): 2.

2. Ibid.

3. Ibid., 4.

4. Agreement, 20 March 1923, typescript, William Rowan Papers, University of Alberta Archives, Edmonton (hereafter WRP).

5. William Rowan to P.A. Taverner, 27 December 1922, P.A. Taverner Papers, Ornithology Division, National Museum of Natural Sciences, Ottawa (hereafter PATP).

6. "As The Crow Flies," typescript, WRP.

7. Reta Rowan to Julian Rowan, 5–6 February 1958, Rowan family papers.

8. W.O. Rowan conversation with author.

9. William Rowan, "The Status of the Dowitchers with a Description of a New Subspecies From Alberta and Manitoba." *Auk* 49 (1932): 14.

10. P.A. Taverner to William Rowan, 23 September 1922, WRP.

11. William Rowan to P.A. Taverner, 27 December 1922, PATP.

12. Thomas Edmund Randall (1886–1974) was a farmer and keen zoologist; Francis (Frank) Farley (1870–1949) of Camrose was a knowledgeable naturalist; A.D. Henderson (1878–1963) was a rancher, trapper, and hunter, and zoologist.

13. Field notes, 25 June 1924, WRP.

14. Ibid., 1 July 1924. The camera apparently belonged to the University of Alberta.

15. Ibid., 6 August 1924; Munro was appointed federal migratory bird officer in 1920. His duties included selecting lands for sanctuaries and public hunting grounds. Rowan returned from this trip just in time to meet with D.M.S. Watson and several other British scientists who were on their way to Vancouver.

16. William Rowan to J.H. Fleming, 13 October 1924, J.H. Fleming Papers, Royal Ontario Museum Archives, Toronto.

17. Ibid., 23 January 1925.

18. Rowan had been corresponding with Elsie Cassels (1865?-1938) since late 1921 or early 1922. She was a well-educated Scottish settler who played the violin. Her husband, W.A. Cassels, was a very frugal man, and no one suspected that he had amassed a sum of ninety thousand dollars. The money was found after W.A. Cassels's death in 1941 (newspaper cutting, Red Deer Archives, Red Deer, Alberta).

19. According to the family, Julian was his father's favourite.

20. William Rowan to Joseph Grinnell, 1 August 1925, Joseph Grinnell Papers, Museum of Vertebrate Zoology Archives, University of California, Berkeley (hereafter JGP).

21. Ibid.

22. William Rowan to Harry Swarth, 29 August 1925, Harry Swarth Papers, Museum of Vertebrate Zoology, University of California, Berkeley (hereafter HSP).

23. William Rowan to P.A. Taverner, 21 June 1925, PATP.

24. Ibid.; field notes, 2 July 1925.

25. William Rowan to Harry Swarth, 13 February 1926, HSP.

26. H.M. Tory to Sir Gregory Foster, 6 December 1920, H.M. Tory Papers, University of Alberta Archives, Edmonton; H.M. Tory to Sir Arthur Currie, 11 January 1932, H.M. Tory Papers, National Research Council Archives, Ottawa.

27. A Canadian Zoologist, "The Passing of the Wood Bison," *Canadian Forum* 6 (1925): 301.

28. William Rowan, "Canada's Buffalo," *Country Life*, 14 September 1929, 358.

29. By December 1920 there were five thousand plains bison at Wainwright Park (see A Canadian Zoologist, "Passing of the Wood Bison").

30. Maxwell Graham, "Finding Range for Canada's Buffalo," *Canadian Field-Naturalist* 38 (1924): 189. In addition to individual scientists, several natural-history organizations protested against the move (see letter from Brodie Club to government, 12 May 1925, National Archives of Canada, RG 84, vol. 52, BU 232–1; B. Potyondi, *Wood Buffalo National Park: An Historical Overview and Source Study*, Parks Canada Manuscript Report, no. 345 [1979].

31. Field notes, 26 April 1925.

32. William Rowan to P.A. Taverner, 9 May 1925, PATP.

33. Field notes, 31 August 1925.
34. Ibid., 1 September 1925.
35. Ibid., 2 September 1925.
36. Ibid., 3 September 1925.
37. Ibid., 8 September 1925.
38. Ibid., 9 September 1925.
39. Ibid., 10 September 1925.
40. Ibid., 10–11 September 1925.
41. Ibid., 12–15 September 1925.
42. Ibid., 17 September 1925.
43. Ibid., 22 September 1925.
44. Ibid., 23 September 1925.
45. Ibid.
46. Ibid., 24 September 1925.
47. H.M. Tory to Sir Arthur Currie, 11 January 1932, H.M. Tory Papers, National Research Council, Ottawa.
48. Winnie Hughes was working on her doctorate at the University of Chicago.
49. P.A. Taverner to William Rowan, 11 November 1926, WRP.
50. F.G. Roe, *The North American Buffalo: A Critical Study of the Species in Its Wild State* (Toronto: University of Toronto Press, 1951), 839.
51. Field notes, 30 May 1926.

Chapter 10: **Further Experiments and Graduate Research**

1. Julian Huxley to William Rowan, 16 September 1925, William Rowan Papers, University of Alberta Archives, Edmonton (hereafter WRP).
2. A copy of the original application for a Royal Society Research Grant ($748) is attached to a letter Rowan wrote to J.P. Hill, 19 June 1926, WRP.
3. William Rowan to J.P. Hill, 19 June 1926, WRP.
4. Ibid.
5. A copy of a second application for a Royal Society Research Grant ($151) is also attached to the letter Rowan wrote to J.P. Hill, 19 June 1926, WRP.
6. F.A. Towle to William Rowan, 13 July 1926, WRP.
7. The actual costs incurred were $172.07, which included $10 for electricity in Rowan's home, $4.00 for a birdbath, and $3.00 for a drinking fountain.
8. William Rowan, "An Alberta Aviary," *Condor* 29 (1927): 133.
9. Junco notebooks, 15 November 1926, WRP..
10. Ibid., 4 January 1927.
11. His canaries, which were also exposed to increased light, sang on a local radio broadcast.
12. Junco notebooks, 30 January 1927.
13. William Rowan to Joseph Grinnell, 1 January 1927, Joseph Grinnell

Papers, Museum of Vertebrate Zoology, University of California, Berkeley (hereafter JGP).

14. William Rowan to Joseph Grinnell, 18 January 1927, JGP.

15. Oscar Riddle to William Rowan, 10 March 1927, WRP.

16. A. Landsborough Thomson to William Rowan, 10 April 1927, WRP.

17. William Rowan to J.P. Hill, 19 June 1926, WRP. At the time there were four species of grebes nesting in western Canada, horned, eared, western, and pied-billed. Recently the western grebe has been split into two new species: Clark's grebe and the western grebe.

18. William Rowan to J.P. Hill, 19 June 1926, WRP. Loons are considered to be the oldest family of birds. They have a primitive structure: their legs, for example, are set well back on their bodies.

19. William Rowan to J.H. Fleming, 30 April 1927, J.H. Fleming Papers, Royal Ontario Museum Archives, Toronto (hereafter JHFP); William Rowan to Joseph Grinnell, 20 April 1927, JGP; William Rowan to P.A. Taverner 10 April 1927, P.A. Taverner Papers, Ornithology Division, National Museum of Natural Sciences, Ottawa (hereafter PATP).

20. William Rowan to J.H. Fleming, 13 October 1927, JHFP.

21. Ibid.

22. William Rowan to H.M. Laing, 30 December 1927, H.M. Laing Papers, British Columbia Provincial Archives, Victoria.

23. Ibid.

24. William Rowan to Joseph Grinnell, 19 October 1927, JGP.

25. William Rowan, "Experiments in Bird Migration I: Manipulation of the Reproductive Cycle: Seasonal Histological Changes in the Gonads," *Proceedings of the Boston Society of Natural History* 39 (1929): 161.

26. Ibid., 168.

27. Ibid., 204.

28. William Rowan to P.A. Taverner, 26 November 1927, PATP.

29. P.A. Taverner to F. Kennard, 19 May 1933, PATP.

30. William Rowan to P.A. Taverner, 15 August 1928, PATP.

31. William Rowan to P.A. Taverner, 22 November 1928, PATP.

32. Julian Rowan to author, [?] February 1986.

33. William Rowan to P.A. Taverner, 22 November 1928, PATP.

34. Winnifred Hughes to William Rowan, 6 January 1929, WRP. T.H. Bissonnette (1885–1951) was born in Ontario. He served in the Army during World War I. He obtained his Ph.D. at the University of Chicago and, from 1925–1951, was teaching at Trinity College, becoming J. Pierpont Morgan Professor of Biology.

35. William Rowan, Presidential Address, University of Alberta Science Association, typescript, 11 October 1928, WRP.

36. Ibid.

37. Ibid.

38. Julian Huxley to William Rowan, 13 December 1928, WRP; A. Landsborough Thomson to William Rowan, 15 December 1928, WRP.

39. G.M. Allen to William Rowan, 7 March 1929, WRP.

40. P.A. Taverner to J.B. Harkin, 6 February 1930, PATP.

41. H.F.L. [Harrison F. Lewis], review of "Experiments in Bird Migration I," by William Rowan, *Canadian Field-Naturalist* 44, no. 2 (1930): 72.

42. Field notes, 4 February 1929.

43. Reta Rowan to Julian Rowan, 5–6 February 1958, Rowan family papers.

44. "Odd Notes on Some Rare British Birds From the Canadian Muskegs," typescript, [article for "Country Life," 1942], WRP.

45. Robert Lister, *The Birds and Birders of Beaverhills Lake* (Edmonton: Edmonton Bird Club, 1979), 69.

46. William Rowan to P.A. Taverner, 30 April 1929, PATP; field notes, 19 May 1929.

47. Field notes, 20 May 1929. Twomey was to become well known as an ornithologist in the United States.

48. Field notes, 21 May 1929.

49. Ibid., 23 May 1929.

50. Ibid., 25 May 1929.

51. Ibid., 26 May 1929.

52. Ibid., 29 May 1929.

53. William Rowan to P.A. Taverner, 16 November 1930, PATP.

54. "As The Crow Flies," typescript, WRP.

55. Field notes, 3 June 1929.

56. William Rowan, "Odd Notes on Some Rare British Birds from the Canadian Muskegs," typescript [article for "Country Life," 1942], WRP.

Chapter 11: As the Crow Flies

1. "As the Crow Flies." typescript, William Rowan Papers, University of Alberta Archives, Edmonton (hereafter WRP).

2. Ibid. Actually, his first encounter with the autumn bird migration occurred in 1917, nearly two years after his discharge from the army.

3. A copy of this application is attached to William Rowan to J.P. Hill, 19 June 1926, WRP.

4. E.B. Wilson to William Rowan, 28 November 1928; H.S. Jennings to William Rowan, 22 July 1929, WRP. The Joseph Henry Fund was administered by Stanford University, the Elizabeth Thompson Science Fund by the American Association for the Advancement of Science, and the Bache Fund by the National Academy of Sciences.

5. William Rowan to Joseph Grinnell, 16 March 1928, Joseph Grinnell Papers, Museum of Vertebrate Zoology, University of California, Berkeley (hereafter JGP).

6. Robert Lister, *The Birds and Birders of Beaverhills Lake* (Edmonton: Edmonton Bird Club, 1979), 119.

7. Ibid.

8. Dr. Walter Cottle, conversation with author.

9. Lister, *Birds and Birders*, 119.

10. Field notes, 23 August 1929, WRP.

11. Press bulletin, 8 November 1929, WRP.

12. Ibid.

13. William Rowan to Joseph Grinnell, 15 November 1929, JGP.

14. William Rowan to Joseph Grinnell, 12 January 1930, JGP.

15. Trevor H. Levere, "What is Canadian about Science in Canadian History?" in *Science, Technology and Canadian History*, ed. R.A. Jarrell and N.R. Ball, (Waterloo, Ont.: Wilfrid Laurier University Press, 1980), 20.

16. In fact the NRC was founded precisely with the mandate to promote industrial and applied scientific research.

17. M.W. Thistle, *The Inner Ring: The Early History of the National Research Council of Canada* (Toronto: University of Toronto Press, 1966), 130–31.

18. Tory was a mathematician by training. In the 1890s he spent time at the Cavendish Laboratory in England learning how a physics laboratory was organized. He did this on behalf of McGill University, which had asked him to set up a physics lab. E.A. Corbett, *Henry Marshall Tory: Beloved Canadian* (Toronto: Ryerson Press, 1954), 44–46.

19. H.M. Tory to Sir Arthur Currie, 11 January 1932, H.M. Tory, Papers, National Research Council Archives, Ottawa.

20. Ibid.

21. Rowan, "Application to the National Research Council of Canada," "Minutes of the Standing Committee on Assisted Research for 1930," *Proceedings of the Eighty-Fourth Meeting of the Council* (1930), 35.

22. National Research Council, "Minutes of the Standing Committee," 36. Tory not only influenced others on the council, but also made unilateral decisions. In 1932 he wrote to British ecologist Charles Elton that the NRC had turned down Elton's application. Elton soon learned, however, that his application had not even been discussed in the council. See Charles Elton to William Rowan, 14 February 1932, WRP.

23. "Minutes of the Standing Committee," 27.

24. Osman James Walker (1892–1958) was recruited to the University of Alberta faculty in 1920. E.H. Gowan (1901–1958), George Hunter (1894–1978), and Ernest Sidney Keeping (1895–1984), joined the faculty of the University of Alberta in 1929. Reta's friendship with George Hunter was a meeting of minds, but, because of Rowan's jealousy, it was to cause many family fights for the next twenty years. As a matter of fact, Reta had always been interested in poetry and by 1930, with her children growing up and a maid (a young immigrant) looking after household matters, she could begin to spend time doing the things she enjoyed. She took up painting again, played the cello, and also became involved in social issues. It was at about his time that she joined the Edmonton chapter of the Women's International League of Peace.

25. R.E. Moreau to William Rowan, 21 August 1930, WRP. R.E. Moreau (1897–1970) later became the editor of *Ibis*. He was one of Rowan's staunch supporters.

26. William Rowan to R.E. Moreau, 16 September 1930, R.E. Moreau Papers, Alexander Library, Oxford (hereafter REMP).

27. Sidgwick and Jackson to William Rowan, 1 April 1930, WRP.

28. William Rowan to Sidgwick and Jackson, 15 April 1930, WRP.

29. The thirty-thousand word "dollar books" were printed in press runs of four thousand; some went through several printings (see E. F. Williams to William Rowan, 15 December 1930, WRP).

30. William Rowan to E.F. Williams, 25 December 1930, WRP.

31. William Rowan to R.E. Moreau, 12 May 1931, REMP.

32. R.E. Moreau to William Rowan, 29 June 1931, WRP. Witmer Stone's omission was particularly glaring because he did have a Ph.D. in biology.

33. *New York Times*, 21 July 1931.

34. See Peter J. Bowler, *The Eclipse of Darwinism* (Baltimore: Johns Hopkins University Press, 1983), 98–106. J.B. Lamarck's theory, first published in 1801, was an important precursor of Darwin's. One must remember that Rowan had never taken a university course in evolution, and that throughout his working life he remained isolated from centres of evolution research. As I have mentioned, the University of Alberta had no proper science library, and Rowan had few chances to have detailed discussions with knowledgeable people about evolution until he visited England in 1933 and 1936–1937, and Huxley visited Edmonton in 1935 (Julian Rowan conversation with author).

35. S.A. Gauthreaux, "The Ecology and Evolution of Avian Migration Systems," in *Avian Biology*, ed. D.S. Farner and J.R. King (New York: Academic Press, 1982), 6: 107.; Martin McNicholl to author, 8 February 1991.

36. Crow notebooks.

37. Field notes, 3 September 1931.

38. Ibid., 8 September 1931.

39. Crow notebooks.

40. Koch told Rowan that "U II-3 contains 5 bird unit per 0.5 cc. It is a solution [of human male urine extract] in olive oil. The dosage is to be 0.5 cc. per day per bird." The other sample, "U II-4," contained "10 bird units per 0.5 cc. . . . in olive oil" and the dosage was to be 0.5 cc per day per bird. F.C. Koch to William Rowan, 22 October 1931, WRP.

41. Crow notebooks.

42. William Rowan to E.B. Wilson, 9 July 1932, WRP.

43. Crow notebooks. The expense sheet, submitted to the trustees of the Elizabeth Thompson Fund (on 9 July 1932), states that Rowan paid $104 for the "hire of airplane," and $5 to "J.H. Weir, sign painter, for Ducoing the tails of 155 crows bright yellow."

44. R.A. Keith, *Bush Pilot with a Briefcase: The Happy-Go-Lucky Story of Grant McConachie* (Toronto: Doubleday Canada, 1972), 45.

45. Crow notebooks.

46. Ibid.

47. "As the Crow Flies."

48. Ibid.

49. William Rowan to P.A. Taverner, 1 December 1931, PATP. Actually the

plane ride cost only $104 (see note 43).

50. William Rowan, "Experiments in Bird Migration III: The Effects of Artificial Light, Castration and Certain Extracts on the Autumn Movements of the American Crow (*Corvus brachyrhynchos*)," *Proceedings of the National Academy of Sciences* 18, no. 11 (1932): 651.

51. Ibid.

52. William Rowan, "Experiments in Bird Migration," *Transactions of the Royal Society of Canada* 3d. ser., sec. 5, 40 (1946): 132.

53. Rowan, "Experiments in Bird Migration III," 652.

54. Ibid.

55. Ibid., 653.

Chapter 12: Depression and Light

1. R.C. Wallace to William Rowan, 27 October 1931, William Rowan Papers, University of Alberta Archives, Edmonton (hereafter WRP).

2. In fact he could consider himself fortunate that it was not until 1933 that salaries at the University of Alberta were reduced by 7 to 15 percent. Rowan's pay fell from $3,800 to $3,340. R.C. Wallace to William Rowan, 13 April 1933, WRP. It remained reduced by 15 percent until 1939.

3. Charles Elton to William Rowan, 8 September 1931; J.B. Collip to William Rowan, 17 December 1931, WRP. Elton (1902–1988) became a famous ecologist.

4. John Tait to William Rowan, 18 December 1931; John Beatty to William Rowan 18 December 1931, WRP. Tait and Beatty invited Rowan to McGill. Dr. John Beatty was in the Department of Anatomy. Rowan actually stayed with Dr. John Tait, from the Department of Physiology.

5. The records, as is often the case, are sketchy on this point, but circumstantial evidence points to Rowan having talked to Currie.

6. H.M. Tory to Sir Arthur Currie, 11 January 1932, H.M. Tory Papers, National Research Council Archives, Ottawa.

7. F.A.E. Crew, letter of recommendation, 8 January 1932, copy in WRP.

8. Julian Huxley, letter of recommendation, 31 January 1932, copy in WRP.

9. Application for the Chair of Zoology at McGill University, March 1932, WRP.

10. Joseph Grinnell to William Rowan, 20 April 1932, WRP.

11. Because of Quebec's Bill 65 which prohibits access to personal information, I could not check the files at the McGill University Archives. See A.P.S. Glassco to William Rowan, 26 May 1932; Ernest MacBride to William Rowan, 5 February 1932; Ernest MacBride to William Rowan, 14 August 1932, WRP.

12. W.T. MacClement to William Rowan, 28 July 1932, WRP. After Klugh's accidental death, Dr. G. Krotkov, a plant physiologist, taught vertebrate anatomy. I thank Dr. A.S. West for this information.

13. Field notes, 26 July 1932, WRP.

15. William Rowan to W.T. MacClement, 17 June 1932, WRP.

16. McGill also cut salaries during the Depression, as did all other Canadian educational institutions. At the University of Manitoba, professors were even ordered not to take vacations. R.A. Wardle to William Rowan, 9 March 1934, WRP.

16. [McGill botanist] Muriel V. Roscoe, conversations with author. In 1946, a British biologist working at McGill wrote "Through lack of equipment [research] has proved impossible" at McGill (W.S. Bullough to William Rowan, 23 January 1946, WRP).

17. From 1924 to 1928 she worked on the junco investigations (she fed the birds and faithfully turned the lights on and off in Bill's absence). From 1929 to 1931 she participated in crow catches. She also made innumerable meals for visiting scientists.

18. Reta Rowan to Julian Rowan, 5–6 February 1958, Rowan family papers.

19. Ibid.

20. Ibid.

21. Ibid.

22. A.B. Klugh had given an extension course on ornithology at the Ontario Agriculture College in 1904.

23. R.C. Wallace to William Rowan, 13 April 1933, WRP.

24. Field notes, 26 May 1933.

25. Fred Kennard to P.A. Taverner, 5 June 1933, P.A. Taverner Papers, Ornithology Division, National Museum of Natural Science, Ottawa. I am grateful to John Cranmer-Byng for having brought this item to my attention.

26. Reta Rowan to William Rowan, 12 July 1933, WRP.

27. Field notes, 30 June 1933.

28. Ibid., 7 July 1933.

29. Ibid., 11 July 1933.

30. Ibid., 3 July 1933.

31. R. Winckworth to William Rowan, 3 November 1933, WRP.

32. A.L. Barrows to William Rowan, 16 November 1933, WRP.

33. W.A. Clemens to William Rowan, 16 November 1933; A.G. Huntsman to William Rowan, 13 November 1933, WRP.

34. Field notes, 3 February 1934.

35. The diaries and correspondence of nineteenth century scientists reveal that a number of them were overworked people who occasionally couldn't cope and had to have a rest on doctors orders. (See, for instance, the correspondence of J.A. Allen, Rare Book Room, Blacker-Wood Library, McGill University, Montreal).

36. Maureen Aytenfishu to author, 25 April 1988.

37. Field notes, 3 February 1934.

38. H.B. Conover to William Rowan, 20 June 1934, WRP.

39. Field notes, 29 May 1934.

40. Ibid., 1 June 1934.

41. Ibid., 3 July 1934.

42. Joan Gregg, interview with author, 25 September 1985.

43. Ibid.

44. Field notes, 12 August 1934.

45. J.S. Huxley to William Rowan, 23 July 1934, WRP.

46. William Rowan to J.B. Collip, 30 January 1935, WRP.

47. Elsie Park Gowan, conversation with author.

48. Julian Rowan, conversation with author.

49. A copy of the testimonial, dated 29 January 1935, is held with the William Rowan Papers.

50. William Rowan to J.B. Collip, 30 January 1935, WRP.

51. Ibid. Although after fourteen years at the University of Alberta Rowan could finally contemplate a sabbatical year, it was obvious that he would need a grant to supplement his sabbatical income, which would be four-fifths of his already reduced annual pay of $3,955. There is no record of his having previously requested a sabbatical.

52. William Rowan, application, 31 January 1935, WRP.

53. Julian Huxley to William Rowan, 3 June 1935, WRP.

54. Julian Huxley to R.C. Wallace, 28 June 1935; William Rowan, staff file, University of Alberta Archives, Edmonton (hereafter William Rowan, staff file).

55. William Rowan to Julian Huxley, 1 September 1935; Julian Huxley to William Rowan, 30 September 1935, WRP.

56. W.A. MacIntosh to William Rowan, 13 January 1936, WRP. Although fifty years after Rowan's original application was sent the selection committee's files could not be located at Queen's University, a copy of the list of the documents originally sent to MacIntosh clearly indicates that it was Kerr and not Wallace who wrote to the Committee in 1935, WRP.

57. R.C. Wallace to W.A. MacIntosh, 3 January 1936, William Rowan, staff file.

58. The cabin was bought with money that Reta inherited after her father's death.

59. William Rowan, "Notes on Lake Edith Railway," WRP; F.G. Roe, "Lake Edith Model Railway," *Canadian National Railway Magazine*, April 1937, 9, 23.

60. William Rowan, "Notes on Lake Edith Railway."

61. Field notes, 16 September 1936.

66. Ibid. 16 September 1936.

Chapter 13: Light and Seasonal Reproduction in Animals

1. Secretary of University College, London to William Rowan, 12 November 1936, William Rowan Papers, University of Alberta Archives, Edmonton (hereafter WRP).

2. William Rowan to W.A. Kerr 28 October 1936, WRP.

3. Ibid.

4. W.A. Kerr to William Rowan, 4 December 1936; E.H. Strickland to William Rowan, 31 December 1936, WRP.

5. A. West to William Rowan, 7 December 1936, WRP.

6. W.R. Brander to William Rowan, 22 February 1937, WRP.

7. William Rowan to Reta Rowan, 18 July 1937, WRP.

8. William Rowan, "Report to the Institute for Animal Behaviour," typescript, WRP.

9. William Rowan, interview with Al Oeming, "Profile," CBC Television, 27 August 1956.

10. Ibid.; Kenneth Clark to William Rowan, 23 January 1937, WRP.

11. The Common Starling (*Sturnus vulgaris*) is an Old World species, and was introduced to New York in 1890. Although by the late 1920s (when Bissonnette began his experiments) the bird had extended its range to many American states and some Canadian provinces, it was still a nonmigratory species. In contrast, the junco is a seasonal migrant. However, by the late 1930s the starling also began short-distance migrations (see William Rowan, "London Starlings and Seasonal Reproduction in Birds," *Proceedings of the Zoological Society of London* 108 [1938]: 380).

12. Later Rowan was to change his own 1928 conclusions concerning the effect on juncos of a moving bar in a dimly illuminated cage.

13. Rowan later established that the light intensity at the very spot where he collected the London starlings was so low that it did not register on a Weston lightometer.

14. In the article Rowan discussed the work of F.H.A. Marshall and coworkers (Cambridge) on the ferret, Jacques Benoit (Strasbourg) on the Rouen drake, Emil Witschi (Iowa) on weaver finches, and Sophia Ivanova (Leningrad) on sparrows, in addition to T.H. Bissonnette (Hartford) on both the starling and the ferret.

15. "London Starlings," 69–70.

16. Ibid., 73. G.M. Riley's research on the "correlation between body-temperatures and the rhythmical mitotic activity of the germ-cells of the sparrow (*P. domesticus*)," and his earlier set of experiments on the tick, conducted in Edmonton with Gregson, convinced him. The work on the rabbit tick, which is usually inactive in winter but "could be induced to feed in January if placed on a rabbit that had first been subjected to increasing illumination," was one of the few exciting findings of the 1934–1935 period.

17. "Light and Seasonal Reproduction in Animals," *Biological Reviews of the Cambridge Philosophical Society* 13 (1938): 374.

18. Ibid., 395.

19. William Rowan to Reta Rowan, 24 March 1937, WRP.

20. Ibid.

21. The results of the study were published as William Rowan and A.M. Batrawi, "Comments on the Gonads of Some European Migrants Collected in East Africa Immediately before Their Spring Departure," *Ibis* ser. 14 no. 3 (1939).

22. William Rowan to Reta Rowan, 21 March 1937, WRP.

23. At Altenberg, Rowan also met a young Dutch scientist, Niko Tinbergen.

24. William Rowan to Reta Rowan, 18 July 1937, WRP.
25. William Rowan to Reta Rowan, 21 March 1937, WRP.
26. William Rowan to Reta Rowan, 24 March 1937, WRP.
27. William Rowan to Reta Rowan, 18 July 1937, WRP.
28. William Rowan to Joseph Grinnell, 3 October 1937, Joseph Grinnell Papers, Museum of Vertebrate Zoology, University of California, Berkeley (hereafter JGP).
29. Joseph Grinnell to William Rowan, 21 October 37, WRP.
30. Joseph Grinnell to William Rowan, 15 November 1937, WRP.
31. J.B. Collip to William Rowan, 8 November 1937, WRP.
32. Julian Huxley to William Rowan, 24 December 1937; J.B. Collip to William Rowan, 23 May 1938, WRP.
33. William Rowan to Joseph Grinnell, 25 October 1937, JGP.
34. "Light and Seasonal Reproduction," 402.
35. Application to the NRC, 26 August 1938, WRP.
36. *Proceedings of the 123rd Meeting of the Council* (1938), Y-2.
37. R.E. Moreau, A.L. Wilk, and W. Rowan, "The Moult and Gonad Cycles of Three Species of Birds at Five Degrees South of the Equator," *Proceedings of the Zoological Society of London* 117 (1946): 345.
38. Ibid.
39. Julian Huxley to William Rowan, 17 December 1940, WRP.
40. Field notes, 23 August 1939, WRP.
41. Field notes, 3 September 1939.
42. Ibid., 11 December 39; 14 March 1940.
43. Ibid., 11 January 1940.
44. Ibid. 2 February 1940.
45. Copy of a letter from F.B. Hanson to W.A.R. Kerr, 7 May 1940, WRP. Rowan originally wanted to apply through the university science association, but the foundation preferred to administer the grant through the university.
46. William Rowan, application to the Rockefeller Foundation, April 1940, WRP.
47. William Rowan to W. Weaver, 12 October 1940, WRP.
48. William Rowan to F.B. Hanson, 26 August 1942, WRP.
49. Ibid.
50. F.B. Hanson to William Rowan, 4 September 1942, WRP.
51. William Rowan to F.B. Hanson b31 December 1942, WRP.
52. William Rowan to Albert Wolfson, 7 November 1946, WRP.
53. Wolfson had been in touch with Rowan since 1937, when Wolfson was a graduate student of Grinnell's. In August 1943 Wolfson inquired whether or not the details of the 1937–1938 experiments had been published? He wrote "we are on the right track as regards wakefulness and the recrudescence of the gonads" (Albert Wolfson to William Rowan, 13 August 1943, WRP).
54. Albert Wolfson to William Rowan, 2 April 1947, WRP.
55. Field notes, 6 March 1946.
56. A copy of the award citation is held in the William Rowan Papers.
57. William Rowan, "Tuck Shop Interview," typescript of an interview

with Clifford Roy, University of Alberta Radio, 23 November 1946, WRP. Actually, in 1939, when Rowan revised "As the Crow Flies," he added to it a pessimistic last chapter. But this amusing, lively manuscript on crows, which had interested a number of British publishers before the war, was not considered a publishing priority during the war years. The last chapter, attached to the original manuscript, had in the meantime, assumed a life of its own: it had developed into a lengthy tome.

58. "Experiments in Bird Migration," *Transactions of the Royal Society of Canada* 3d. ser., sec. 5, 40 (1946): 135.

Chapter 14: Population Cycles

1. "Beloved Wilderness," typescript of a talk given by Rowan at the Diamond Jubilee of the Winnipeg Game Association, 26 April 1957, William Rowan papers, University of Alberta Archives, Edmonton (hereafter WRP).

2. The term *conservation* at the time meant game conservation and management rather than general wildlife and habitat conservation. I thank Dr. Rodger Titman for bringing this distinction to my attention.

3. Charles Elton to William Rowan, 26 February 1925, WRP. Elton was to become a good friend and supporter. By 1987 he was too sick to talk to the author.

4. *Proceedings of the Matamek Conference on Biological Cycles* (Matamek: privately printed, 1932), 295.

5. See M.G. Ainley, "From Natural History to Avian Biology: Canadian Ornithology, 1860–1950," Ph.D. diss., McGill University, 1985.

6. P.A. Taverner to Fred Bradshaw, 6 Nov. 1919, P.A. Taverner Papers, Ornithology Division, National Museum of Natural Sciences, Ottawa (hereafter PATP).

7. William Rowan to P.A. Taverner, 2 December 1930, PATP.

8. One of the major questions was whether or not climate alone could influence the population changes. Elton told Rowan that if they could, all the highs and lows in populations would occur circumpolarly at the same time (Charles Elton to William Rowan, 26 February 1925, WRP).

9. William Rowan to Hudson's Bay Company, 15 March 1925, WRP.

10. Hudson's Bay Company to William Rowan, 17 March 1925, WRP.

11. Charles Elton to William Rowan, 15 November 1925, WRP.

12. *Proceedings*, 2.

13. Charles Elton to William Rowan, 17 February 1931; 7 May 1931, WRP.

14. A.O. Gross to William Rowan, 20 May 1931, WRP.

15. Copley Amory to William Rowan, 24 April 1931; 4 July 1931, WRP.

16. William Rowan, field notes, 14 July 1931, WRP.

17. Ibid., 16 July 1931.

18. Ibid., 18 July 1931.

19. *Proceedings*, 14–17.

20. Ibid., 19.

21. Ibid., 39–41.

22. Ibid., 38.
23. Field notes, 26 July 1931.
24. Ibid.
25. "The Perfect Cycle," Thornton W. Burgess, typescript with Burgess's signature, WRP.
26. Charles Elton to William Rowan, 14 February 1932, WRP.
27. William Rowan to F.E. Clements, 25 December 1932, WRP.
28. Ibid.
29. A copy of this proposal is attached to a letter Rowan wrote to F. E. Clements, 25 December 1932, WRP.
30. Ibid.
31. In fact, he had wanted Amory to invite a biochemist to the Matamek conference, but because of financial constraints this could not be done.
32. R. Winckworth to William Rowan, 3 November 1933, WRP.
33. R.A. Wardle to William Rowan, 9 March 1933; D. McLachlan to William Rowan, 8 March 1933, WRP.
34. William Rowan to Seth Gordon, 13 October 1935, WRP.
35. Ibid.. By 1935, his friend Alex Lawrence had sent similar questionnaires to people in Manitoba.
36. J.D. Gregson to William Rowan, September 1934. Gregson worked during the summer at the Dominion Entomological Branch at Kamloops, British Columbia.
37. William Rowan to J.B. Collip, 30 January 1935, WRP.
38. Ibid.
39. Field notes, 7 October 1933.
40. Ibid., 1 December 1934.
41. Ibid., 4 September 1931; William Rowan to Seth Gordon, 13 October 1935, WRP.
42. Frustrated by this pigheadedness, he wrote to the American Wildlife Institute and suggested that they make the topic of cycles "a special phase" of one of the meetings at their forthcoming February 1936 conference. Rowan also hinted that funds were needed "so that scientists [who] have already taken an active interest in the problem, could have something tangible to draw on to carry on their work." William Rowan to Seth Gordon, 13 October 1935, WRP.
43. Fred Bradshaw, "Museum Report," in Government of the Province of Saskatchewan, *Annual Report*, 1929–30, 11.
44. Fred Bradshaw to William Rowan, 18 March 1930, WRP.
45. In 1955, Wood Buffalo National Park was discovered as the nesting ground of this threatened species.
46. Rowan's stamp of the endangered whooping crane was issued by Canada Post in April 1955.
47. Richard Mackie, *Hamilton Mack Laing: Hunter-Naturalist.* (Victoria: Sono Nis Press, 1985), 142.
48. "Beloved Wilderness."

Chapter 15: Conservation Problems

1. "Beloved Wilderness," typescript of a talk given at the Diamond Jubilee of the Winnipeg Game Association, 26 April 1957, William Rowan Papers, University of Alberta Archives, Edmonton (hereafter WRP).

2. A human population explosion had destroyed formerly widespread wildlife habitats in the United States.

3. Field notes, 27 September 1932, WRP.

4. J.F. Bell to William Rowan, 18 May 1933; 1 September 1934, WRP.

5. Edward Ward to William Rowan, 2 April 1934, WRP.

6. J.F. Bell to William Rowan, 1 September 1934, WRP.

7. J.F. Bell to William Rowan, 26 December 1935, WRP.

8. F. Fraser-Darling to William Rowan, 14 August 1937, WRP.

9. H.A. Hochbaum, interview with author, 16 August 1985.

10. H.A. Hochbaum to William Rowan, 10 December 1943, WRP.

11. Most of Rowan's trips were paid for with Delta Station funds; advisers' transportation and subsistence were included in the budget.

12. H.A. Hochbaum, interview with author, 16 August 1985.

13. H.A. Hochbaum, *The Canvasback on a Prairie Marsh*, 2d. ed. (Lincoln: University of Nebraska Press, 1981), 2.

14. William Rowan to acting controller, National Parks Bureau, 28 December 1941, WRP; see also Peter Crowcroft, *Elton's Ecologists: A History of the Bureau of Animal Population.* (Chicago: University of Chicago Press, 1991), 28.

15. H.E. Rawlinson, "letter to hunting-licence vendors," 31 August 1942, typescript, WRP.

16. William Rowan to H.A. Hochbaum, 25 January 1943, WRP.

17. William Rowan to Austin de B. Winter 22 January 1944, Austin de B. Winter Papers, Glenbow-Alberta Institute Archives, Calgary.

18. William Rowan to H.A. Hochbaum, 21 November 1945, WRP.

19. William Rowan to H.A. Hochbaum, 28 May 1948, WRP.

20. Rowan's correspondence with Hochbaum, Lawrence, and others during 1948 contains numerous references to his schemes to escape from the zoology department at the University of Alberta (see, especially, William Rowan to A.G. Lawrence, 3 March 1948; A.G. Lawrence to William Rowan, 20 March 1948; William Rowan to Isaac Pitbaldo, 5 May 1948; E.B. Pitbaldo to William Rowan, 8 May 1948; E.B. Pitbaldo to William Rowan, 12 May 1948; A.G. Lawrence to William Rowan 14 June 1948; as well as William Rowan to C.R. Gutermuth, 18 June 1948; William Rowan to C.R. Gutermuth, 5 July 1948; William Rowan to H.A. Hochbaum 6 June 1948, WRP).

21. William Rowan to H.A. Hochbaum, 29 May 1949, WRP.

22. Rowan needed the extra cash to help pay for Josephine's studies at the Peabody Academy of Music in Baltimore — a hefty two hundred dollars per month (William Rowan to H.A. Hochbaum, 6 August 1950, WRP).

23. The group included his assistant David Stelfox, and other favoured students, such as Roy Anderson and Lloyd Keith.

24. Field notes, 1 July 1949.

25. See, for instance William Rowan to Charles Elton, 18 December 1949, WRP.

26. Michiel Horn, "Academic Freedom and the Dismissal of George Hunter," *Dalhousie Review* 69, no. 3 (1989): 427.

27. Bruce Collier, interview with author, 24 July 1985.

28. Field notes, 5 August 1950.

29. "Peace River Luck," *New Trail* 10, no. 4. (1952), [1].

30. Ibid., [1].

31. "Why Birds, Animals Disappear," *Edmonton Journal* 16 April 1949.

32 Ibid.

33. William Rowan, "The Coming Peak of the Ten-Year Cycle in Alberta," *Transactions of the Fifteenth North American Wildlife Conference* (1952): 379, 382.

34. William Rowan, "Canada's Premier Problem of Animal Conservation: A Question of Cycles," *New Biology* 9 (1950): 49.

35. Charles Elton to William Rowan, 24 November 1949, WRP.

36. A.G. Huntsman to William Rowan, 7 November 1949, WRP.

37. William Rowan to Roy Gibson, 20 October 1949, WRP.

38. Roy Gibson to William Rowan, 18 November 1949, WRP.

39. William Rowan to A.G. Huntsman, 17 April 1950, WRP.

40. Roy Gibson to William Rowan, 21 April 1950, WRP.

41. William Rowan, "Biological Cycles," Progress Report (1952), typescript, WRP.

42. Ibid.

43. William Rowan to George Templeton, 18 March 1953, WRP.

44. Field notes, 15 August 1953.

45. Ibid., 3 January 1953.

46. Oliver Hewitt to William Rowan, 13 July 1953, WRP.

47. Rowan had asked Cole to explain his reasoning in 1951, but Cole had not bothered to reply to his letter.

48. The other authors on this international panel included British ecologist David Lack, Finnish game researcher Lauri Siivonen, Canadian fish zoologist W.E. Ricker, Australian statistician P.A.P. Moran, and several American scientists. Cole, a zoologist at Cornell University, updated his earlier controversial paper that prompted the panel. Ecologists Paul Errington and G.E. Huthinson, and wildlife biologists J.J. Hickey and W.H. Marshall, were divided in their approaches to the study of cycles, as in fact were all the authors. The two camps consisted of scientists "who require no periodicity in their definitions of cyclic behaviour, and those who consider as cyclic only those species which exhibit fairly regular fluctuation in number" (O.H. Hewitt, "A Symposium on Cycles in Animal Populations," *Journal of Wildlife Management* 18 [1954]: 1).

49. William Rowan, "Reflections on the Biology of Animal Cycles," *Journal of Wildlife Management* 18 (1952): 52.

50. Ibid., 54.

51. Ibid., 59–60.

52. Talk given to the Alberta Fish and Game Association, Calgary, type-

script, 18 February 1955, WRP.

53. Ibid.

54. Copy of brief by the Predator Committee, 14 January 1956, WRP.

55. William Rowan to B. Dean, 30 January 1956, WRP. A new book on birds of prey by Alexander Sprunt substantiated Rowan's arguments.

56. William Rowan to the Honourable E.C. Manning, 4 March 1956, WRP.

57. William Rowan and L.B. Keith, "Reproductive Potential and Sex Ratios of Snowshoe Hares in Northern Alberta," *Canadian Journal of Zoology* 34, no. 4 (1956): 273.

Chapter 16: Warring Humanity

1. William Rowan to Reta Rowan, 24 March 1937, William Rowan Papers, University of Alberta Archives, Edmonton (hereafter WRP).

2. Ibid.

3. William Rowan to Reta Rowan, 18 July 1937, WRP.

4. Gerdine McPhee, Julian Rowan, and Josephine Traugott, conversations with author.

5. J.R. Baker to William Rowan, December 1941, WRP. Support grew among the members of the larger scientific community and by late 1942 the President of the Royal Society "endorsed the notion of free science and *Nature* brought the problem before the public." See J.R. Baker, Society for Freedom in Science, "Notice to Members," October 1942, WRP.

6. "Warring Humanity" had its origins in the last chapter Rowan wrote, in 1939, to "As the Crow Flies." It dealt with human biology and integrity. *Integrity* was a key word for Rowan's father, and, increasingly, for Rowan as well. Allee showed the manuscript to several colleagues at the University of Chicago and asked for their comments (see William Rowan to W.C. Allee, 9 May 1943; 10 July 1943, WRP).

7. In addition to Allee, Rowan discussed his philosophical concerns with a number of other people, including anthropologist Ashley Montague, American judge Thurman Arnold, and his own favourite brother, Fred. The letters he wrote to these people detailed his fears and worries about the war and the future of humanity, and allow us a good insight into his thoughts and feelings about a number of important issues.

8. "Warring Humanity: A Biologists's View: Integrity Is Key to World Peace," *Calgary Herald*, 3 July 1943.

9. Ibid.

10. Ibid.

11. William Rowan to W.C. Allee, 15 February 1944, WRP.

12. William Rowan to T. Arnold, 4 May 1944, WRP.

13. William Rowan to Fred Rowan, 16 August 1944, WRP.

14. William Rowan to W.C. Allee, 5 December 1945, WRP.

15. William Rowan to Fred Rowan, 30 March 1947, WRP. This was a philosophy Reta had advocated since World War I.

16. William Rowan to W.C. Allee, 5 December 1945, WRP.

17. Ibid. In spite of the fact that there were a number of female atomic physicists, including Lise Meitner the co-discoverer of nuclear fission, and the fact that women had long shown pacifist leanings, women were never mentioned by Rowan in his discussions of these issues.

18. William Rowan to W.C. Allee, 5 December 1945, WRP.

19. The book consisted of an introduction and three major parts. These dealt with evolution (animal and human); the biology of the human constitution (including hormones, the nervous system, sex, heredity, variation, selection, and environment); and man as builder of his own environment — the thinker (science), the schemer (politics and economics), the modernist (art), the master of speech (education), and the man of the future. This last chapter of "The Last Chapter" dealt with the ideal of integrity.

20. Field notes, 4 January 1941, WRP.

21. Ibid., 26 May 1941.

22. Ibid., 30 May 1941.

23. Ibid., 20–23 June 1941.

24. Ibid., 11 May 1942; 24 May 1942.

25. Ibid., 19 May 1942; 1 June 1942.

26. Rowan included $1,166.62 for a lecturer's salary in his 1939–1940 departmental estimates. The appointment was ratified in March 1939 (see R.B. Miller to William Rowan, 2 April 1939; W.A. Kerr to William Rowan, 12 April 1939, WRP).

27. R.B. Miller to William Rowan, 7 January 1939; 2 April 1939, WRP.

28. By 1941 the Alberta government had become interested in improving whitefish breeding, and during the following summer Miller, with a government grant, was sent to Lesser Slave Lake to study whitefish breeding biology. Rowan was pleased for his young colleague. In fact, he felt that Miller had "fully vindicated [Rowan's] estimates of his ability" because it was evident that the young scientist had done a good job both at the university and in the field (see Rowan to Dymond, 6 March 1944, WRP).

29. William Rowan to G.M. Smith, 15 October 1941, WRP.

30. Ibid.

31. William Rowan to Robert Newton, 17 October 1941, WRP.

32. Ibid.

33. William Rowan to G.M. Smith, 5 November 1941, WRP. In 1941, Hughes was still only earning $2,600, Miller, the new lecturer, was earning $2,000, and Rowan was earning only $4,600.

34. William Rowan to J.R. Dymond, 6 March 1944, WRP. Although enrollment had decreased after the onset of World War II, there were still thirty hours of lecturing and demonstrating to be performed by a staff of three and a student demonstrator, and Lister had to prepare and organize all the teaching material and help in the labs.

35. In March 1942, Dean Smith notified Rowan that Assistant Professor Hughes would receive $2,700 per annum, and that lecturer R.B. Miller would receive $ 2,100 (G.M. Smith to William Rowan, 21 March 1942, WRP.

36. William Rowan to Robert Newton, 6 November 1942, WRP.

37. William Rowan to G.M. Smith, 30 October 1943, WRP. Rowan also requested other things for the department, such as desks, chairs, and even a typewriter, as Hughes's ancient machine, used by the department for fifteen years, had finally given up the ghost.

38. R.K. Gordon to William Rowan, 1 April 1944, WRP.

39. John Macdonald to William Rowan, 25 March 1946, WRP; Robert Newton to J.E. Moore, 8 May 1946, Records of the President, University of Alberta Archives, Edmonton (hereafter RPUA).

40. William Rowan to John Macdonald, 13 April 1946, WRP.

41. Robert Newton to John Macdonald, 29 April 1946, RPUA.

42. William Rowan to Fred Rowan, 30 March 1947, WRP.

43. A visit from American nature artist Francis Lee Jacques and his wife livened up his days at Jasper. There was also a family occasion: the marriage of his firstborn, Gerdine, to a young doctor, Gordon McPhee, on 13 July 1946 brought together most of the family. Only Oliver could not attend.

44. William Rowan to Winnifred Hughes, 4 May 1947, WRP.

45. Ibid.

46. Field notes, 9 May 1947.

47. Ibid., 30 May 1947

48. Winnifred Hughes to William Rowan, 24 May 1947, WRP.

49. Field notes, 2–28 June 1947.

50. William Rowan to Winnifred Hughes, 7 June 1947, WRP.

51. William Rowan to A.W. Bell, 2 June 1947, WRP.

52. William Rowan to Robert Newton, 10 June 1947; also A.W. Bell to William Rowan, 5 June 1947; William Rowan to A. W. Bell, 7 June 1947, WRP.

53. Field notes, 18 July 1947.

54. William Rowan to Robert Newton, 20 August 1947, WRP.

55. John Macdonald to William Rowan, 4 September 1947, WRP.

56. William Rowan to John Macdonald, 14 September 1947, WRP.

57. Ibid.

58. William Rowan to J. Gilmour, 16 January 1949, WRP.

59. John Macdonald to William Rowan 28 October 1949, WRP.

60. Robert Newton to R.B. Miller 29 March 1950, PRUA.

61. R.B. Miller to William Rowan, 22 December 1951, WRP.

62. F.A. Oeming, 27 July 1985; David Stelfox, 30 July 1985; Cy Hampson, 8 August 1985, interviews with author.

63. Wilk had been a graduate student in the department in the late 1930s, and had worked with Rowan on a research project on the gonads of African birds. He later became a diviner. David A. Boag, conversation with author.

64. Organized in December 1944, the committee was part of the council.

65. Field notes, 23 September 1947.

66. Ibid., 29 November 1947.

67. Ibid., 24 December 1947.

Chapter 17: **Science, Ethics, and Peace: "A Biologist Looks Forward"**

1. On the same day, 15 March, he also gave a talk entitled, "The Riddle of Migration."

2. "Science and World Peace," *Blue Print*, December 1948, 1.

3. Ibid., 2.

4. Ibid., 3–4, 5.

5. Ibid., 6.

6. "A Biologist Looks Back," CBC Radio, 18 February 1951.

7. "A Biologist Looks Forward," CBC Radio, 25 February 1951.

8. According to Barbara Moon, he made five hundred dollars per year on his radio talks (see note 9).

9. Barbara Moon, "The Acid-Minded Professor," *Maclean's*, 15 May 1952, 21.

10. Ibid.

11. Field notes, 21 March 1952, William Rowan Papers, University of Alberta Archives, Edmonton (hereafter WRP).

12. William Rowan to Reta Rowan, 8 June 1952, WRP.

13. Field notes, 8 September 1952.

14. Ibid.

15. Field notes, 26 June 1953.

16. Ibid., 13 September 1953.

17. Donald Cameron to William Rowan, 4 August 1953, WRP.

18. Field notes, 13 September 1953.

19. William Rowan to R.D. Gibbs, 21 February 1954, WRP. Rowan had several reasons for suggesting these topics, one of which was the unpleasant experience he had when attending the society's Kingston meeting in the early 1950s: members "got served up . . . American war propaganda . . . a series of anti-Russian smears that might have come direct from Washington." Rowan was one of the many people who left the meeting, about 60 percent of the audience walked out.

20. William Rowan to R.D. Gibbs, 21 February 1954, WRP.

21. "Intellect and Human Survival," typescript, WRP.

22. W.M. Sibley, the chairman, had already asked Rowan for an advance copy of the paper to "facilitate intelligent treatment of your address by the press and radio assigned to the Conference" (W.M. Sibley to William Rowan, 13 May 1953, WRP).

23. "Rule by Scientists Termed 'Doomed' World's Only Hope," *Winnipeg Free Press*, 1 June 1954.

24. Whether or not this was the case is not clear. The Royal Society of Canada Archives have recently been transferred to the National Archives and I could get no information on this.

25. By contrast, British scientist A.V. Hill's presidential address to the British Association for the Advancement of Science, given a few years earlier, which also discussed the responsibilities of scientists, was practically ignored by the press (see "Intellect and Human Survival").

26. Field notes, 4 June 1954.

27. William Rowan to Editor, *Winnipeg Free Press*, 1 June 1954, WRP.

28. Bruce Collier, interview with author, 22 July 1985.

29. Field notes, 3–10 July 1954.

30. Ibid., 22 July 1954.

31. William Rowan to J.B. Marshall, 4 September 1954, WRP. A longtime correspondent of Rowan's, Bullough had published extensively on avian endocrinology. Rowan liked and respected the young scientist and, in 1949, had tried to persuade him to apply to the zoology department at the University of Alberta. In 1952 Rowan had hoped that Bullough would go the University of British Columbia, but Bullough had already accepted a more prestigious position at Birkbeck College, London.

32. Because of last-minute changes, not all papers were given as originally scheduled. Some were cancelled, while others, such as Rowan's, served as replacements.

33. William Rowan to J.B. Marshall, 4 September 1954, WRP.

34. William Rowan to R.E. Moreau, 10 September 1954, WRP. Actually, Rowan had already discovered this in the early 1930s, when Bissonnette's results on starlings differed substantially from his own on juncos.

35. William Rowan to R.E. Moreau, 10 September 1954, WRP.

36. Field notes, 13 September 1954.

37. William Boyd to William Rowan, 20 November 1954, WRP.

38. Austin Smith to William Rowan, 12 October 1954, WRP.

39. A handwritten version of Rowan's will, 15 July 1954, is to be found in the William Rowan Papers. After Rowan's death, Dr. Ray Salt from the Department of Anatomy supervised the extraction of the brain and the cleaning of the skeleton (Ray Salt to Josephine Traugott, 17 May 1988, Rowan family papers).

40. "Birthday Ode," 29 July 1955, WRP.

41. Field notes, 10 August 1956.

42. Introduction, "Beloved Wilderness," typescript, WRP. Macmillan expressed interest in publishing it in 1953.

43. Two of the fourteen council members were women: British crystallographer Kathleen Lonsdale and American physiological chemist M. Jane Oesterling.

44. Field notes, 22 September 1955. This is the first mention of any heart problem since the First World War, but apparently Rowan used to worry about his heart. I thank Julian Rowan for this information.

45. William Rowan to J.B. Marshall, 21 January 1956, WRP.

46. William Rowan to Roy Anderson, 8 April 1956, WRP.

47. Ibid.

48. William Rowan to "Kids," [1 September 1956], WRP.

49. Field notes, 1 September 1956.

50. Field notes, 28 April 1957.

51. William Rowan to "Dearly Beloveds," 12 May 1957, WRP.

52. Field notes, 13 May 1957.

53. William Rowan to "Dearly Beloveds," 12 May 1957, WRP.

54. William Rowan to "Kids," 20 May 1957, WRP.
55. Field notes, 19 May 1957.
56. William Rowan to "Dearly Beloveds," 26 May 1957, WRP.
57. H.A. Hochbaum, interview with author, 16 August 1985.
58. Al Oeming, interview with author, 27 July 1985.
59. Cy Hampson, interview with author, 8 August 1985.
60. Josephine Traugott, conversation with author.
61. Ibid.
62. Nancy Eddis, conversation with author; Charles Eddis, "Memorial Service for Dr. Wm. Rowan," The Unitarian Church of Edmonton, Alberta, July 3, 1957, Rowan family papers.

Selected Bibliography of the Works of William Rowan

Rowan, W. "Unpigmented Eggs of Ringed Plover." *British Birds* 6, no. 5 (1912): 160.

———. "Note on the Food Plants of Rabbits on Blakeney Point, Norfolk." *Journal of Ecology* 1 (1913): 273–76.

———. "Breeding Habits of Oyster Catchers." *British Birds* 5, no. 7 (1913): 200.

———. "Some Observations on a Tern Colony." *Journal of Ecology* 2 (1914): 18–21.

———. "The Blakeney Point Ternery." *British Birds* 8, no 11 (1915): 250–66.

———. "Annotated List of the Birds of Blakeney Point, Norfolk." Norfolk and Norwich Naturalists' Society, 1916–1917.

———. "Notes on the Kingfisher (*Alcedo ispida ispida*)." *British Birds* 11, no. 10 (1918): 218–25.

———. "Birds of the Eastby District, Yorkshire." *Naturalist* 45 (1920): 103–6, 133–36, 153–54.

———. "Breeding of the Evening Grosbeak in Manitoba." *Auk* 37, no. 4 (1920): 585–86.

———. "Some Notes on the Belted Kingfisher." *Canadian Field-Naturalist* 38, no. 1 (1921): 30–33.

———. "Observations on the Breeding-Habits of the Merlin."
"I: General Environment." *British Birds* 15, no. 6 (1921–1922): 122–29.
"II: Incubations." *British Birds* 15, no. 9 (1921–1922): 194–202.
"III: Rearing of the Young." *British Birds* 15, no. 10 (1921–1922): 222–31.
"IV: The Young." *British Birds* 15, no. 11 (1921–1922): 246–49.

———. "Some bird notes from Indian Bay, Manitoba." *Auk* 39, no. 2 (1922): 255–60.

———. "Ecological Note on the Birds Observed at the Biological Station of the University of Manitoba." *Ecology* 3, no. 3 (1922): 253–60.

——. "An Unusual Wapiti Head." *Journal of Mammalogy* 4, no. 2 (1923): 112.

——. "Migrations of the Golden and Black-bellied Plovers in Alberta." *Condor* 25, no. 1 (1923): 21–23.

——. "Danger in Bird Traps." *Auk* 42, no. 1 (1925): 171–73.

——. "Relation of Light to Bird Migration and Developmental Changes." *Nature* 115 (1925): 494–95.

——. "A Practical Method of Recording Bird-Calls." *British Birds* 18, no. 1 (1925): 14–18.

——. "On the Effects of Extreme Cold on Birds." *British Birds* 18, no. 11 (1925): 296–99.

——. "On the Wintering of *Perdix perdix* in Alberta." *Canadian Field-Naturalist*. 39, no. 1 (1925): 114–15.

——. ["A Canadian Zoologist"]. "On the Passing of the Wood Bison." *Canadian Forum* 58 (1925): 301–5.

——. "Bird Protection in Canada." *Ibis* 67, 12 ser., no. 1 (1925): 994–95.

——. "Editions of the 'Check-List.'" *Auk* 43, no. 1 (1926): 136.

——. "Comments on Two Hybrid Grouse and the Occurrence of *Tympanuchus americanus americanus* in the Province of Alberta." *Auk* 43, no. 3 (1926): 333–36.

——. "Notes on Alberta Waders Included in the British List":

"I: Semipalmated and Killdeer Plovers." *British Birds* 20, no. 1 (1926): 1–10.

"II: Golden and Grey Plovers." *British Birds* 20, no. 2 (1926): 34–42.

"III: Turnstone, Bartram's Sandpiper, Sanderling, Knot and Dunlin." *British Birds* 20, no. 4 (1926): 82–90.

"IV: Sandpipers." *British Birds* 20, no. 6 (1926): 138–45.

——. "On Photoperiodism, Reproductive Periodicity, and the Annual Migrations of Birds and Certain Fishes." *Proceedings of the Boston Society of Natural History* 38 (1926): 147–89.

——. "Details of the Release of the Hungarian Partridge (*Perdix perdix*) in Central Alberta." *Canadian Field-Naturalist* 41, no. 1 (1927): 98–101.

——. "An Alberta Aviary." *Condor* 29, no.3 (1927): 133–39.

——. "Banding Franklin's Gulls in Alberta." *Wilson Bulletin* 34, no. 1 (1927): 44–49.

——. "Notes on Alberta Waders Included in the British List":

"V: Buff-Breasted Sandpiper." *British Birds* 20, no. 8 (1927): 186–92.

"VI: Dowitcher and Spotted Sandpiper." *British Birds* 20, no. 9 (1927): 210–22.

——. "Migration and Reproductive Rhythm in Birds." *Nature* 119 (1928): 351–52.

——. "Bird Feathers and the Antirachitic Vitamin D." *Nature* 121 (1928): 323–24.

——. "Reproductive Rhythm in Birds." *Nature* 122 (1928): 11–12.

——. "The Scientific Aspects of Bird Banding." *Bulletin of the Northeastern*

Bird-Banding Association 4, no. 2 (1928): 31–42.

——. "A Hermaphrodite Spiny Dogfish (*Squalus sucklei*)." *Proceedings of the Zoological Society of London* 1–2 (1929): 441–43.

——. "Notes on Alberta Waders Included in the British List":

——. "VII: Yellowshank." *British Birds* 23, no. 1 (1929): 2–17.

——. "Migration in Relation to Barometric and Temperature Changes." *Bulletin of the Northeastern Bird-Banding Association* 5, no. 3 (1929): 85–92.

——. "Experiments in Bird Migration I: Manipulation of the Reproductive Cycle: Seasonal Histological Changes in the Gonads." *Proceedings of the Boston Society of Natural History* 39, no. 5 (1929): 151–208.

——. "Experiments in Bird Migration II: Reversed Migration." *Proceedings of the National Academy of Sciences* 16, no. 7 (1930): 520–25.

——. "A Unique Type of Follicular Atresia in the Avian Ovary." *Transactions of the Royal Society of Canada*, 3d ser., sec. 5, 24 (1930): 157–64.

——. "On a New Hydra from Alberta." *Transactions of the Royal Society of Canada* 3d ser., sec. 5, 24 (1930): 165–75.

——. "The Mechanism of Bird Migration." *Science Progress* 97 (1930): 70–78.

——. *The Riddle of Migration*. Baltimore: Williams and Wilkins Co., 1931.

——. "Experiments in Bird Migration III: The Effects of Artificial Light, Castration and Certain Extracts on the Autumn Movements of the American Crow (*Corvus brachyrhynchos*)." *Proceedings of the National Academy of Sciences* 18, no. 11 (1932): 639–54.

——. "The Status of the Dowitchers with a Description of a New Subspecies from Alberta and Manitoba." *Auk* 49, no. 1 (1932): 14–35.

——. "Fifty Years of Bird Migration." In *Fifty Years' Progress of American Ornithology, 1883–1933*, ed. F.M. Chapman and T.S. Palmer, 51–63. Lancaster, Pa.: American Ornithologists' Union, 1933.

——. "The Effect of Controlled Illumination on the Reproductive Activities of Birds." *Kongressbericht d. Weltflugelkongresses* 1, no. 16 (1936): 142–52.

——. "The Partridge Situation in Western Canada." *Sportsman* 20, no. 5 (1936): 43, 63.

——. "Effects of Traffic Disturbance and Night Illumination on London Starlings." *Nature* 139 (1937): 668–69.

——. "London Starlings and Seasonal Reproductions in Birds." *Proceedings of the Zoological Society of London* 108 (1938): 51–77.

——. "Light and Seasonal Reproduction in Animals." *Biological Reviews of the Cambridge Philosophical Society* 13 (1938): 374–402.

——. "The Hungarian Partridge on the Canadian Prairies." *Outdoor America* 3, no. 4 (1938): 6–7.

——. "Homing, Migration and Instinct." *Science* 102, no. 2643 (1945): 210–11.

——. "Inheritance and Acquired Characteristics." *Nature* 156 (1945): 236.

———. "Numbers of Young in the Common Black and Grizzly Bears in Western Canada." *Journal of Mammalogy* 26, no. 2 (1945): 197–99.

———. "Experiments in Bird Migration." *Transactions of the Royal Society of Canada*, 3d ser., sec. 5, 40 (1946): 123–35.

———. "Migration of Birds" [1947]. *Encyclopedia Britannica.*

———. "The Ten-Year Cycle: Outstanding Problem of Canadian Conservation." Edmonton: Department of Extension Publications, University of Alberta, 1948.

———. "Science and World Peace." *Blueprint* [British Columbia Academy of Science], December 1948, n.p.

———. "The Northern Migration of Birds" [1949], *Encyclopedia Arctica.*

———. "Some Comments on the Lysenko Controversy." *New Trail* (August 1949), n.p.

———. "Canada's Premier Problem of Animal Conservation: A Question of Cycles." *New Biology* 9 (1950): 38–57.

———. "Winter Habits and Numbers of Timber Wolves." *Journal of Mammalogy* 31, no. 2 (1950): 167–69.

———. "Some Effects of Settlement on Wildlife in Alberta." *Transactions of the Canadian Conservation Association* (1952): 31–39.

———. "Peace River Luck." *New Trail* 10, no. 4 (1952): 1–6.

———. "The Coming Peak of the Ten-Year Cycle in Alberta." *Transactions of the 15th North American Wildlife Conference* (1952): 379–83.

———. "Reflections on the Biology of Animal Cycles." *Journal of Wildlife Management* 18, no. 1 (1954): 52–60.

———. "A Layman Challenges Medicine." *Historical Bulletin of the Calgary Associate Clinic* 22, no. 1 (1957): 145–53.

———, K.M. Parker, and J. Bell. "On Homotyposis and Allied Characters in the Eggs of the Common Tern." *Biometrika* 10 (1914): 144–66.

———, et al. "On the Nest and Eggs of the Common Tern (*S. fluviatilis*): A Cooperative Study." *Biometrika* 12 (1919): 308–53.

——— and J.D. Gregson. "Winter Feeding of the Tick *Dermacentor anderssoni* Styles." *Nature* 135 (1935): 652.

——— and A.M. Batrawi. "Comments on the Gonads of Some European Migrants Collected in East Africa Immediately Before Their Spring Departure." *Ibis* 14th ser., 3 (1939): 58–65.

Moreau, R.E., A.L. Wilk, and W. Rowan. "The Moult and Gonad Cycles of Three Species of Birds at Five Degrees South of the Equator." *Proceedings of the Zoological Society of London* 117 (1947): 345–64.

——— and L.B. Keith. "Reproductive Potential and Sex Ratios of Snowshoe Hares in Northern Alberta." *Canadian Journal of Zoology* 34, no. 4 (1956): 273–81.

——— and L.B. Keith. "Monthly Weights of Snowshoe Hares in North-Central Alberta." *Journal of Mammalogy* 40, no. 2 (1959): 221–26.

Selected Bibliography of Works on William Rowan

Ainley, Marianne G. "William Rowan: Canada's First Avian Biologist." *Picoides* 1 (1987): 6–8.

——. "Rowan vs. Tory – Conflicting Views of Scientific Research in Canada, 1920–1935." *Scientia Canadensis* 12, no. 1 (1988): 3–21.

——. "William Rowan and the Experimental Approach in Ornithology." *Acta XIX Congressus Internationalis Ornithologici* (1988): 2737–45.

——. "William Rowan, 1891–1957. *Bulletin of the Canadian Society of Zoologists* 22 (1991): 33–35.

Babkin, B. P. "Flavelle Medal: William Rowan." *Proceedings of the Royal Society of Canada*. 3d ser., sec. 5, 40 (1962): 48.

Carlisle, N. "He Made Crows Fly Backwards." *True: The Man's Magazine*, September 1962: 88b– 88h.

Corbett. E. A. "The Battle of the Crows and Other Rowan Escapades." *New Trail* 31, no. 2 (1975): 2–5.

Gauthreaux, S. A., Jr. "Avian Migration Systems." *Avian Biology* 6 (1982): 93–168.

Gillese, John P. "William Rowan: Outdoor Man of the Month." *Forest and Outdoors*, April 1949: 17, 26.

——. "The Wildlife Journals of William Rowan." *Beaver* 289 Autumn 1958: 46–53.

Halliday, Hugh M. "Academic Rebel." *Star Weekly*, 3 November 1956: 8.

Hohn, Otto. " Professor William Rowan: Ornithologist and Artist." *Alberta Naturalist* 14, no. 4 (1984): 126–30.

Keith, R. A. *Bush Pilot with a Briefcase: The Happy-Go-Lucky Story of Grant McConachie*. Toronto: Doubleday Canada, 1972, 43–47.

Lewis, M. *To Conserve a Heritage*. Calgary: Alberta Fish and Game Association, 1979.

Lister, Robert. *The Birds and Birders of Beaverhills Lake.* Edmonton: Edmonton Bird Club, 1979.

Moon, Barbara. "The Acid-Minded Professor." *Maclean's*, 15 May 1952: 20–21, 56-59.

Salt, Ray W. "In Memoriam: William Rowan." *Auk* 75, no.4 (1958): 387–90.

Stresemann, E. *Ornithology: From Aristotle to the Present.* Cambridge: Harvard University Press, 1975, 355–56.

Walkinshaw, L. "A New Sandhill Crane from Central Canada." *Canadian Field-Naturalist* 79, no. (1965): 181–84.

Index